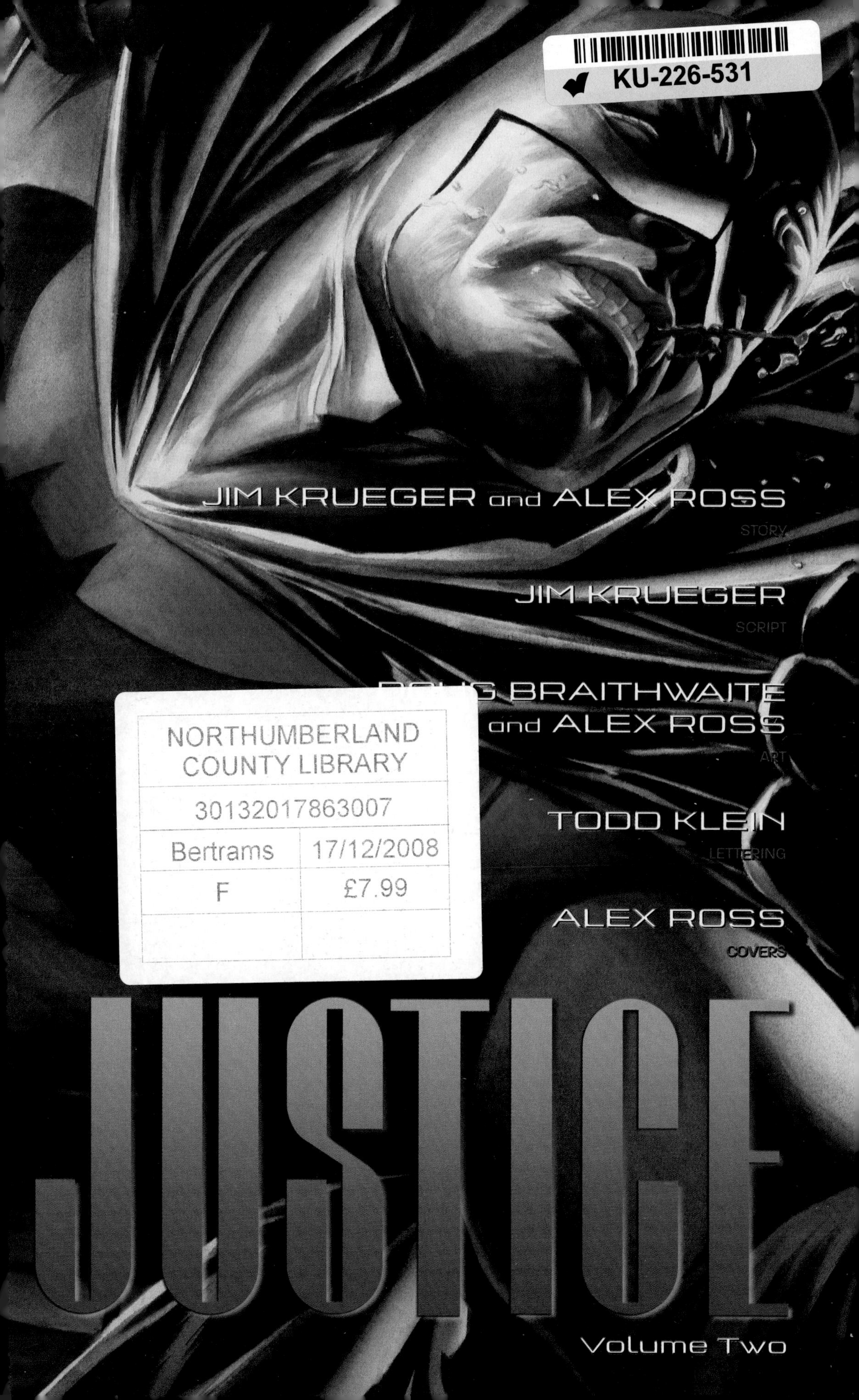

JIM KRUEGER and ALEX ROSS
STORY

JIM KRUEGER
SCRIPT

DOUG BRAITHWAITE
and ALEX ROSS
ART

TODD KLEIN
LETTERING

ALEX ROSS
COVERS

JUSTICE

Volume Two

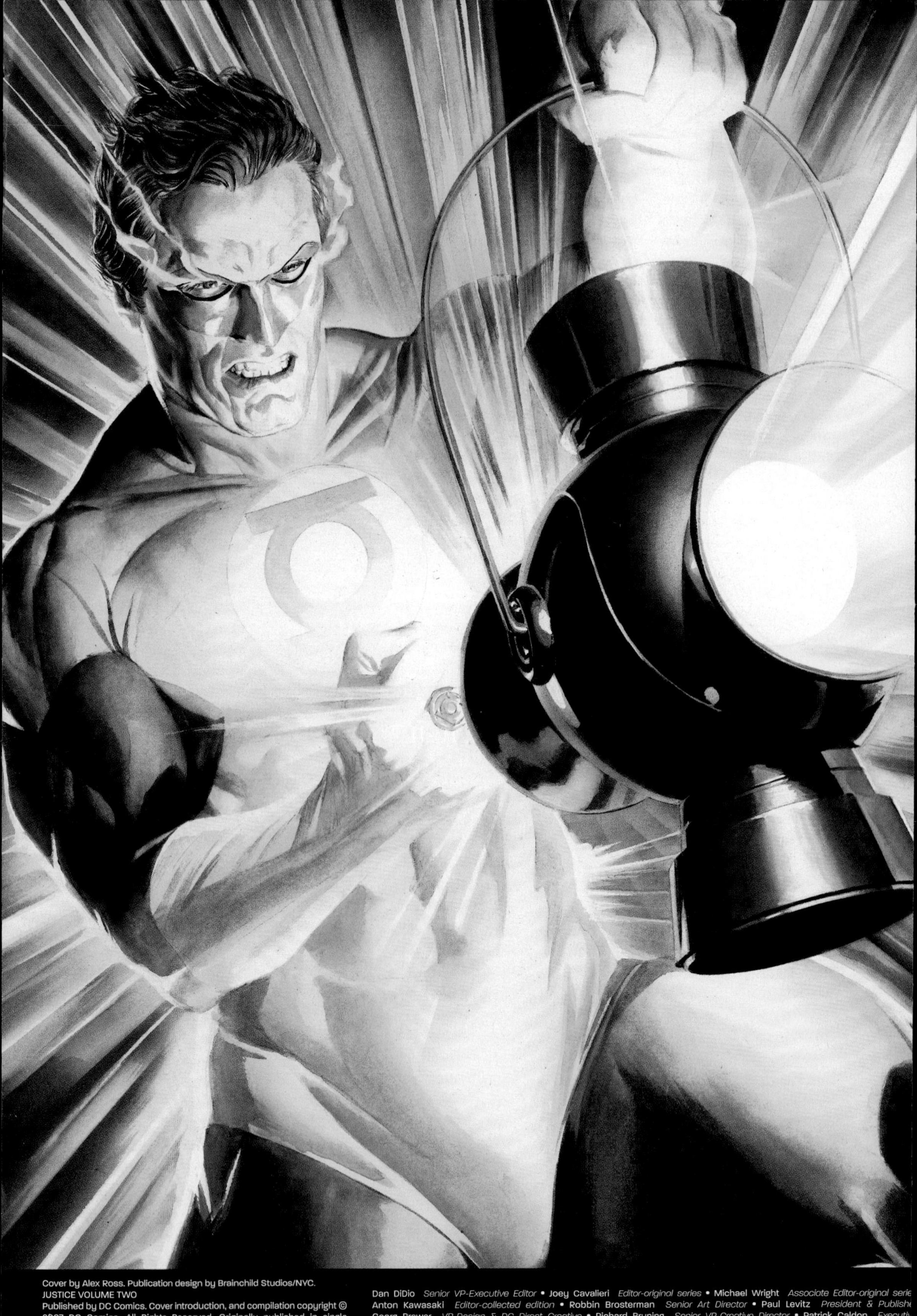

Cover by Alex Ross. Publication design by Brainchild Studios/NYC.
JUSTICE VOLUME TWO
Published by DC Comics.

DC Comics, 1700 Broadway, New York, NY 10019
A Warner Bros. Entertainment Company
Printed in Canada. First Printing.
HC ISBN: 1-4012-1207-7 HC ISBN 13: 978-1-4012-1207-0
ISBN: 1-4012-1206-9 ISBN 13: 978-1-4012-1206-3

INTRODUCTION

by Doug Braithwaite

Has it really been two years since this whole JUSTICE thing started? It only seems like yesterday that I was having a conversation with Alex on a cold September night about the prospect of our working together on this.

JUSTICE starts with a dream, and for me it *has* been a dream to work on. And I suppose you could look at it as something I have been practicing for my whole life. I'm sure everyone reading this has a memory of their first experience of comic books. My own is when I was about three or four years old. My dad would take me with him when he went to the newsagents to buy his newspaper. In the corner of the shop was a spin rack filled with comic books. That comic rack drew me like a magnet, and one character in particular grabbed my attention. I'm not sure whether it was the red and blue costume or the flowing cape that attracted me, or maybe it was the strange emblem on his chest — the "S" symbol on Superman looked to me like two yellow fish swimming 'round each other. I remember my dad looking over at me at the rack, then he let me choose a comic, a choice based purely on what I saw as I hadn't yet been taught to read. When we got home, I settled down next to dad and he read the comic to me — complete with all the sound effects! I was transfixed — this was better than all the other children's stories read to me so far in my short life! The strange thing is I have no recollection of what issue it was — the only thing I can remember is the image of Superman flying through outer space, towing a line of planets with a gigantic chain.

After this early introduction to the world of superheroes, I was obsessed with attempting to draw them and, seeing my interest, the teachers at my infant's school gave me a big canvas to work on — when they allowed me to paint superheroes all over one of the walls of the school! I remember reading the Justice League of America when I was about seven, and one issue in particular made a huge impression on me — issue #137, Superman versus Shazam. The image on the cover of those two going head to head, one of them gone bad, was mind-blowing to me. It is still amazing for me to realize, thirty-odd years later, that I'm involved in creating similar imagery in JUSTICE.

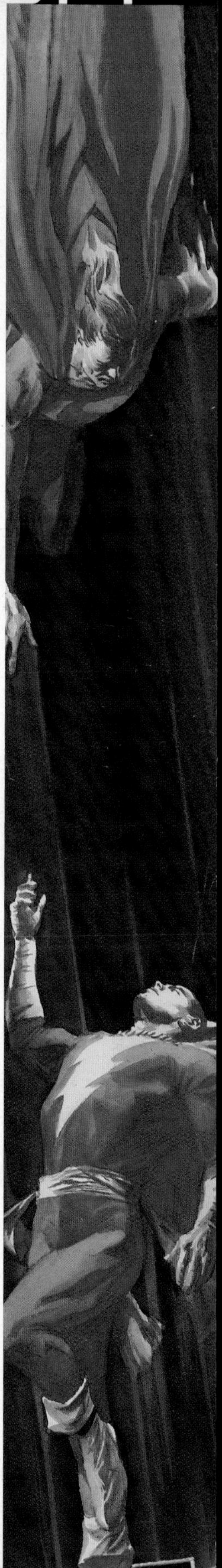

The compulsion to draw stayed with me, despite the obvious distractions of sports and girls (and not necessarily in that order). It sounds obsessive, I know, but in my early teens, it was quite usual for me to sit up until 3 a.m. drawing stuff — most of it superheroes. My intention was to go to art college, but it didn't work out that way because a teacher happened to see some of my superhero drawings in the back of my schoolbook and he said the words that probably got me where I am today: "You know, you could do that for a living." I had never dreamt of that as an option for me, as the comics I loved were produced in America, which may as well have been a million miles away as I had no way of getting there. However, with help from the same teacher, Steve Medway, I ended up walking into the Marvel UK office in London

Yes they're superheroes, and yes, they have special powers, but equally we can relate to them because they're just like people we've known all our lives.

at the age of 15. Two years later after attending classes at the London Cartoon Centre, Marvel gave me my first paid work. I've been in it for the long haul since then, and I have to thank goodness for some of the older guys in the business, people like the late, great Archie Goodwin and the genius Al Williamson — both of whom had faith in me at a time when my classic style of drawing wasn't so fashionable. I suppose the result of that faith was when Alex, someone whom I had long admired, asked me to pencil JUSTICE.

And you know, after 20 years in the business, I still get an enormous kick out of drawing the characters I loved as a kid. It's the best job in the world as far as I'm concerned: it tests the skills I've been working on virtually all my life, but it's not just about the art, it's about the things these superheroes represent for all of us. Yes, they're superheroes, and yes, they have special powers, but equally we can relate to them because they're just like people we've known all our lives. We know them, warts and all, and we respond to them knowing both sides of the coin. We have the writers to thank for that relationship with the characters. I marvel that a writer of Jim's talent can make you empathize with them and in the next breath make you think they're utter jerks. I love the fact that in the writing the characters reflect the problems we all have in relating to others, whether it is our friends, family, colleagues or lovers. But most of all, I love the fact that they live the

...knowing that he would use his superb talent to bring the pencils to life, in a way all his own, made me secure in the knowledge that what we were producing would be something we could all be proud of.

lives most of us never do: I don't know about you, but being a super-fit specimen will — for me, anyway — continue to be a fantasy, and in reality, very few of us have the guts to take on the job of fighting the bad guys. The one thing we may get the chance to experience is to fly, free as a bird, but even that will remain the dream we dream only when we are asleep.

Working on JUSTICE has allowed me to pay tribute to all those who worked on the classic JLA of my childhood, and the story Jim and Alex have put together is as gripping as they ever were to me back then. Pencilling the great scripts Jim has produced has probably been the biggest challenge of my career so far — I know I have never worked so hard in my life. Then to hand the work to Alex, knowing that he would use his superb talent to bring the pencils to life, in a way all his own, made me secure in the knowledge that what we were producing would be something we could all be proud of. It's great that the fans are excited by the series. But they are not the only ones — you wouldn't believe the excitement generated in our house every time a package of Alex's completed painted

artwork is delivered. And believe it or not, as I'm writing this, I don't know how this whole story pans out. I haven't seen the final script — I didn't want to. This way I respond to the story as much as I did as a kid. So, it's still a dream — I just hope there's a seven-year-old out there who is inspired by JUSTICE to live his dream one day too.

DOUG BRAITHWAITE
November, 2006

Working on JUSTICE has allowed me to pay tribute to all those who worked on the classic JLA of my childhood, and the story Jim and Alex have put together is as gripping as they ever were to me back then.

WHAT HAS COME BEFORE

It begins with a dream...or rather a nightmare.

The world's vilest villains all wake up from the same feverish glimpse of a possible near-future: one where the combined might of the fabled Justice League of America is not enough to save the world from total disaster. Humanity has relied too much on its heroes, and has become too weak to defend itself. So now the greatest criminal minds on Earth have decided that the only way to save the world is by taking down the members of the Justice League...one by one.

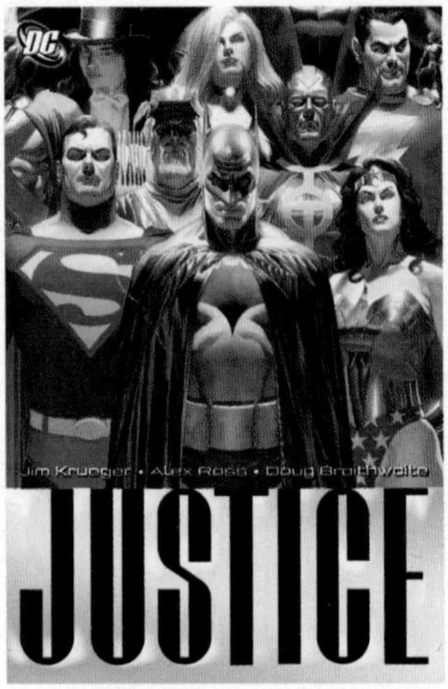
DC
Jim Krueger • Alex Ross • Doug Braithwaite
JUSTICE

The first hero to fall is Aquaman, thanks to the deadly Black Manta. Taken to the villain group's underwater base, the King of the Seas is subjected to experiments by the alien Brainiac. Meanwhile, the villains begin their plan to change the world around them in dramatic ways that the JLA couldn't or wouldn't — as desert wastelands bloom with life, people with disabilities walk again, and world hunger has an end in sight.

But the criminals' deeds are not entirely altruistic, as they discover the secret identities of the heroes, and more of the JLA falls by their hand. Gorilla Grodd makes the Martian Manhunter believe he is being consumed by his greatest weakness...fire. The Red Tornado finds himself being taken over by an uncontrollable force that rips him apart. Green Lantern is transported far away via a Boom Tube by Sinestro. Green Arrow and Black Canary become victims of Scarecrow and Clayface. The Cheetah attacks Wonder Woman at a women's conference. The Toyman targets Hawkman and Hawkgirl at the museum they work in. Ray Palmer, the Atom, is shot by a sniper. The Flash finds that he can't stop running. And Superman is overwhelmed by the combined forces of Bizarro, Solomon Grundy, Metallo and the Parasite.

And once the World's Greatest Heroes are defeated, the villains present to the Earth's population their plan to change the world. Accusing the heroes of being absent and unable to make the real changes needed for a better society, the villains build "perfect" cities without disease or poverty, and invite the people they've cured to live in them. It's looking like there's no hope left for the Justice League.

But they're not the *only* heroes left in the world...

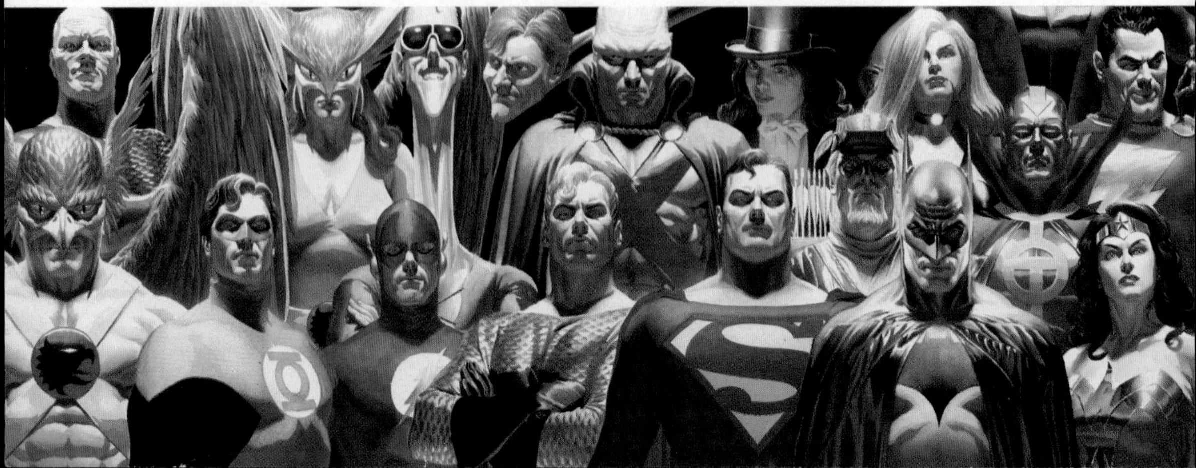

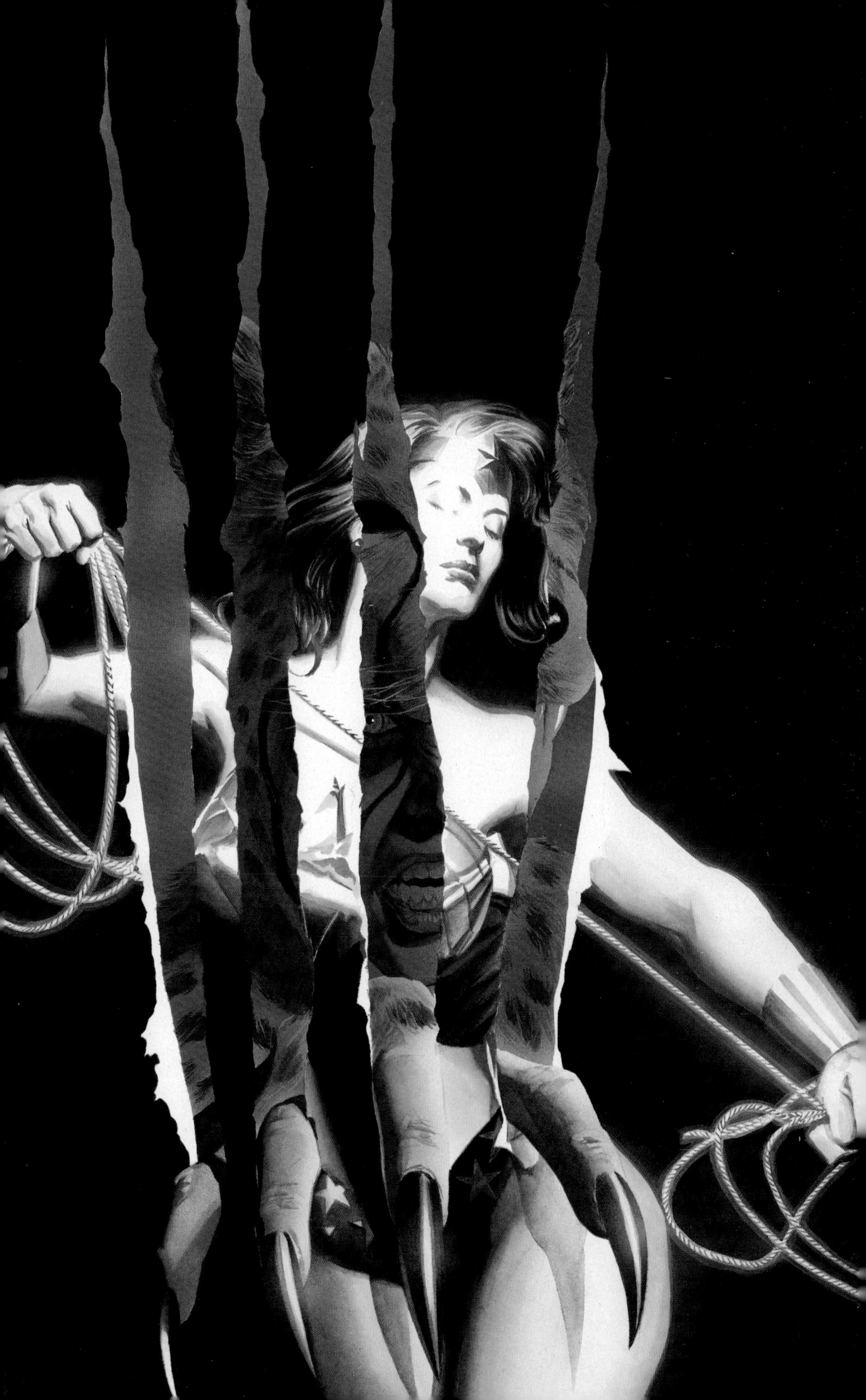

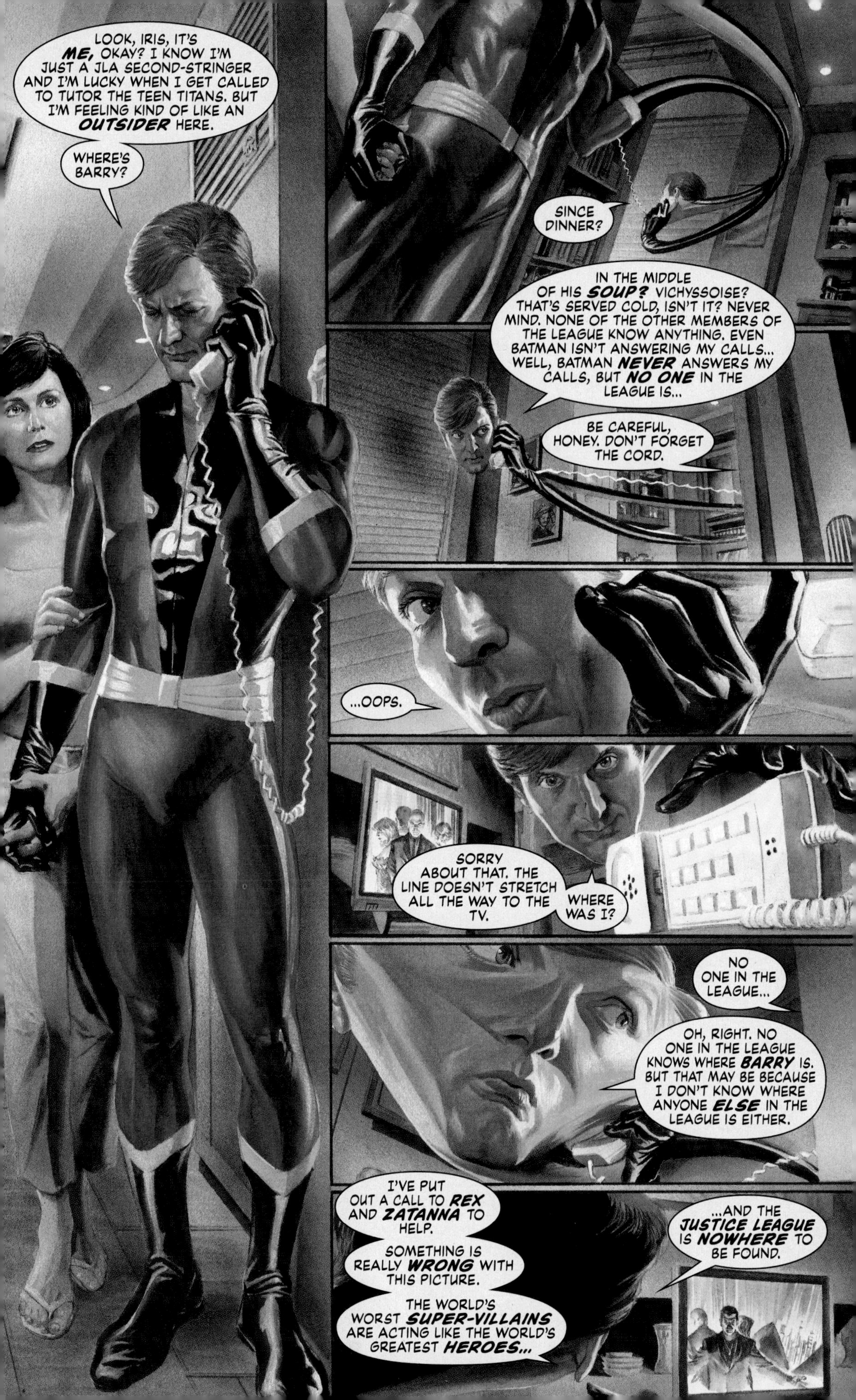
LOOK, IRIS, IT'S ME, OKAY? I KNOW I'M JUST A JLA SECOND-STRINGER AND I'M LUCKY WHEN I GET CALLED TO TUTOR THE TEEN TITANS. BUT I'M FEELING KIND OF LIKE AN OUTSIDER HERE.
WHERE'S BARRY?
SINCE DINNER?
IN THE MIDDLE OF HIS SOUP? VICHYSSOISE? THAT'S SERVED COLD, ISN'T IT? NEVER MIND. NONE OF THE OTHER MEMBERS OF THE LEAGUE KNOW ANYTHING. EVEN BATMAN ISN'T ANSWERING MY CALLS... WELL, BATMAN NEVER ANSWERS MY CALLS, BUT NO ONE IN THE LEAGUE IS...
BE CAREFUL, HONEY. DON'T FORGET THE CORD.
...OOPS.
SORRY ABOUT THAT. THE LINE DOESN'T STRETCH ALL THE WAY TO THE TV.
WHERE WAS I?
NO ONE IN THE LEAGUE...
OH, RIGHT. NO ONE IN THE LEAGUE KNOWS WHERE BARRY IS. BUT THAT MAY BE BECAUSE I DON'T KNOW WHERE ANYONE ELSE IN THE LEAGUE IS EITHER.
I'VE PUT OUT A CALL TO REX AND ZATANNA TO HELP.
SOMETHING IS REALLY WRONG WITH THIS PICTURE.
THE WORLD'S WORST SUPER-VILLAINS ARE ACTING LIKE THE WORLD'S GREATEST HEROES...
...AND THE JUSTICE LEAGUE IS NOWHERE TO BE FOUND.

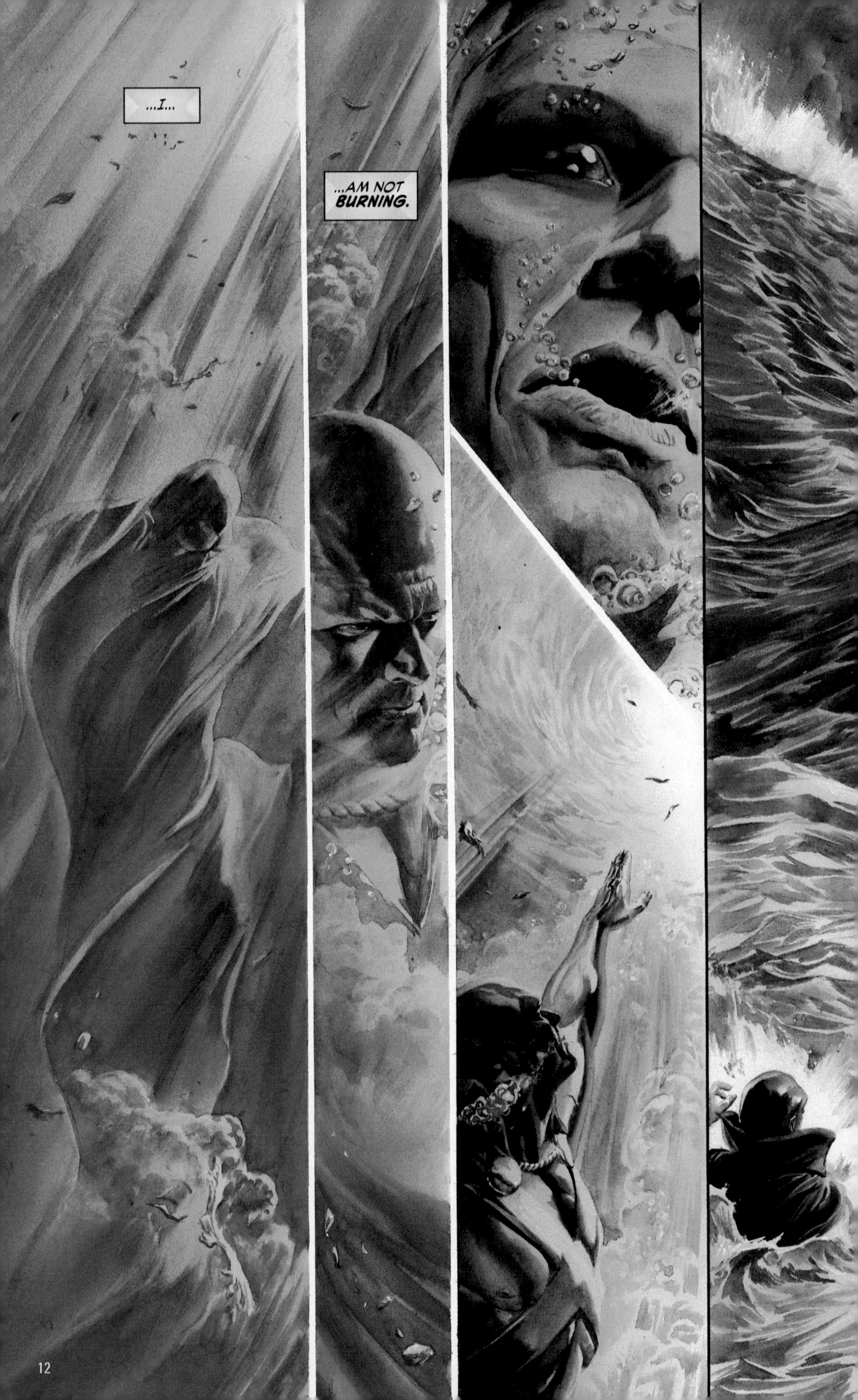
...I...
...AM NOT BURNING.

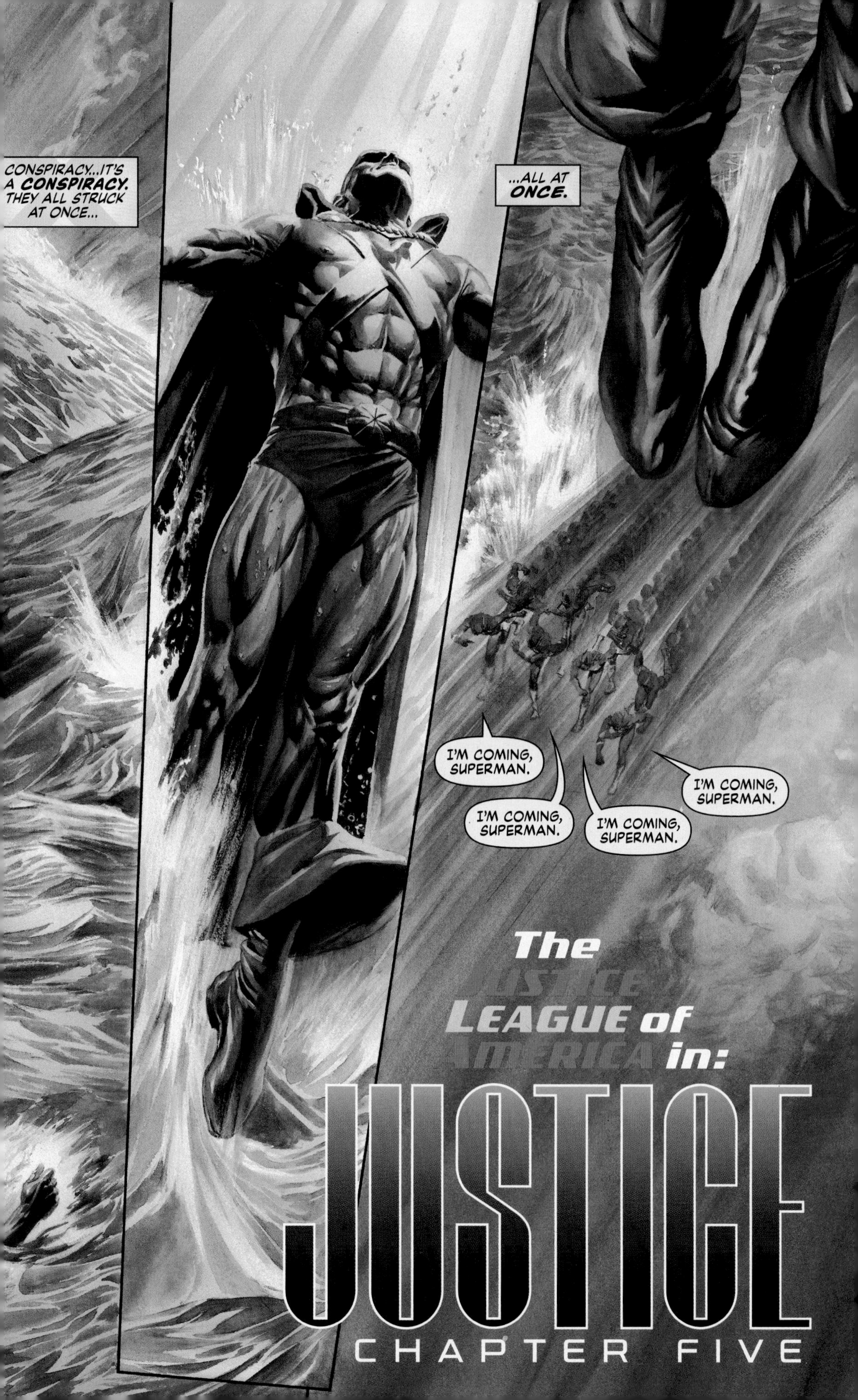
CONSPIRACY...IT'S A CONSPIRACY. THEY ALL STRUCK AT ONCE...
...ALL AT ONCE.
I'M COMING, SUPERMAN.
I'M COMING, SUPERMAN.
I'M COMING, SUPERMAN.
I'M COMING, SUPERMAN.
The JUSTICE LEAGUE of AMERICA in:
JUSTICE
CHAPTER FIVE

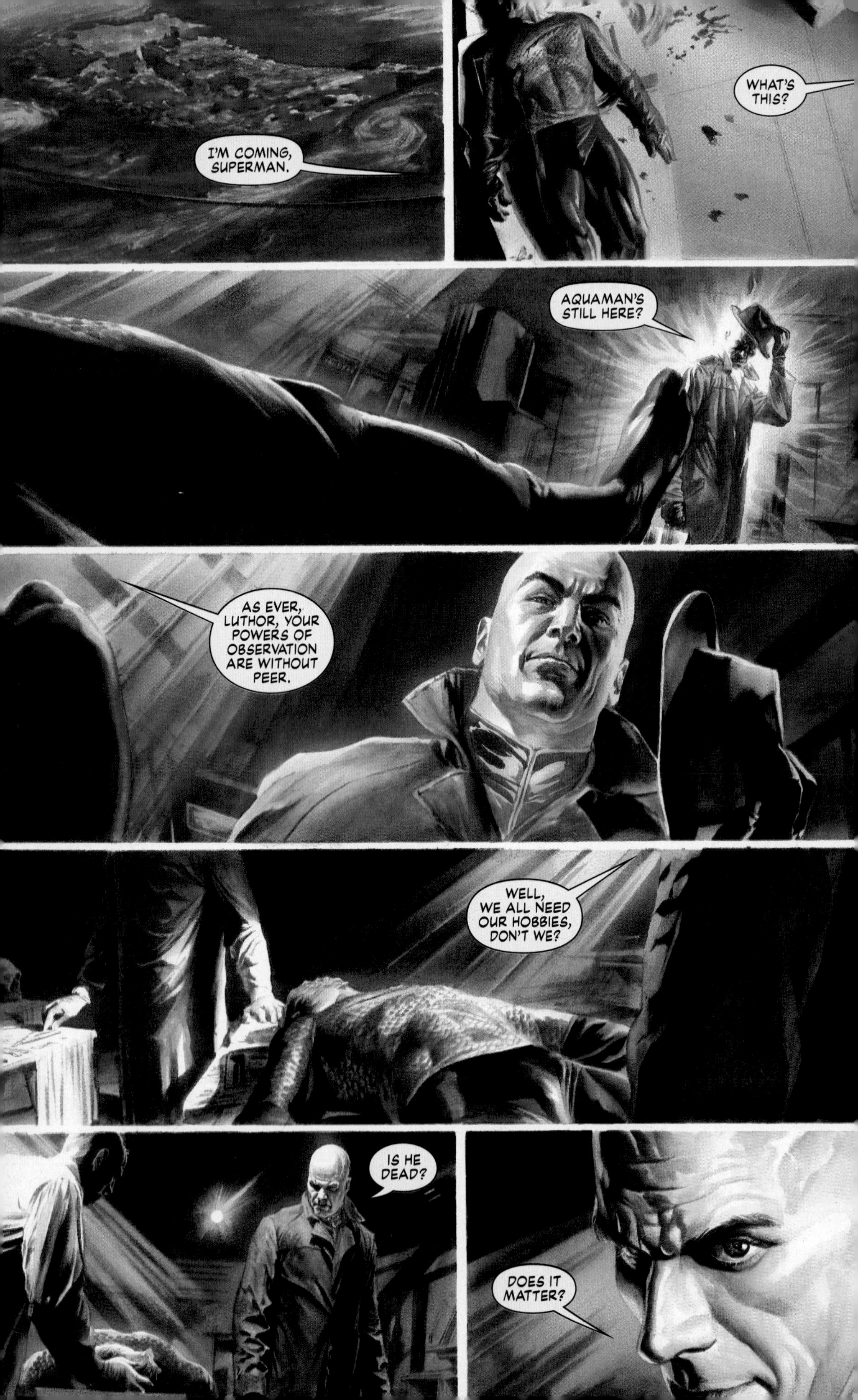
I'M COMING, SUPERMAN.
WHAT'S THIS?
AQUAMAN'S STILL HERE?
AS EVER, LUTHOR, YOUR POWERS OF OBSERVATION ARE WITHOUT PEER.
WELL, WE ALL NEED OUR HOBBIES, DON'T WE?
IS HE DEAD?
DOES IT MATTER?

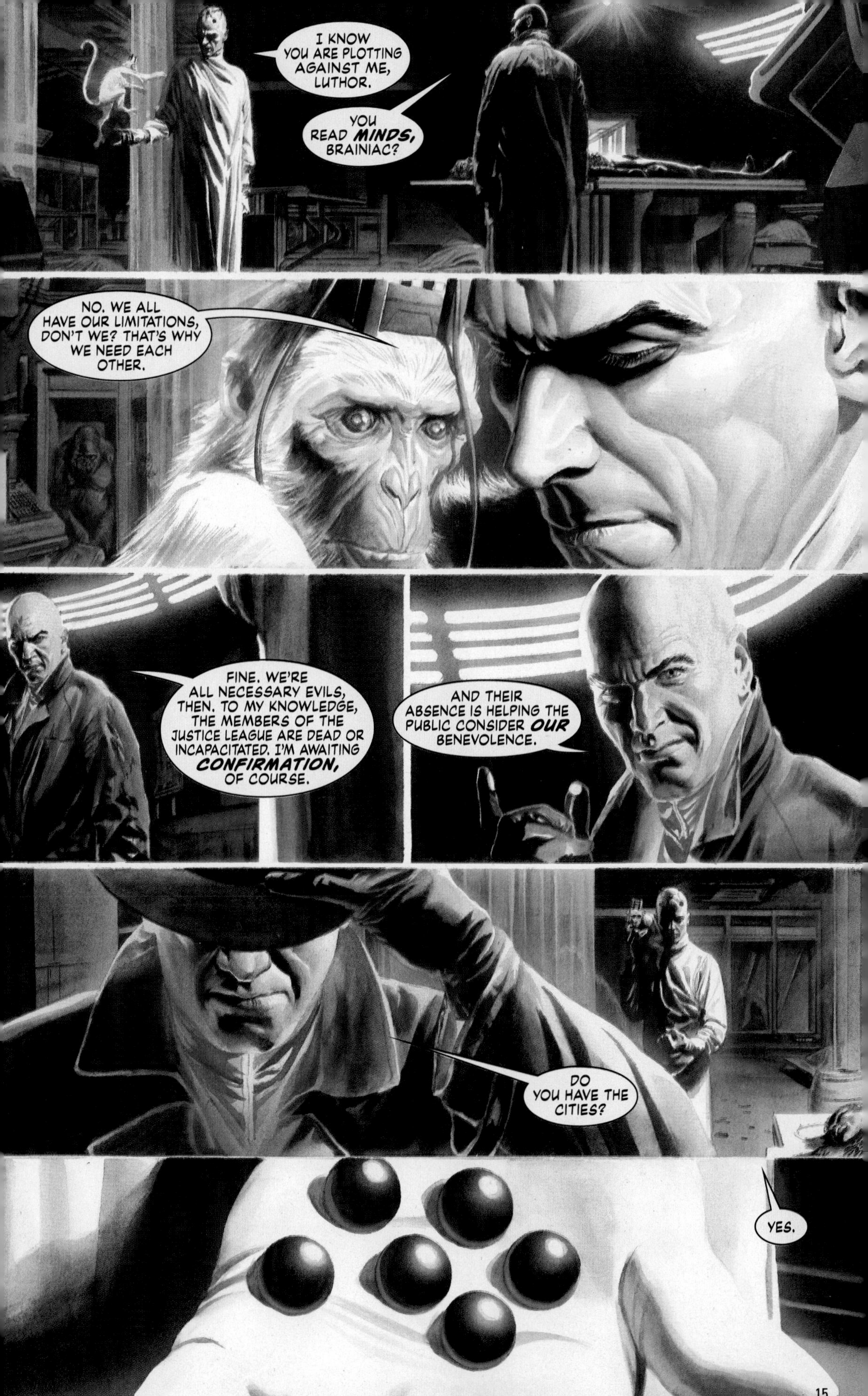

I KNOW YOU ARE PLOTTING AGAINST ME, LUTHOR.
YOU READ MINDS, BRAINIAC?
NO. WE ALL HAVE OUR LIMITATIONS, DON'T WE? THAT'S WHY WE NEED EACH OTHER.
FINE. WE'RE ALL NECESSARY EVILS, THEN. TO MY KNOWLEDGE, THE MEMBERS OF THE JUSTICE LEAGUE ARE DEAD OR INCAPACITATED. I'M AWAITING CONFIRMATION, OF COURSE.
AND THEIR ABSENCE IS HELPING THE PUBLIC CONSIDER OUR BENEVOLENCE.
DO YOU HAVE THE CITIES?
YES.

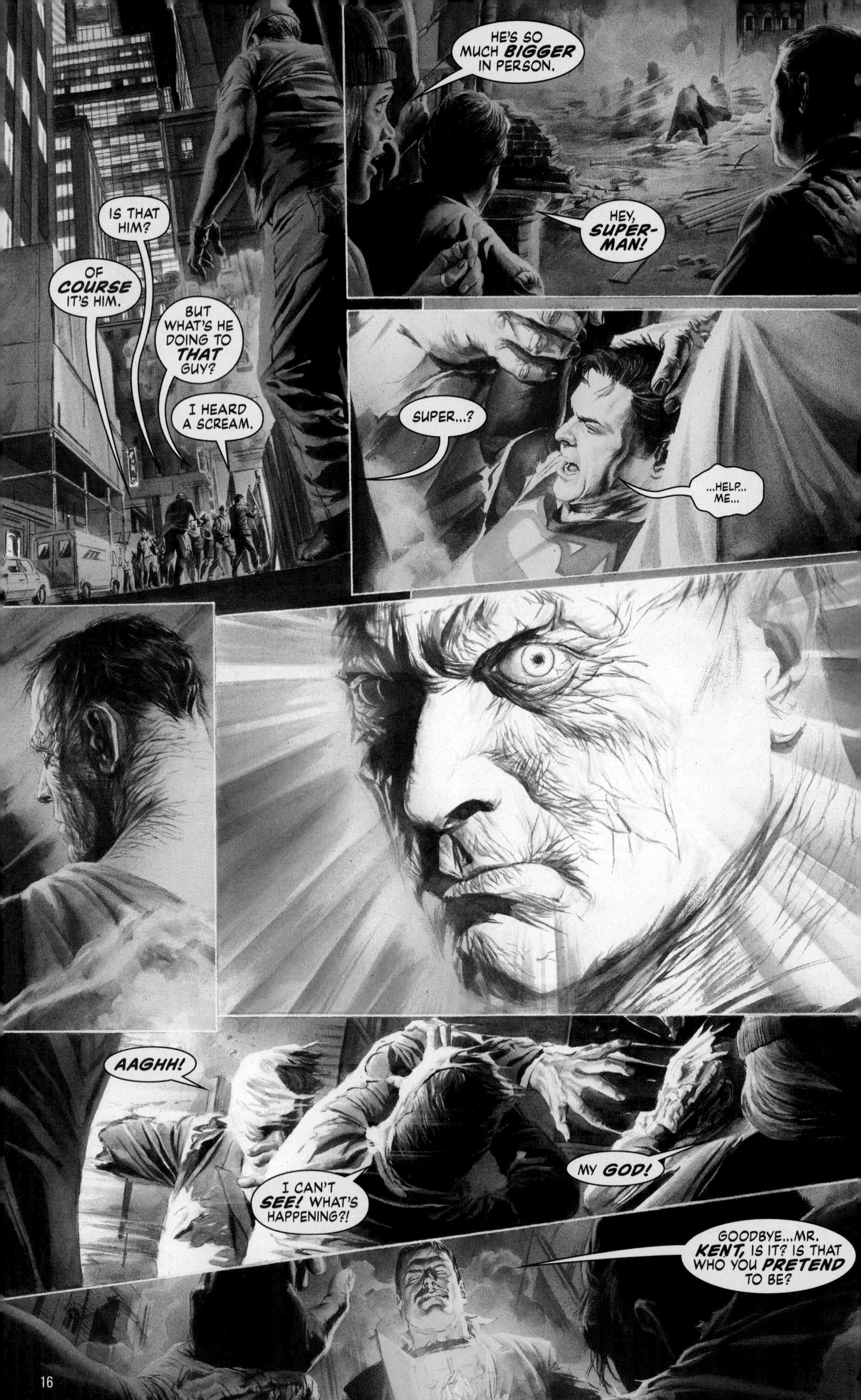
IS THAT HIM?
OF COURSE IT'S HIM.
BUT WHAT'S HE DOING TO THAT GUY?
I HEARD A SCREAM.
HE'S SO MUCH BIGGER IN PERSON.
HEY, SUPER-MAN!
SUPER...?
...HELP... ME...
AAGHH!
I CAN'T SEE! WHAT'S HAPPENING?!
MY GOD!
GOODBYE...MR. KENT, IS IT? IS THAT WHO YOU PRETEND TO BE?

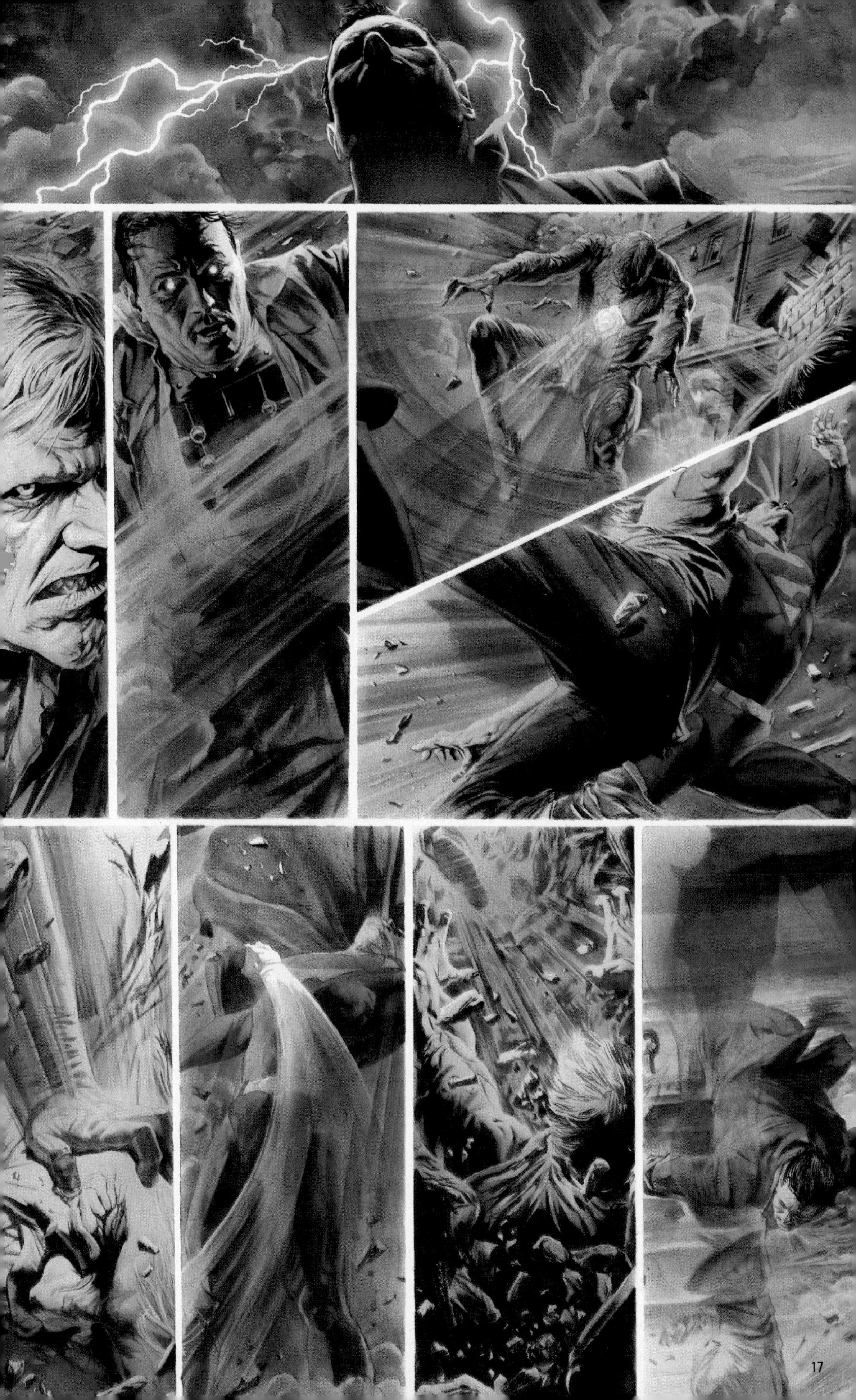

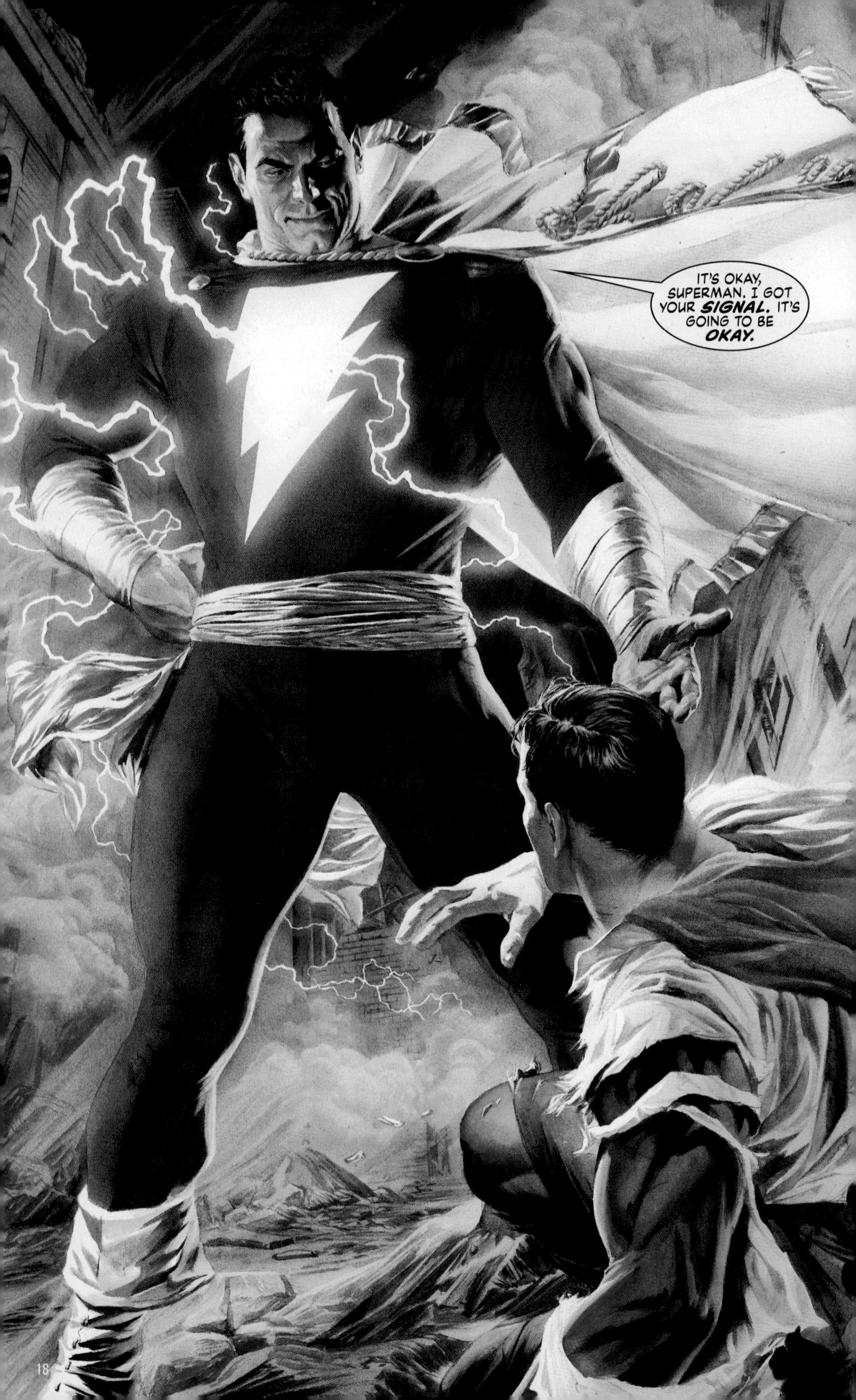
IT'S OKAY, SUPERMAN. I GOT YOUR SIGNAL. IT'S GOING TO BE OKAY.

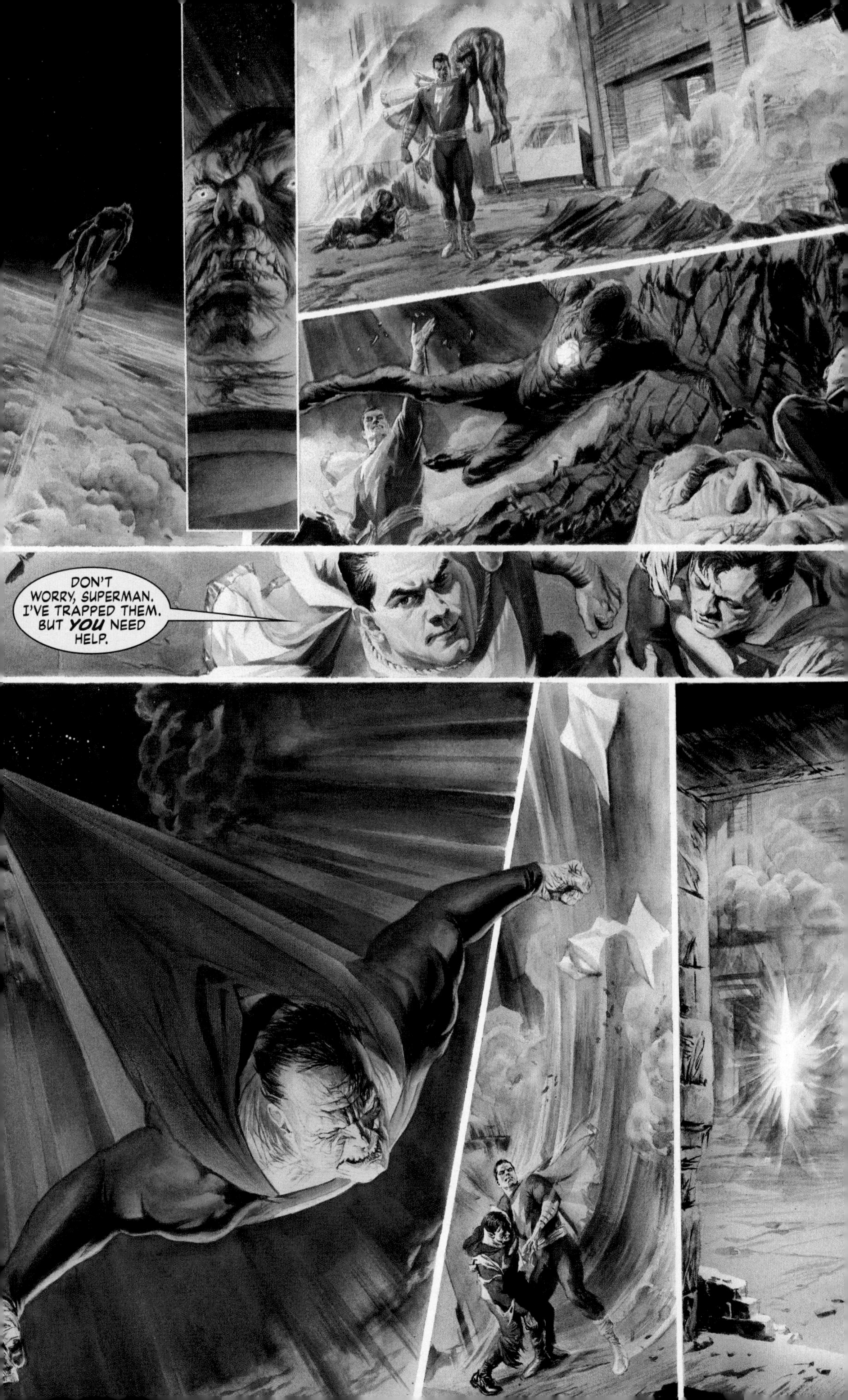
DON'T WORRY, SUPERMAN. I'VE TRAPPED THEM. BUT YOU NEED HELP.

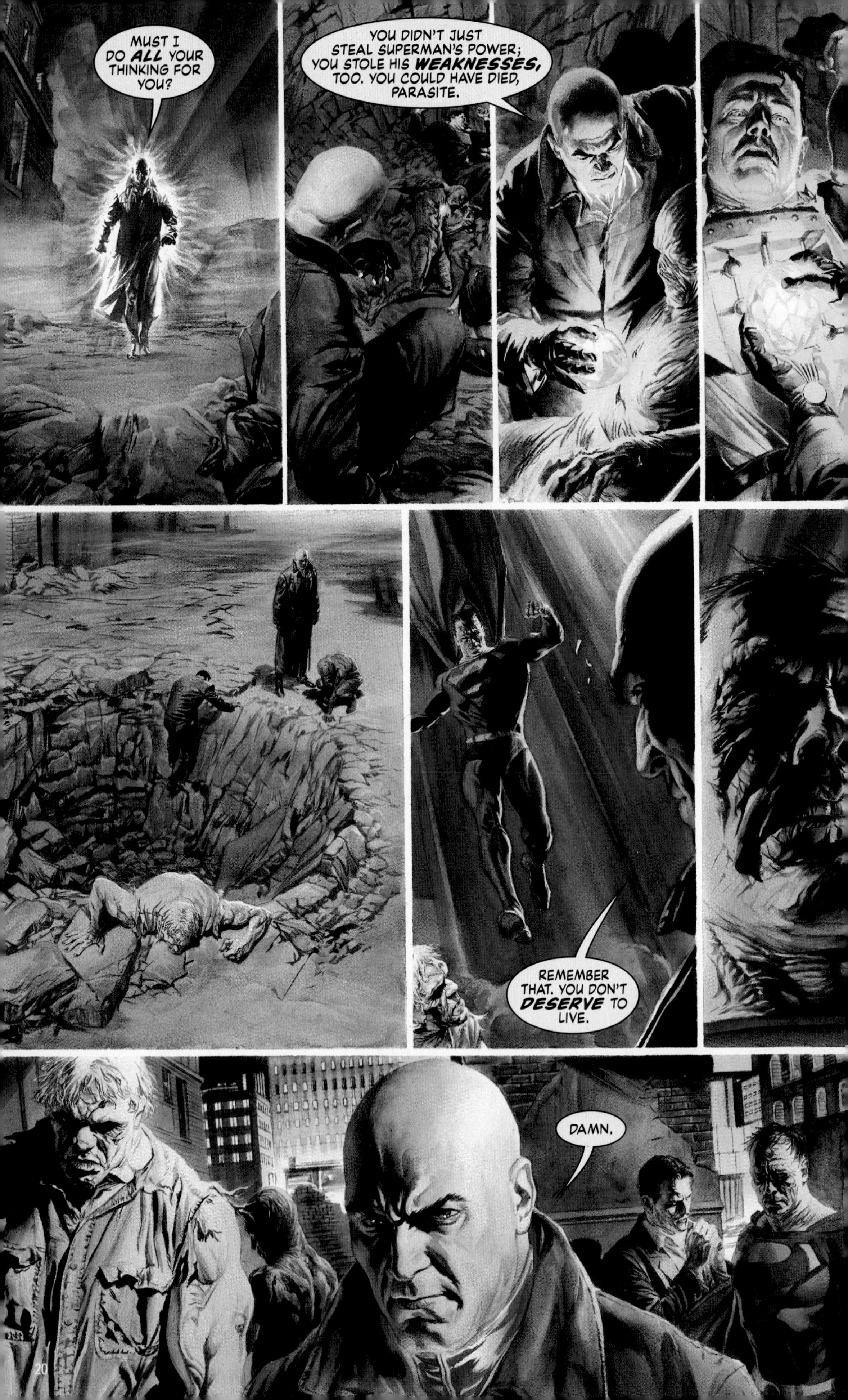
MUST I DO ALL YOUR THINKING FOR YOU?
YOU DIDN'T JUST STEAL SUPERMAN'S POWER; YOU STOLE HIS WEAKNESSES, TOO. YOU COULD HAVE DIED, PARASITE.
REMEMBER THAT. YOU DON'T DESERVE TO LIVE.
DAMN.

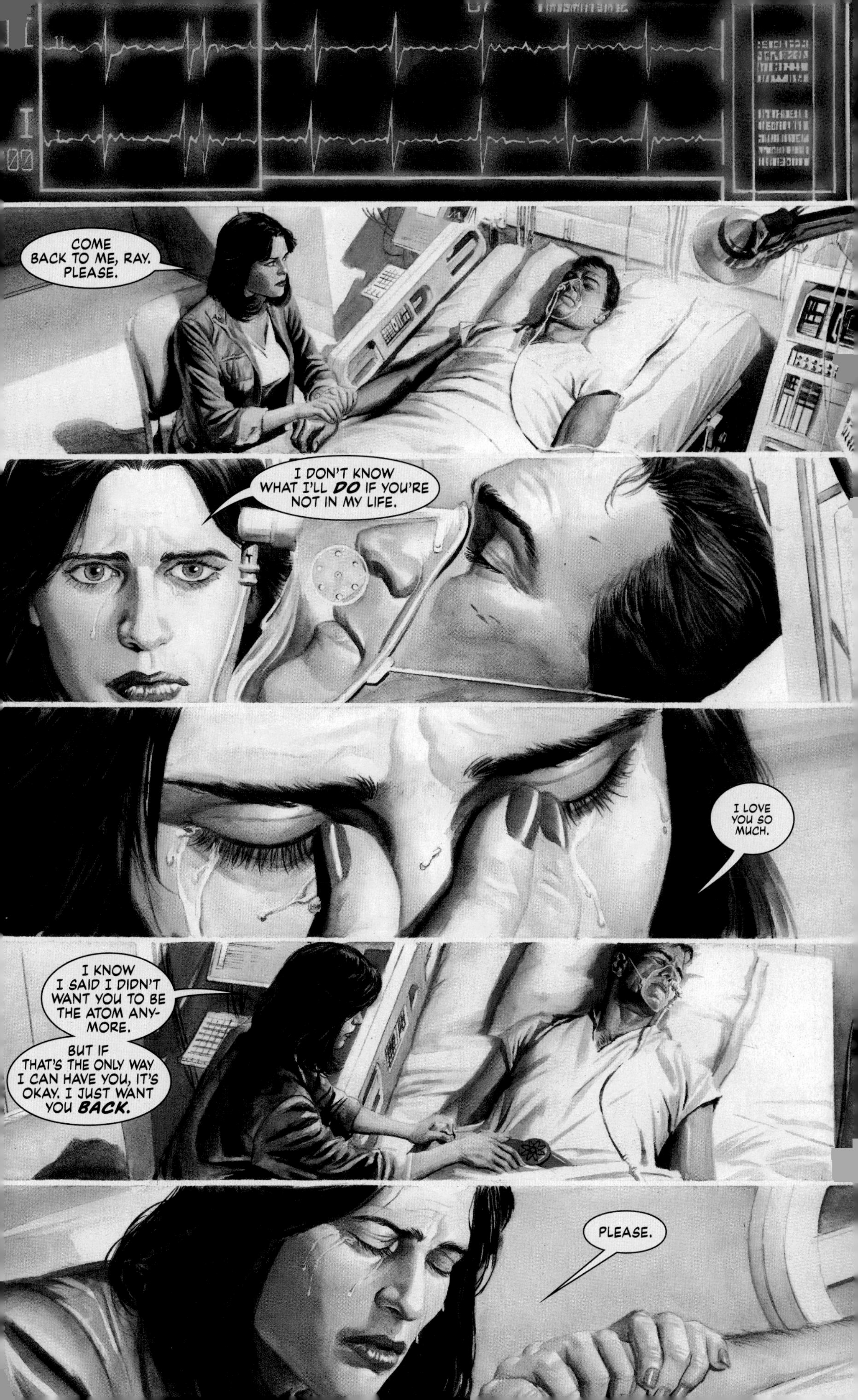
COME BACK TO ME, RAY. PLEASE.
I DON'T KNOW WHAT I'LL **DO** IF YOU'RE NOT IN MY LIFE.
I LOVE YOU SO MUCH.
I KNOW I SAID I DIDN'T WANT YOU TO BE THE ATOM ANY-MORE.
BUT IF THAT'S THE ONLY WAY I CAN HAVE YOU, IT'S OKAY. I JUST WANT YOU **BACK.**
PLEASE.

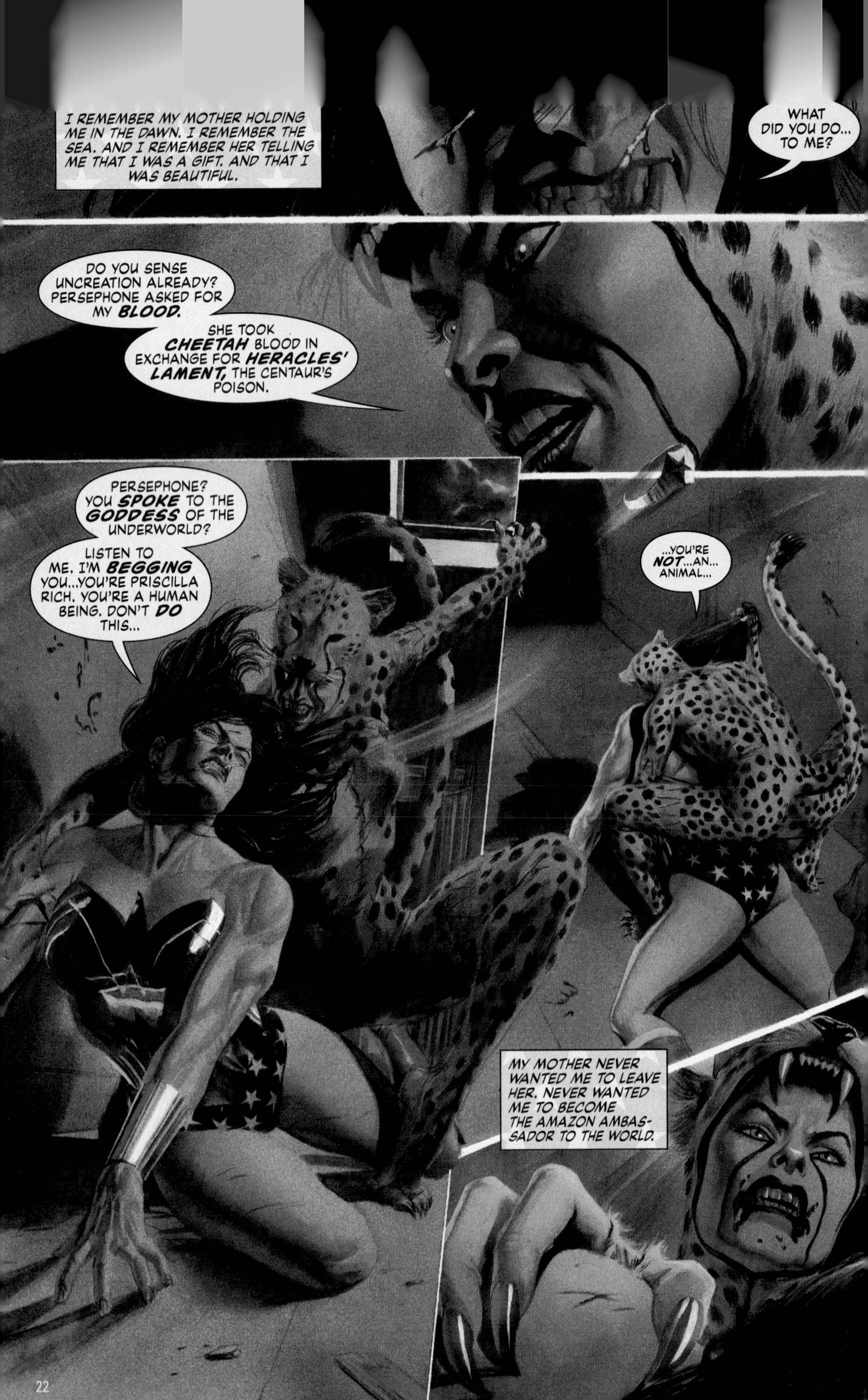
I REMEMBER MY MOTHER HOLDING ME IN THE DAWN. I REMEMBER THE SEA. AND I REMEMBER HER TELLING ME THAT I WAS A GIFT. AND THAT I WAS BEAUTIFUL.
WHAT DID YOU DO... TO ME?
DO YOU SENSE UNCREATION ALREADY? PERSEPHONE ASKED FOR MY BLOOD.
SHE TOOK CHEETAH BLOOD IN EXCHANGE FOR HERACLES' LAMENT, THE CENTAUR'S POISON.
PERSEPHONE? YOU SPOKE TO THE GODDESS OF THE UNDERWORLD?
LISTEN TO ME. I'M BEGGING YOU...YOU'RE PRISCILLA RICH. YOU'RE A HUMAN BEING. DON'T DO THIS...
...YOU'RE NOT...AN... ANIMAL...
MY MOTHER NEVER WANTED ME TO LEAVE HER. NEVER WANTED ME TO BECOME THE AMAZON AMBASSADOR TO THE WORLD.

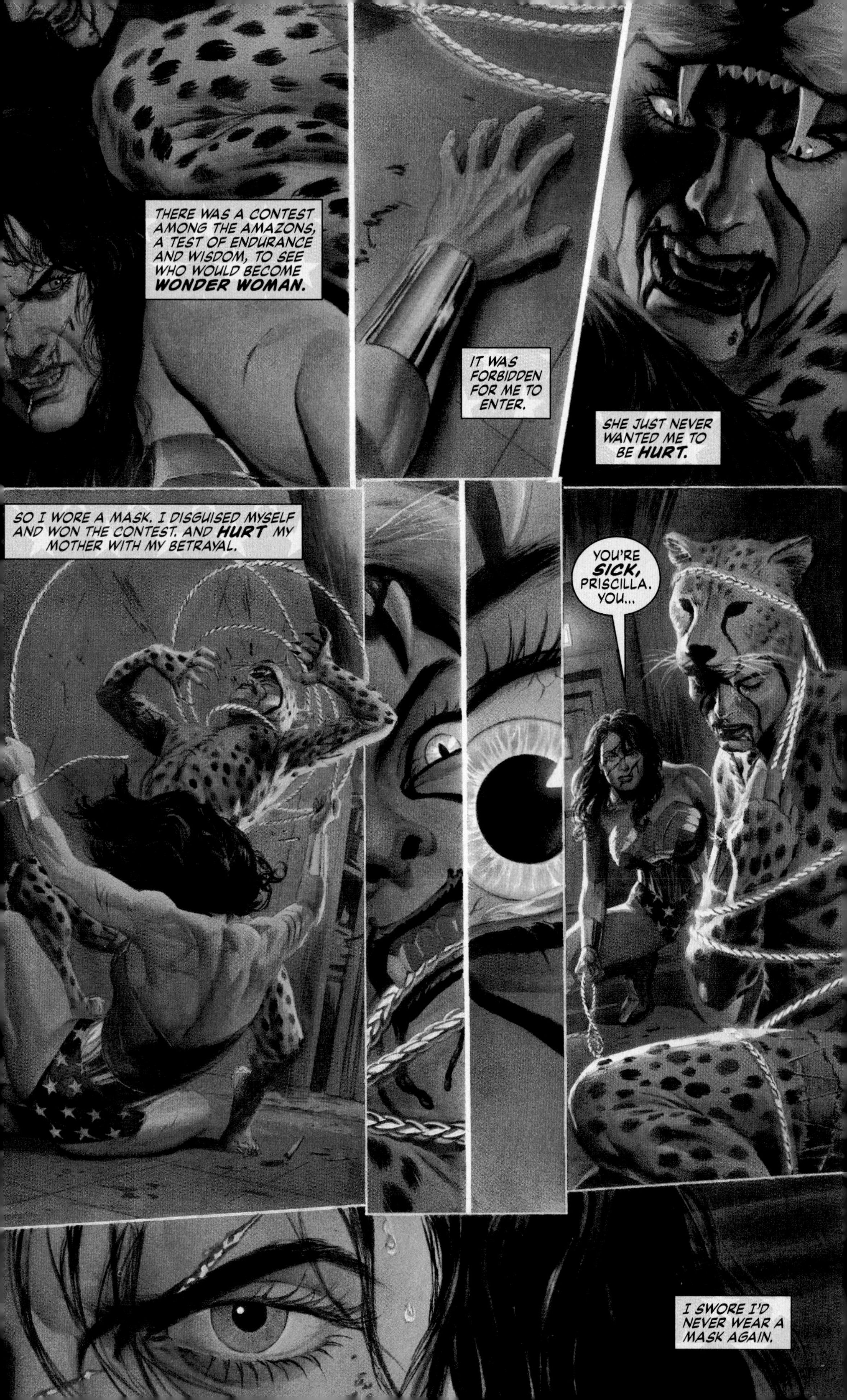
THERE WAS A CONTEST AMONG THE AMAZONS, A TEST OF ENDURANCE AND WISDOM, TO SEE WHO WOULD BECOME **WONDER WOMAN.**
IT WAS FORBIDDEN FOR ME TO ENTER.
SHE JUST NEVER WANTED ME TO BE **HURT.**
SO I WORE A MASK. I DISGUISED MYSELF AND WON THE CONTEST. AND **HURT** MY MOTHER WITH MY BETRAYAL.
YOU'RE **SICK,** PRISCILLA. YOU...
I SWORE I'D NEVER WEAR A MASK AGAIN.

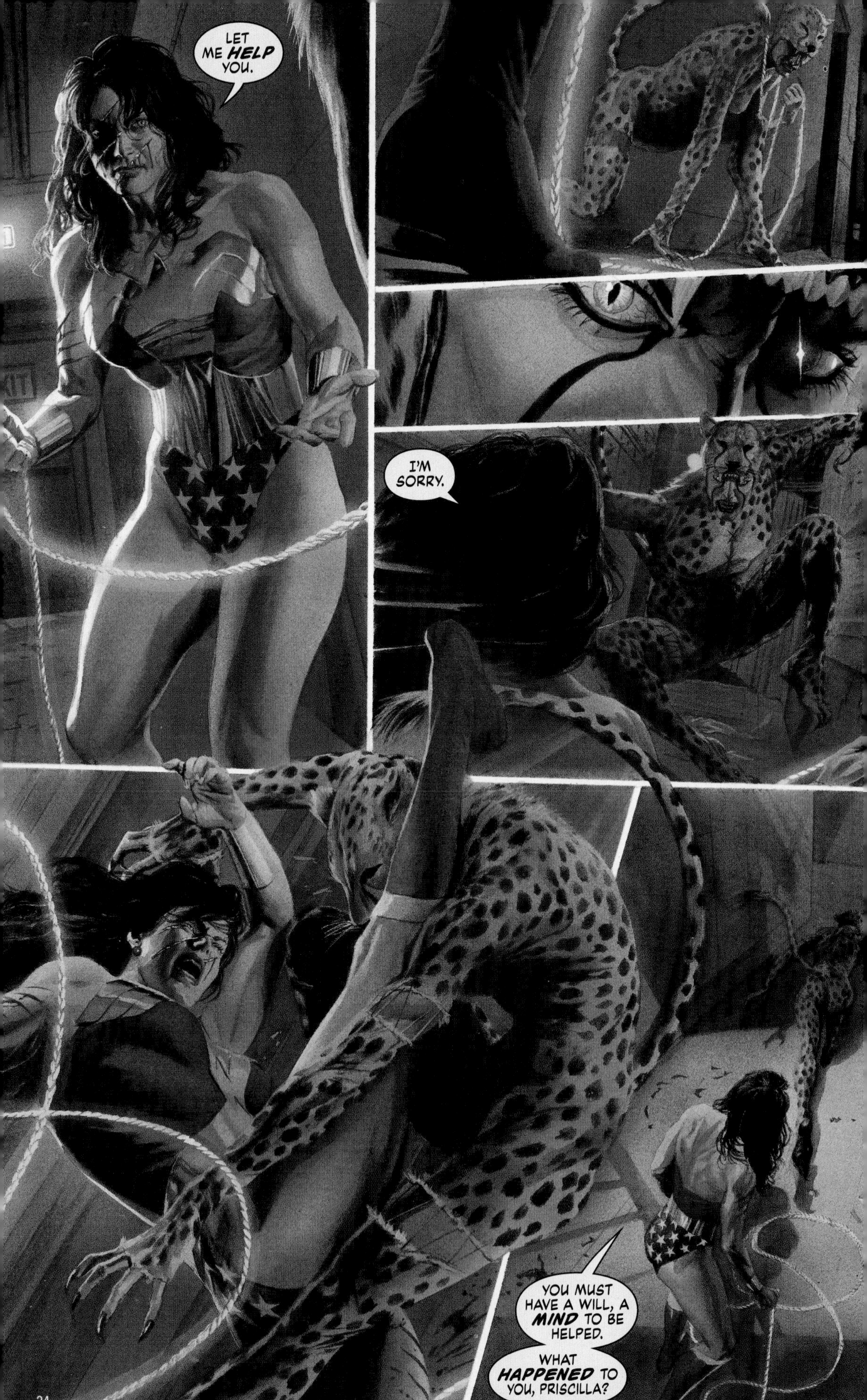
LET ME HELP YOU.
I'M SORRY.
YOU MUST HAVE A WILL, A MIND TO BE HELPED.
WHAT HAPPENED TO YOU, PRISCILLA?

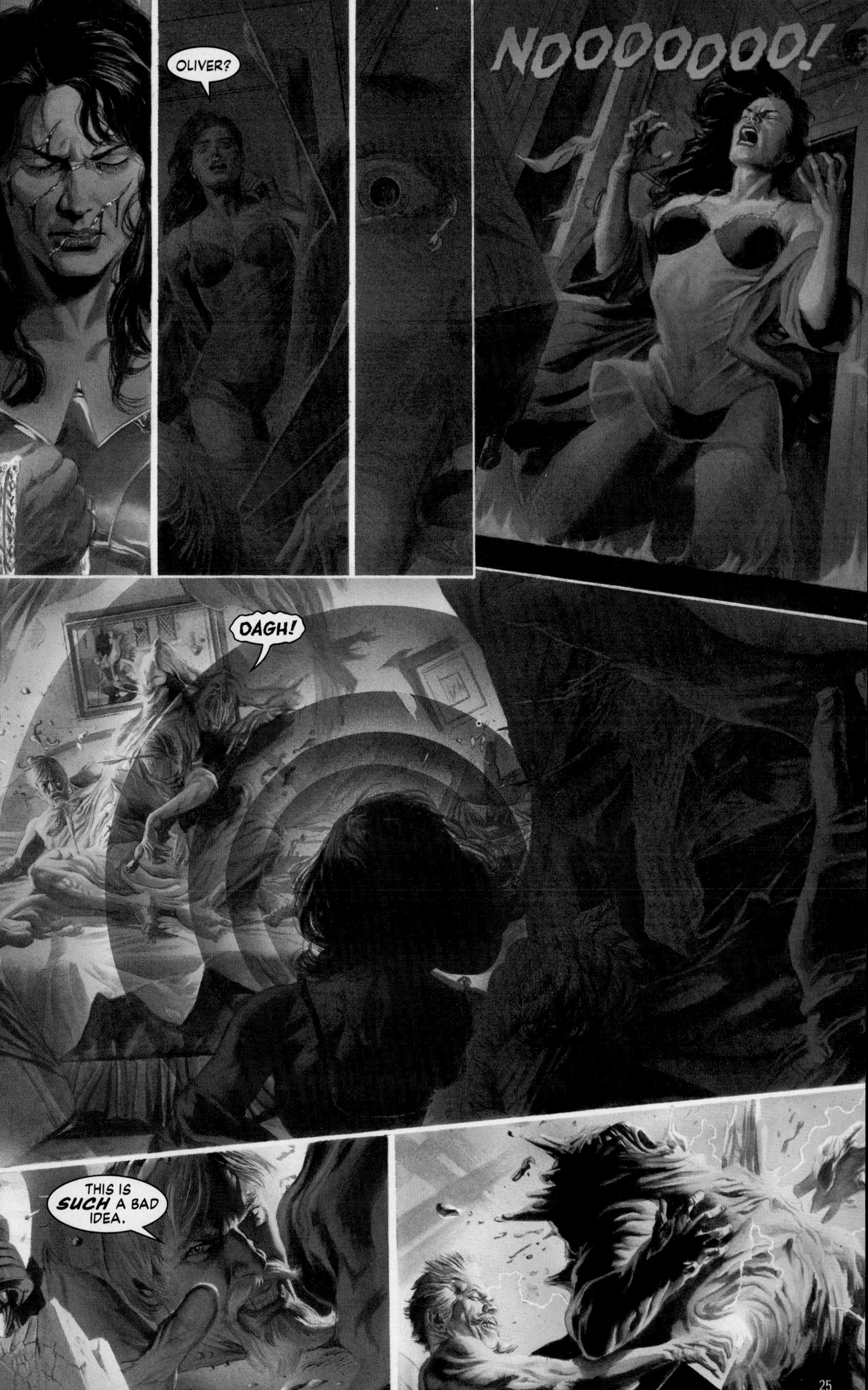
OLIVER?
NOOOOOOO!
DAGH!
THIS IS SUCH A BAD IDEA.

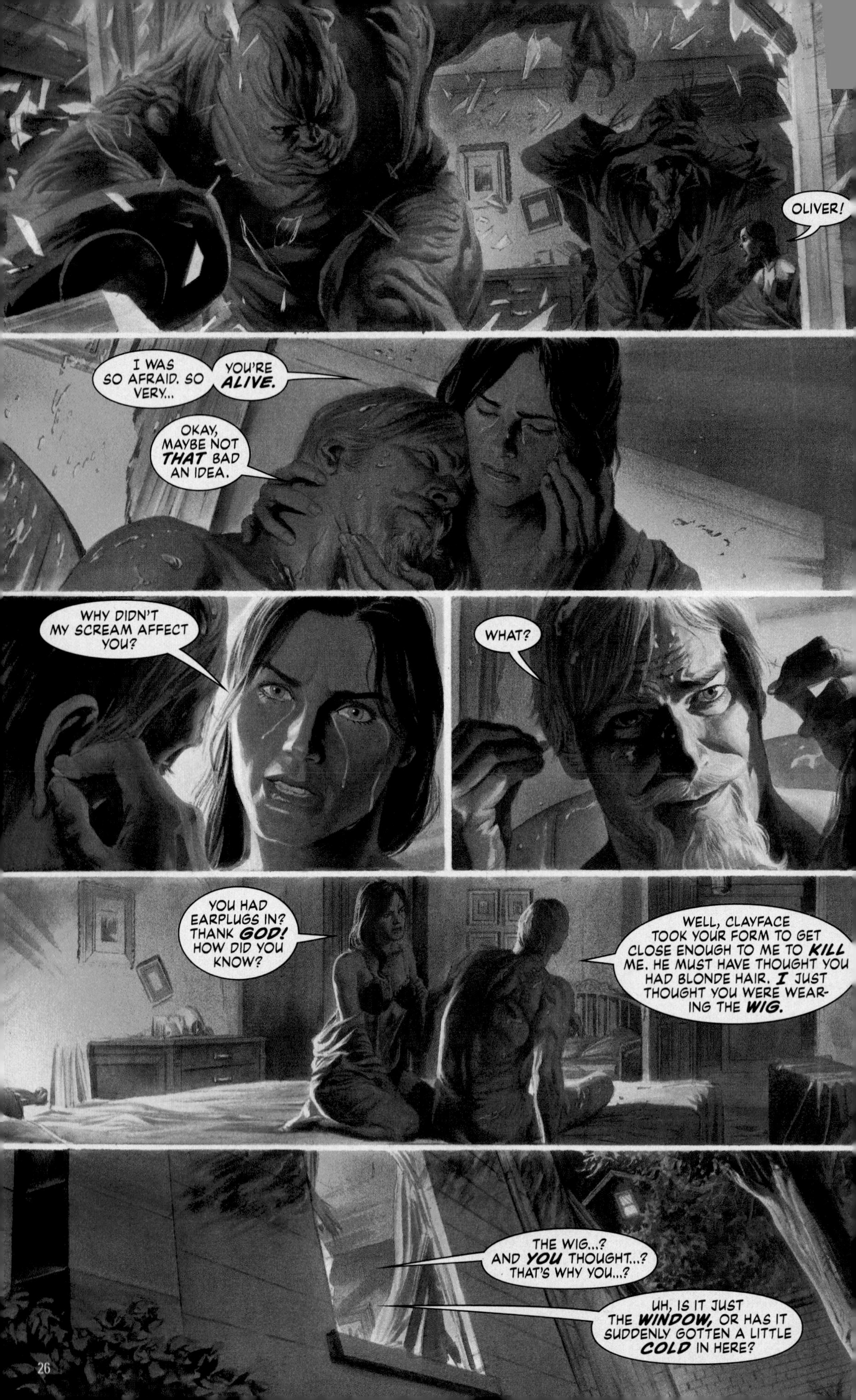
OLIVER!
I WAS SO AFRAID. SO VERY...
YOU'RE ALIVE.
OKAY, MAYBE NOT THAT BAD AN IDEA.
WHY DIDN'T MY SCREAM AFFECT YOU?
WHAT?
YOU HAD EARPLUGS IN? THANK GOD! HOW DID YOU KNOW?
WELL, CLAYFACE TOOK YOUR FORM TO GET CLOSE ENOUGH TO ME TO KILL ME. HE MUST HAVE THOUGHT YOU HAD BLONDE HAIR. I JUST THOUGHT YOU WERE WEARING THE WIG.
THE WIG...? AND YOU THOUGHT...? THAT'S WHY YOU...?
UH, IS IT JUST THE WINDOW, OR HAS IT SUDDENLY GOTTEN A LITTLE COLD IN HERE?

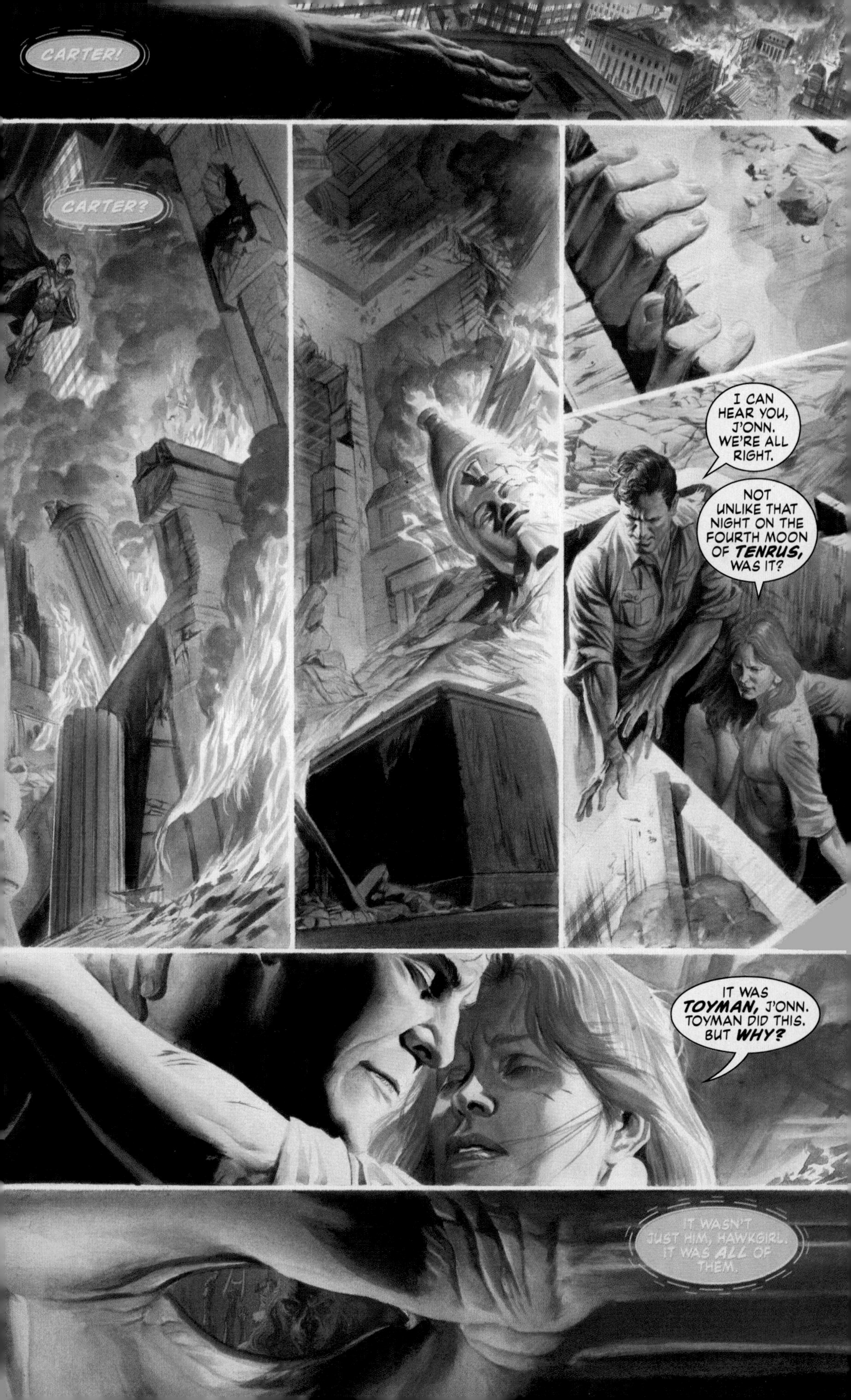
CARTER!
CARTER?
I CAN HEAR YOU, J'ONN. WE'RE ALL RIGHT.
NOT UNLIKE THAT NIGHT ON THE FOURTH MOON OF **TENRUS,** WAS IT?
IT WAS **TOYMAN,** J'ONN. TOYMAN DID THIS. BUT **WHY?**
IT WASN'T JUST HIM, HAWKGIRL. IT WAS **ALL** OF THEM.

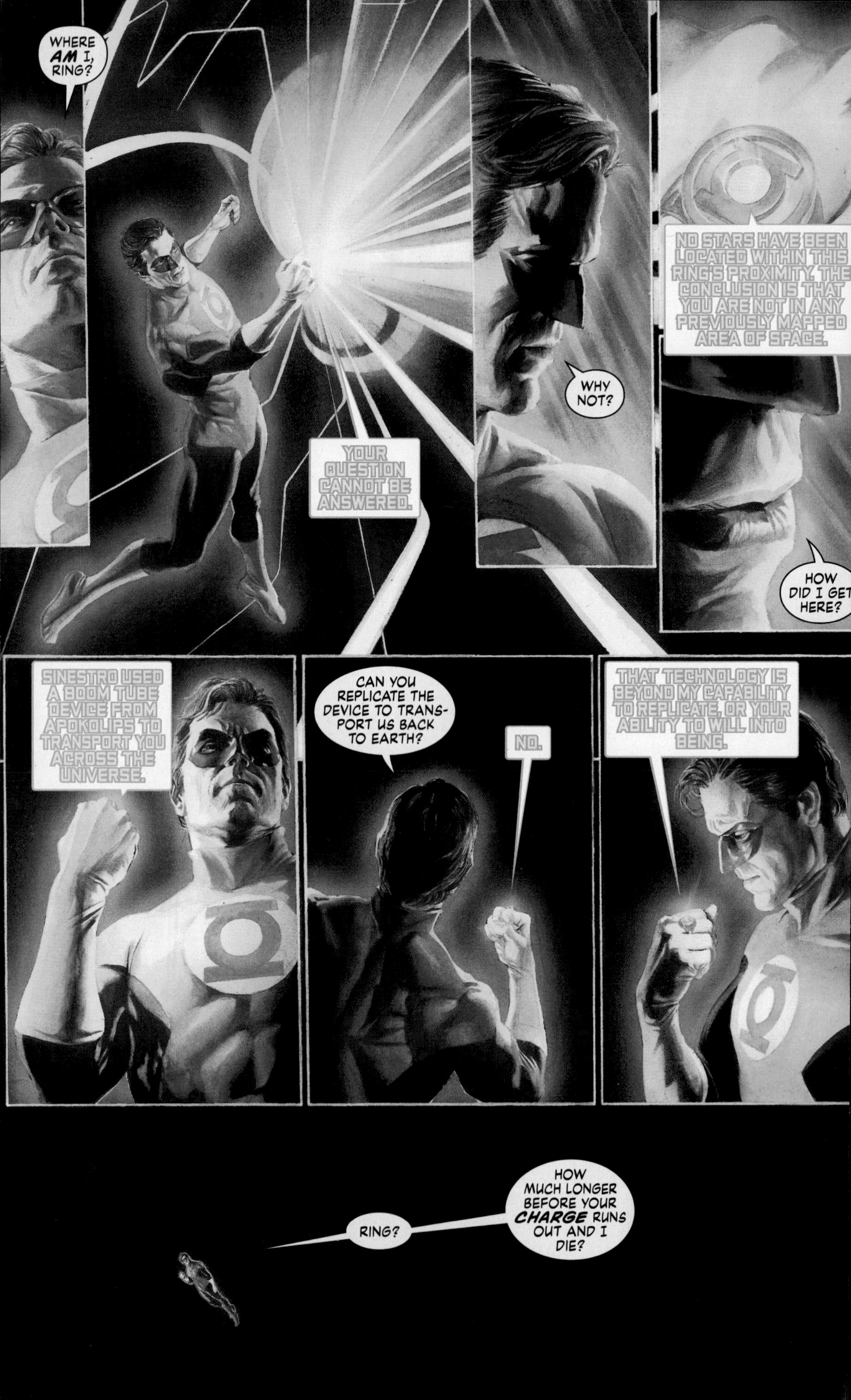
WHERE AM I, RING?
YOUR QUESTION CANNOT BE ANSWERED.
WHY NOT?
NO STARS HAVE BEEN LOCATED WITHIN THIS RING'S PROXIMITY. THE CONCLUSION IS THAT YOU ARE NOT IN ANY PREVIOUSLY MAPPED AREA OF SPACE.
HOW DID I GET HERE?
SINESTRO USED A BOOM TUBE DEVICE FROM APOKOLIPS TO TRANSPORT YOU ACROSS THE UNIVERSE.
CAN YOU REPLICATE THE DEVICE TO TRANSPORT US BACK TO EARTH?
NO.
THAT TECHNOLOGY IS BEYOND MY CAPABILITY TO REPLICATE, OR YOUR ABILITY TO WILL INTO BEING.
RING?
HOW MUCH LONGER BEFORE YOUR CHARGE RUNS OUT AND I DIE?

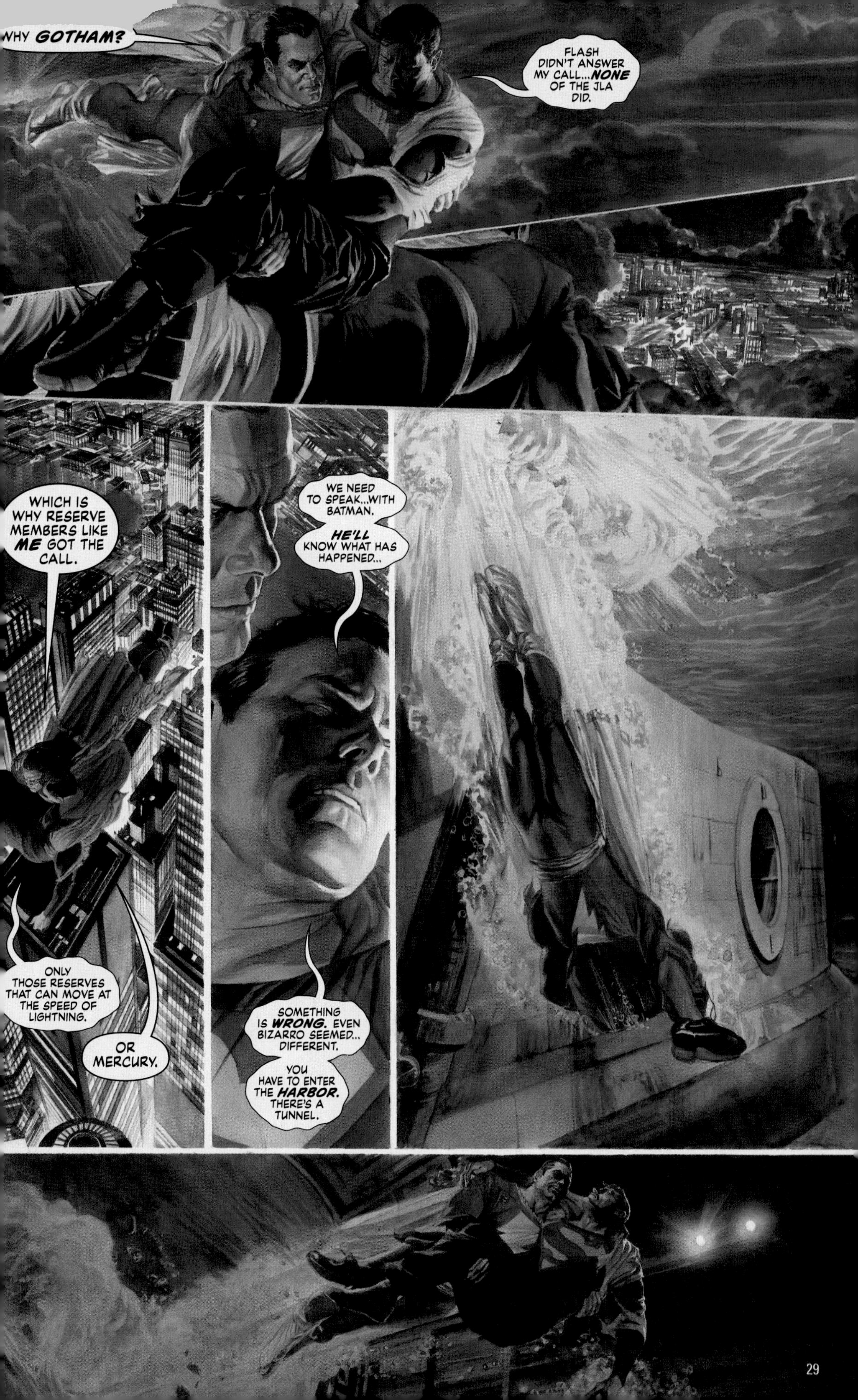
WHY GOTHAM?
FLASH DIDN'T ANSWER MY CALL...NONE OF THE JLA DID.
WHICH IS WHY RESERVE MEMBERS LIKE ME GOT THE CALL.
ONLY THOSE RESERVES THAT CAN MOVE AT THE SPEED OF LIGHTNING.
OR MERCURY.
WE NEED TO SPEAK...WITH BATMAN.
HE'LL KNOW WHAT HAS HAPPENED...
SOMETHING IS WRONG. EVEN BIZARRO SEEMED... DIFFERENT.
YOU HAVE TO ENTER THE HARBOR. THERE'S A TUNNEL.

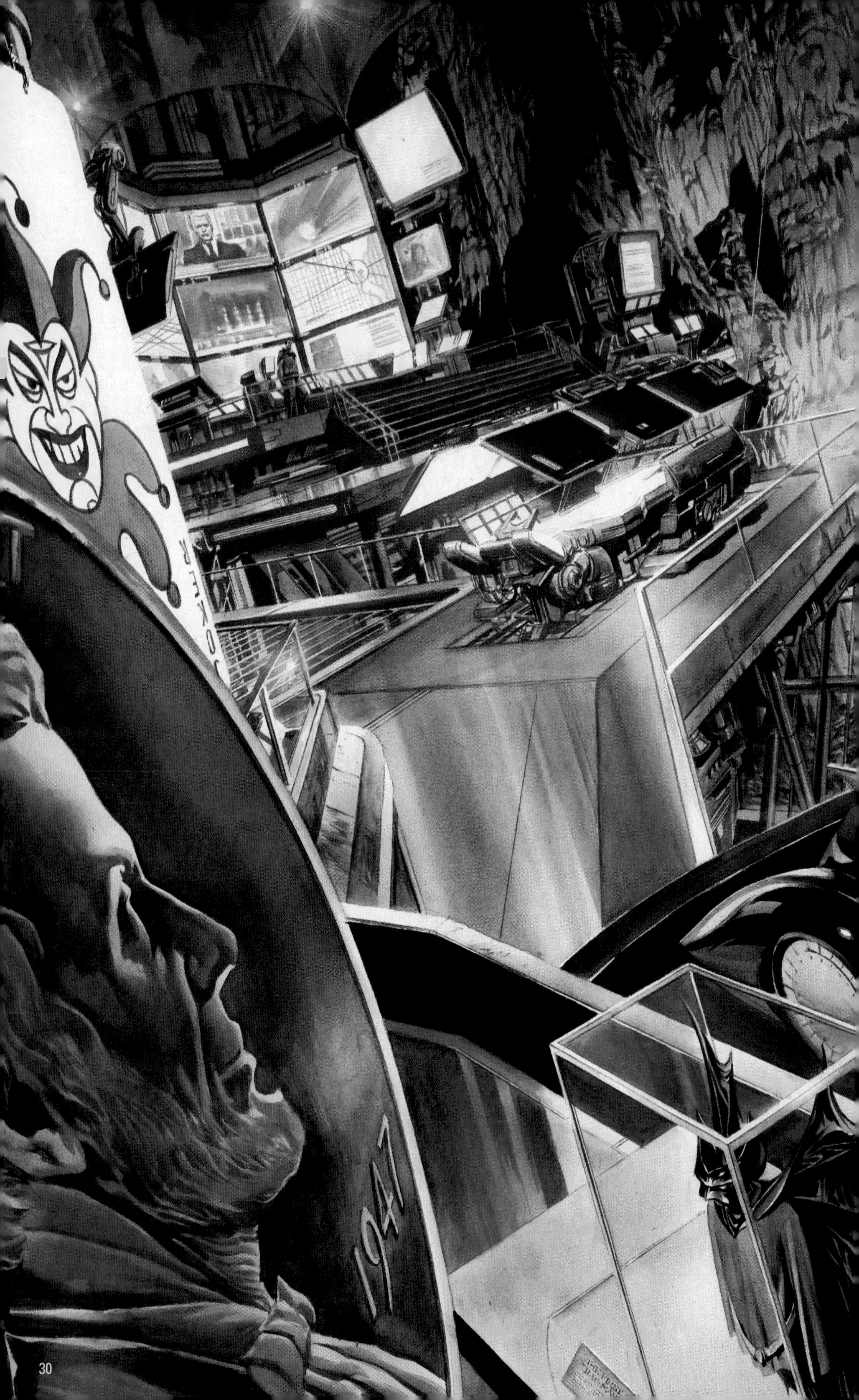
JOKER
1947

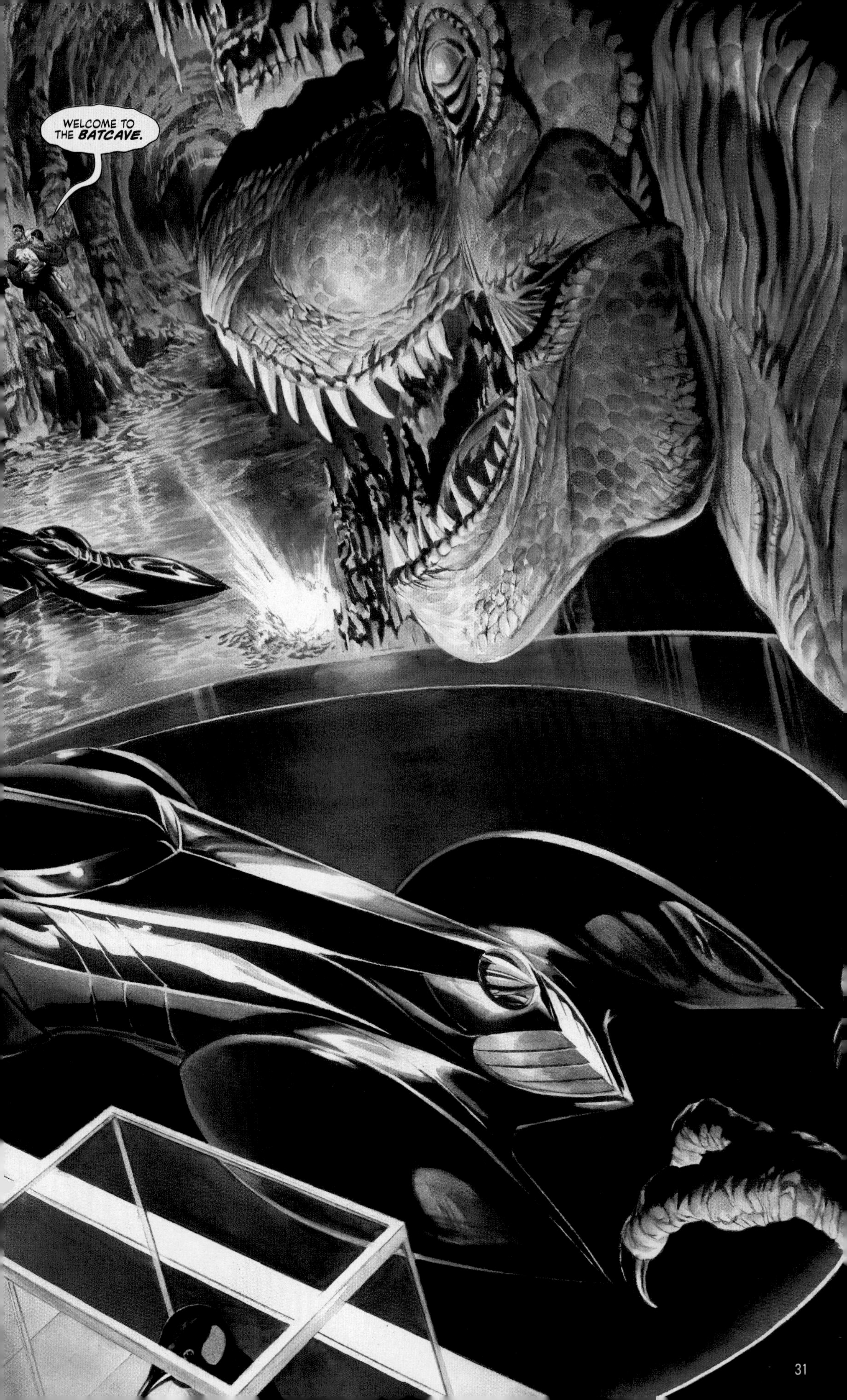
WELCOME TO THE *BATCAVE.*

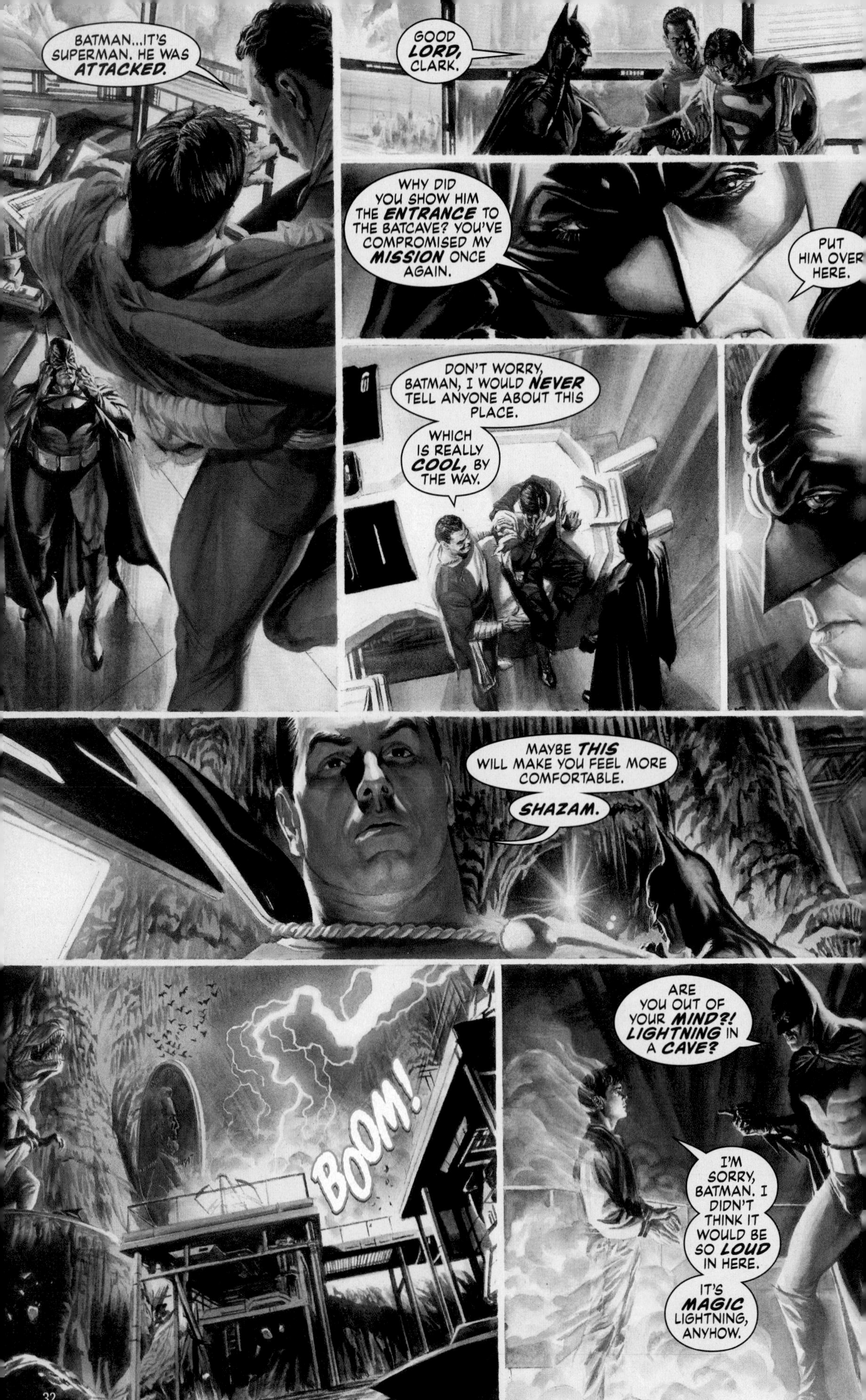

BATMAN...IT'S SUPERMAN. HE WAS ATTACKED.
GOOD LORD, CLARK.
WHY DID YOU SHOW HIM THE ENTRANCE TO THE BATCAVE? YOU'VE COMPROMISED MY MISSION ONCE AGAIN.
PUT HIM OVER HERE.
DON'T WORRY, BATMAN, I WOULD NEVER TELL ANYONE ABOUT THIS PLACE.
WHICH IS REALLY COOL, BY THE WAY.
MAYBE THIS WILL MAKE YOU FEEL MORE COMFORTABLE.
SHAZAM.
BOOM!
ARE YOU OUT OF YOUR MIND?! LIGHTNING IN A CAVE?
I'M SORRY, BATMAN. I DIDN'T THINK IT WOULD BE SO LOUD IN HERE.
IT'S MAGIC LIGHTNING, ANYHOW.

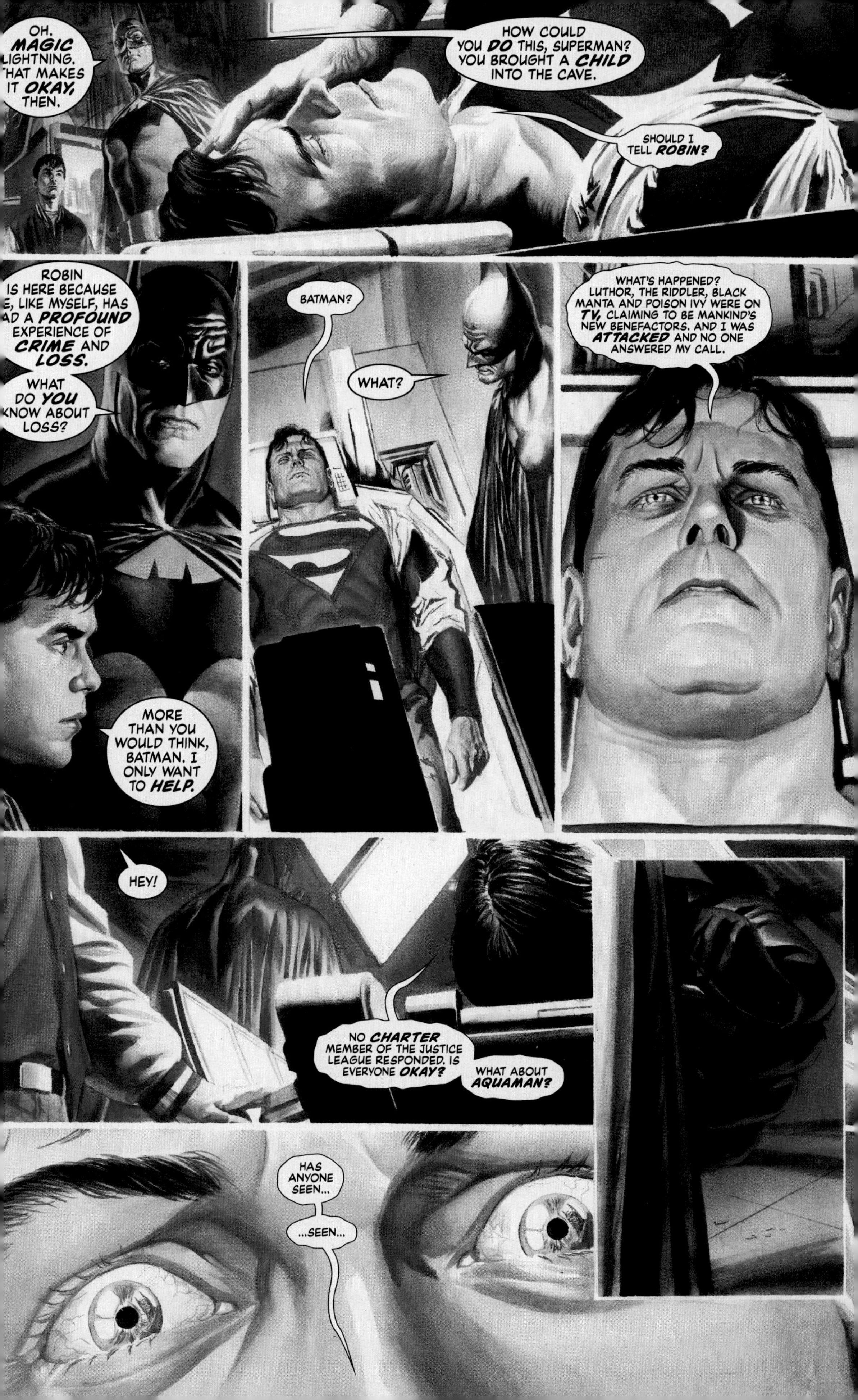
OH. MAGIC LIGHTNING. THAT MAKES IT OKAY, THEN.
HOW COULD YOU DO THIS, SUPERMAN? YOU BROUGHT A CHILD INTO THE CAVE.
SHOULD I TELL ROBIN?
ROBIN IS HERE BECAUSE HE, LIKE MYSELF, HAS HAD A PROFOUND EXPERIENCE OF CRIME AND LOSS.
WHAT DO YOU KNOW ABOUT LOSS?
MORE THAN YOU WOULD THINK, BATMAN. I ONLY WANT TO HELP.
BATMAN?
WHAT?
WHAT'S HAPPENED? LUTHOR, THE RIDDLER, BLACK MANTA AND POISON IVY WERE ON TV, CLAIMING TO BE MANKIND'S NEW BENEFACTORS. AND I WAS ATTACKED AND NO ONE ANSWERED MY CALL.
HEY!
NO CHARTER MEMBER OF THE JUSTICE LEAGUE RESPONDED. IS EVERYONE OKAY?
WHAT ABOUT AQUAMAN?
HAS ANYONE SEEN...
...SEEN...

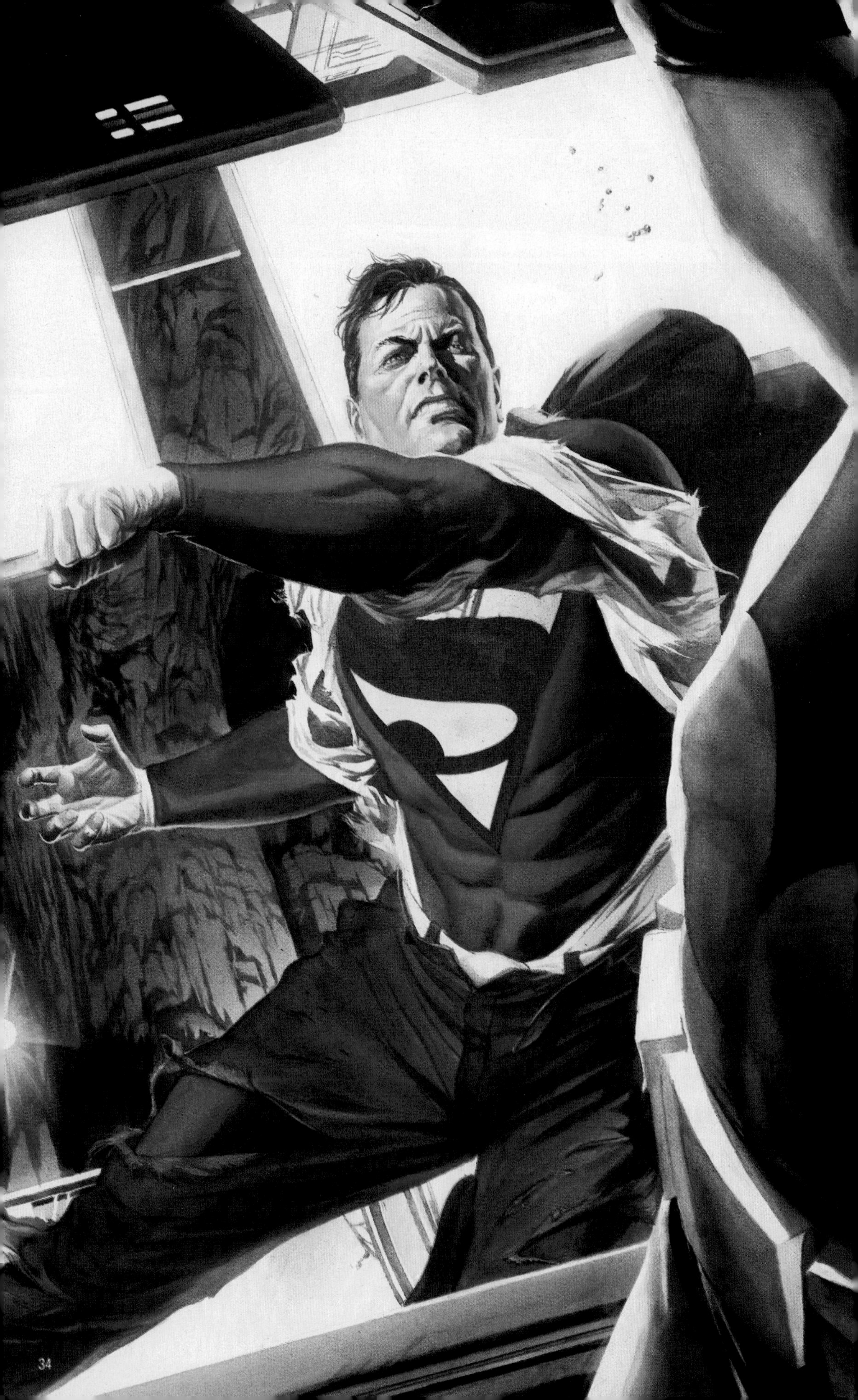

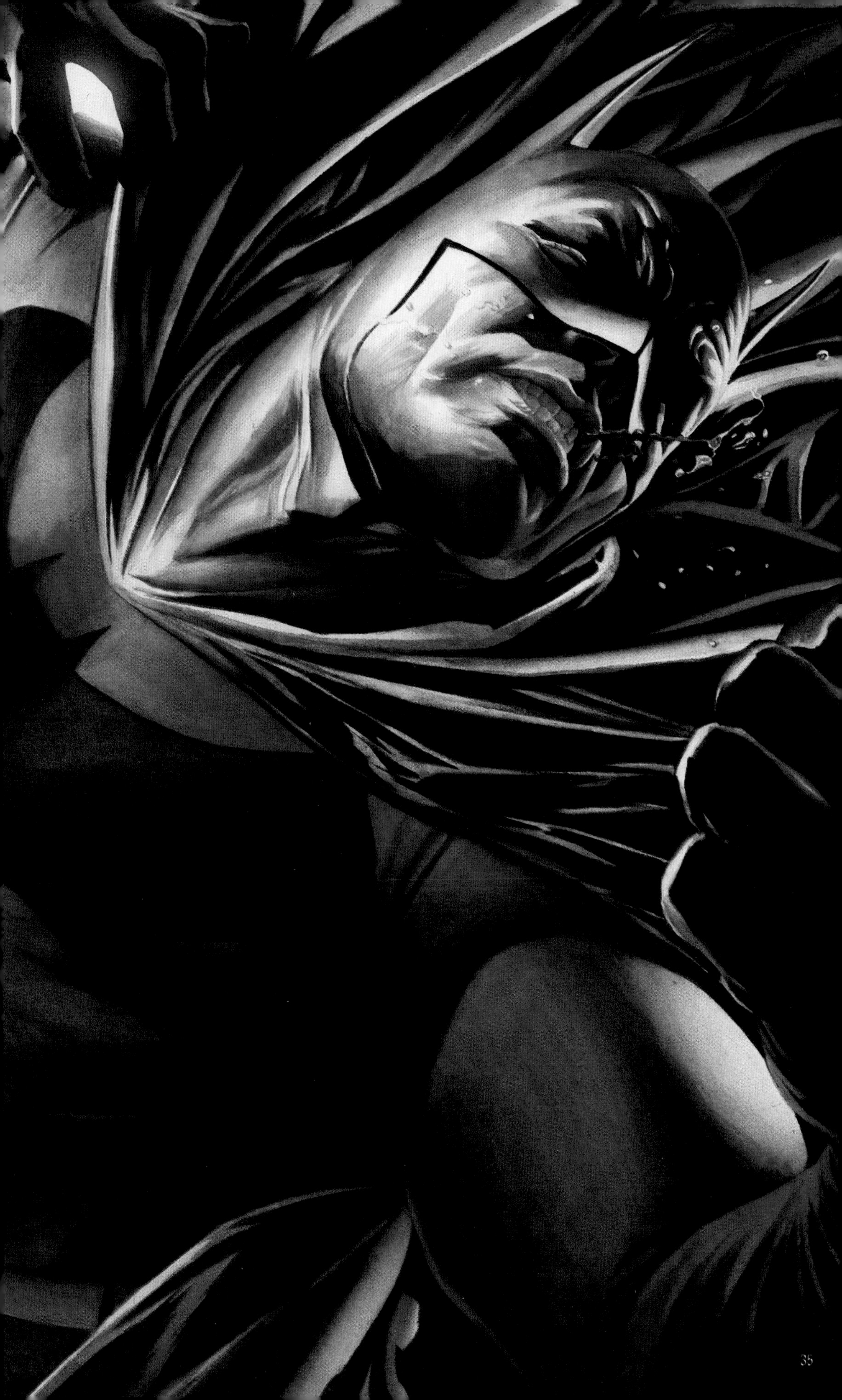

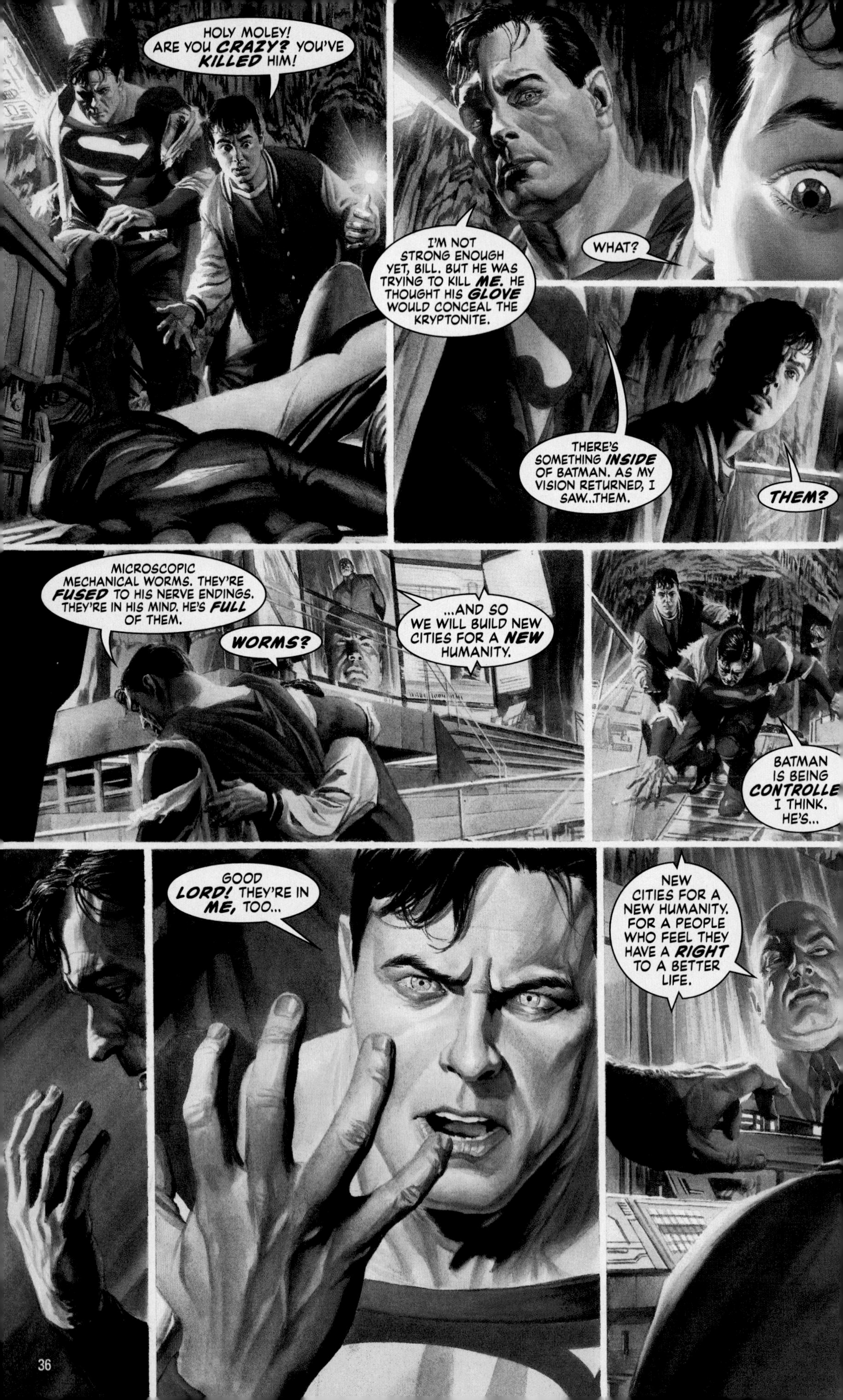
HOLY MOLEY! ARE YOU CRAZY? YOU'VE KILLED HIM!
I'M NOT STRONG ENOUGH YET, BILL. BUT HE WAS TRYING TO KILL ME. HE THOUGHT HIS GLOVE WOULD CONCEAL THE KRYPTONITE.
WHAT?
THERE'S SOMETHING INSIDE OF BATMAN. AS MY VISION RETURNED, I SAW...THEM.
THEM?
MICROSCOPIC MECHANICAL WORMS. THEY'RE FUSED TO HIS NERVE ENDINGS. THEY'RE IN HIS MIND. HE'S FULL OF THEM.
WORMS?
...AND SO WE WILL BUILD NEW CITIES FOR A NEW HUMANITY.
BATMAN IS BEING CONTROLLE I THINK. HE'S...
GOOD LORD! THEY'RE IN ME, TOO...
NEW CITIES FOR A NEW HUMANITY. FOR A PEOPLE WHO FEEL THEY HAVE A RIGHT TO A BETTER LIFE.

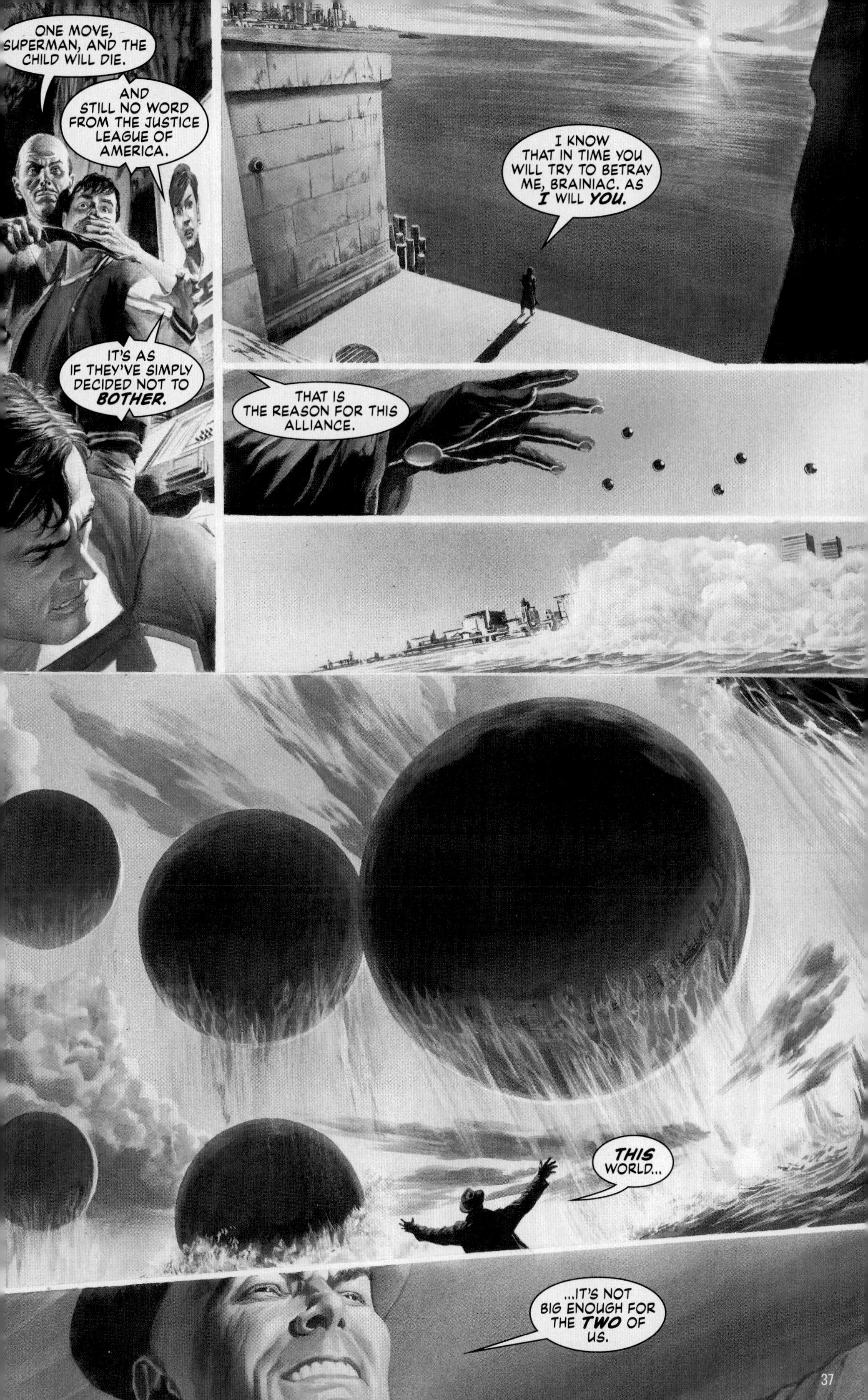
ONE MOVE, SUPERMAN, AND THE CHILD WILL DIE.
AND STILL NO WORD FROM THE JUSTICE LEAGUE OF AMERICA.
IT'S AS IF THEY'VE SIMPLY DECIDED NOT TO **BOTHER.**
I KNOW THAT IN TIME YOU WILL TRY TO BETRAY ME, BRAINIAC. AS ***I*** WILL ***YOU.***
THAT IS THE REASON FOR THIS ALLIANCE.
THIS WORLD...
...IT'S NOT BIG ENOUGH FOR THE ***TWO*** OF US.

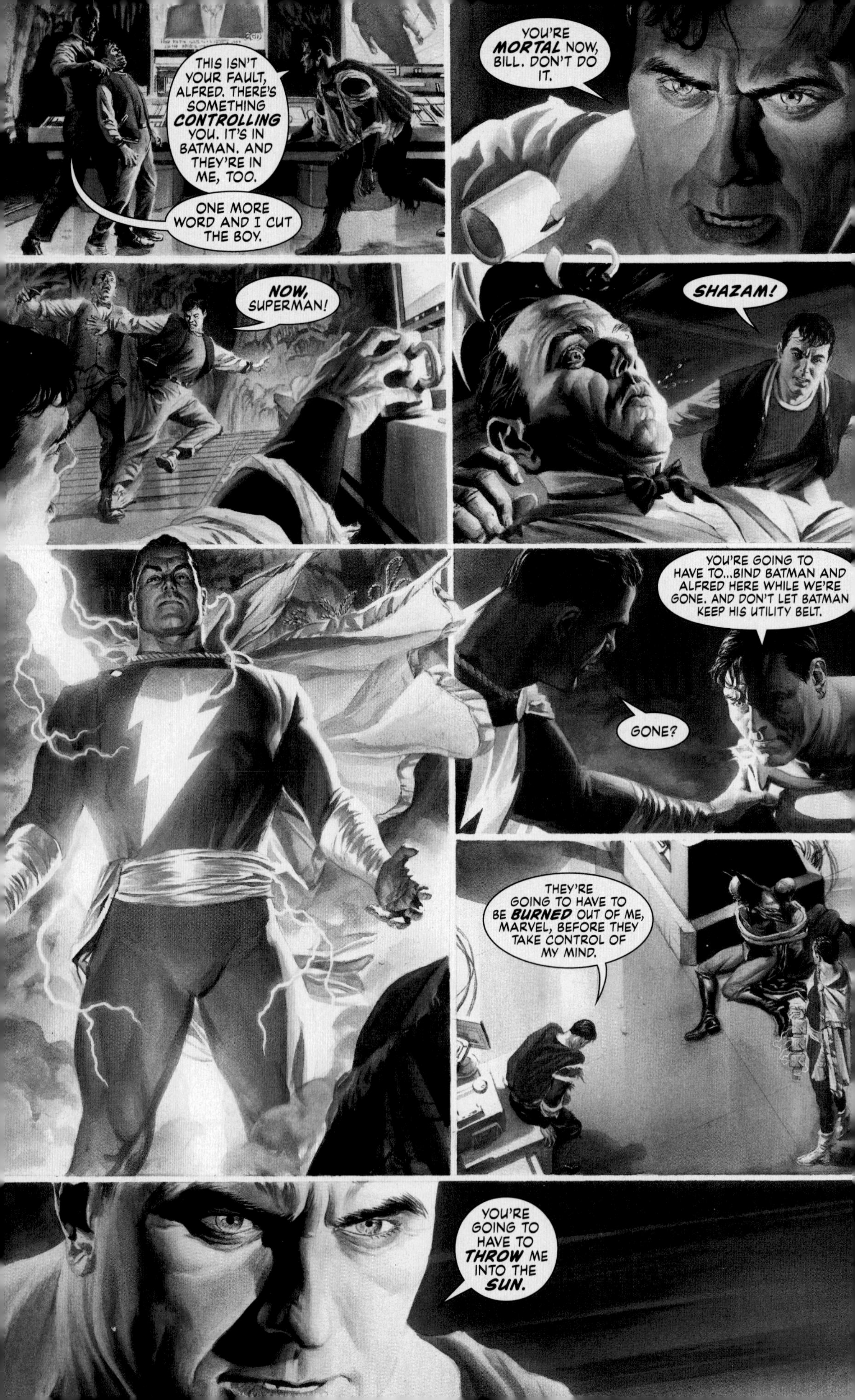
THIS ISN'T YOUR FAULT, ALFRED. THERE'S SOMETHING CONTROLLING YOU. IT'S IN BATMAN. AND THEY'RE IN ME, TOO.
ONE MORE WORD AND I CUT THE BOY.
YOU'RE MORTAL NOW, BILL. DON'T DO IT.
NOW, SUPERMAN!
SHAZAM!
YOU'RE GOING TO HAVE TO...BIND BATMAN AND ALFRED HERE WHILE WE'RE GONE. AND DON'T LET BATMAN KEEP HIS UTILITY BELT.
GONE?
THEY'RE GOING TO HAVE TO BE BURNED OUT OF ME, MARVEL, BEFORE THEY TAKE CONTROL OF MY MIND.
YOU'RE GOING TO HAVE TO THROW ME INTO THE SUN.

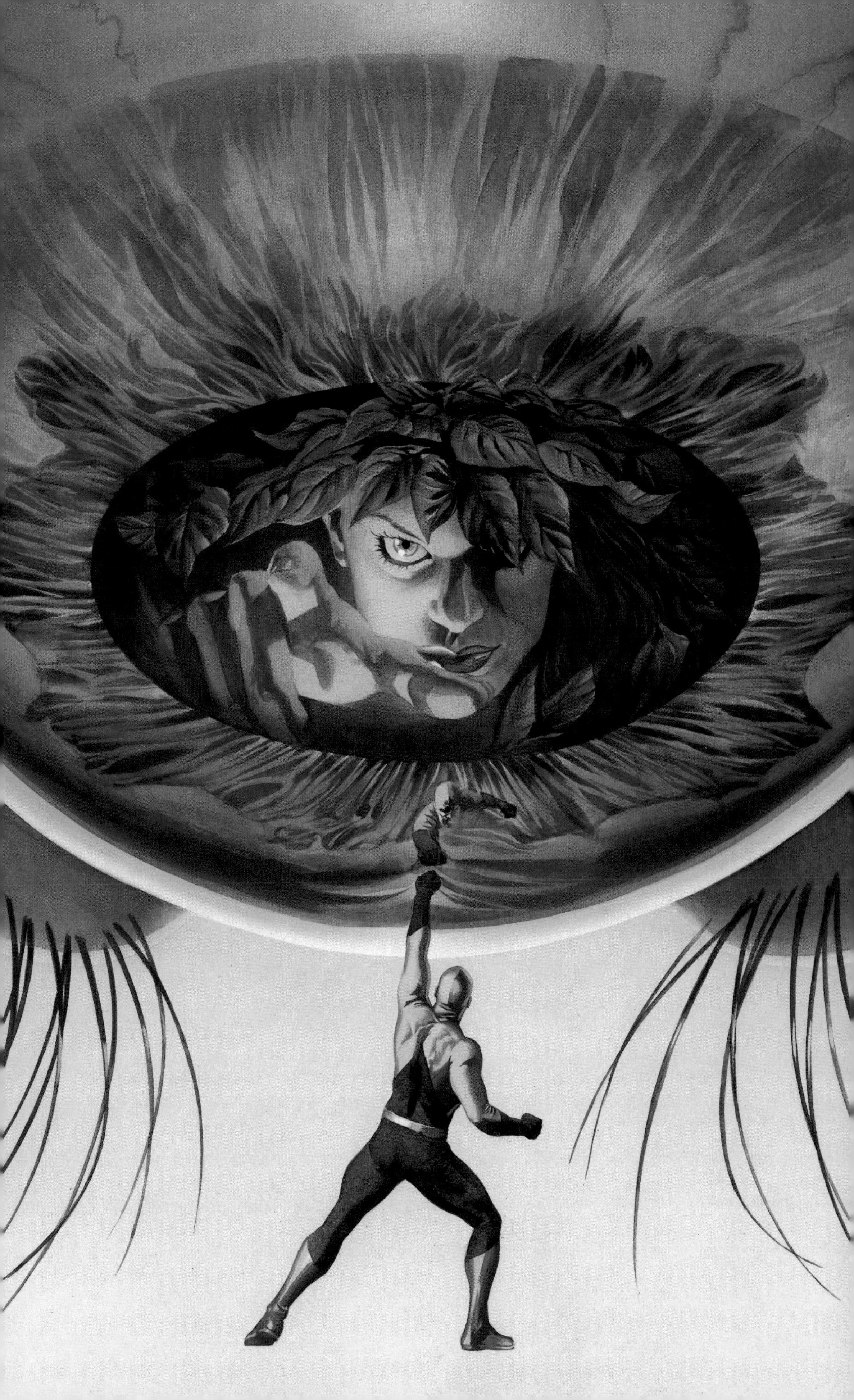

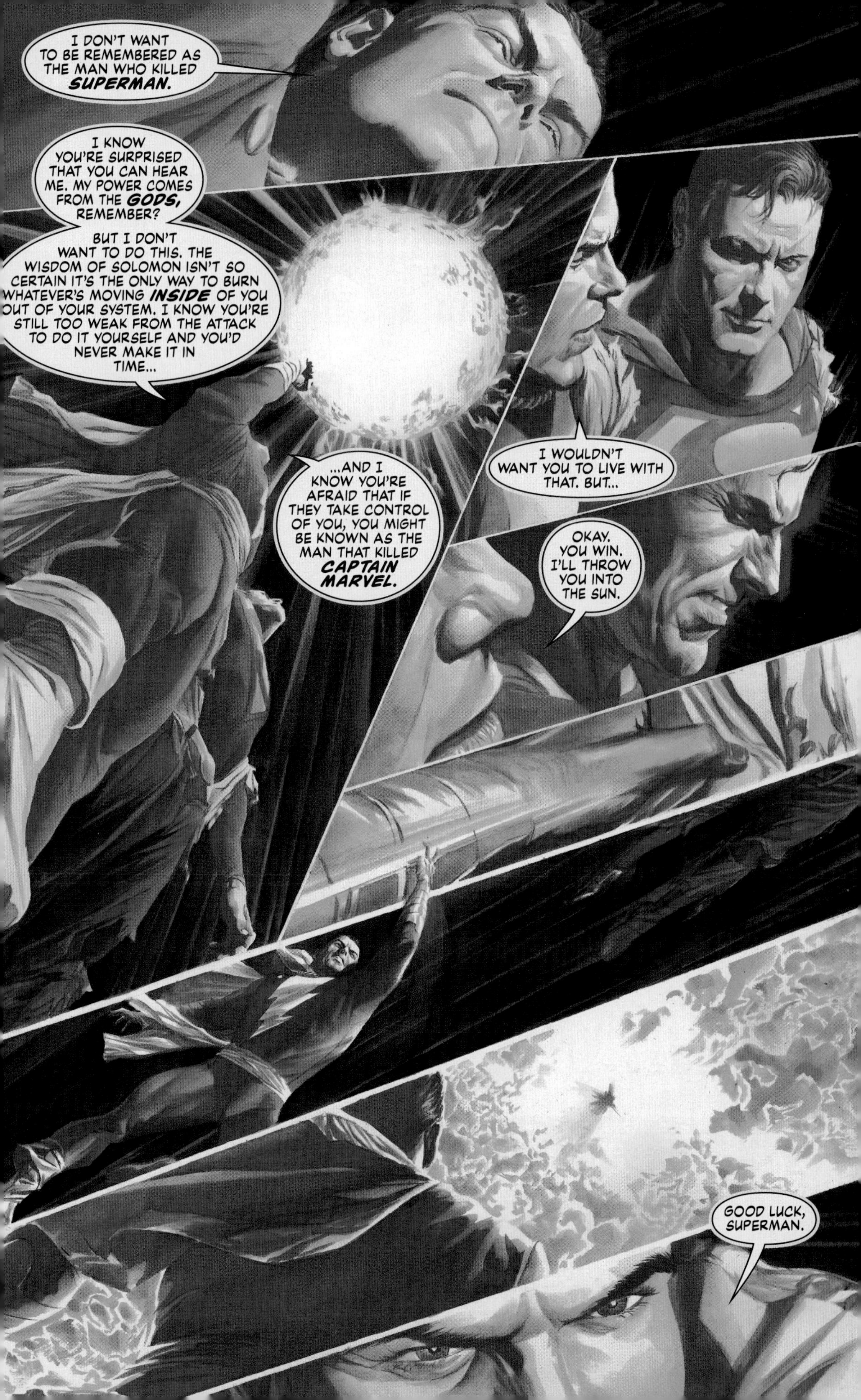
I DON'T WANT TO BE REMEMBERED AS THE MAN WHO KILLED ***SUPERMAN.***
I KNOW YOU'RE SURPRISED THAT YOU CAN HEAR ME. MY POWER COMES FROM THE ***GODS,*** REMEMBER?
BUT I DON'T WANT TO DO THIS. THE WISDOM OF SOLOMON ISN'T SO CERTAIN IT'S THE ONLY WAY TO BURN WHATEVER'S MOVING ***INSIDE*** OF YOU OUT OF YOUR SYSTEM. I KNOW YOU'RE STILL TOO WEAK FROM THE ATTACK TO DO IT YOURSELF AND YOU'D NEVER MAKE IT IN TIME...
...AND I KNOW YOU'RE AFRAID THAT IF THEY TAKE CONTROL OF YOU, YOU MIGHT BE KNOWN AS THE MAN THAT KILLED ***CAPTAIN MARVEL.***
I WOULDN'T WANT YOU TO LIVE WITH THAT. BUT...
OKAY. YOU WIN. I'LL THROW YOU INTO THE SUN.
GOOD LUCK, SUPERMAN.

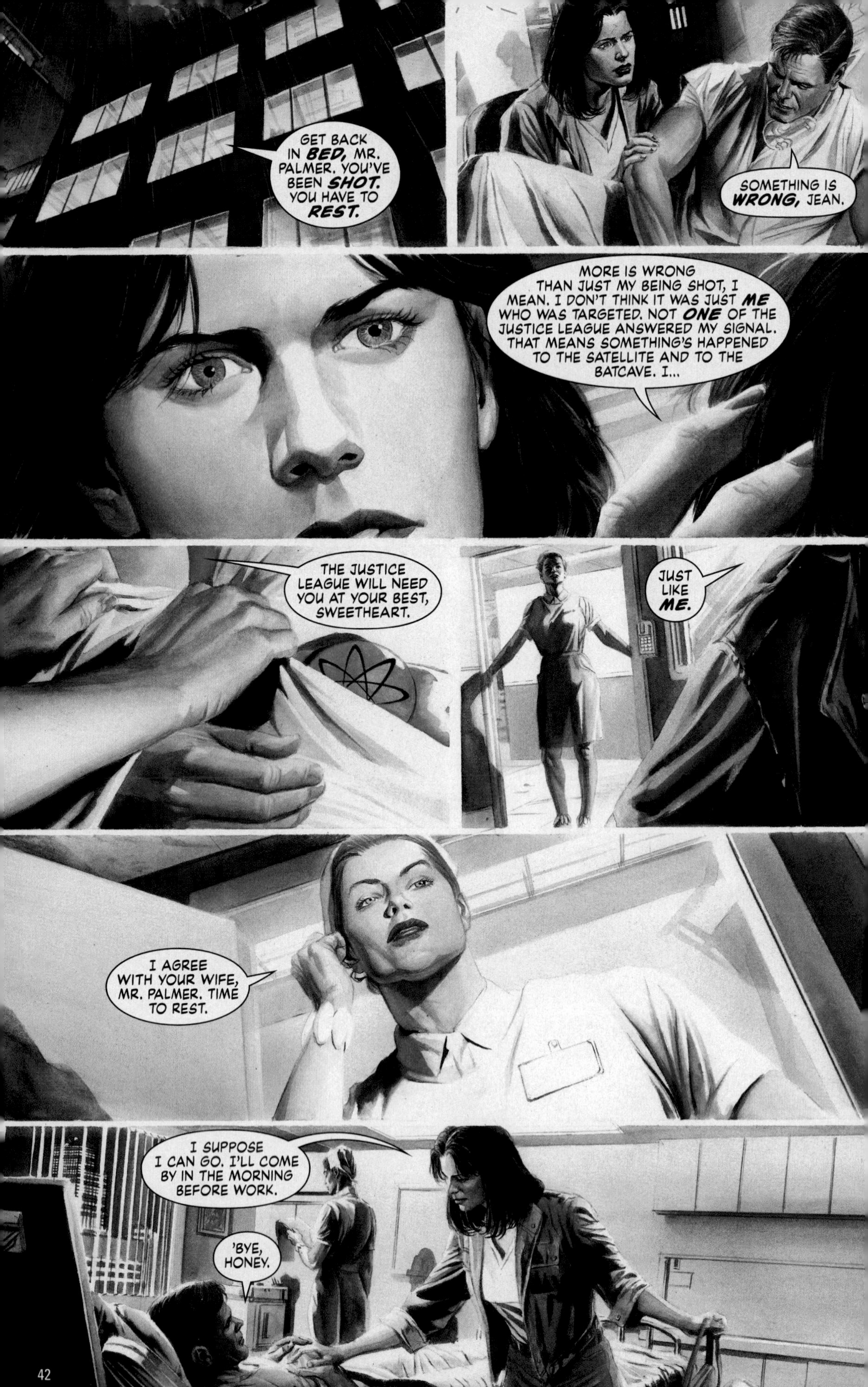
GET BACK IN BED, MR. PALMER. YOU'VE BEEN SHOT. YOU HAVE TO REST.
SOMETHING IS WRONG, JEAN.
MORE IS WRONG THAN JUST MY BEING SHOT, I MEAN. I DON'T THINK IT WAS JUST ME WHO WAS TARGETED. NOT ONE OF THE JUSTICE LEAGUE ANSWERED MY SIGNAL. THAT MEANS SOMETHING'S HAPPENED TO THE SATELLITE AND TO THE BATCAVE. I...
THE JUSTICE LEAGUE WILL NEED YOU AT YOUR BEST, SWEETHEART.
JUST LIKE ME.
I AGREE WITH YOUR WIFE, MR. PALMER. TIME TO REST.
I SUPPOSE I CAN GO. I'LL COME BY IN THE MORNING BEFORE WORK.
'BYE, HONEY.

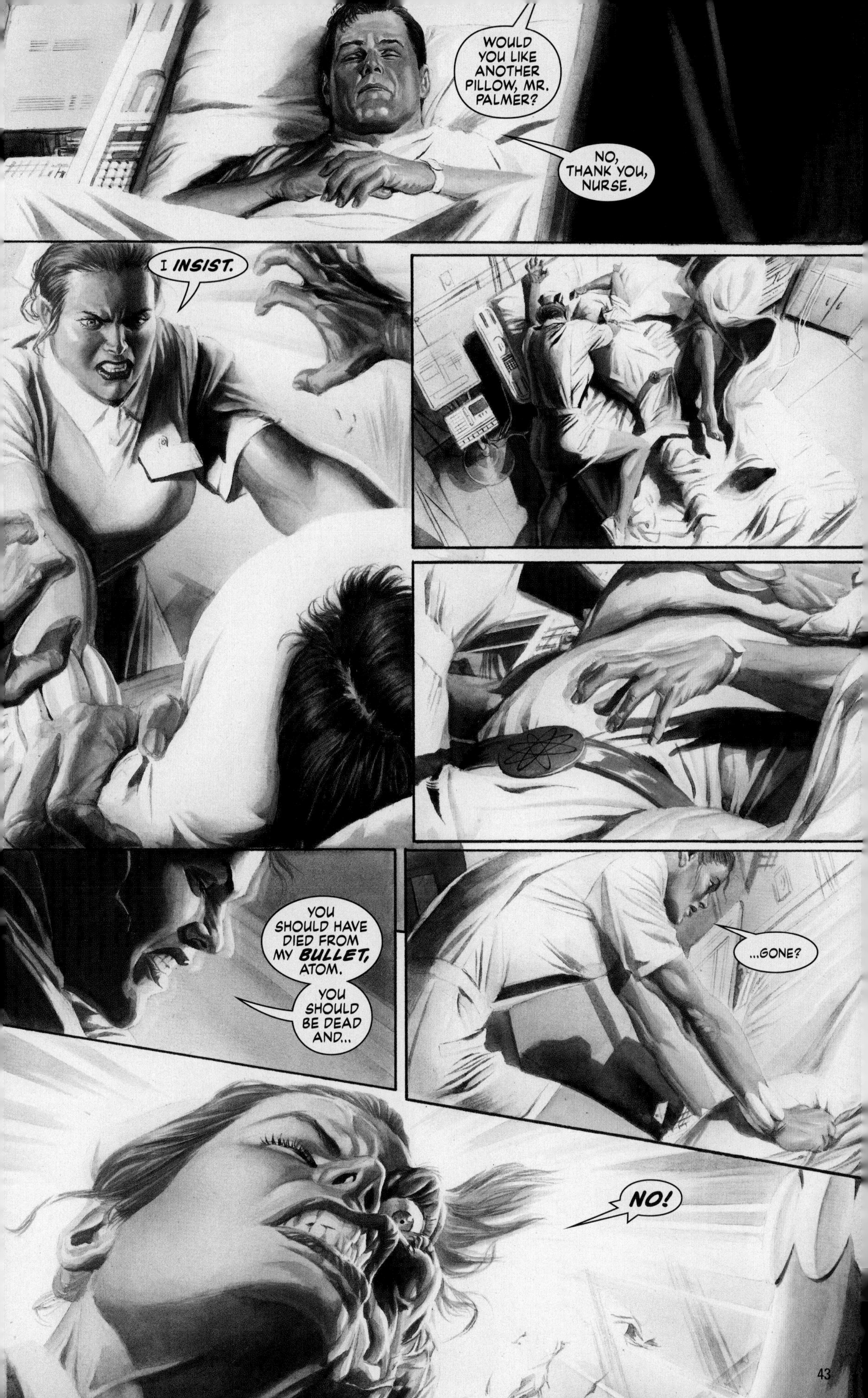
WOULD YOU LIKE ANOTHER PILLOW, MR. PALMER?
NO, THANK YOU, NURSE.
I INSIST.
YOU SHOULD HAVE DIED FROM MY BULLET, ATOM.
YOU SHOULD BE DEAD AND...
...GONE?
NO!

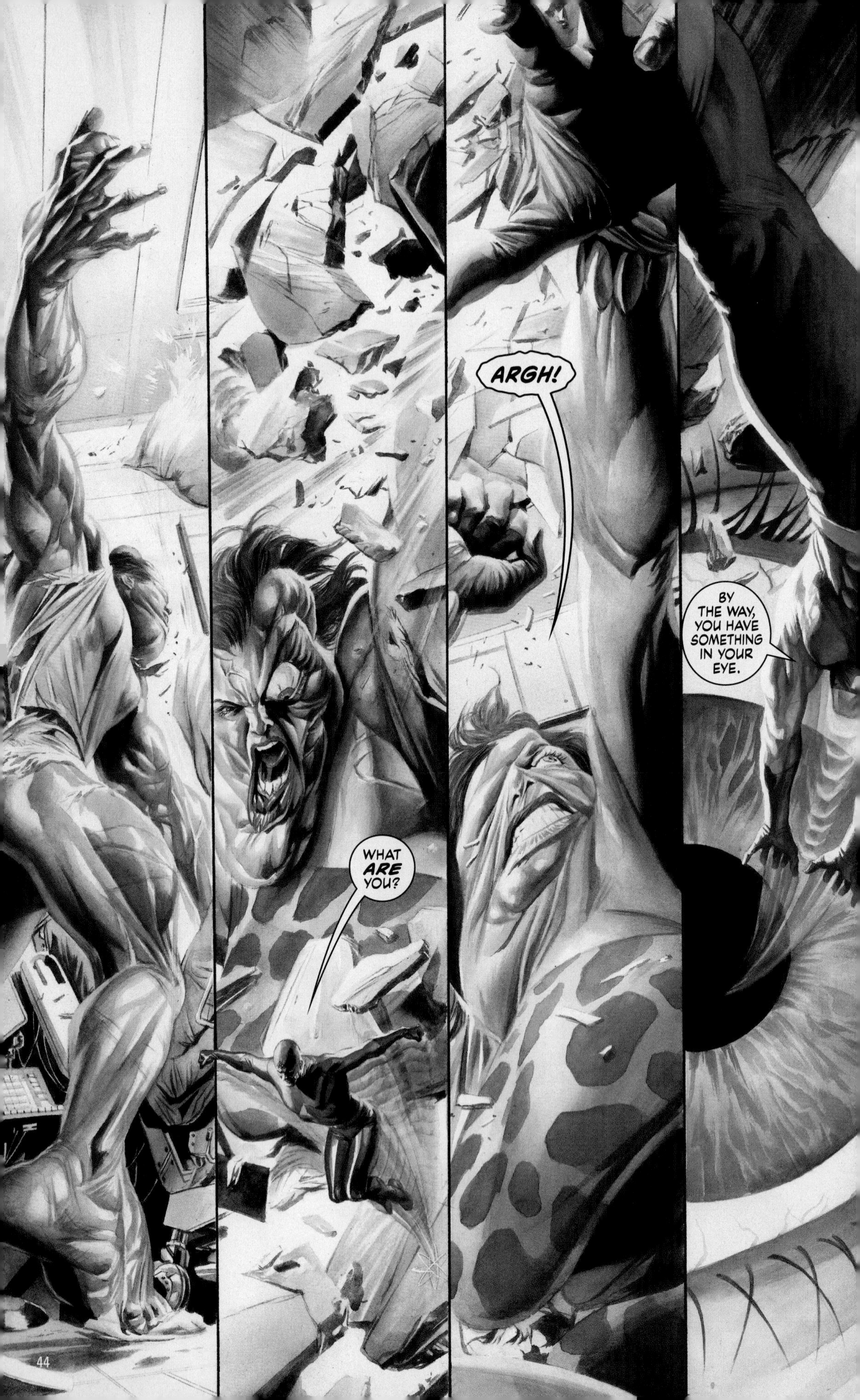
ARGH!
BY THE WAY, YOU HAVE SOMETHING IN YOUR EYE.
WHAT ARE YOU?

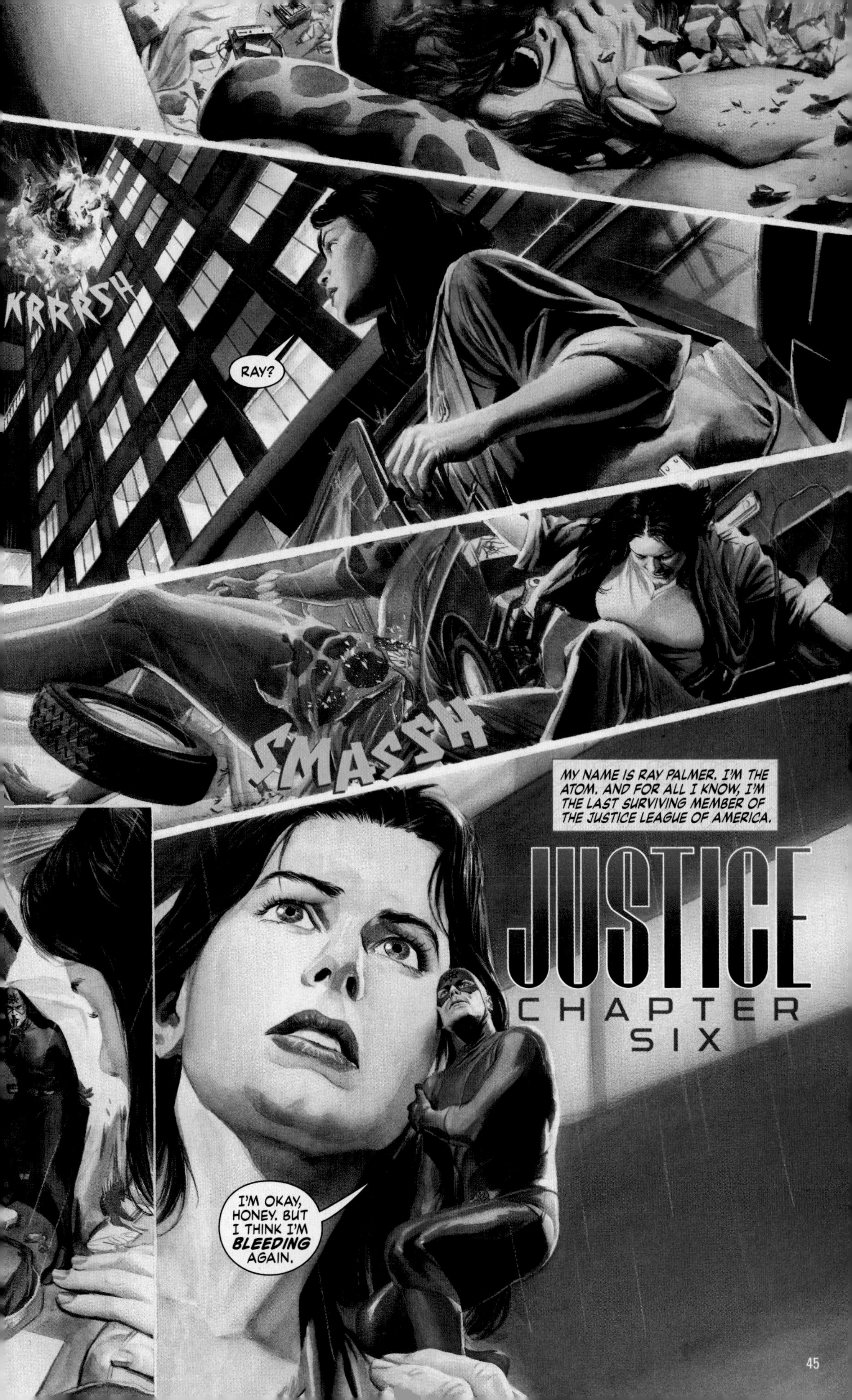
KRRRSH
RAY?
SMASSH
MY NAME IS RAY PALMER. I'M THE ATOM. AND FOR ALL I KNOW, I'M THE LAST SURVIVING MEMBER OF THE JUSTICE LEAGUE OF AMERICA.
JUSTICE
CHAPTER SIX
I'M OKAY, HONEY. BUT I THINK I'M BLEEDING AGAIN.

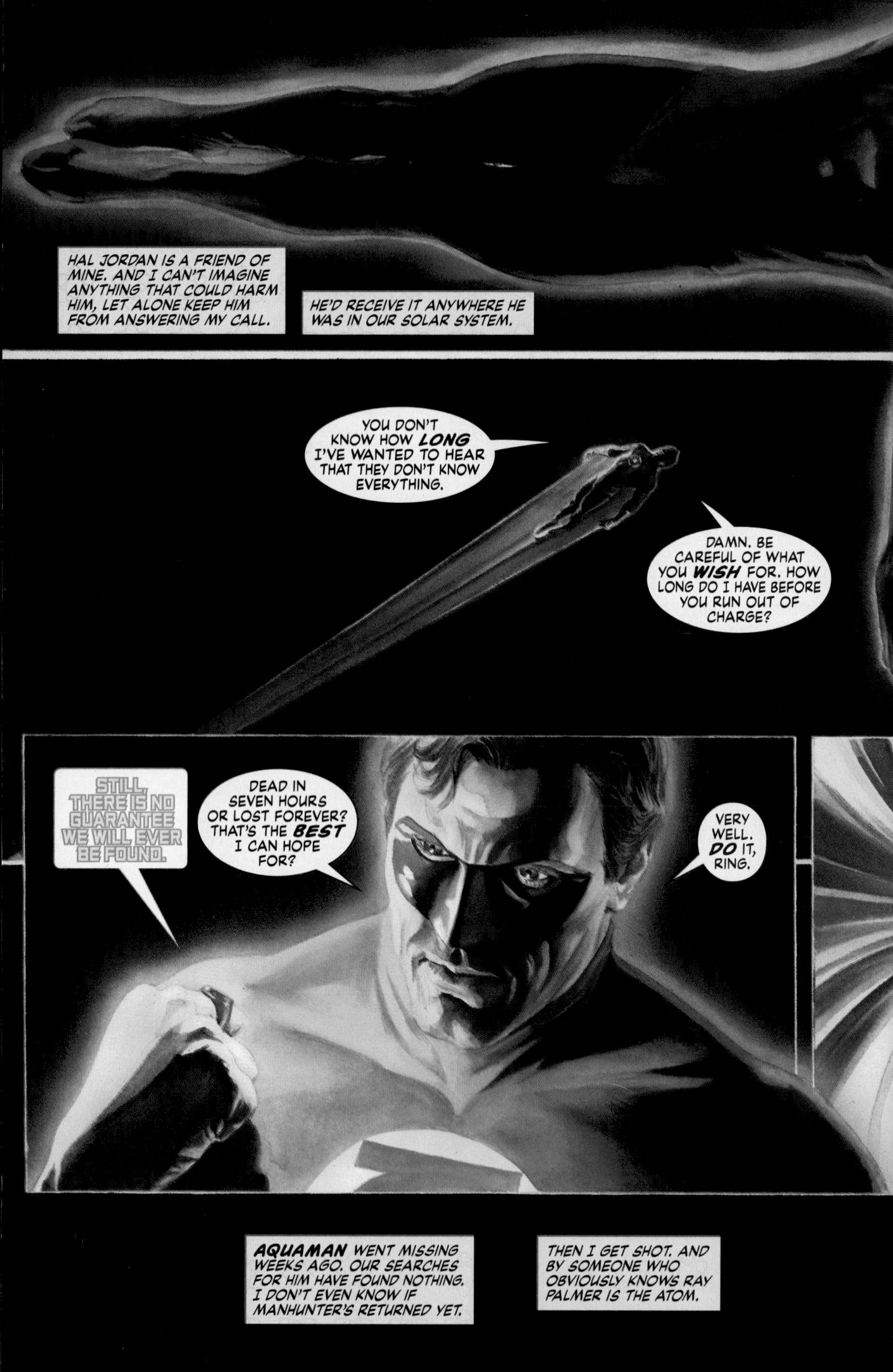
HAL JORDAN IS A FRIEND OF MINE. AND I CAN'T IMAGINE ANYTHING THAT COULD HARM HIM, LET ALONE KEEP HIM FROM ANSWERING MY CALL.
HE'D RECEIVE IT ANYWHERE HE WAS IN OUR SOLAR SYSTEM.
YOU DON'T KNOW HOW LONG I'VE WANTED TO HEAR THAT THEY DON'T KNOW EVERYTHING.
DAMN. BE CAREFUL OF WHAT YOU WISH FOR. HOW LONG DO I HAVE BEFORE YOU RUN OUT OF CHARGE?
STILL, THERE IS NO GUARANTEE WE WILL EVER BE FOUND.
DEAD IN SEVEN HOURS OR LOST FOREVER? THAT'S THE BEST I CAN HOPE FOR?
VERY WELL. DO IT, RING.
AQUAMAN WENT MISSING WEEKS AGO. OUR SEARCHES FOR HIM HAVE FOUND NOTHING. I DON'T EVEN KNOW IF MANHUNTER'S RETURNED YET.
THEN I GET SHOT. AND BY SOMEONE WHO OBVIOUSLY KNOWS RAY PALMER IS THE ATOM.

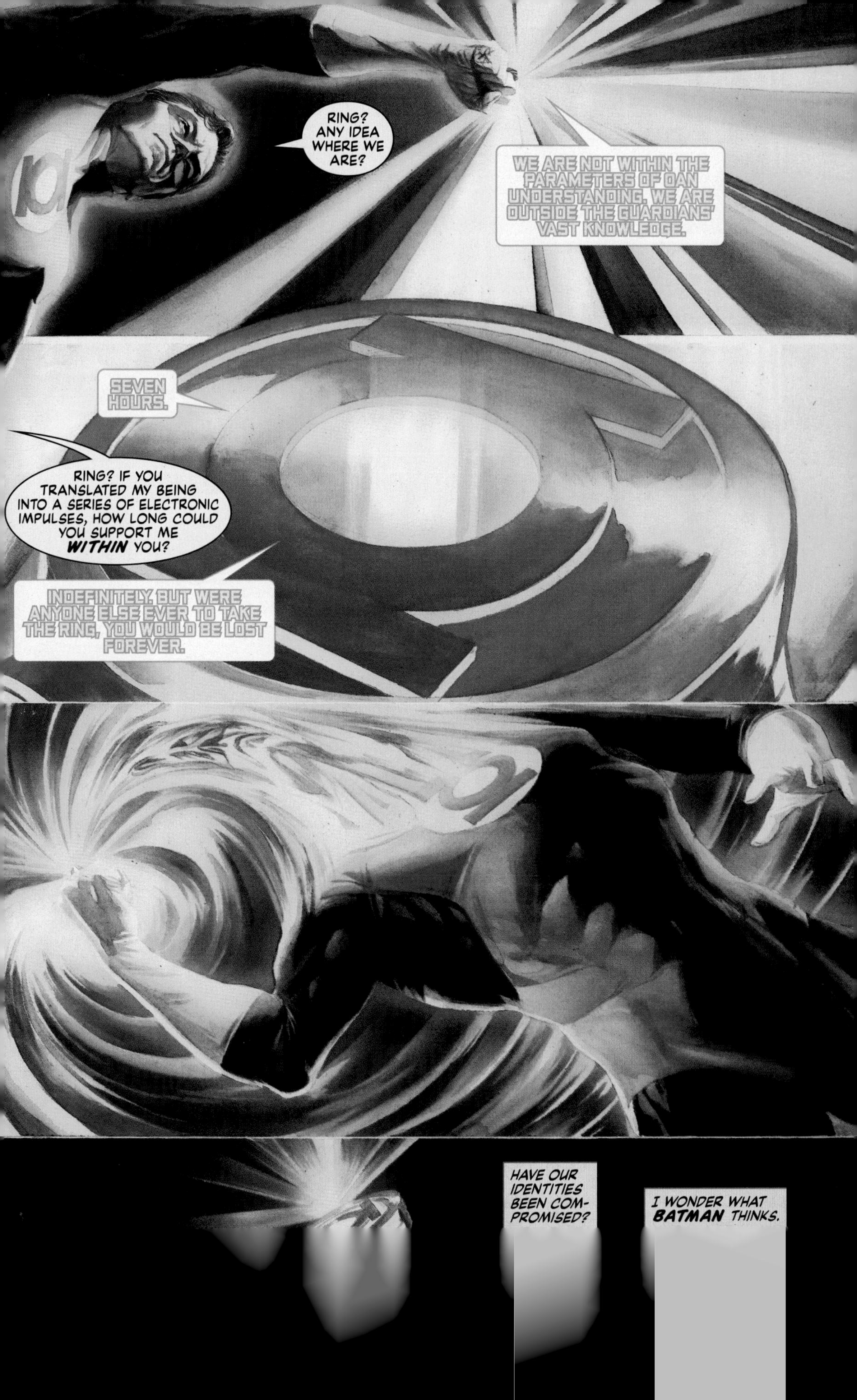
RING? ANY IDEA WHERE WE ARE?
WE ARE NOT WITHIN THE PARAMETERS OF OAN UNDERSTANDING. WE ARE OUTSIDE THE GUARDIANS' VAST KNOWLEDGE.
RING? IF YOU TRANSLATED MY BEING INTO A SERIES OF ELECTRONIC IMPULSES, HOW LONG COULD YOU SUPPORT ME WITHIN YOU?
SEVEN HOURS.
INDEFINITELY. BUT WERE ANYONE ELSE EVER TO TAKE THE RING, YOU WOULD BE LOST FOREVER.
HAVE OUR IDENTITIES BEEN COM-PROMISED?
I WONDER WHAT BATMAN THINKS.

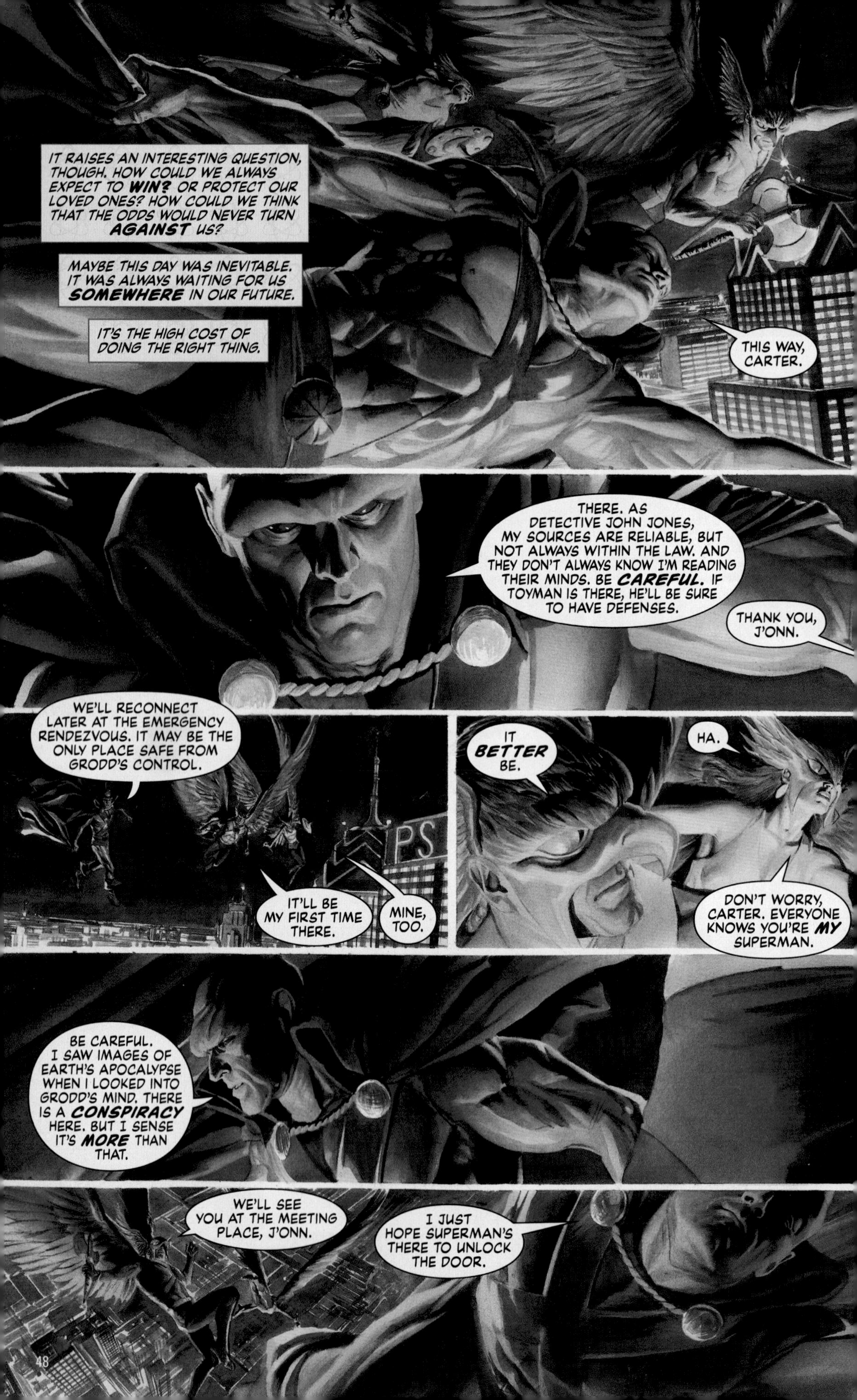
IT RAISES AN INTERESTING QUESTION, THOUGH. HOW COULD WE ALWAYS EXPECT TO WIN? OR PROTECT OUR LOVED ONES? HOW COULD WE THINK THAT THE ODDS WOULD NEVER TURN AGAINST US?
MAYBE THIS DAY WAS INEVITABLE. IT WAS ALWAYS WAITING FOR US SOMEWHERE IN OUR FUTURE.
IT'S THE HIGH COST OF DOING THE RIGHT THING.
THIS WAY, CARTER.
THERE. AS DETECTIVE JOHN JONES, MY SOURCES ARE RELIABLE, BUT NOT ALWAYS WITHIN THE LAW. AND THEY DON'T ALWAYS KNOW I'M READING THEIR MINDS. BE CAREFUL. IF TOYMAN IS THERE, HE'LL BE SURE TO HAVE DEFENSES.
THANK YOU, J'ONN.
WE'LL RECONNECT LATER AT THE EMERGENCY RENDEZVOUS. IT MAY BE THE ONLY PLACE SAFE FROM GRODD'S CONTROL.
IT'LL BE MY FIRST TIME THERE.
MINE, TOO.
IT BETTER BE.
HA.
DON'T WORRY, CARTER. EVERYONE KNOWS YOU'RE MY SUPERMAN.
BE CAREFUL. I SAW IMAGES OF EARTH'S APOCALYPSE WHEN I LOOKED INTO GRODD'S MIND. THERE IS A CONSPIRACY HERE. BUT I SENSE IT'S MORE THAN THAT.
WE'LL SEE YOU AT THE MEETING PLACE, J'ONN.
I JUST HOPE SUPERMAN'S THERE TO UNLOCK THE DOOR.

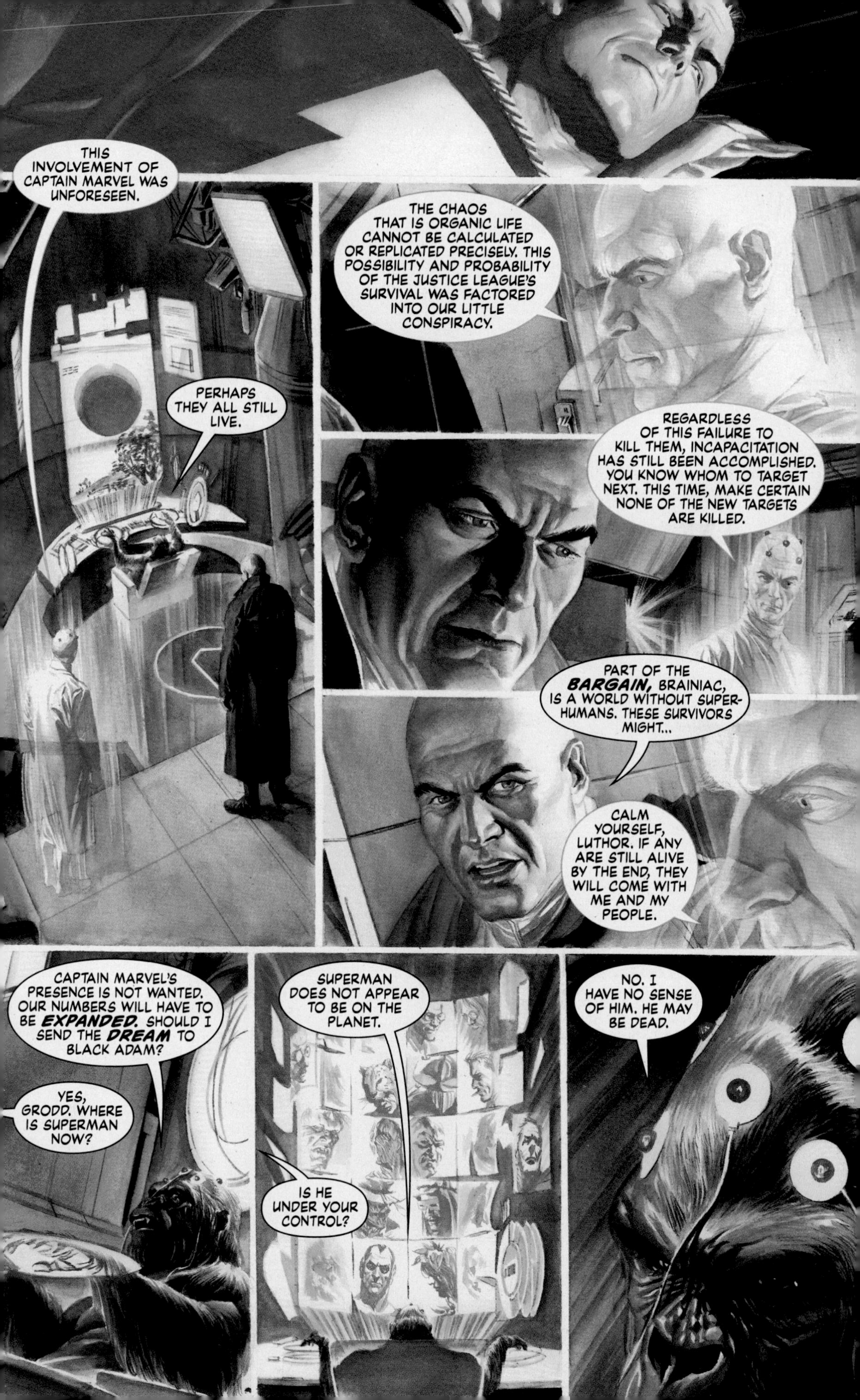

THIS INVOLVEMENT OF CAPTAIN MARVEL WAS UNFORESEEN.
THE CHAOS THAT IS ORGANIC LIFE CANNOT BE CALCULATED OR REPLICATED PRECISELY. THIS POSSIBILITY AND PROBABILITY OF THE JUSTICE LEAGUE'S SURVIVAL WAS FACTORED INTO OUR LITTLE CONSPIRACY.
PERHAPS THEY ALL STILL LIVE.
REGARDLESS OF THIS FAILURE TO KILL THEM, INCAPACITATION HAS STILL BEEN ACCOMPLISHED. YOU KNOW WHOM TO TARGET NEXT. THIS TIME, MAKE CERTAIN NONE OF THE NEW TARGETS ARE KILLED.
PART OF THE **BARGAIN,** BRAINIAC, IS A WORLD WITHOUT SUPER-HUMANS. THESE SURVIVORS MIGHT...
CALM YOURSELF, LUTHOR. IF ANY ARE STILL ALIVE BY THE END, THEY WILL COME WITH ME AND MY PEOPLE.
CAPTAIN MARVEL'S PRESENCE IS NOT WANTED. OUR NUMBERS WILL HAVE TO BE **EXPANDED.** SHOULD I SEND THE **DREAM** TO BLACK ADAM?
YES, GRODD. WHERE IS SUPERMAN NOW?
SUPERMAN DOES NOT APPEAR TO BE ON THE PLANET.
IS HE UNDER YOUR CONTROL?
NO. I HAVE NO SENSE OF HIM. HE MAY BE DEAD.

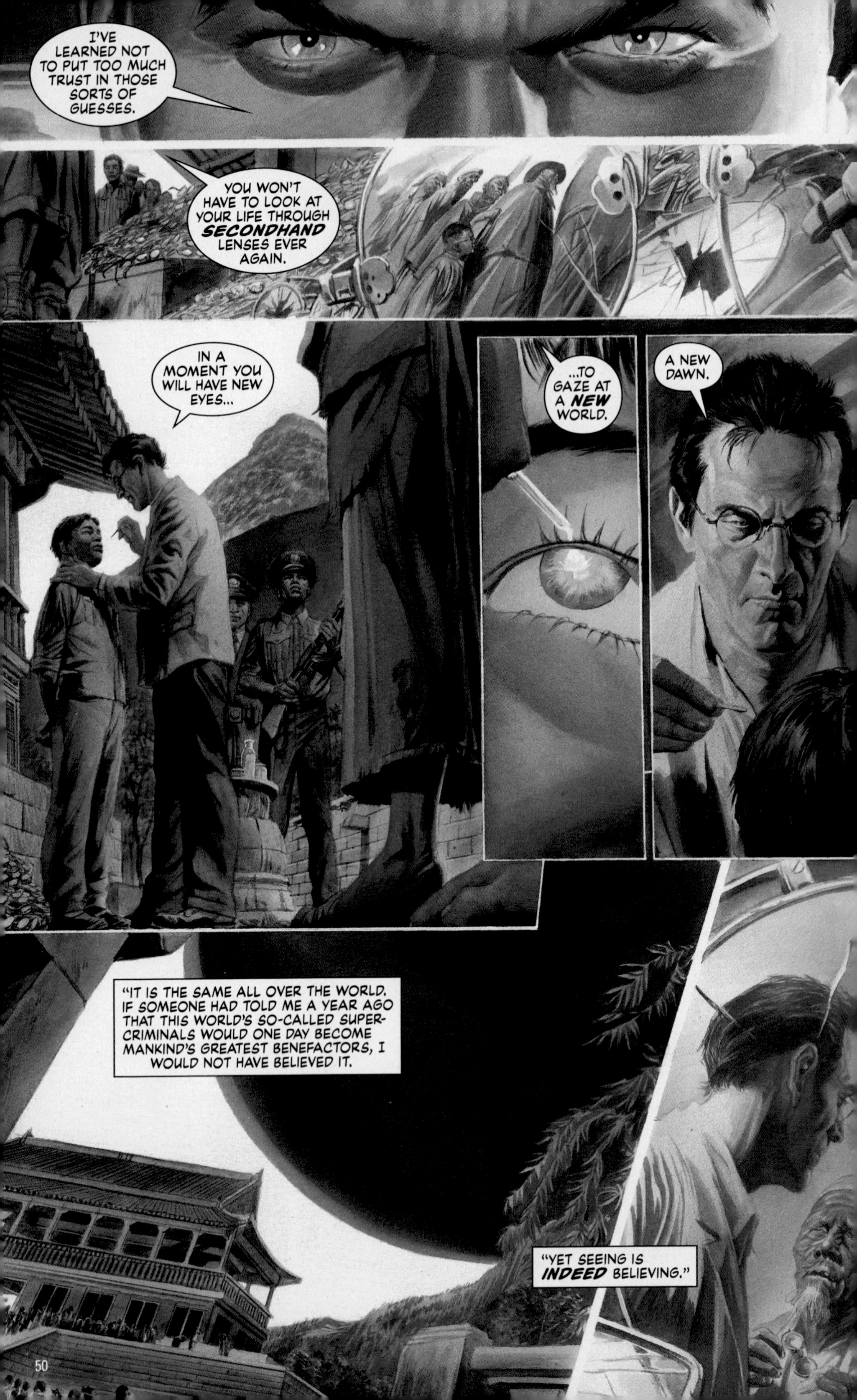
I'VE LEARNED NOT TO PUT TOO MUCH TRUST IN THOSE SORTS OF GUESSES.
YOU WON'T HAVE TO LOOK AT YOUR LIFE THROUGH ***SECONDHAND*** LENSES EVER AGAIN.
IN A MOMENT YOU WILL HAVE NEW EYES...
...TO GAZE AT A ***NEW*** WORLD.
A NEW DAWN.
"IT IS THE SAME ALL OVER THE WORLD. IF SOMEONE HAD TOLD ME A YEAR AGO THAT THIS WORLD'S SO-CALLED SUPER-CRIMINALS WOULD ONE DAY BECOME MANKIND'S GREATEST BENEFACTORS, I WOULD NOT HAVE BELIEVED IT.
"YET SEEING IS ***INDEED*** BELIEVING."

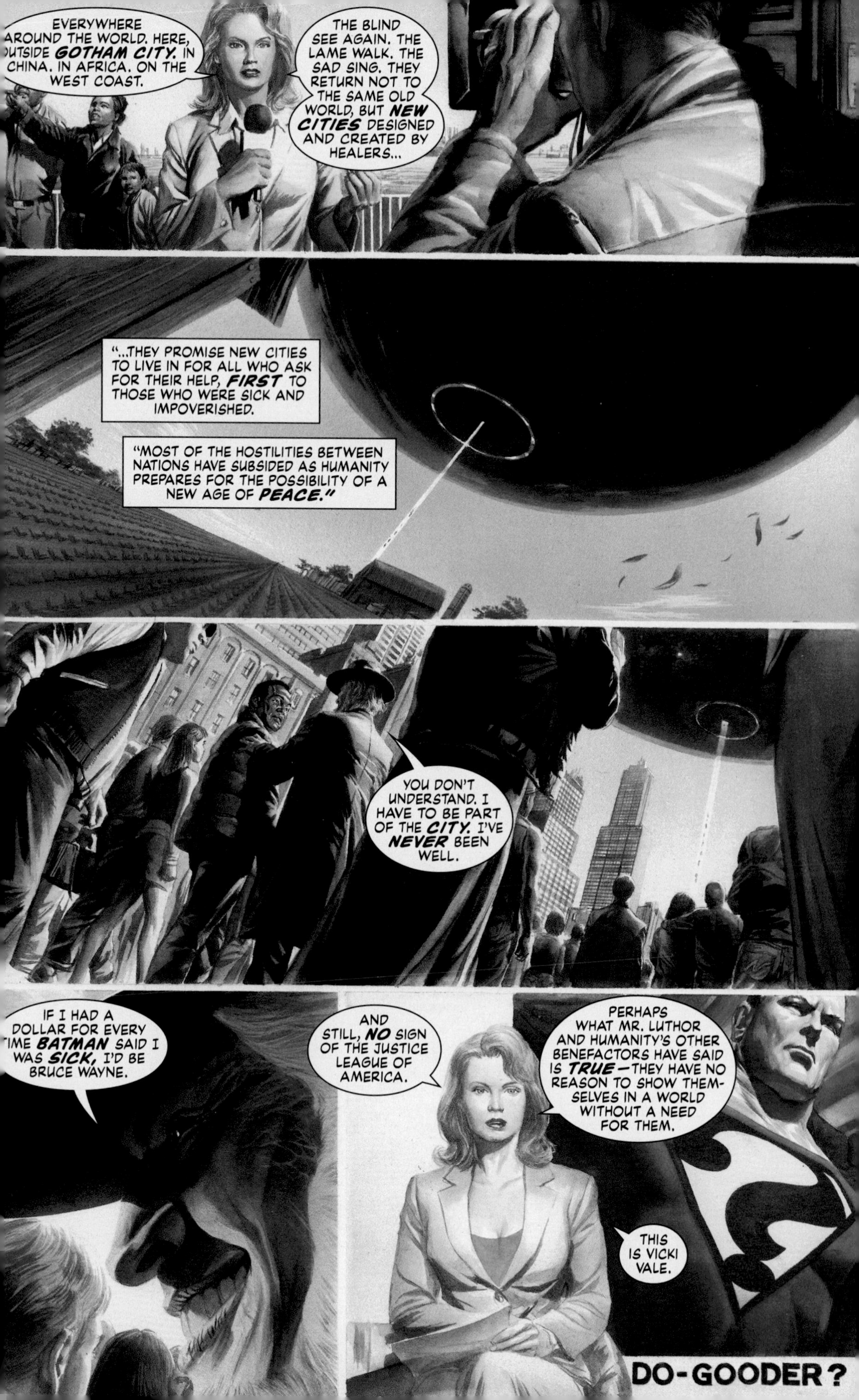
EVERYWHERE AROUND THE WORLD. HERE, OUTSIDE GOTHAM CITY. IN CHINA. IN AFRICA. ON THE WEST COAST.
THE BLIND SEE AGAIN. THE LAME WALK. THE SAD SING. THEY RETURN NOT TO THE SAME OLD WORLD, BUT NEW CITIES DESIGNED AND CREATED BY HEALERS...
"...THEY PROMISE NEW CITIES TO LIVE IN FOR ALL WHO ASK FOR THEIR HELP, FIRST TO THOSE WHO WERE SICK AND IMPOVERISHED.
"MOST OF THE HOSTILITIES BETWEEN NATIONS HAVE SUBSIDED AS HUMANITY PREPARES FOR THE POSSIBILITY OF A NEW AGE OF PEACE."
YOU DON'T UNDERSTAND. I HAVE TO BE PART OF THE CITY. I'VE NEVER BEEN WELL.
IF I HAD A DOLLAR FOR EVERY TIME BATMAN SAID I WAS SICK, I'D BE BRUCE WAYNE.
AND STILL, NO SIGN OF THE JUSTICE LEAGUE OF AMERICA.
PERHAPS WHAT MR. LUTHOR AND HUMANITY'S OTHER BENEFACTORS HAVE SAID IS TRUE—THEY HAVE NO REASON TO SHOW THEM-SELVES IN A WORLD WITHOUT A NEED FOR THEM.
THIS IS VICKI VALE.
DO-GOODER?

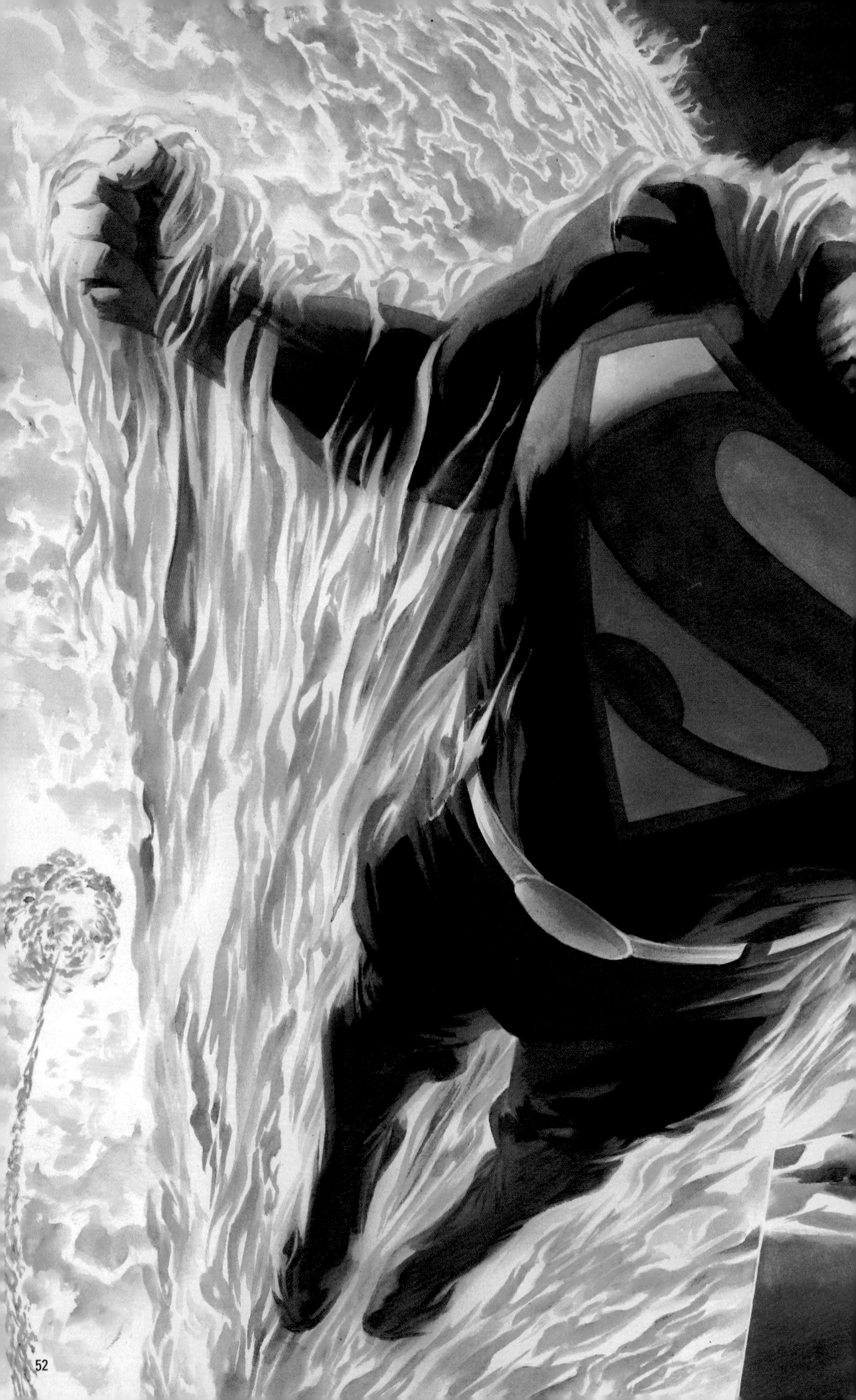

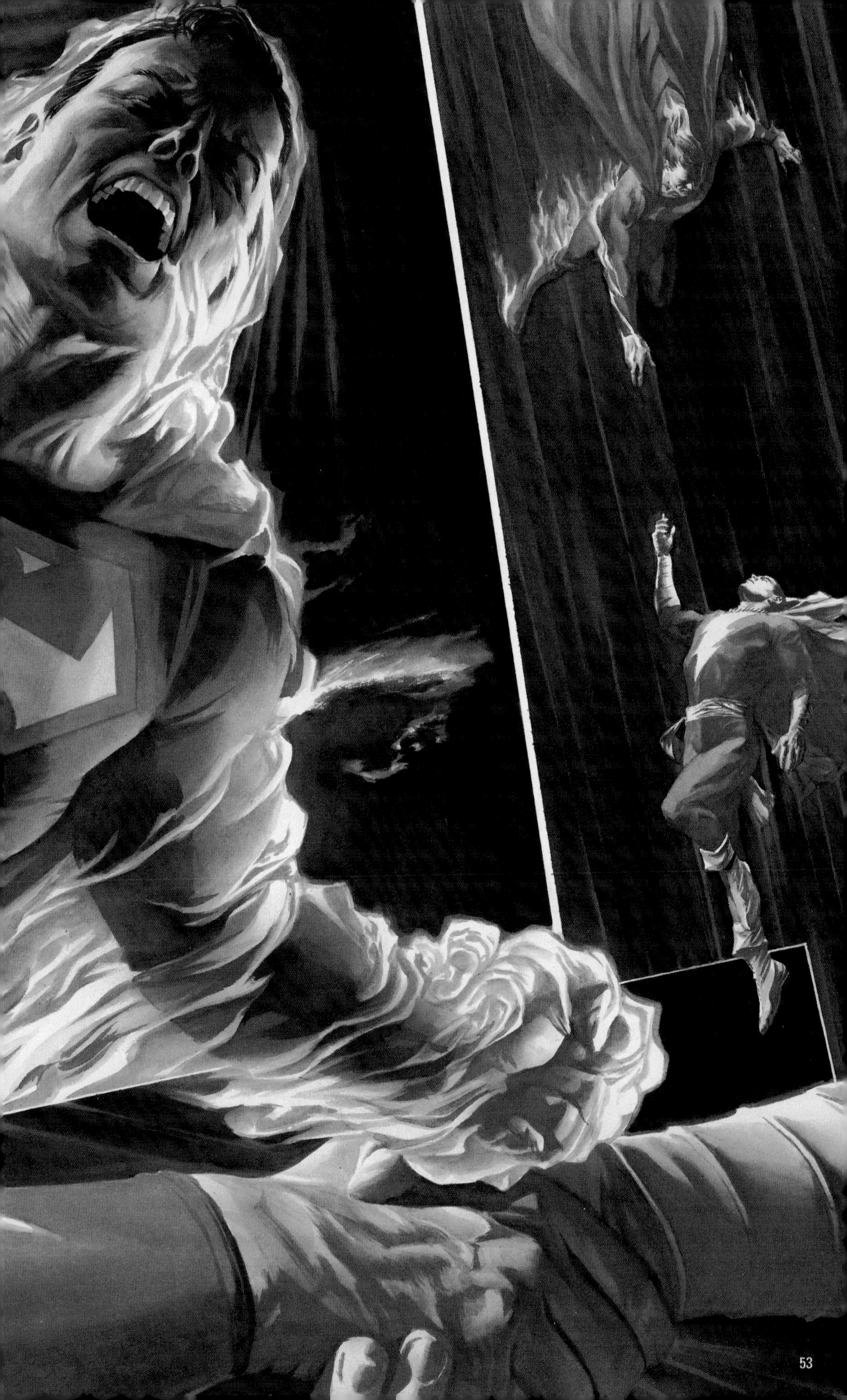

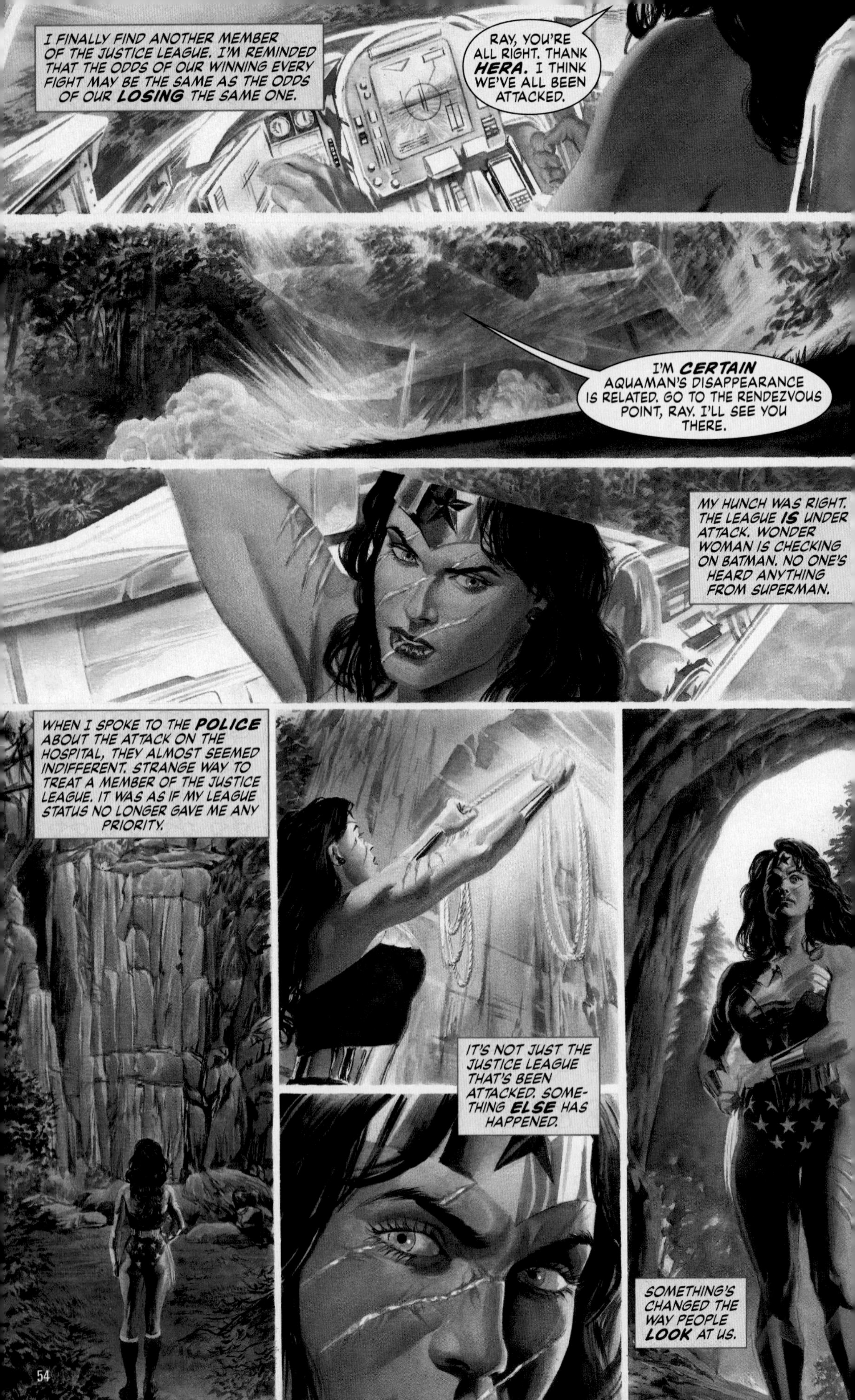
I FINALLY FIND ANOTHER MEMBER OF THE JUSTICE LEAGUE. I'M REMINDED THAT THE ODDS OF OUR WINNING EVERY FIGHT MAY BE THE SAME AS THE ODDS OF OUR LOSING THE SAME ONE.
RAY, YOU'RE ALL RIGHT. THANK HERA. I THINK WE'VE ALL BEEN ATTACKED.
I'M CERTAIN AQUAMAN'S DISAPPEARANCE IS RELATED. GO TO THE RENDEZVOUS POINT, RAY. I'LL SEE YOU THERE.
MY HUNCH WAS RIGHT. THE LEAGUE IS UNDER ATTACK. WONDER WOMAN IS CHECKING ON BATMAN. NO ONE'S HEARD ANYTHING FROM SUPERMAN.
WHEN I SPOKE TO THE POLICE ABOUT THE ATTACK ON THE HOSPITAL, THEY ALMOST SEEMED INDIFFERENT. STRANGE WAY TO TREAT A MEMBER OF THE JUSTICE LEAGUE. IT WAS AS IF MY LEAGUE STATUS NO LONGER GAVE ME ANY PRIORITY.
IT'S NOT JUST THE JUSTICE LEAGUE THAT'S BEEN ATTACKED. SOMETHING ELSE HAS HAPPENED.
SOMETHING'S CHANGED THE WAY PEOPLE LOOK AT US.

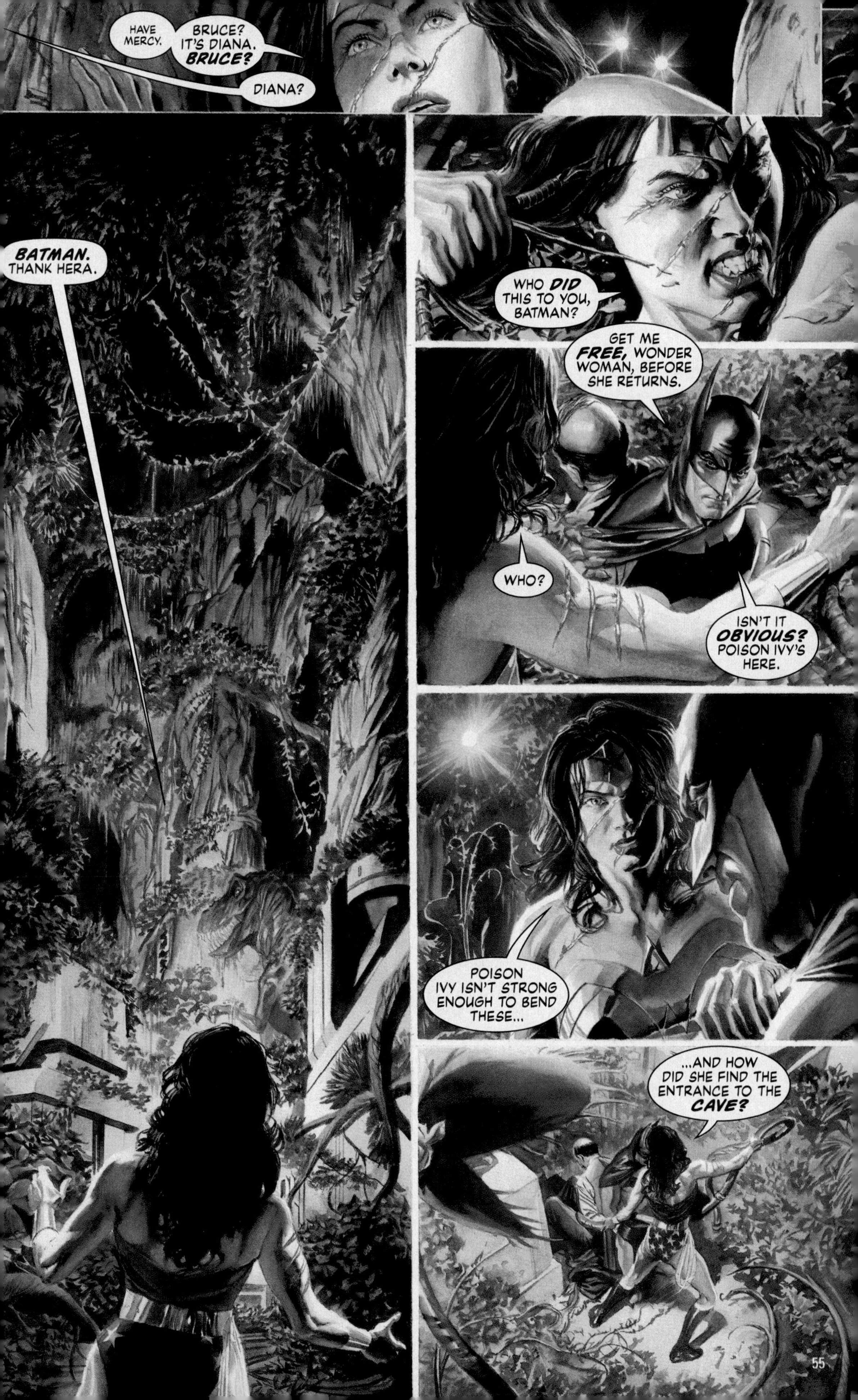
HAVE MERCY.
BRUCE? IT'S DIANA. BRUCE?
DIANA?
BATMAN. THANK HERA.
WHO DID THIS TO YOU, BATMAN?
GET ME FREE, WONDER WOMAN, BEFORE SHE RETURNS.
WHO?
ISN'T IT OBVIOUS? POISON IVY'S HERE.
POISON IVY ISN'T STRONG ENOUGH TO BEND THESE...
...AND HOW DID SHE FIND THE ENTRANCE TO THE CAVE?

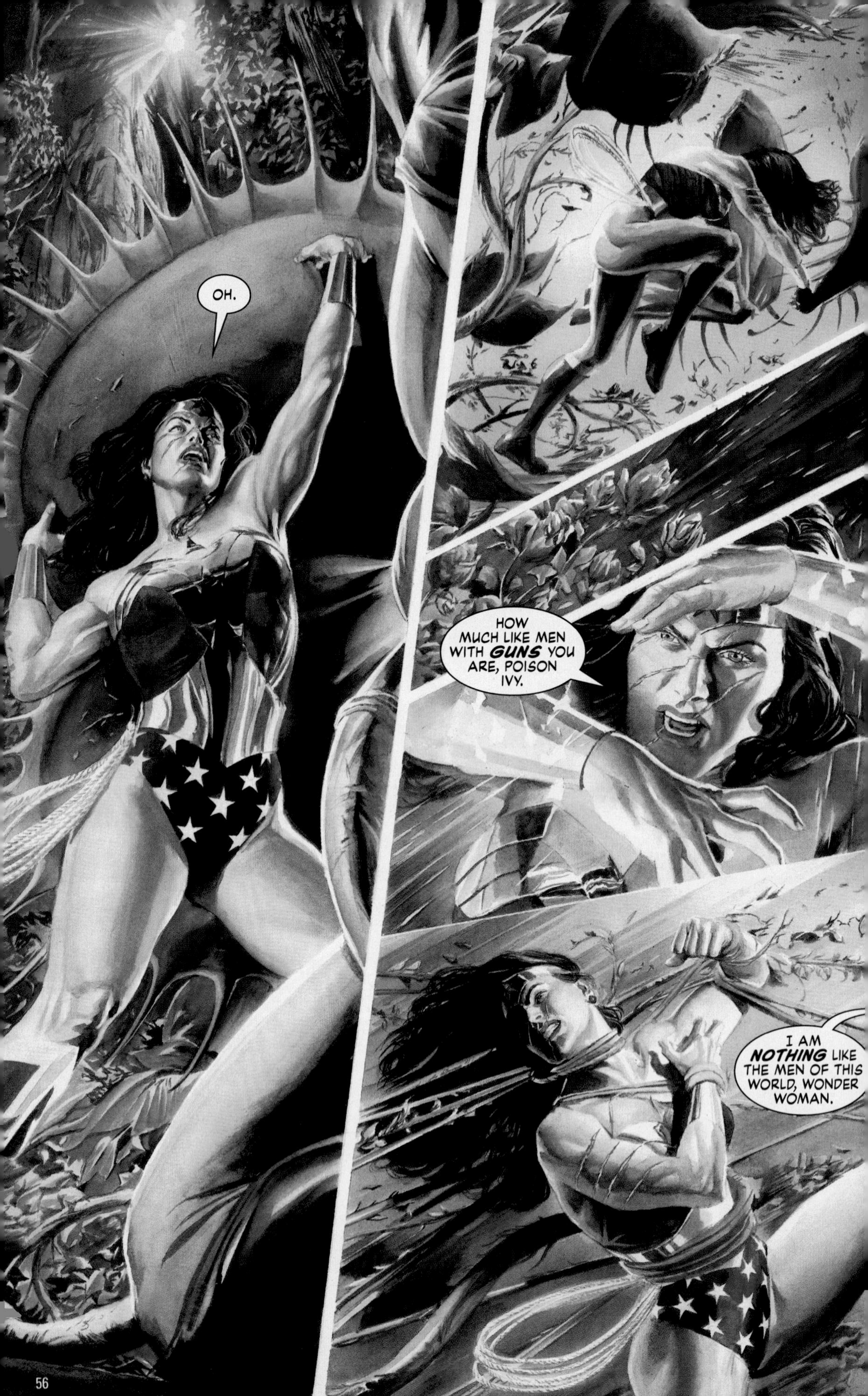
OH.
HOW MUCH LIKE MEN WITH **GUNS** YOU ARE, POISON IVY.
I AM **NOTHING** LIKE THE MEN OF THIS WORLD, WONDER WOMAN.

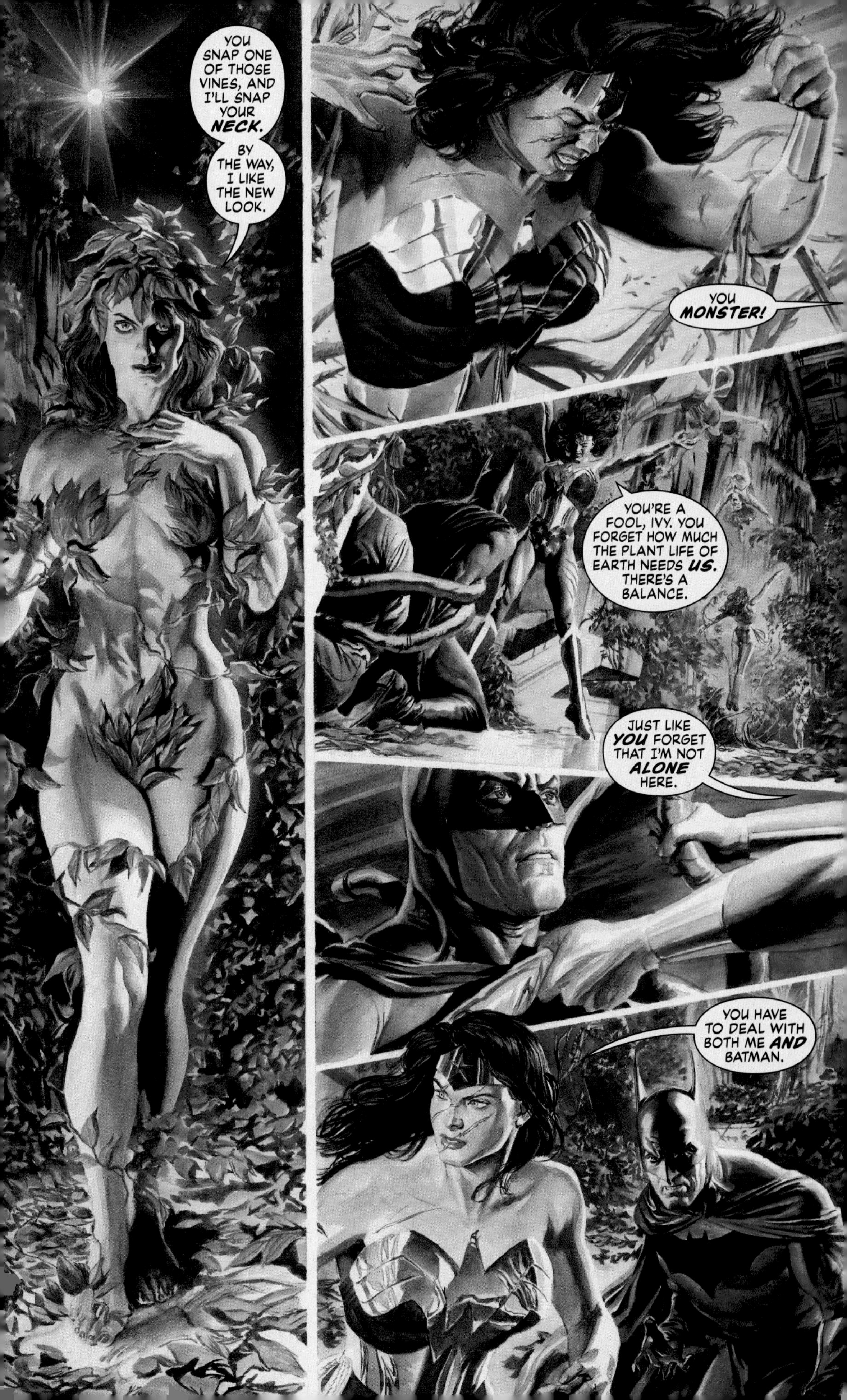
YOU SNAP ONE OF THOSE VINES, AND I'LL SNAP YOUR **NECK.**
BY THE WAY, I LIKE THE NEW LOOK.
YOU **MONSTER!**
YOU'RE A FOOL, IVY. YOU FORGET HOW MUCH THE PLANT LIFE OF EARTH NEEDS **US.** THERE'S A BALANCE.
JUST LIKE **YOU** FORGET THAT I'M NOT **ALONE** HERE.
YOU HAVE TO DEAL WITH BOTH ME **AND** BATMAN.

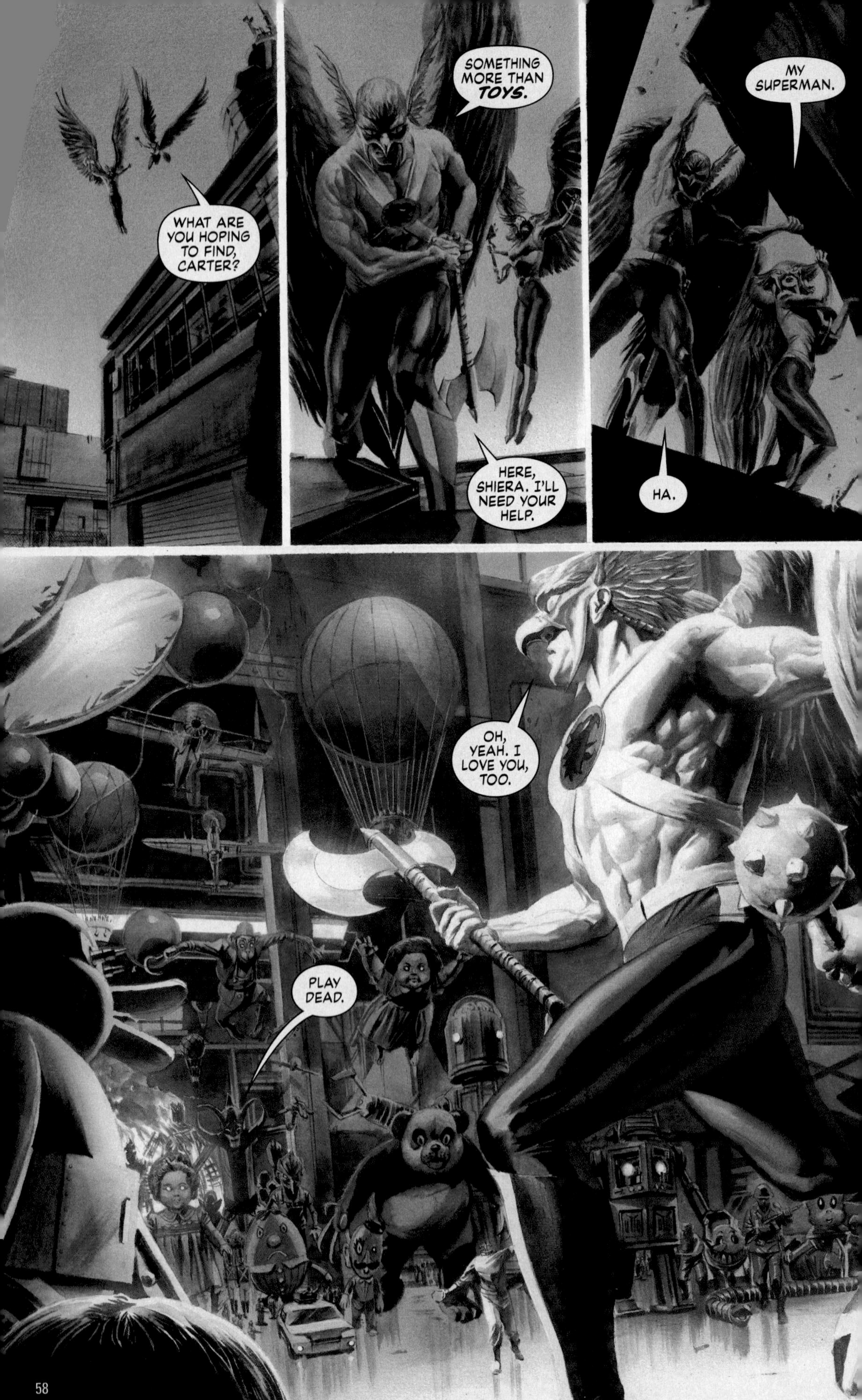
WHAT ARE YOU HOPING TO FIND, CARTER?
SOMETHING MORE THAN TOYS.
HERE, SHIERA. I'LL NEED YOUR HELP.
MY SUPERMAN.
HA.
OH, YEAH. I LOVE YOU, TOO.
PLAY DEAD.

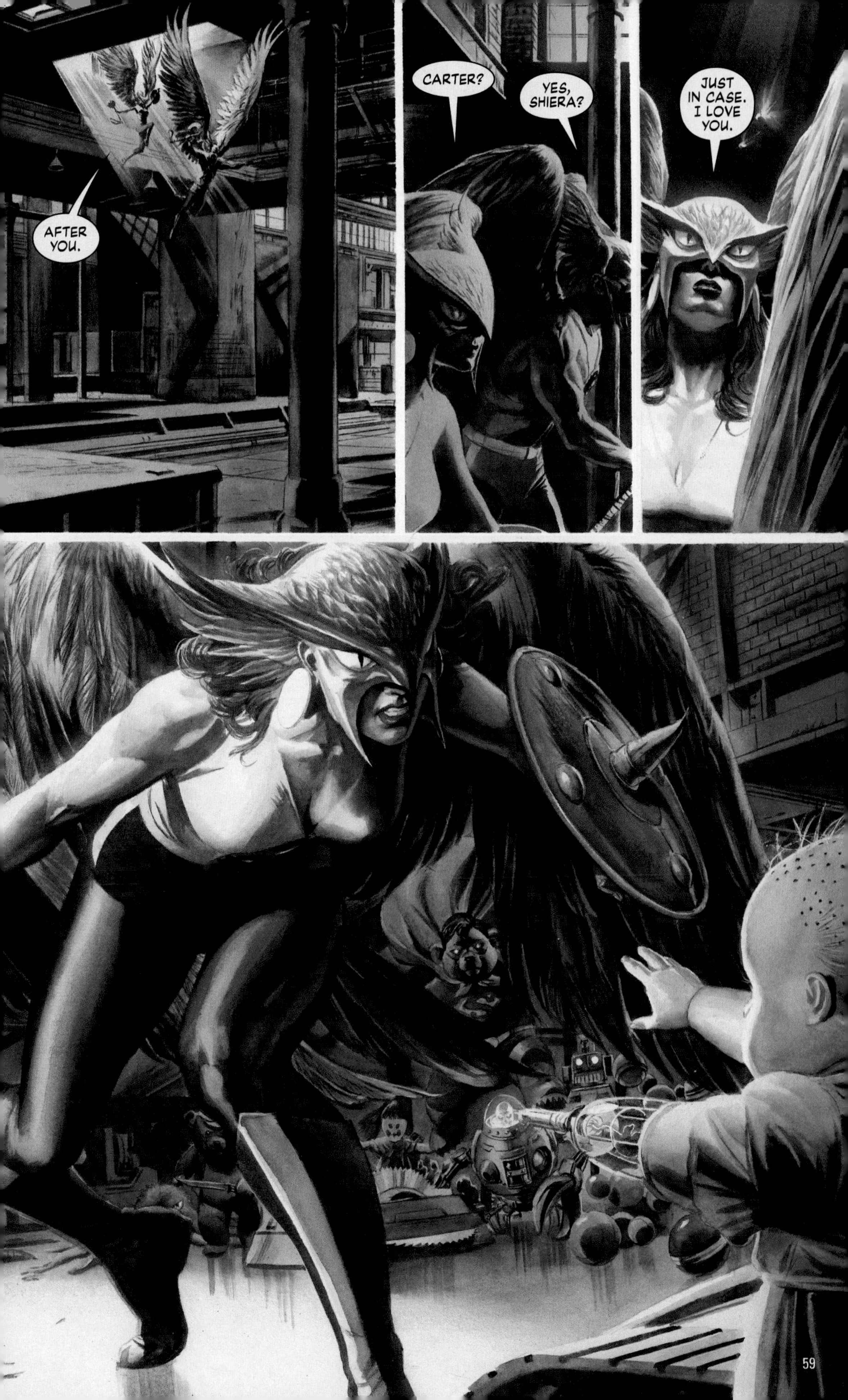
AFTER YOU.
CARTER?
YES, SHIERA?
JUST IN CASE. I LOVE YOU.

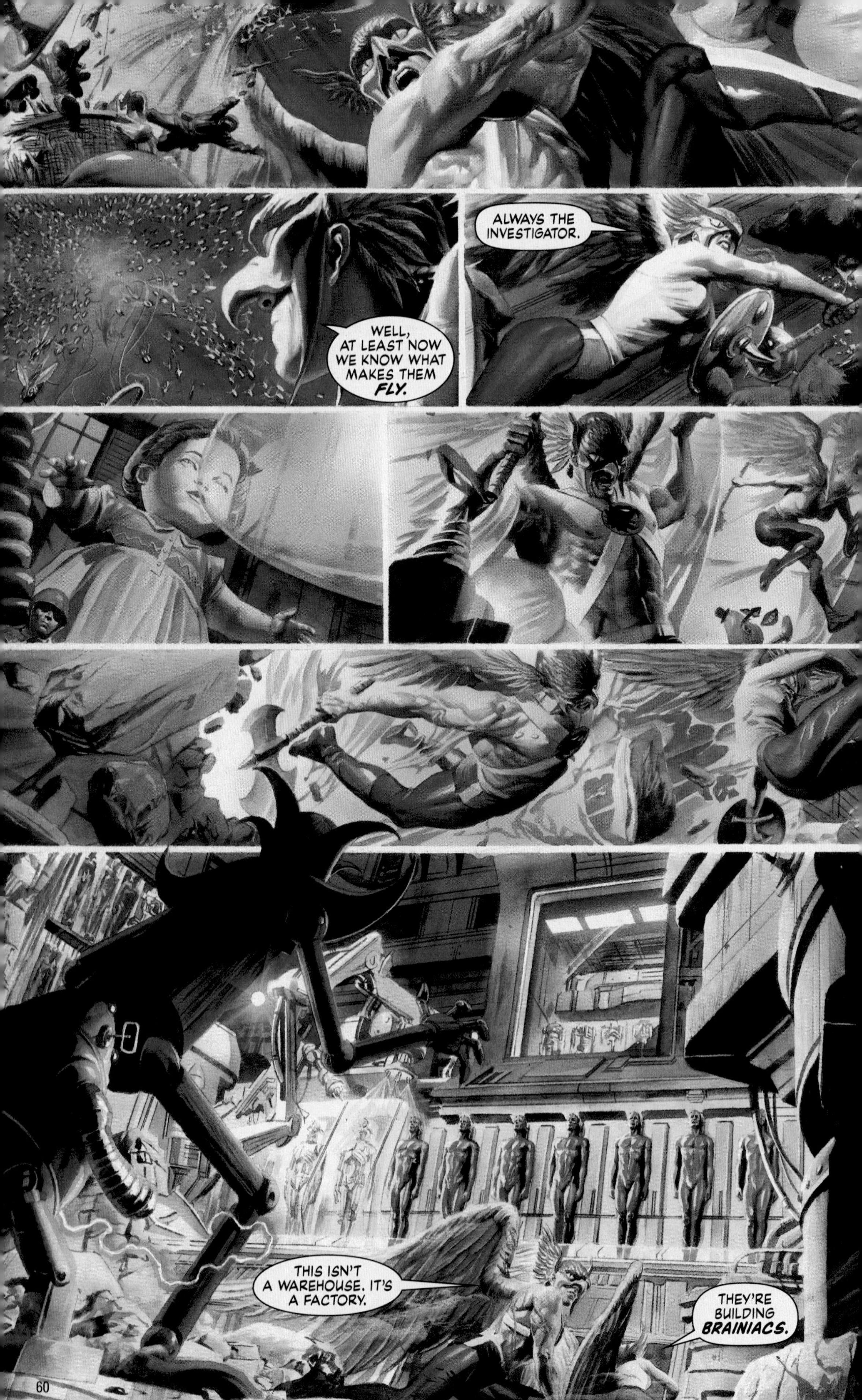
WELL, AT LEAST NOW WE KNOW WHAT MAKES THEM FLY.
ALWAYS THE INVESTIGATOR.
THIS ISN'T A WAREHOUSE. IT'S A FACTORY.
THEY'RE BUILDING BRAINIACS.

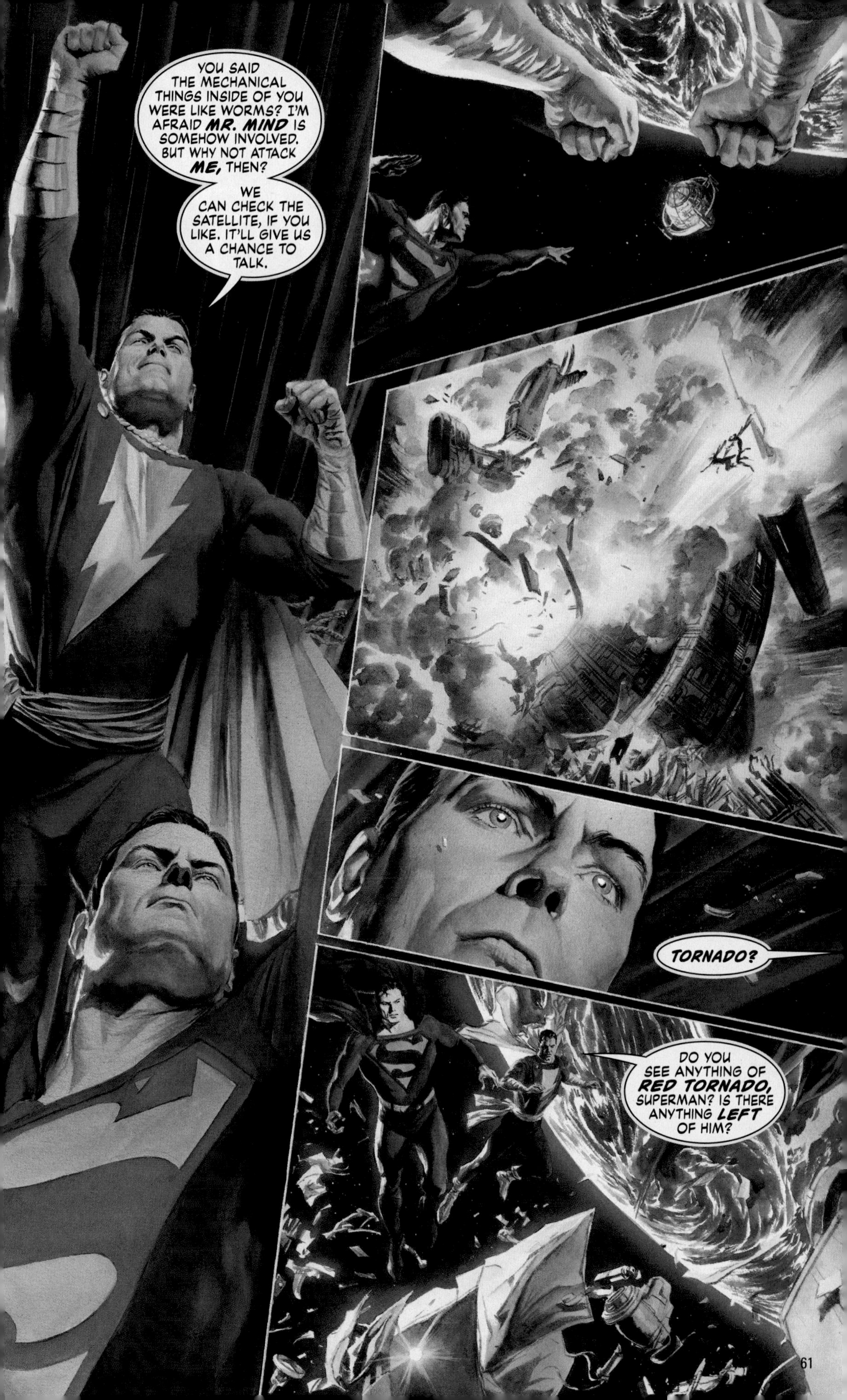
YOU SAID THE MECHANICAL THINGS INSIDE OF YOU WERE LIKE WORMS? I'M AFRAID MR. MIND IS SOMEHOW INVOLVED. BUT WHY NOT ATTACK ME, THEN?
WE CAN CHECK THE SATELLITE, IF YOU LIKE. IT'LL GIVE US A CHANCE TO TALK.
TORNADO?
DO YOU SEE ANYTHING OF RED TORNADO, SUPERMAN? IS THERE ANYTHING LEFT OF HIM?

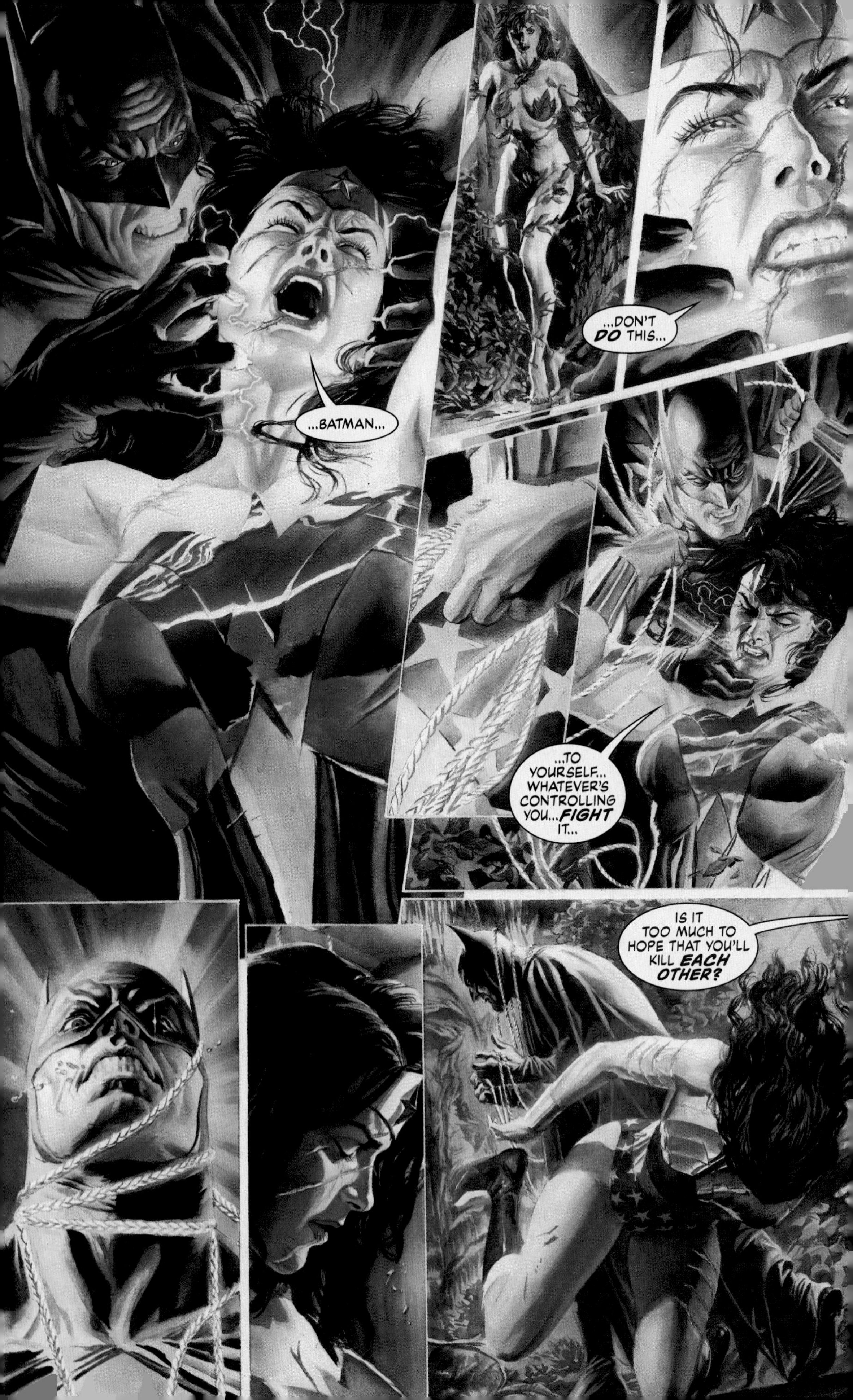
...BATMAN...
...DON'T DO THIS...
...TO YOURSELF... WHATEVER'S CONTROLLING YOU...FIGHT IT...
IS IT TOO MUCH TO HOPE THAT YOU'LL KILL EACH OTHER?

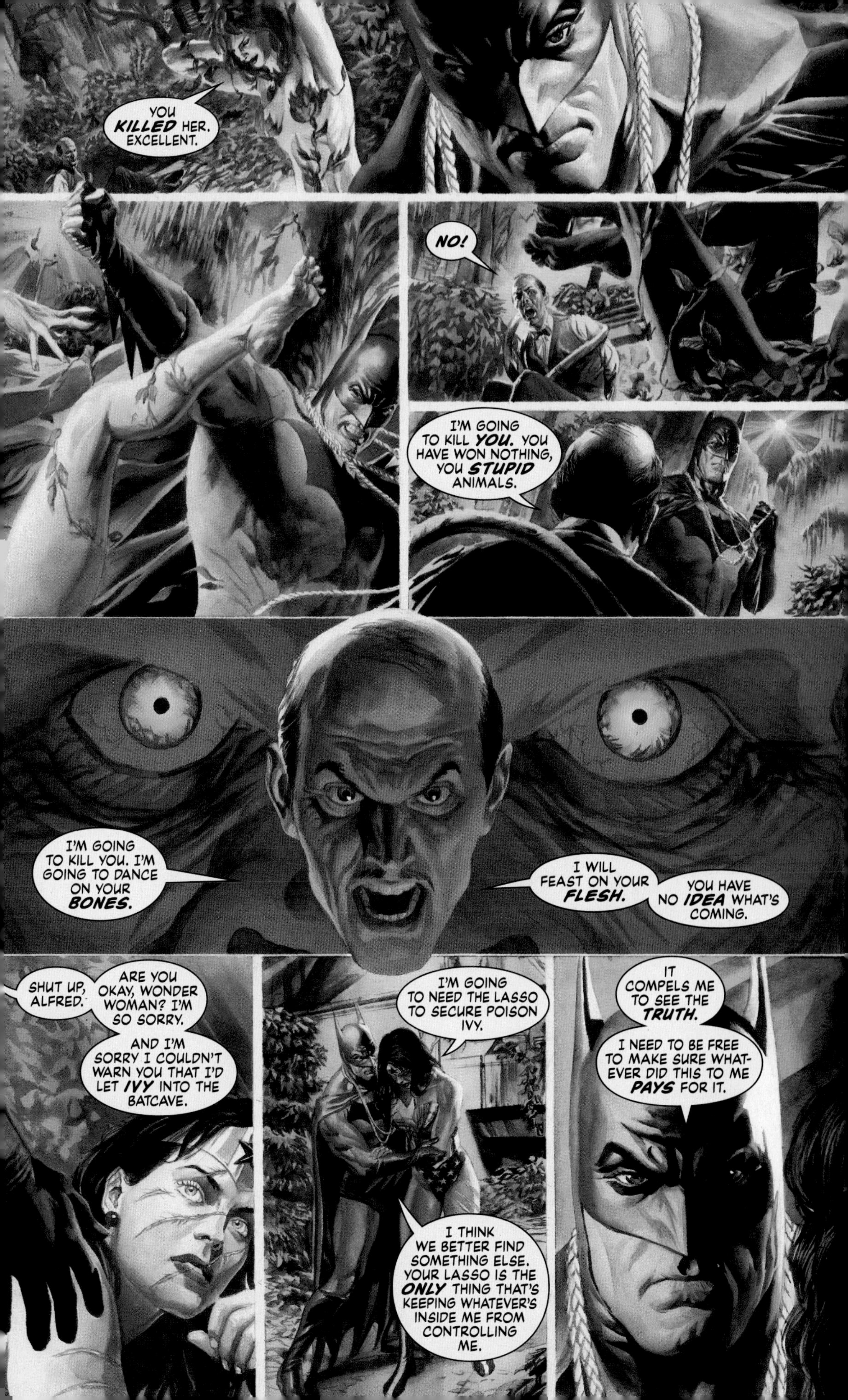
YOU KILLED HER. EXCELLENT.
NO!
I'M GOING TO KILL YOU. YOU HAVE WON NOTHING, YOU STUPID ANIMALS.
I'M GOING TO KILL YOU. I'M GOING TO DANCE ON YOUR BONES.
I WILL FEAST ON YOUR FLESH.
YOU HAVE NO IDEA WHAT'S COMING.
SHUT UP, ALFRED.
ARE YOU OKAY, WONDER WOMAN? I'M SO SORRY.
AND I'M SORRY I COULDN'T WARN YOU THAT I'D LET IVY INTO THE BATCAVE.
I'M GOING TO NEED THE LASSO TO SECURE POISON IVY.
I THINK WE BETTER FIND SOMETHING ELSE. YOUR LASSO IS THE ONLY THING THAT'S KEEPING WHATEVER'S INSIDE ME FROM CONTROLLING ME.
IT COMPELS ME TO SEE THE TRUTH.
I NEED TO BE FREE TO MAKE SURE WHATEVER DID THIS TO ME PAYS FOR IT.

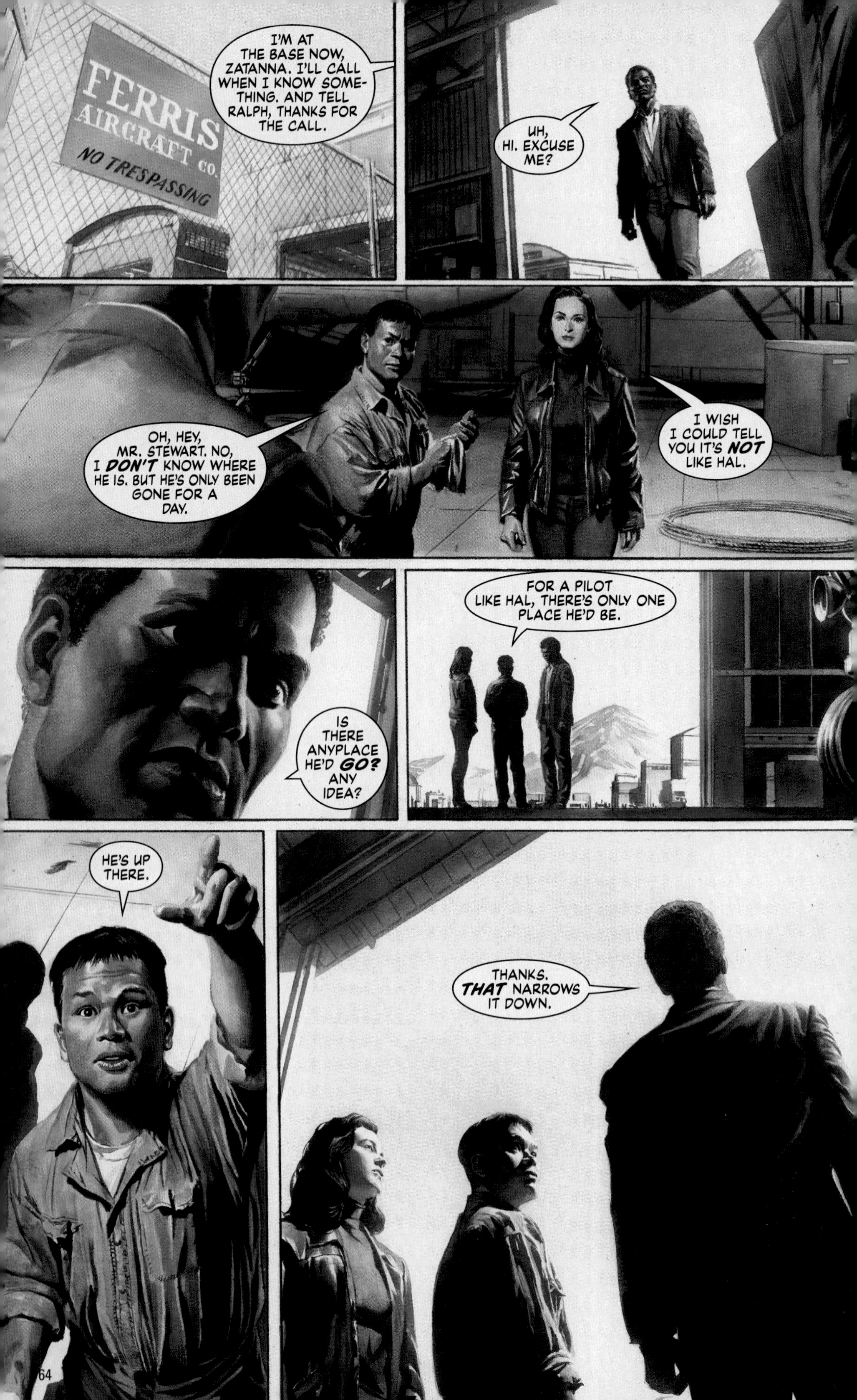
FERRIS AIRCRAFT CO.
NO TRESPASSING
I'M AT THE BASE NOW, ZATANNA. I'LL CALL WHEN I KNOW SOMETHING. AND TELL RALPH, THANKS FOR THE CALL.
UH, HI. EXCUSE ME?
OH, HEY, MR. STEWART. NO, I DON'T KNOW WHERE HE IS. BUT HE'S ONLY BEEN GONE FOR A DAY.
I WISH I COULD TELL YOU IT'S NOT LIKE HAL.
IS THERE ANYPLACE HE'D GO? ANY IDEA?
FOR A PILOT LIKE HAL, THERE'S ONLY ONE PLACE HE'D BE.
HE'S UP THERE.
THANKS. THAT NARROWS IT DOWN.

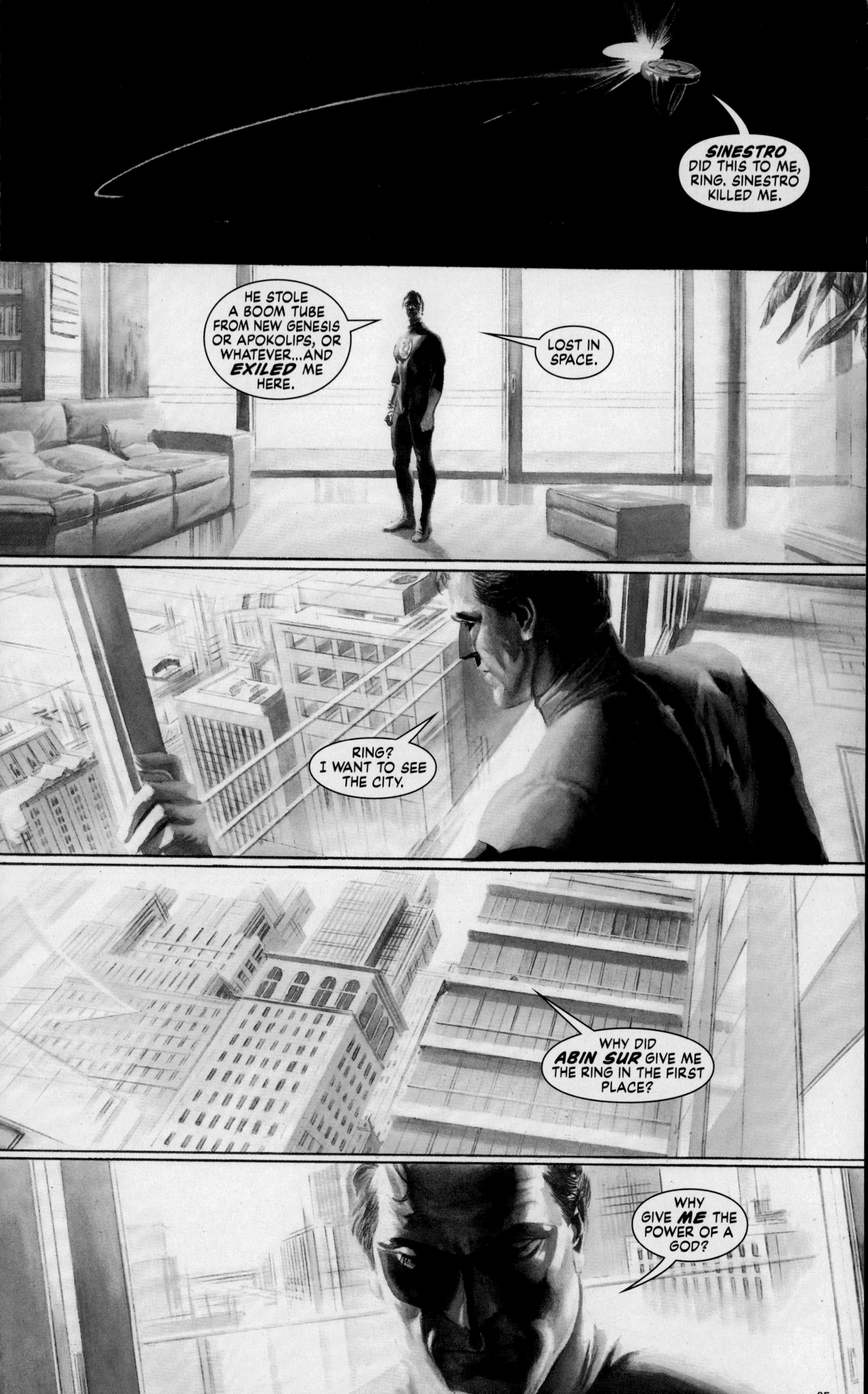
SINESTRO DID THIS TO ME, RING. SINESTRO KILLED ME.
HE STOLE A BOOM TUBE FROM NEW GENESIS OR APOKOLIPS, OR WHATEVER...AND EXILED ME HERE.
LOST IN SPACE.
RING? I WANT TO SEE THE CITY.
WHY DID ABIN SUR GIVE ME THE RING IN THE FIRST PLACE?
WHY GIVE ME THE POWER OF A GOD?

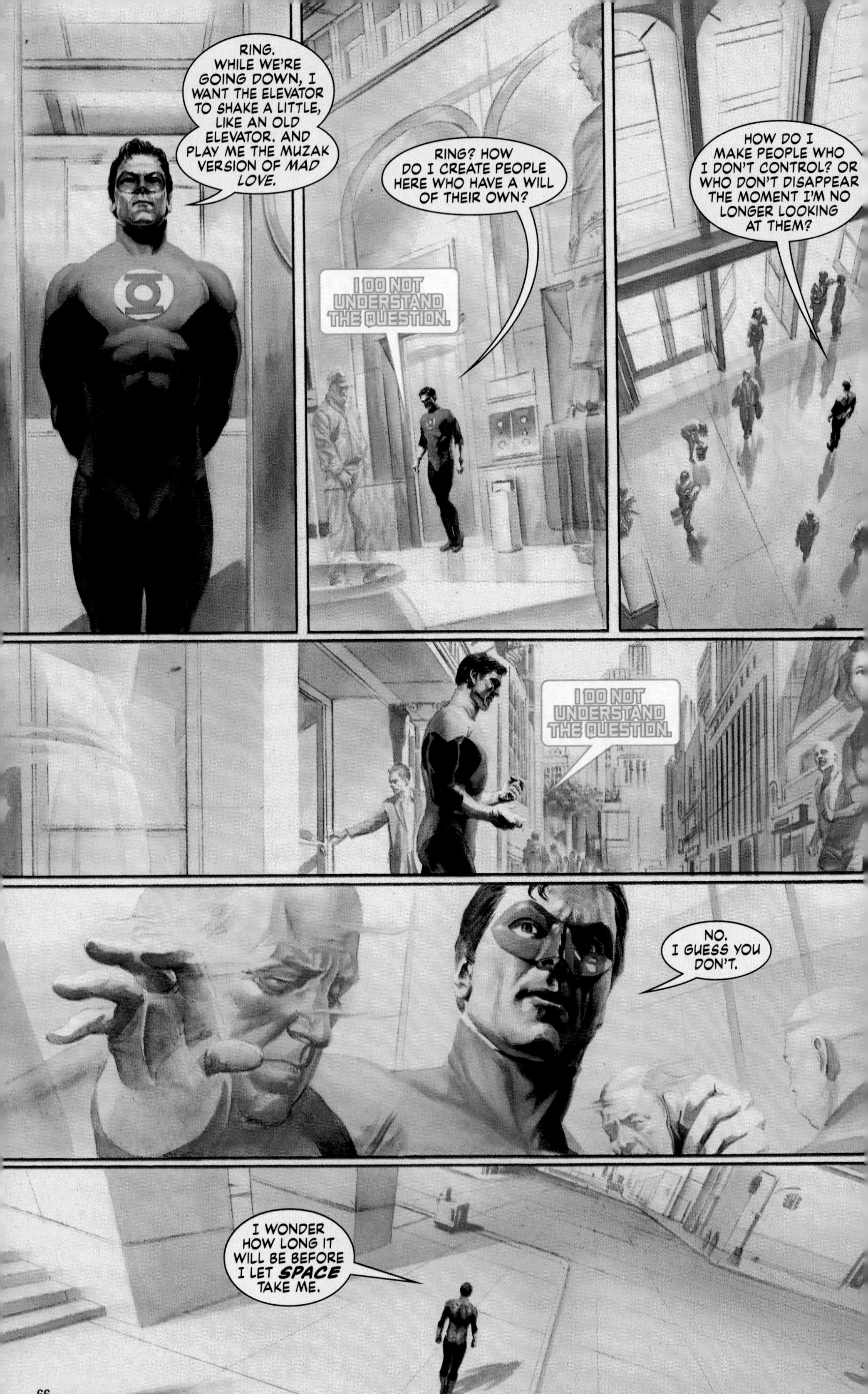
RING. WHILE WE'RE GOING DOWN, I WANT THE ELEVATOR TO SHAKE A LITTLE, LIKE AN OLD ELEVATOR. AND PLAY ME THE MUZAK VERSION OF *MAD LOVE*.
RING? HOW DO I CREATE PEOPLE HERE WHO HAVE A WILL OF THEIR OWN?
I DO NOT UNDERSTAND THE QUESTION.
HOW DO I MAKE PEOPLE WHO I DON'T CONTROL? OR WHO DON'T DISAPPEAR THE MOMENT I'M NO LONGER LOOKING AT THEM?
I DO NOT UNDERSTAND THE QUESTION.
NO. I GUESS YOU DON'T.
I WONDER HOW LONG IT WILL BE BEFORE I LET ***SPACE*** TAKE ME.

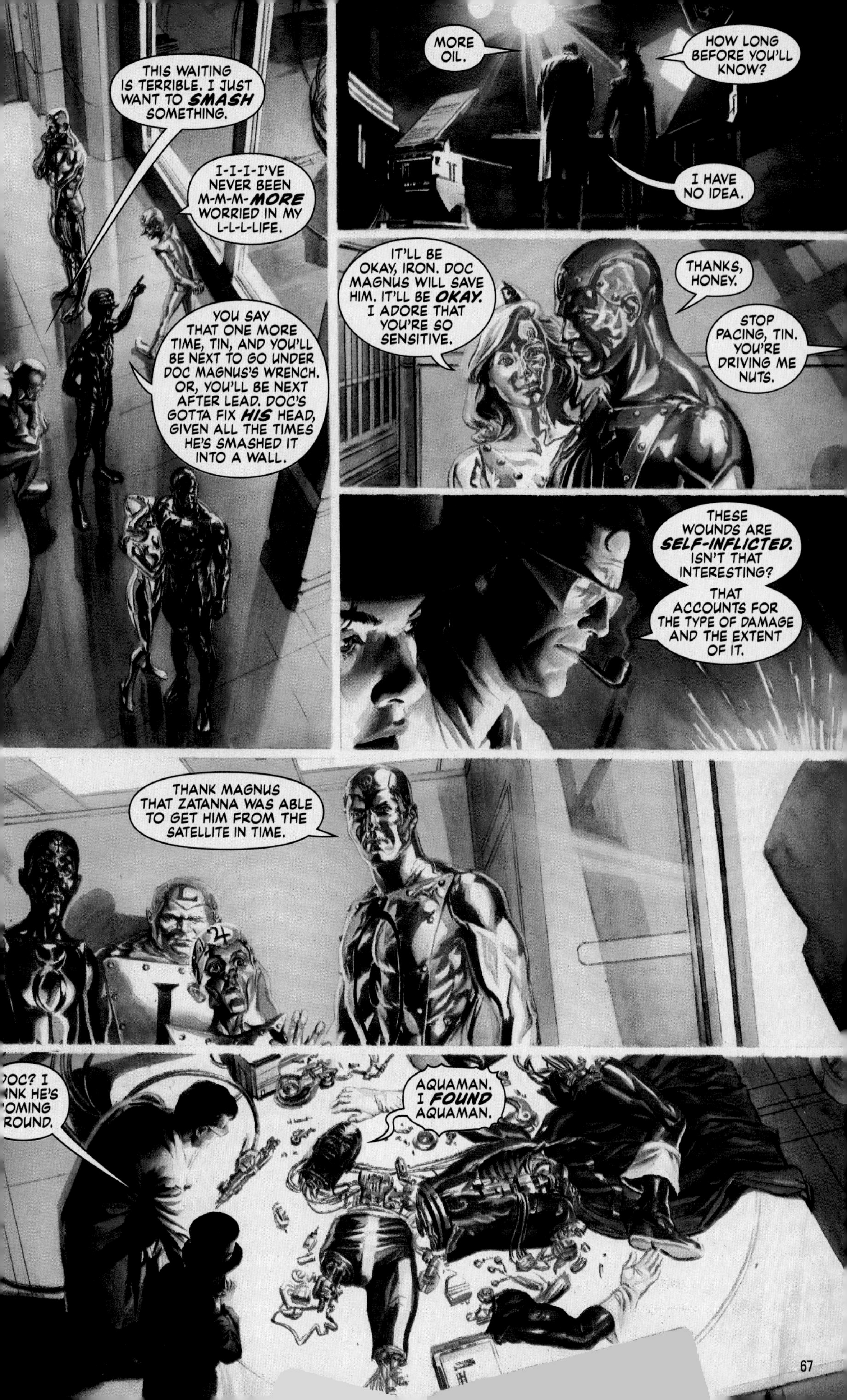
THIS WAITING IS TERRIBLE. I JUST WANT TO *SMASH* SOMETHING.
I-I-I-I'VE NEVER BEEN M-M-M-*MORE* WORRIED IN MY L-L-L-LIFE.
YOU SAY THAT ONE MORE TIME, TIN, AND YOU'LL BE NEXT TO GO UNDER DOC MAGNUS'S WRENCH. OR, YOU'LL BE NEXT AFTER LEAD. DOC'S GOTTA FIX *HIS* HEAD, GIVEN ALL THE TIMES HE'S SMASHED IT INTO A WALL.
MORE OIL.
HOW LONG BEFORE YOU'LL KNOW?
I HAVE NO IDEA.
IT'LL BE OKAY, IRON. DOC MAGNUS WILL SAVE HIM. IT'LL BE *OKAY.* I ADORE THAT YOU'RE SO SENSITIVE.
THANKS, HONEY.
STOP PACING, TIN. YOU'RE DRIVING ME NUTS.
THESE WOUNDS ARE *SELF-INFLICTED.* ISN'T THAT INTERESTING?
THAT ACCOUNTS FOR THE TYPE OF DAMAGE AND THE EXTENT OF IT.
THANK MAGNUS THAT ZATANNA WAS ABLE TO GET HIM FROM THE SATELLITE IN TIME.
?OC? I INK HE'S OMING ROUND.
AQUAMAN. I *FOUND* AQUAMAN.

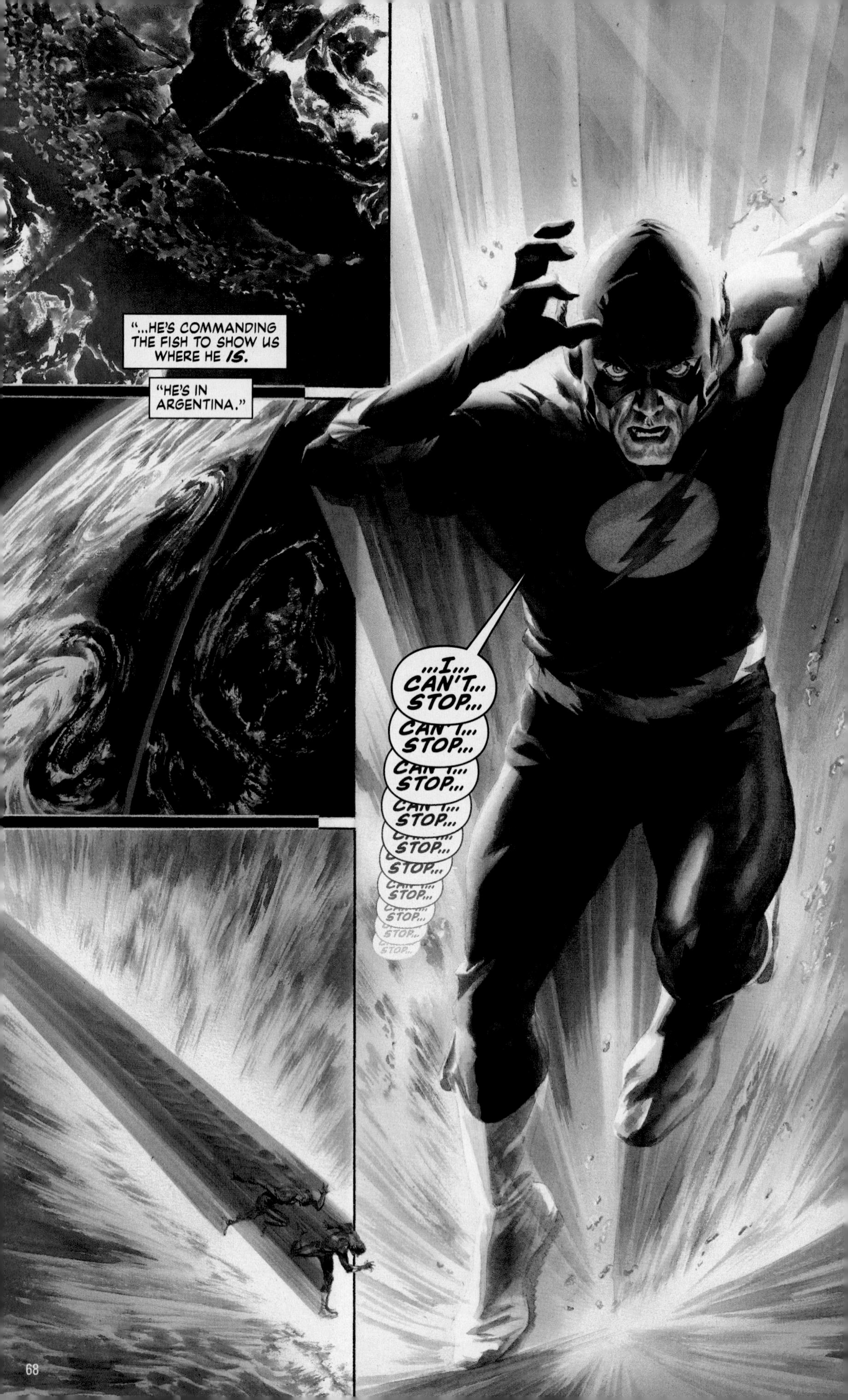
"...HE'S COMMANDING THE FISH TO SHOW US WHERE HE *IS*.
"HE'S IN ARGENTINA."
...I... CAN'T... STOP...
CAN'T... STOP...
CAN'T... STOP...
CAN'T... STOP...
STOP...
STOP...
STOP...
STOP...
STOP...

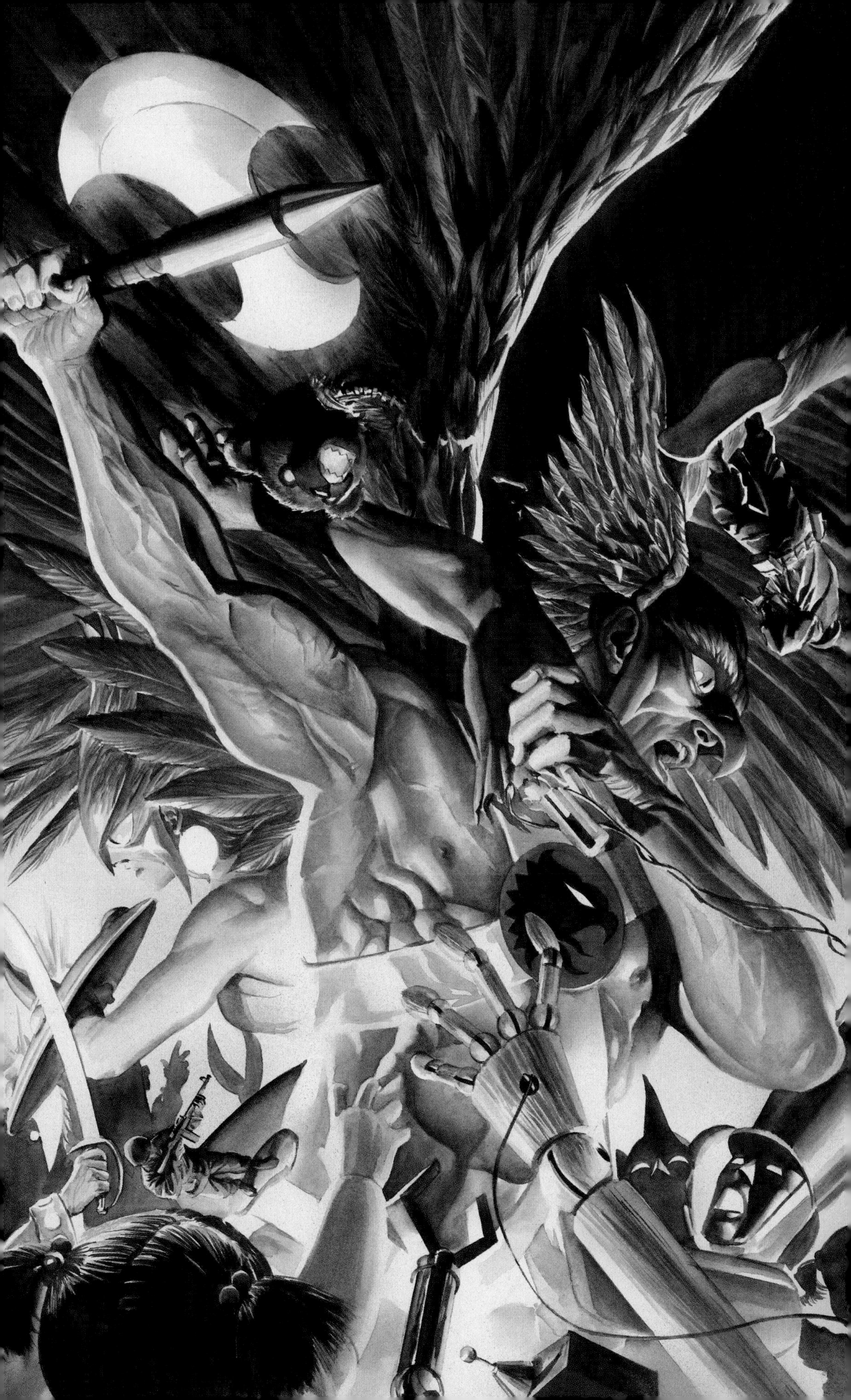

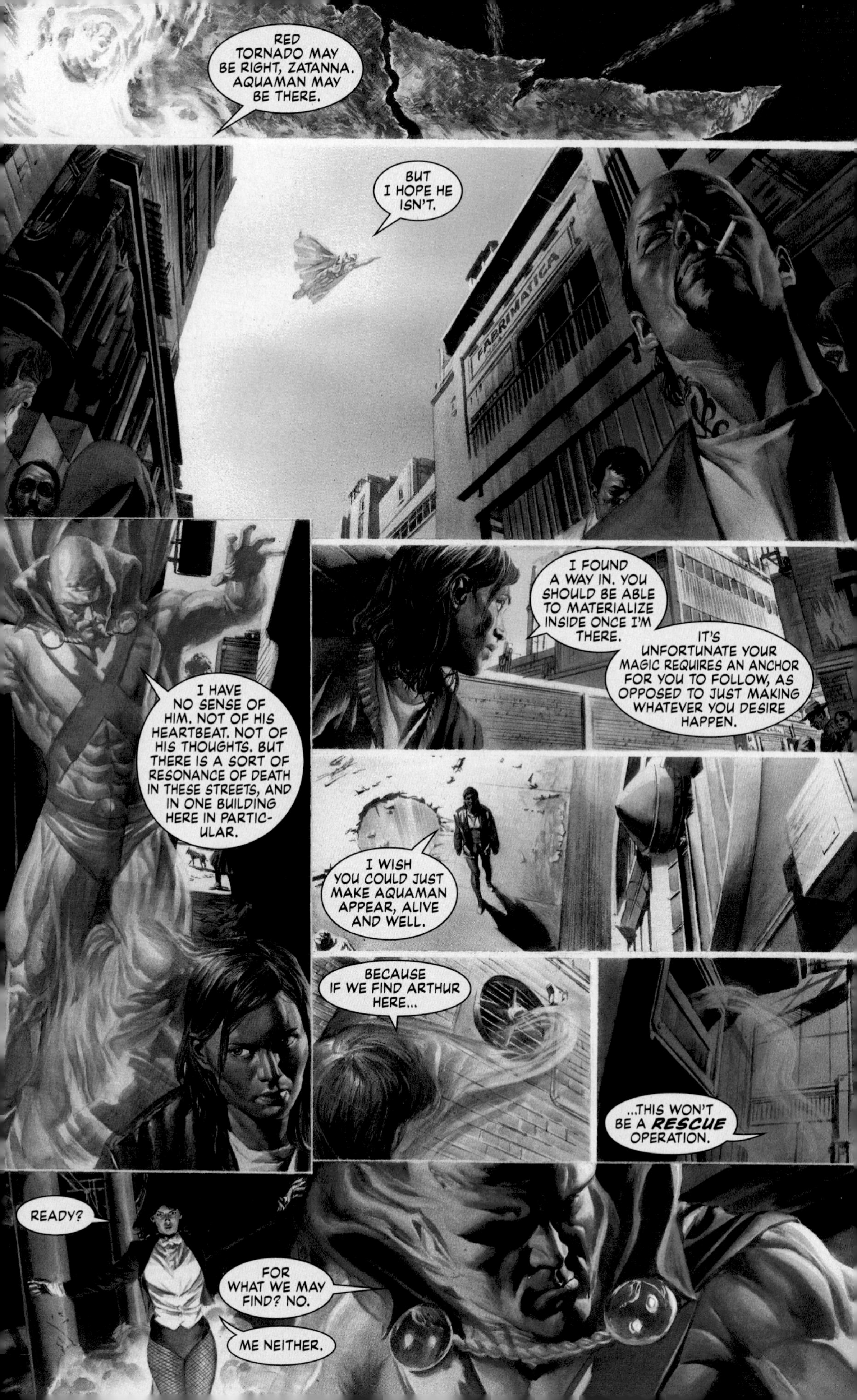
RED TORNADO MAY BE RIGHT, ZATANNA. AQUAMAN MAY BE THERE.
BUT I HOPE HE ISN'T.
FABRIMATICA
I HAVE NO SENSE OF HIM. NOT OF HIS HEARTBEAT. NOT OF HIS THOUGHTS. BUT THERE IS A SORT OF RESONANCE OF DEATH IN THESE STREETS, AND IN ONE BUILDING HERE IN PARTIC-ULAR.
I FOUND A WAY IN. YOU SHOULD BE ABLE TO MATERIALIZE INSIDE ONCE I'M THERE.
IT'S UNFORTUNATE YOUR MAGIC REQUIRES AN ANCHOR FOR YOU TO FOLLOW, AS OPPOSED TO JUST MAKING WHATEVER YOU DESIRE HAPPEN.
I WISH YOU COULD JUST MAKE AQUAMAN APPEAR, ALIVE AND WELL.
BECAUSE IF WE FIND ARTHUR HERE...
...THIS WON'T BE A ***RESCUE*** OPERATION.
READY?
FOR WHAT WE MAY FIND? NO.
ME NEITHER.

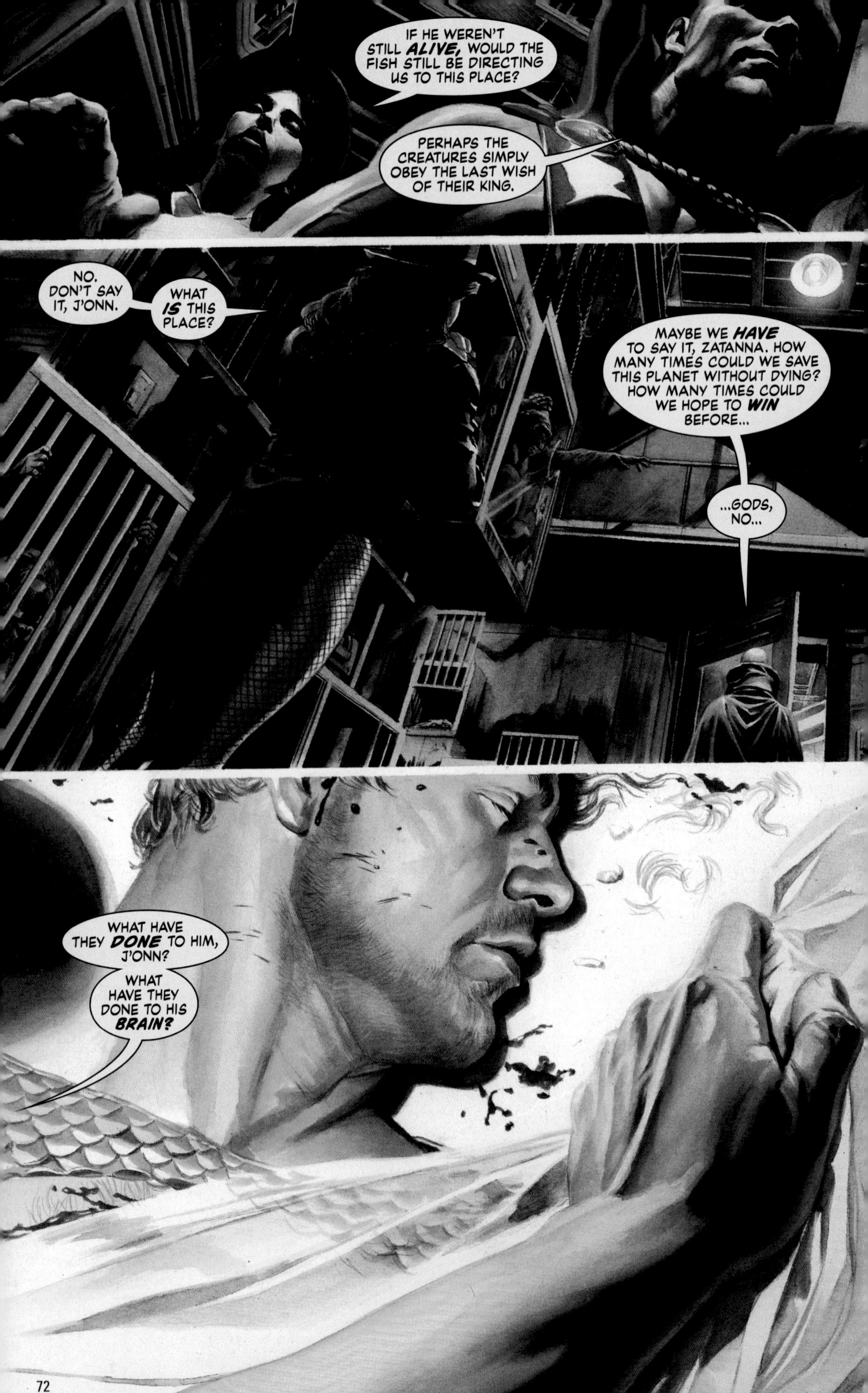
IF HE WEREN'T STILL ALIVE, WOULD THE FISH STILL BE DIRECTING US TO THIS PLACE?
PERHAPS THE CREATURES SIMPLY OBEY THE LAST WISH OF THEIR KING.
NO. DON'T SAY IT, J'ONN.
WHAT IS THIS PLACE?
MAYBE WE HAVE TO SAY IT, ZATANNA. HOW MANY TIMES COULD WE SAVE THIS PLANET WITHOUT DYING? HOW MANY TIMES COULD WE HOPE TO WIN BEFORE...
...GODS, NO...
WHAT HAVE THEY DONE TO HIM, J'ONN?
WHAT HAVE THEY DONE TO HIS BRAIN?

PERHAPS THEY HAVE NO KNOWLEDGE OF HIS...

HERE, ZATANNA. HE'S IN HERE.

OH, NO.

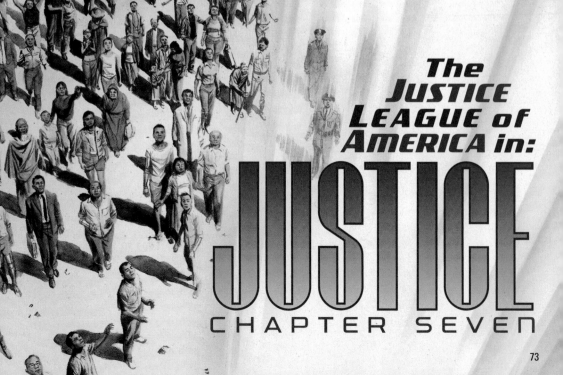

The JUSTICE LEAGUE of AMERICA in:

JUSTICE

CHAPTER SEVEN

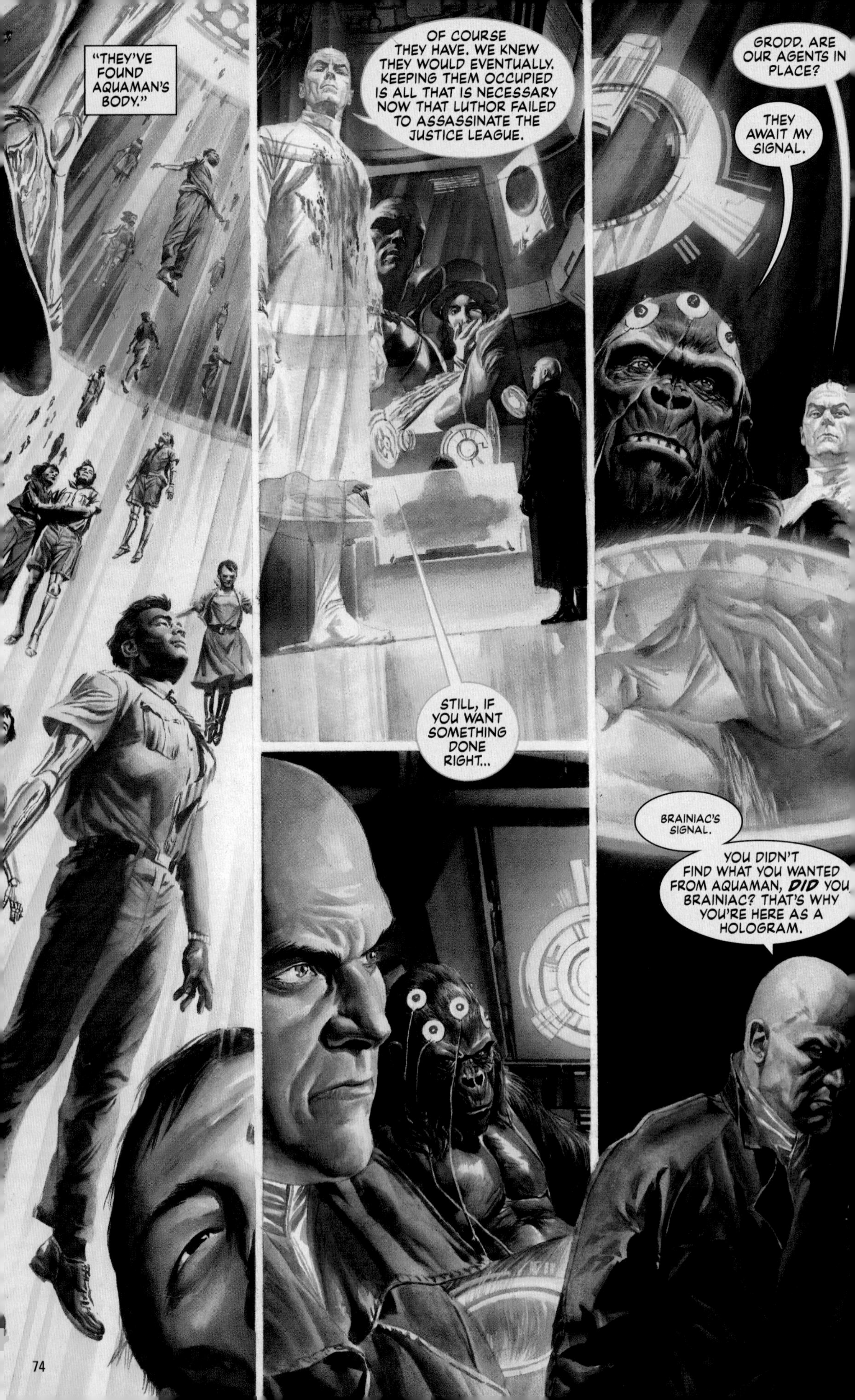
"THEY'VE FOUND AQUAMAN'S BODY."
OF COURSE THEY HAVE. WE KNEW THEY WOULD EVENTUALLY. KEEPING THEM OCCUPIED IS ALL THAT IS NECESSARY NOW THAT LUTHOR FAILED TO ASSASSINATE THE JUSTICE LEAGUE.
GRODD. ARE OUR AGENTS IN PLACE?
THEY AWAIT MY SIGNAL.
STILL, IF YOU WANT SOMETHING DONE RIGHT...
BRAINIAC'S SIGNAL.
YOU DIDN'T FIND WHAT YOU WANTED FROM AQUAMAN, *DID* YOU BRAINIAC? THAT'S WHY YOU'RE HERE AS A HOLOGRAM.

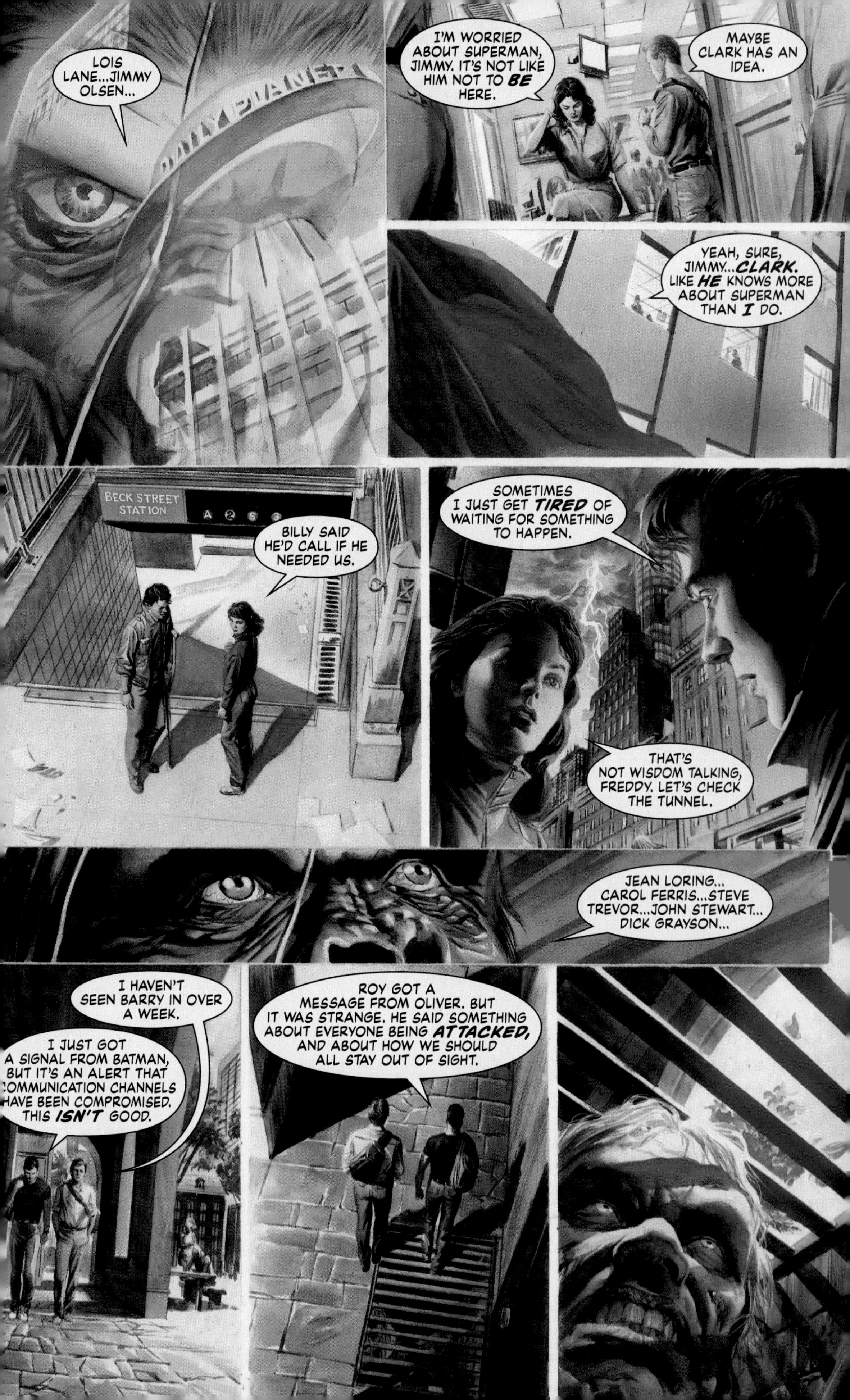
LOIS LANE...JIMMY OLSEN...
I'M WORRIED ABOUT SUPERMAN, JIMMY. IT'S NOT LIKE HIM NOT TO BE HERE.
MAYBE CLARK HAS AN IDEA.
YEAH, SURE, JIMMY...CLARK. LIKE HE KNOWS MORE ABOUT SUPERMAN THAN I DO.
BECK STREET STATION
BILLY SAID HE'D CALL IF HE NEEDED US.
SOMETIMES I JUST GET TIRED OF WAITING FOR SOMETHING TO HAPPEN.
THAT'S NOT WISDOM TALKING, FREDDY. LET'S CHECK THE TUNNEL.
JEAN LORING... CAROL FERRIS...STEVE TREVOR...JOHN STEWART... DICK GRAYSON...
I HAVEN'T SEEN BARRY IN OVER A WEEK.
I JUST GOT A SIGNAL FROM BATMAN, BUT IT'S AN ALERT THAT COMMUNICATION CHANNELS HAVE BEEN COMPROMISED. THIS ISN'T GOOD.
ROY GOT A MESSAGE FROM OLIVER. BUT IT WAS STRANGE. HE SAID SOMETHING ABOUT EVERYONE BEING ATTACKED, AND ABOUT HOW WE SHOULD ALL STAY OUT OF SIGHT.

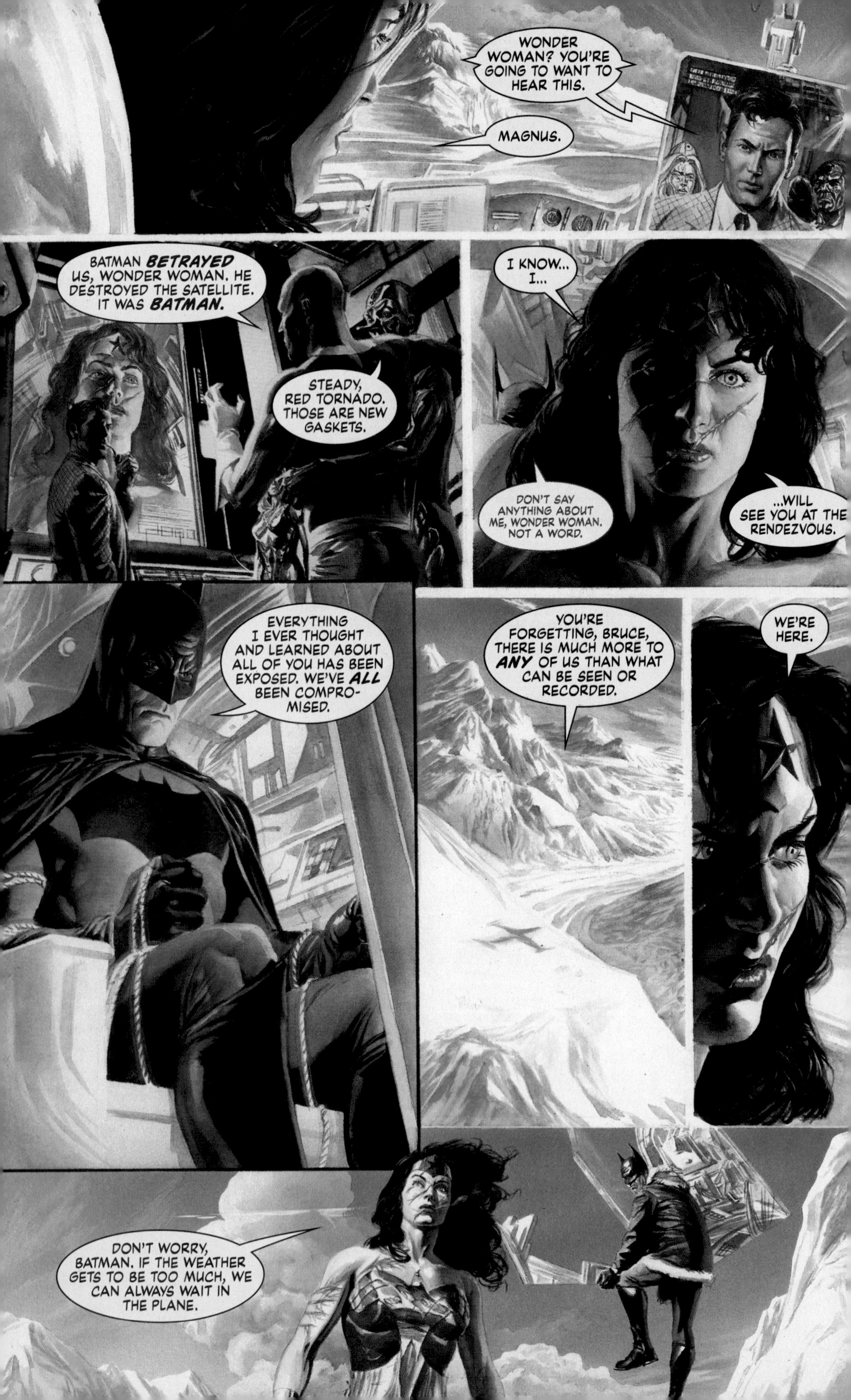
WONDER WOMAN? YOU'RE GOING TO WANT TO HEAR THIS.
MAGNUS.
BATMAN BETRAYED US, WONDER WOMAN. HE DESTROYED THE SATELLITE. IT WAS BATMAN.
STEADY, RED TORNADO. THOSE ARE NEW GASKETS.
I KNOW... I...
DON'T SAY ANYTHING ABOUT ME, WONDER WOMAN. NOT A WORD.
...WILL SEE YOU AT THE RENDEZVOUS.
EVERYTHING I EVER THOUGHT AND LEARNED ABOUT ALL OF YOU HAS BEEN EXPOSED. WE'VE ALL BEEN COMPRO-MISED.
YOU'RE FORGETTING, BRUCE, THERE IS MUCH MORE TO ANY OF US THAN WHAT CAN BE SEEN OR RECORDED.
WE'RE HERE.
DON'T WORRY, BATMAN. IF THE WEATHER GETS TO BE TOO MUCH, WE CAN ALWAYS WAIT IN THE PLANE.

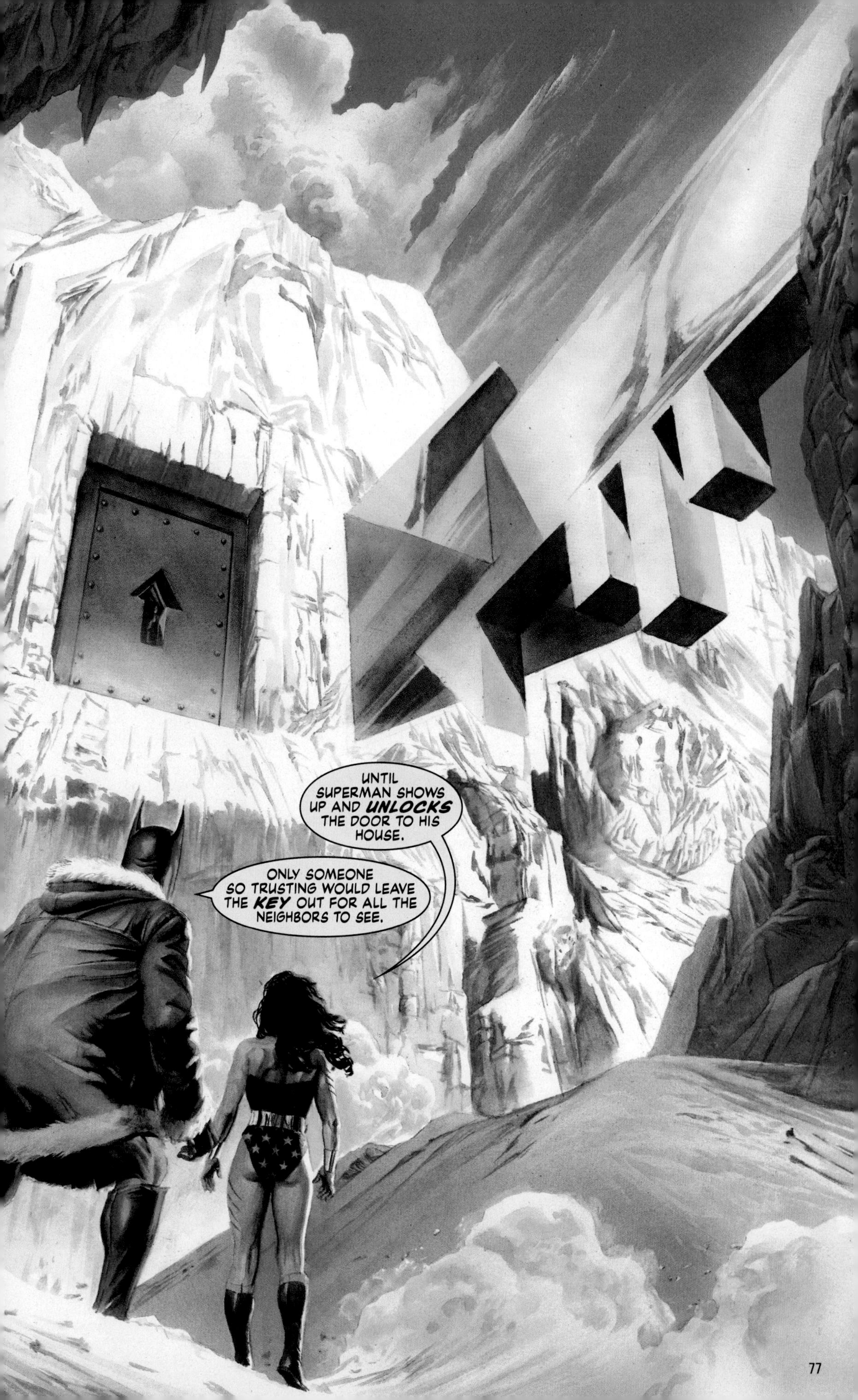
ONLY SOMEONE SO TRUSTING WOULD LEAVE THE KEY OUT FOR ALL THE NEIGHBORS TO SEE.
UNTIL SUPERMAN SHOWS UP AND UNLOCKS THE DOOR TO HIS HOUSE.

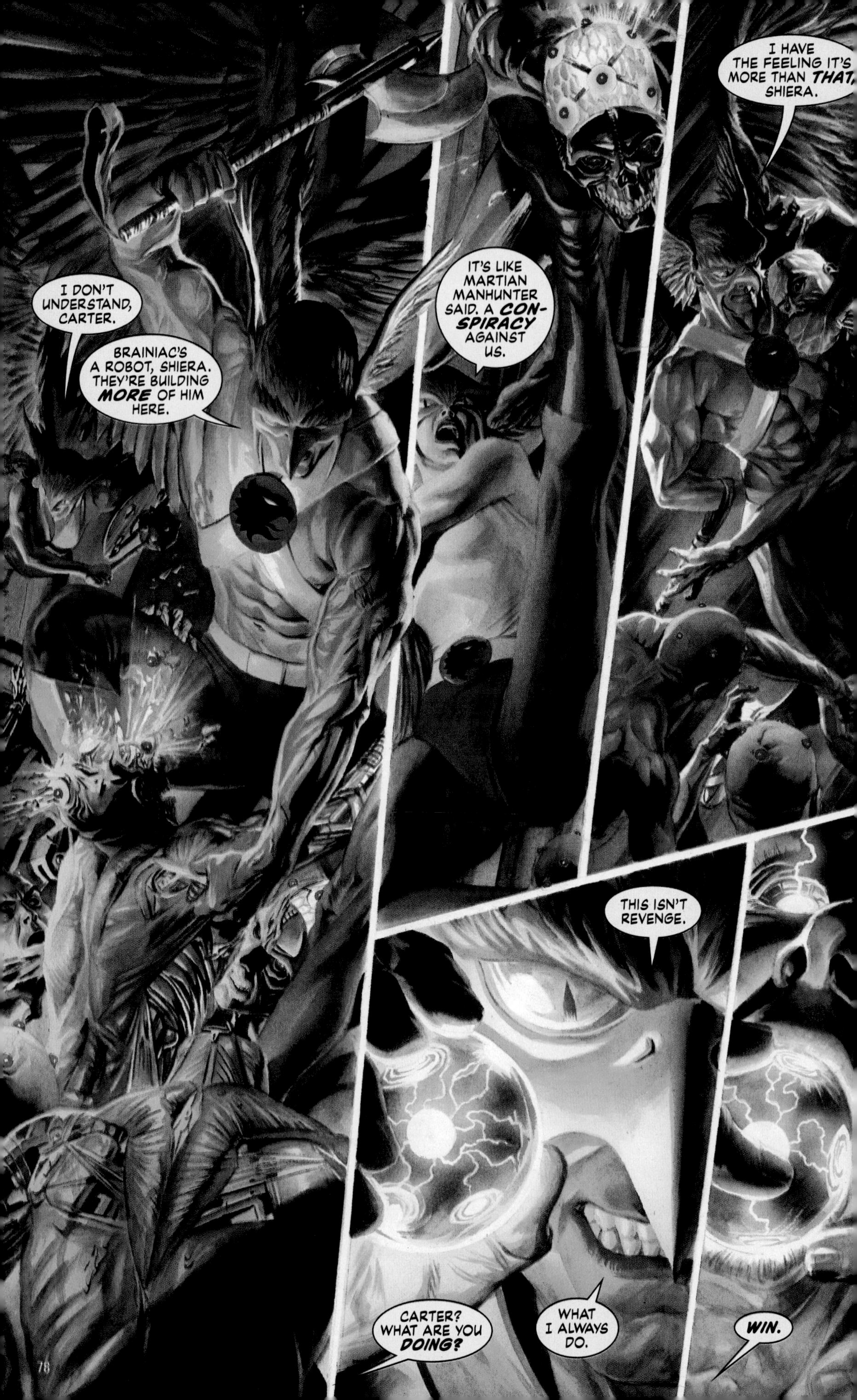
I DON'T UNDERSTAND, CARTER.
BRAINIAC'S A ROBOT, SHIERA. THEY'RE BUILDING MORE OF HIM HERE.
IT'S LIKE MARTIAN MANHUNTER SAID. A CONSPIRACY AGAINST US.
I HAVE THE FEELING IT'S MORE THAN THAT, SHIERA.
THIS ISN'T REVENGE.
CARTER? WHAT ARE YOU DOING?
WHAT I ALWAYS DO.
WIN.

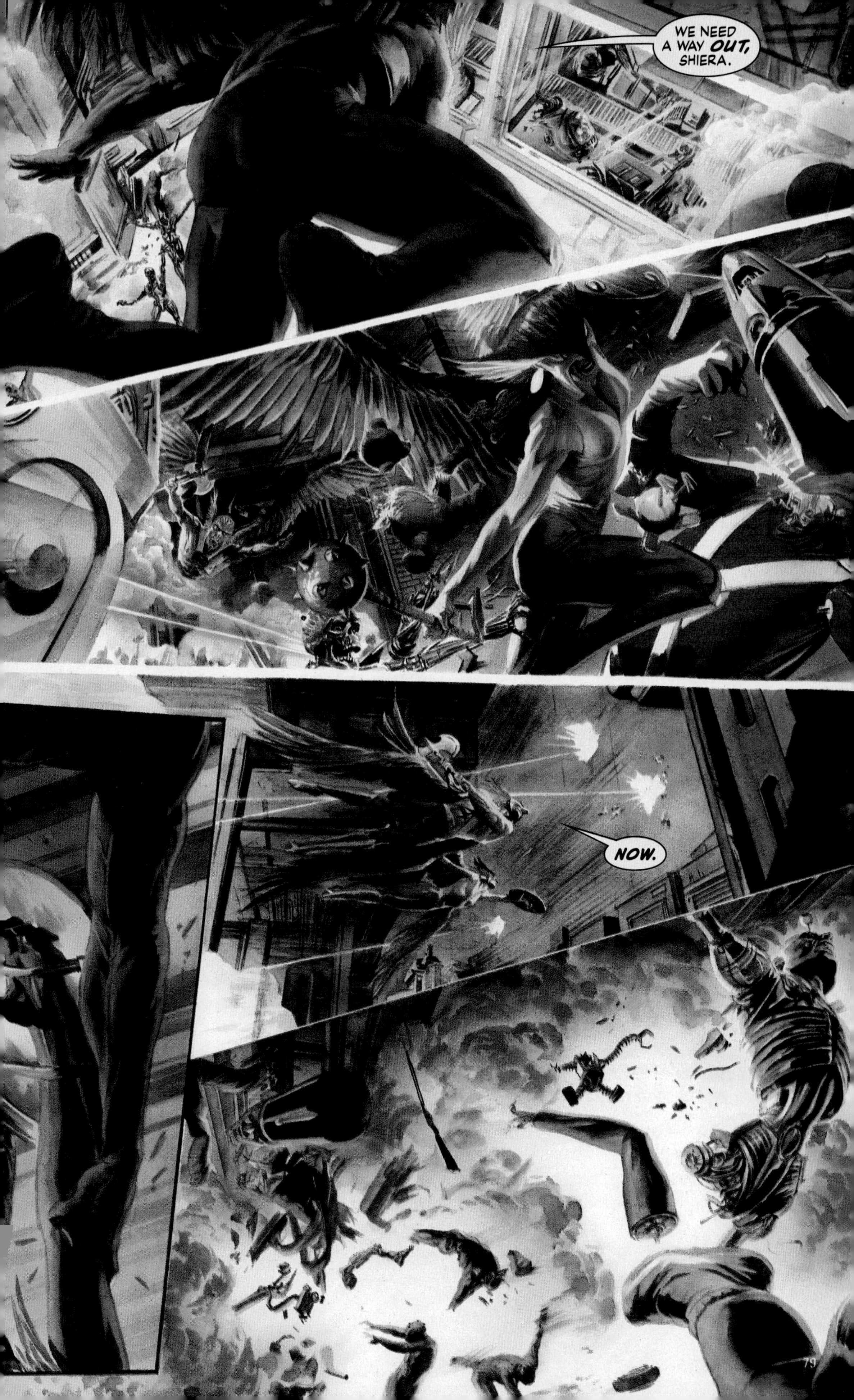
WE NEED A WAY OUT, SHIERA.
NOW.

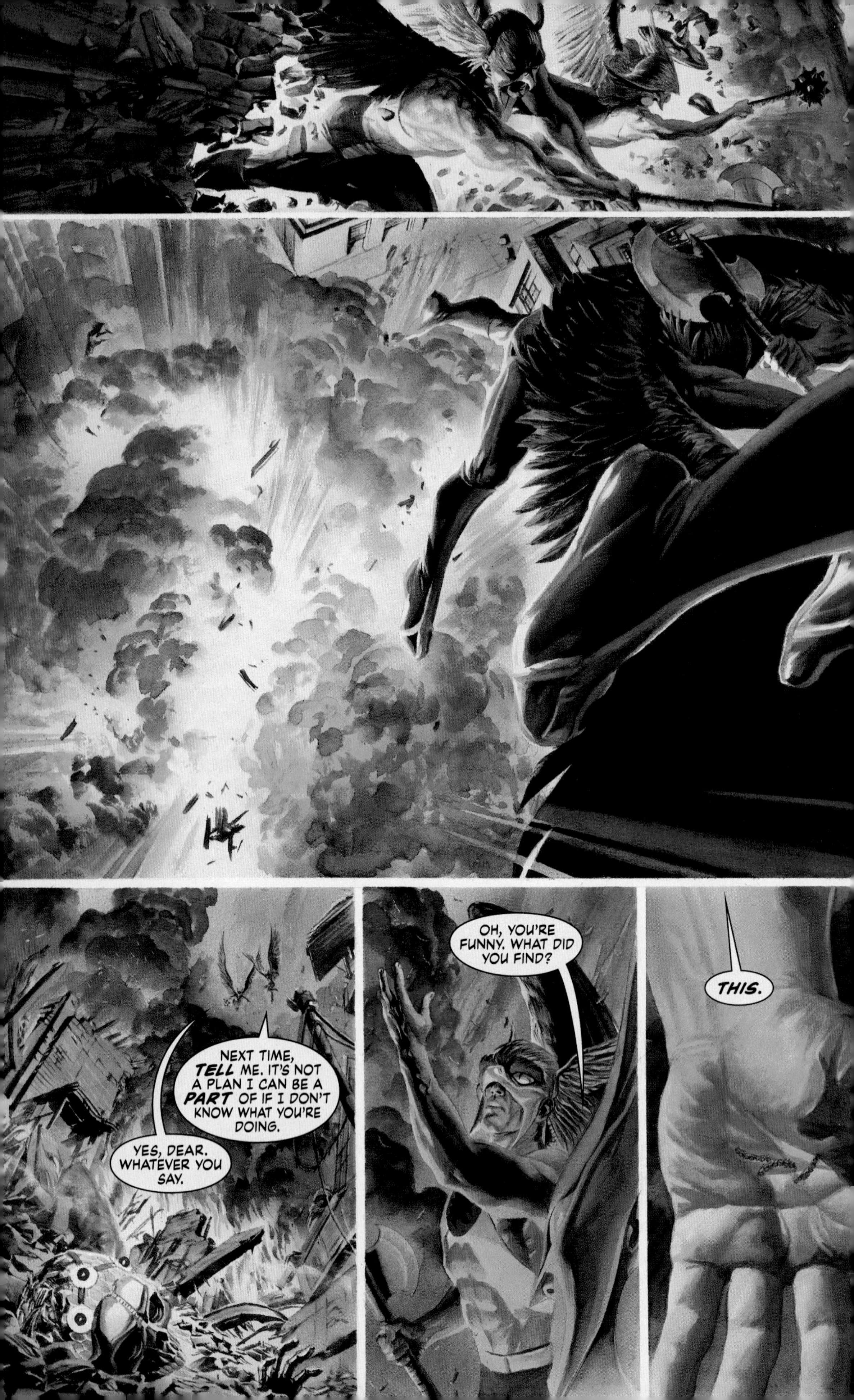
NEXT TIME, TELL ME. IT'S NOT A PLAN I CAN BE A PART OF IF I DON'T KNOW WHAT YOU'RE DOING.
YES, DEAR. WHATEVER YOU SAY.
OH, YOU'RE FUNNY. WHAT DID YOU FIND?
THIS.

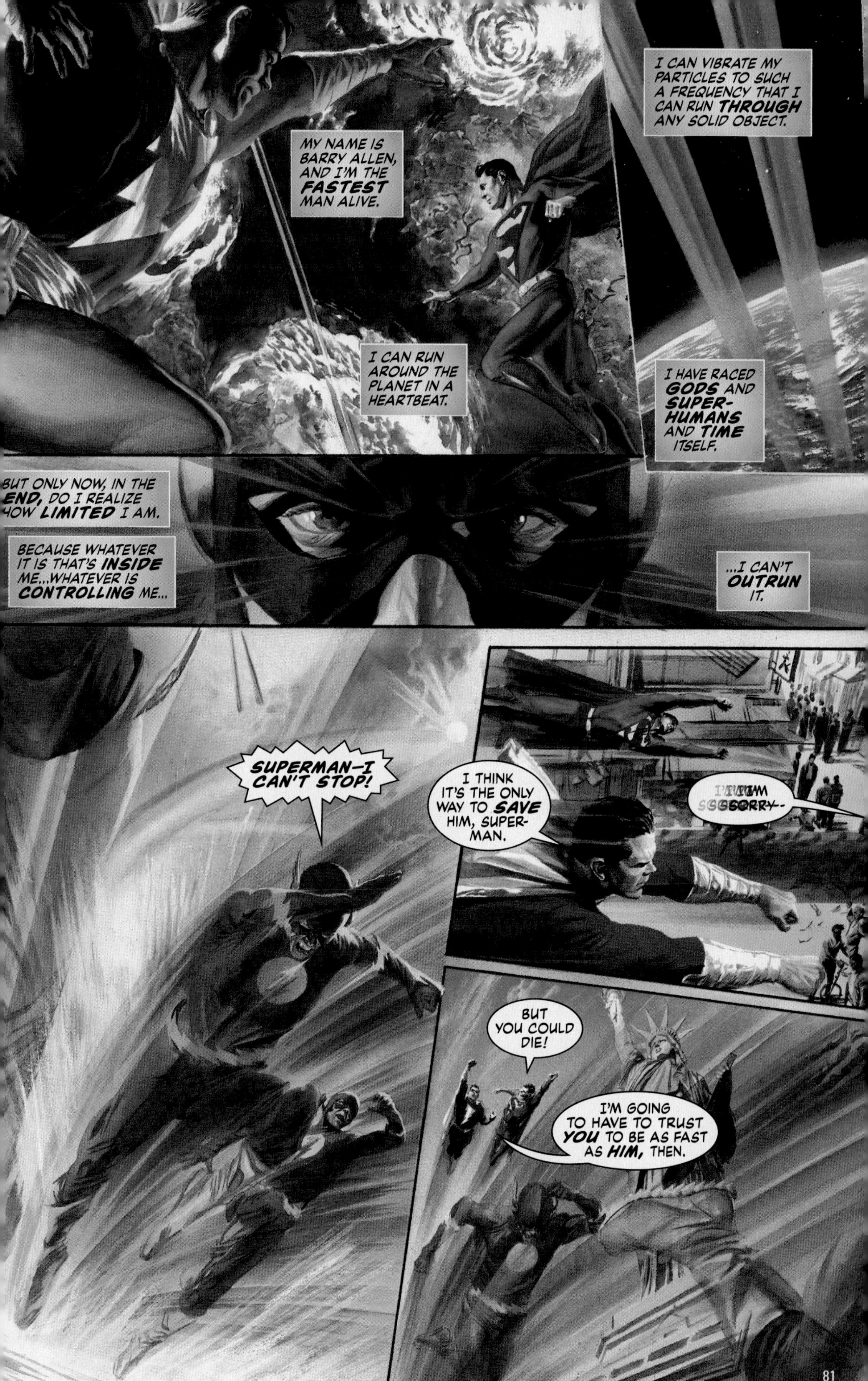

MY NAME IS BARRY ALLEN, AND I'M THE FASTEST MAN ALIVE.
I CAN RUN AROUND THE PLANET IN A HEARTBEAT.
I CAN VIBRATE MY PARTICLES TO SUCH A FREQUENCY THAT I CAN RUN THROUGH ANY SOLID OBJECT.
I HAVE RACED GODS AND SUPER-HUMANS AND TIME ITSELF.
BUT ONLY NOW, IN THE END, DO I REALIZE HOW LIMITED I AM.
BECAUSE WHATEVER IT IS THAT'S INSIDE ME...WHATEVER IS CONTROLLING ME...
...I CAN'T OUTRUN IT.
SUPERMAN—I CAN'T STOP!
I THINK IT'S THE ONLY WAY TO SAVE HIM, SUPER-MAN.
I'M SORRY--
BUT YOU COULD DIE!
I'M GOING TO HAVE TO TRUST YOU TO BE AS FAST AS HIM, THEN.

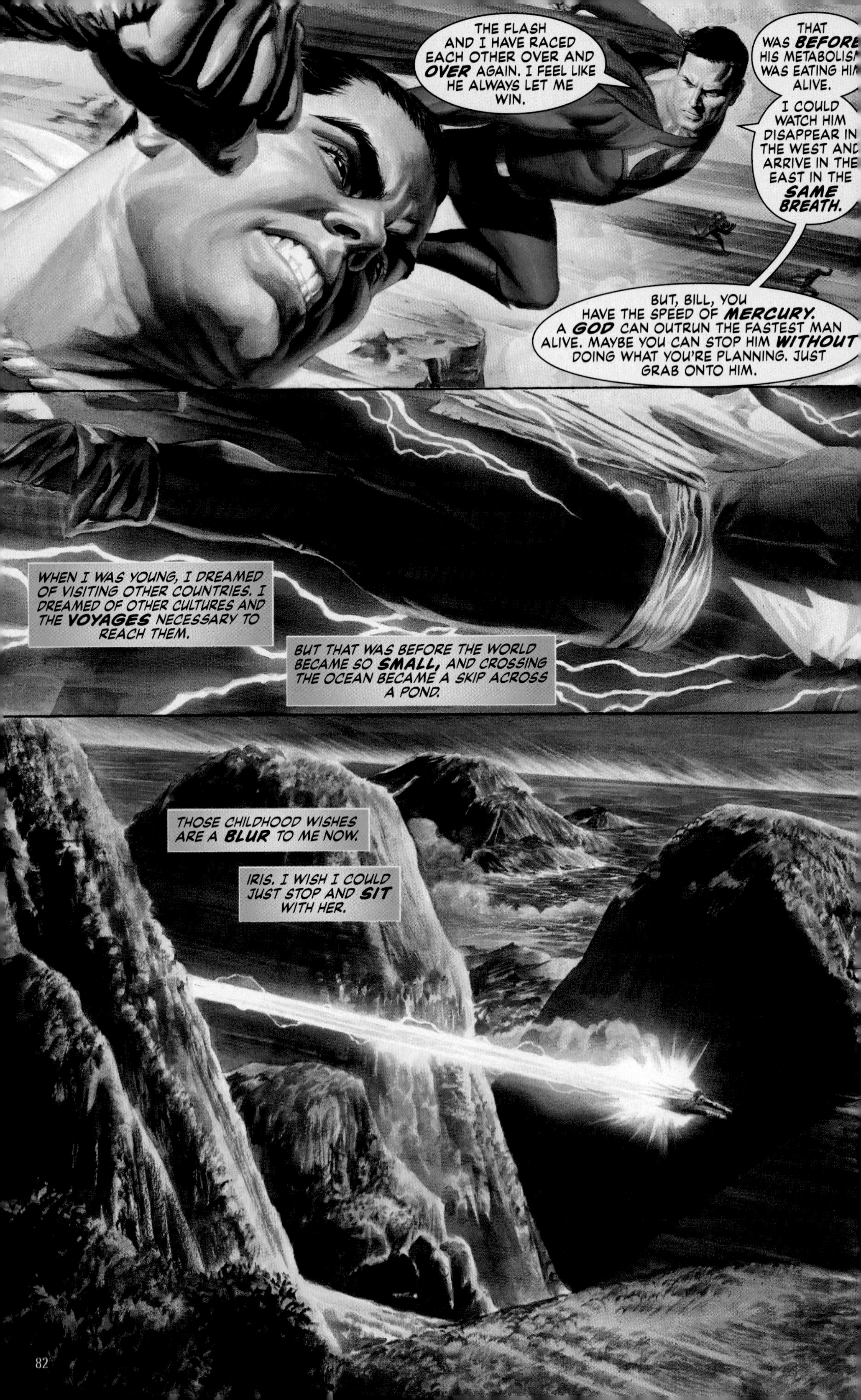
THE FLASH AND I HAVE RACED EACH OTHER OVER AND OVER AGAIN. I FEEL LIKE HE ALWAYS LET ME WIN.
THAT WAS BEFORE HIS METABOLISM WAS EATING HIM ALIVE.
I COULD WATCH HIM DISAPPEAR IN THE WEST AND ARRIVE IN THE EAST IN THE SAME BREATH.
BUT, BILL, YOU HAVE THE SPEED OF MERCURY. A GOD CAN OUTRUN THE FASTEST MAN ALIVE. MAYBE YOU CAN STOP HIM WITHOUT DOING WHAT YOU'RE PLANNING. JUST GRAB ONTO HIM.
WHEN I WAS YOUNG, I DREAMED OF VISITING OTHER COUNTRIES. I DREAMED OF OTHER CULTURES AND THE VOYAGES NECESSARY TO REACH THEM.
BUT THAT WAS BEFORE THE WORLD BECAME SO SMALL, AND CROSSING THE OCEAN BECAME A SKIP ACROSS A POND.
THOSE CHILDHOOD WISHES ARE A BLUR TO ME NOW.
IRIS. I WISH I COULD JUST STOP AND SIT WITH HER.

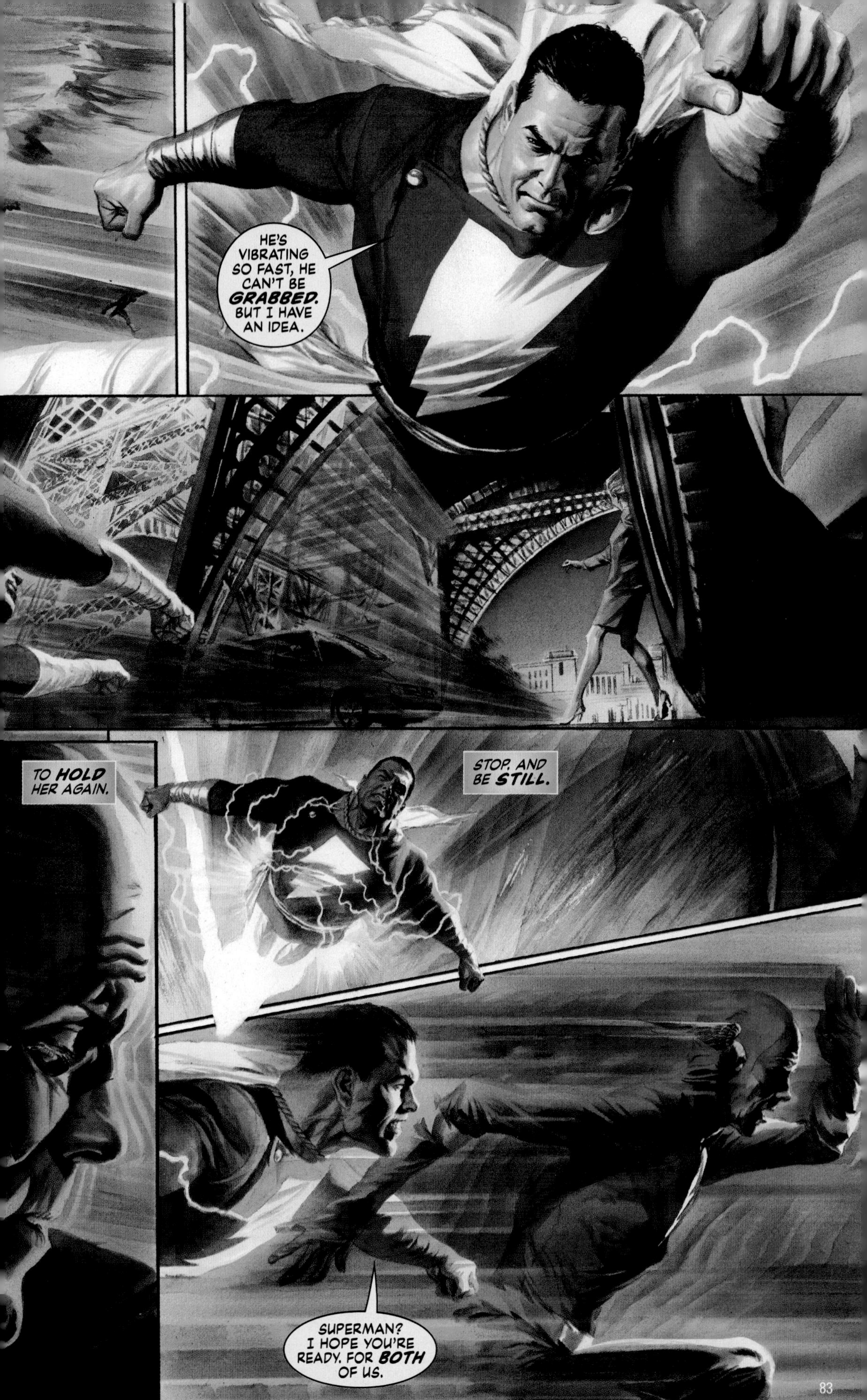
HE'S VIBRATING SO FAST, HE CAN'T BE **GRABBED.** BUT I HAVE AN IDEA.
TO **HOLD** HER AGAIN.
STOP. AND BE **STILL.**
SUPERMAN? I HOPE YOU'RE READY. FOR **BOTH** OF US.

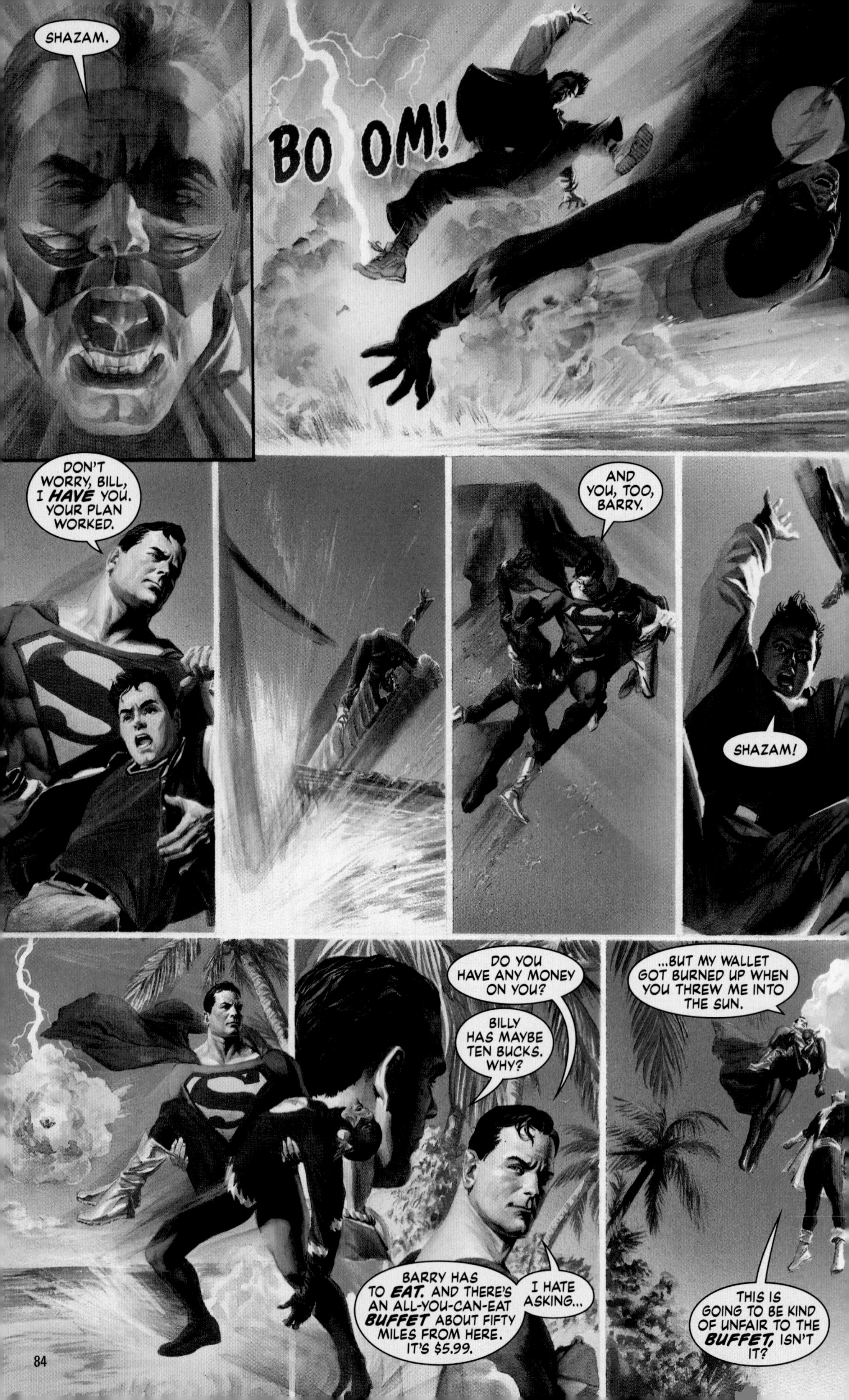
SHAZAM.
BOOM!
DON'T WORRY, BILL, I HAVE YOU. YOUR PLAN WORKED.
AND YOU, TOO, BARRY.
SHAZAM!
DO YOU HAVE ANY MONEY ON YOU?
BILLY HAS MAYBE TEN BUCKS. WHY?
I HATE ASKING...
BARRY HAS TO EAT. AND THERE'S AN ALL-YOU-CAN-EAT BUFFET ABOUT FIFTY MILES FROM HERE. IT'S $5.99.
...BUT MY WALLET GOT BURNED UP WHEN YOU THREW ME INTO THE SUN.
THIS IS GOING TO BE KIND OF UNFAIR TO THE BUFFET, ISN'T IT?

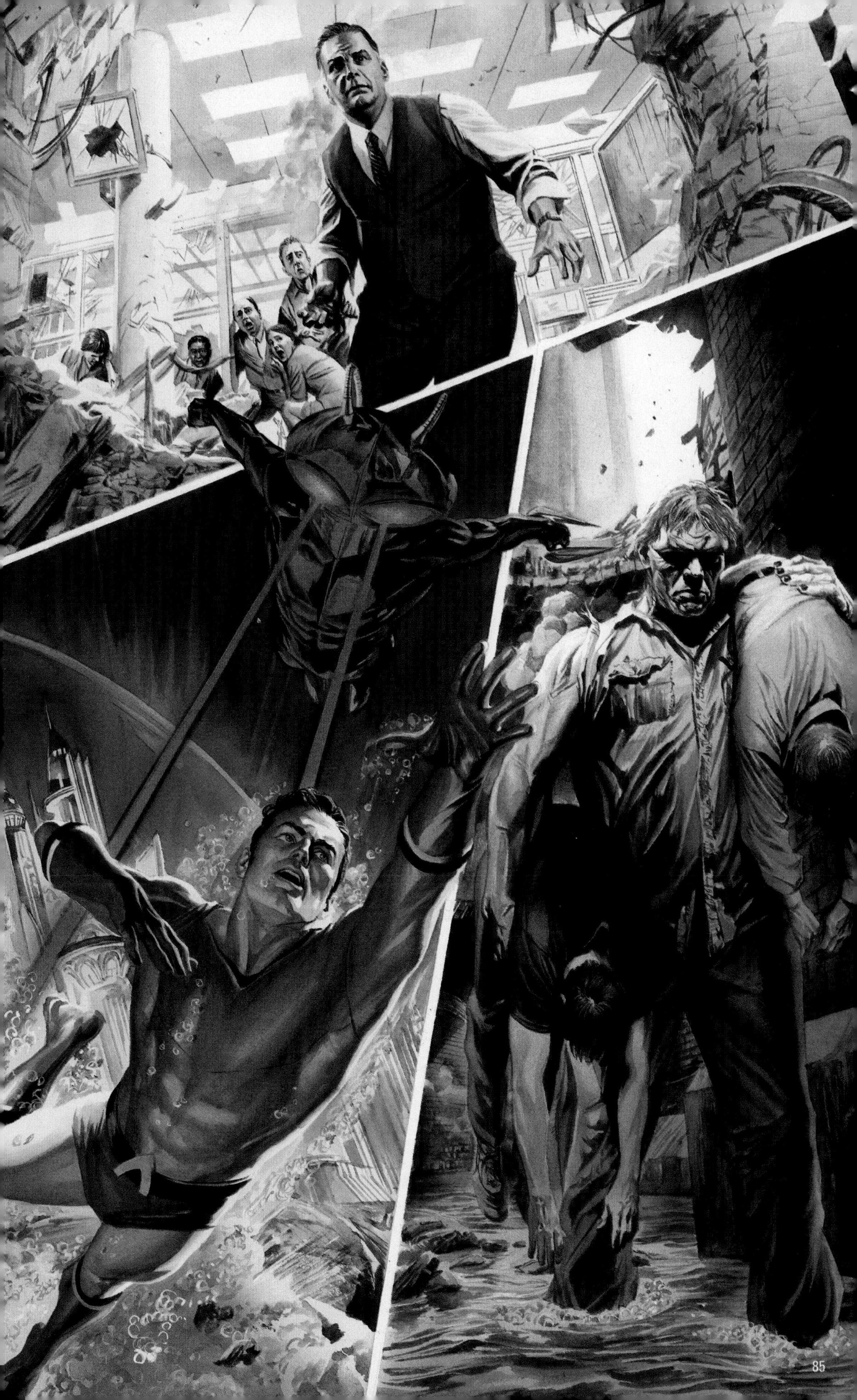

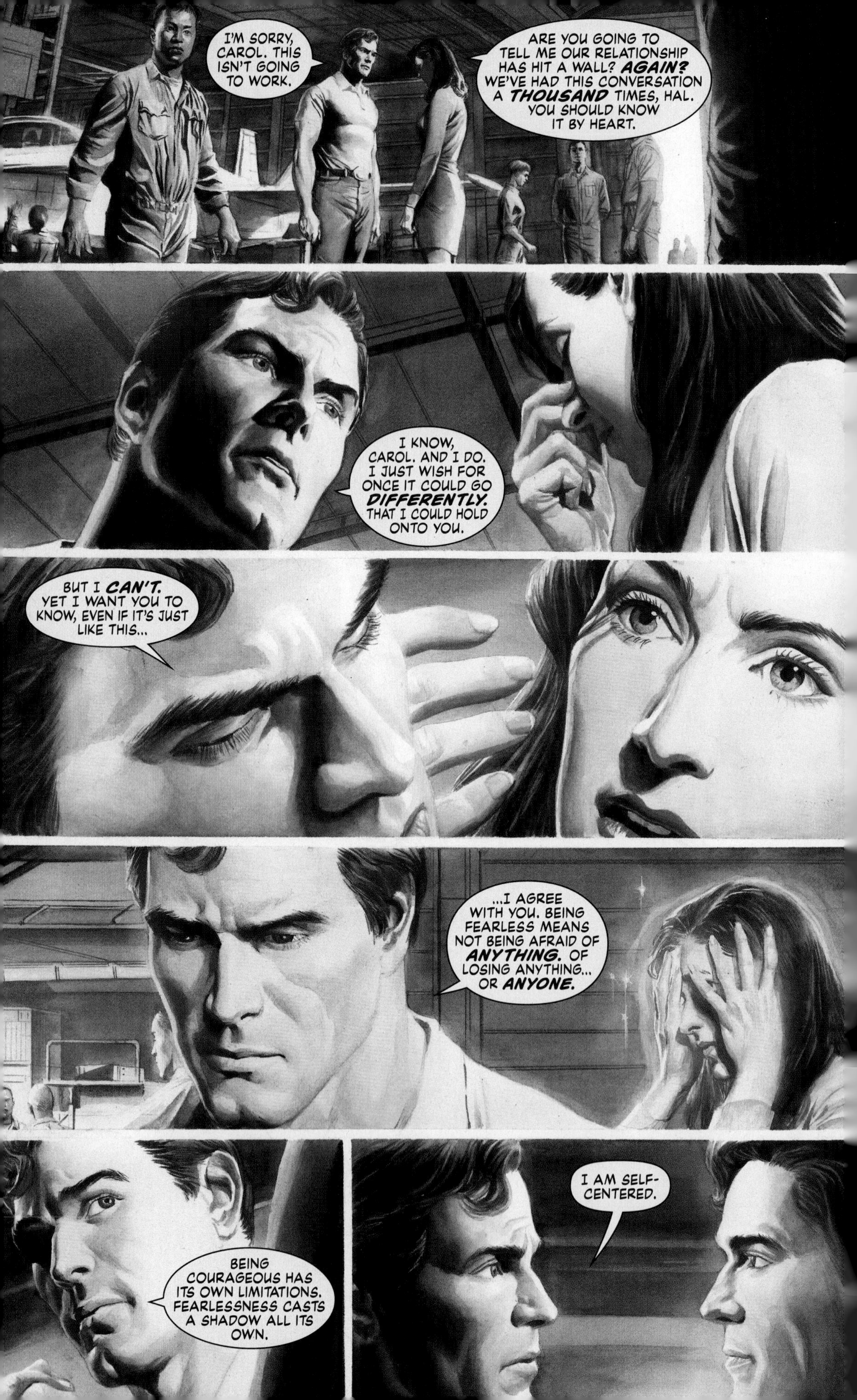
I'M SORRY, CAROL. THIS ISN'T GOING TO WORK.
ARE YOU GOING TO TELL ME OUR RELATIONSHIP HAS HIT A WALL? **AGAIN?** WE'VE HAD THIS CONVERSATION A **THOUSAND** TIMES, HAL. YOU SHOULD KNOW IT BY HEART.
I KNOW, CAROL. AND I DO. I JUST WISH FOR ONCE IT COULD GO **DIFFERENTLY.** THAT I COULD HOLD ONTO YOU.
BUT I **CAN'T.** YET I WANT YOU TO KNOW, EVEN IF IT'S JUST LIKE THIS...
...I AGREE WITH YOU. BEING FEARLESS MEANS NOT BEING AFRAID OF **ANYTHING.** OF LOSING ANYTHING... OR **ANYONE.**
BEING COURAGEOUS HAS ITS OWN LIMITATIONS. FEARLESSNESS CASTS A SHADOW ALL ITS OWN.
I AM SELF-CENTERED.

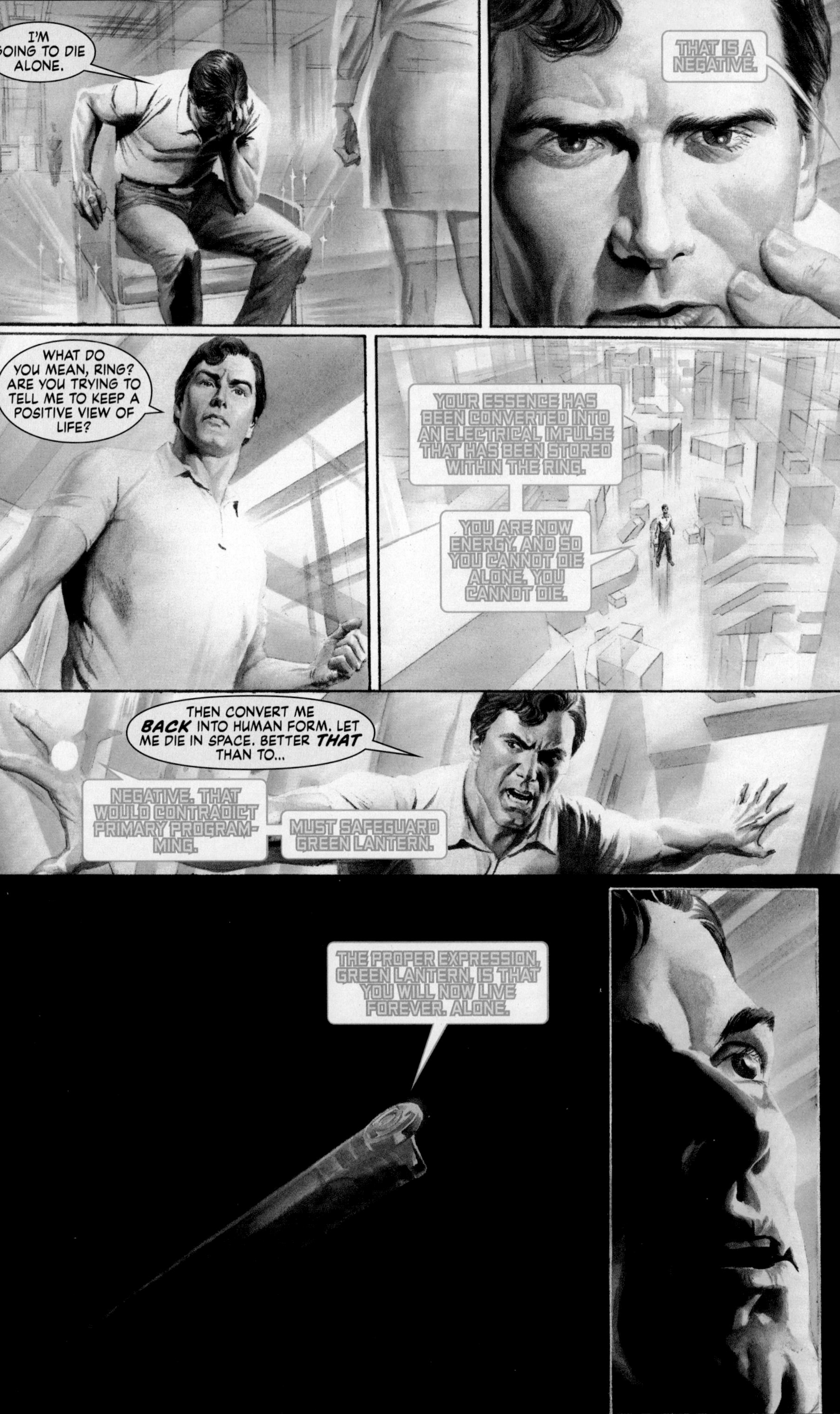
I'M GOING TO DIE ALONE.
THAT IS A NEGATIVE.
WHAT DO YOU MEAN, RING? ARE YOU TRYING TO TELL ME TO KEEP A POSITIVE VIEW OF LIFE?
YOUR ESSENCE HAS BEEN CONVERTED INTO AN ELECTRICAL IMPULSE THAT HAS BEEN STORED WITHIN THE RING.
YOU ARE NOW ENERGY. AND SO YOU CANNOT DIE ALONE. YOU CANNOT DIE.
THEN CONVERT ME BACK INTO HUMAN FORM. LET ME DIE IN SPACE. BETTER THAT THAN TO...
NEGATIVE. THAT WOULD CONTRADICT PRIMARY PROGRAMMING.
MUST SAFEGUARD GREEN LANTERN.
THE PROPER EXPRESSION, GREEN LANTERN, IS THAT YOU WILL NOW LIVE FOREVER. ALONE.

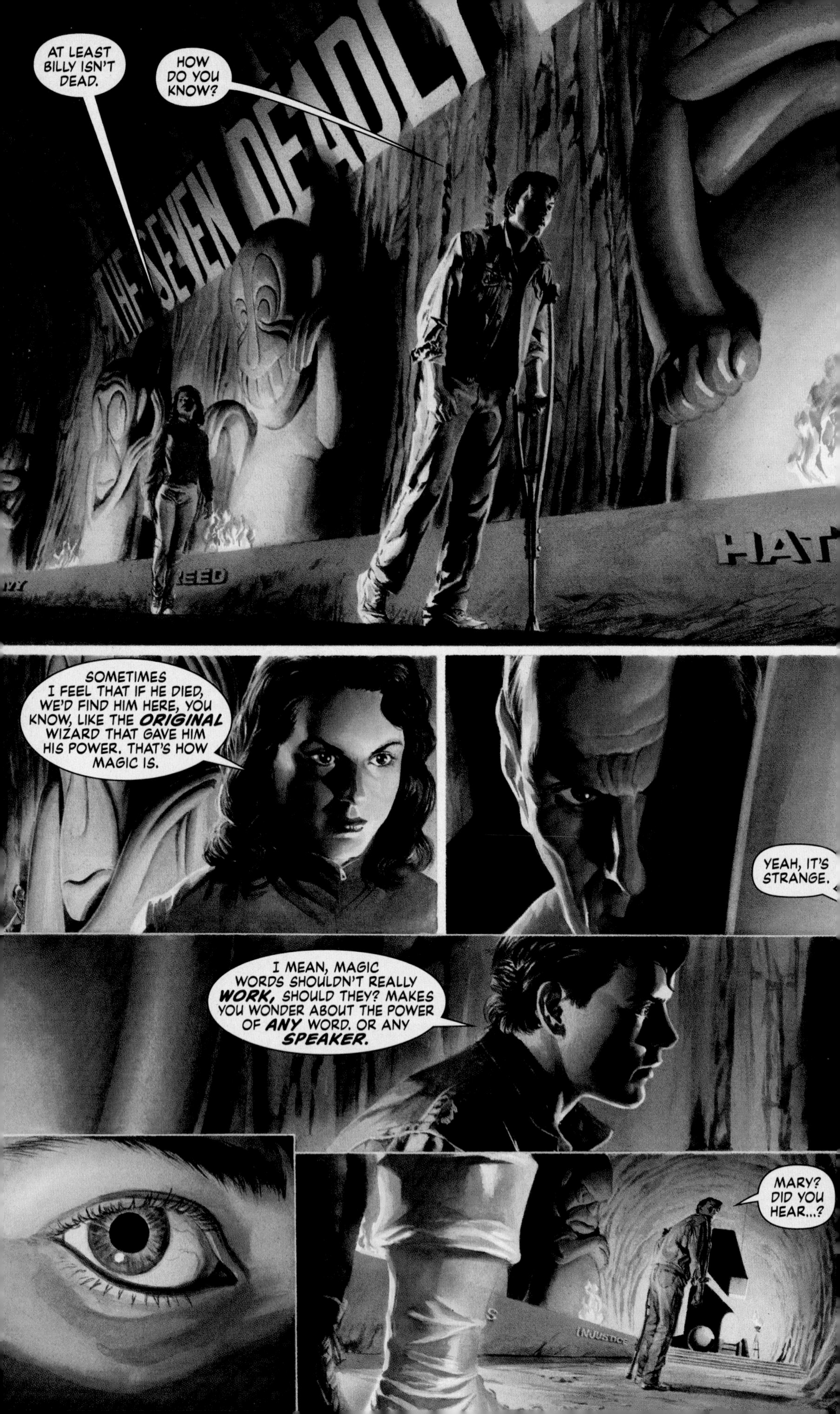
AT LEAST BILLY ISN'T DEAD.
HOW DO YOU KNOW?
THE SEVEN DEADLY
REED
HAT
SOMETIMES I FEEL THAT IF HE DIED, WE'D FIND HIM HERE, YOU KNOW, LIKE THE ORIGINAL WIZARD THAT GAVE HIM HIS POWER. THAT'S HOW MAGIC IS.
YEAH, IT'S STRANGE.
I MEAN, MAGIC WORDS SHOULDN'T REALLY WORK, SHOULD THEY? MAKES YOU WONDER ABOUT THE POWER OF ANY WORD. OR ANY SPEAKER.
MARY? DID YOU HEAR...?
INJUSTICE

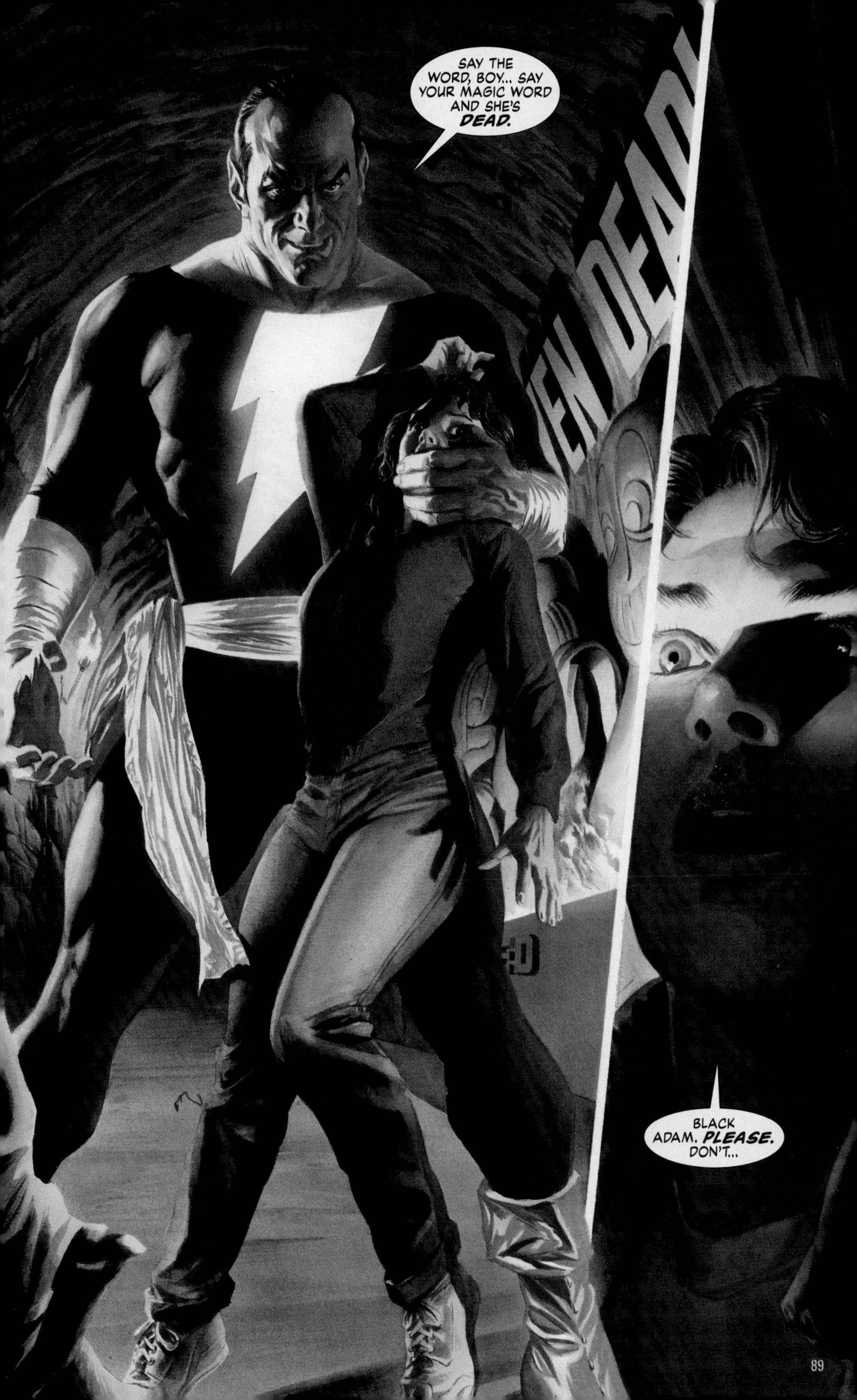
SAY THE WORD, BOY... SAY YOUR MAGIC WORD AND SHE'S *DEAD.*
BLACK ADAM. *PLEASE.* DON'T...

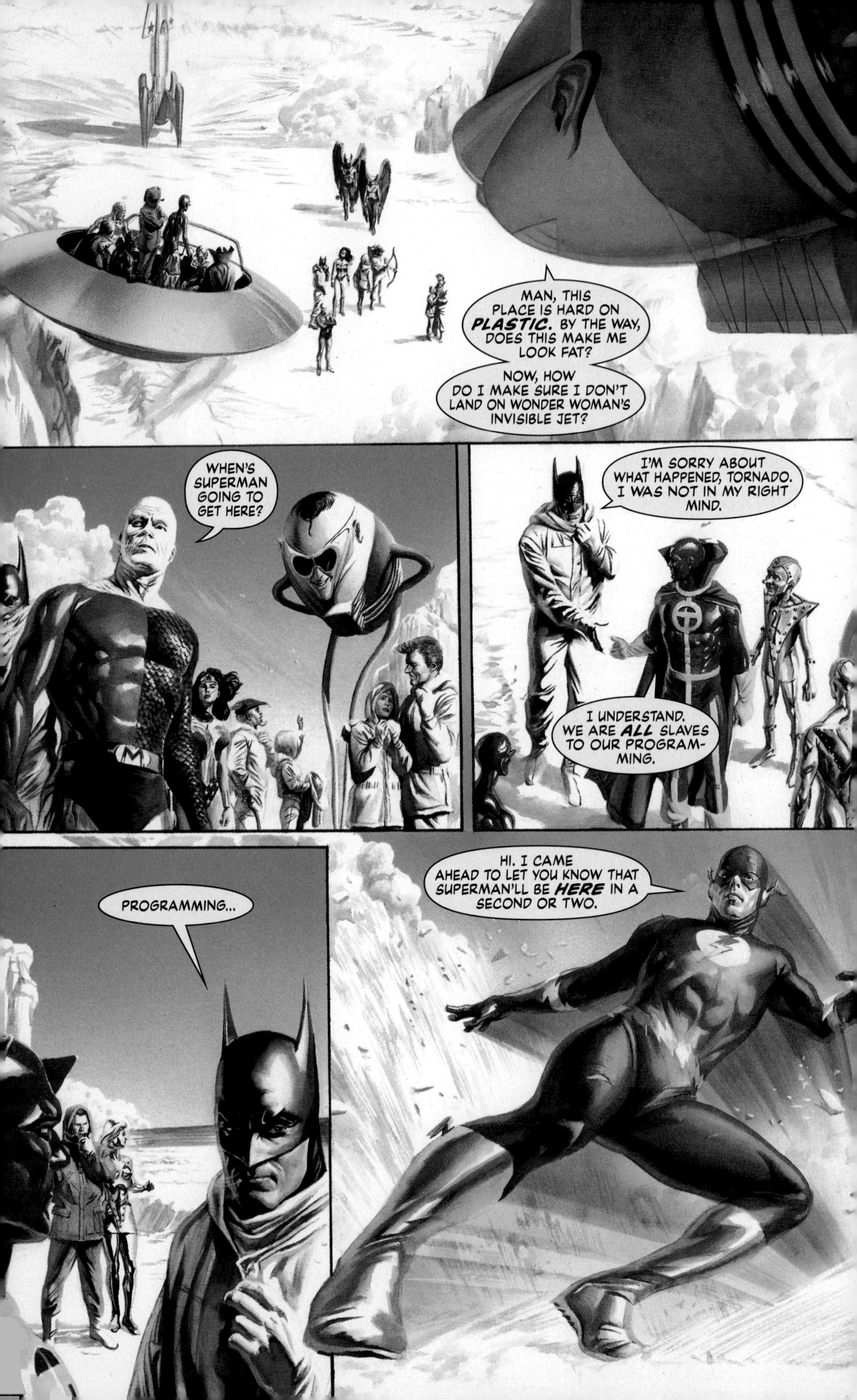
MAN, THIS PLACE IS HARD ON PLASTIC. BY THE WAY, DOES THIS MAKE ME LOOK FAT?
NOW, HOW DO I MAKE SURE I DON'T LAND ON WONDER WOMAN'S INVISIBLE JET?
WHEN'S SUPERMAN GOING TO GET HERE?
I'M SORRY ABOUT WHAT HAPPENED, TORNADO. I WAS NOT IN MY RIGHT MIND.
I UNDERSTAND. WE ARE ALL SLAVES TO OUR PROGRAM-MING.
PROGRAMMING...
HI. I CAME AHEAD TO LET YOU KNOW THAT SUPERMAN'LL BE HERE IN A SECOND OR TWO.

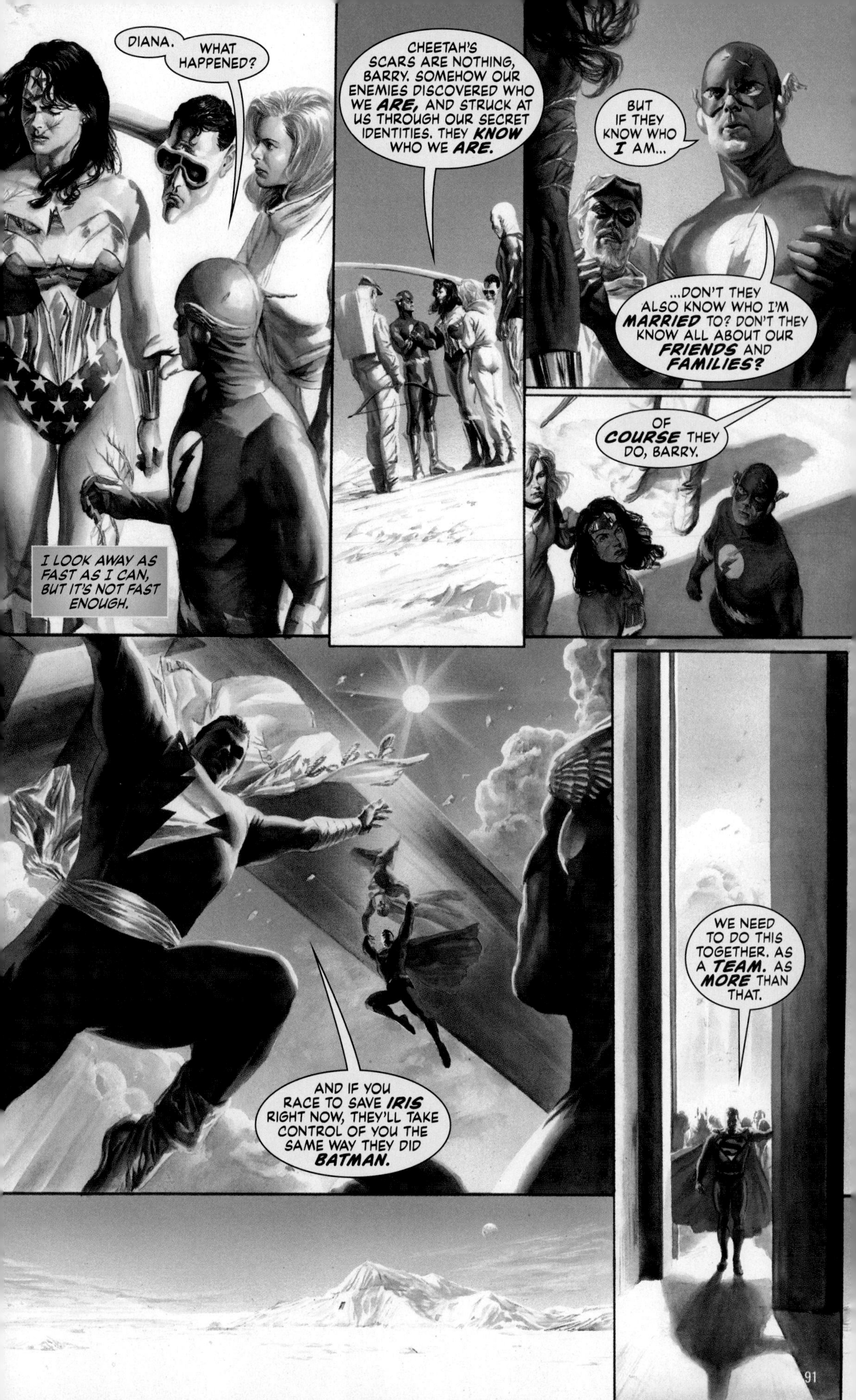
DIANA.
WHAT HAPPENED?
I LOOK AWAY AS FAST AS I CAN, BUT IT'S NOT FAST ENOUGH.
CHEETAH'S SCARS ARE NOTHING, BARRY. SOMEHOW OUR ENEMIES DISCOVERED WHO WE ARE, AND STRUCK AT US THROUGH OUR SECRET IDENTITIES. THEY KNOW WHO WE ARE.
BUT IF THEY KNOW WHO I AM...
...DON'T THEY ALSO KNOW WHO I'M MARRIED TO? DON'T THEY KNOW ALL ABOUT OUR FRIENDS AND FAMILIES?
OF COURSE THEY DO, BARRY.
AND IF YOU RACE TO SAVE IRIS RIGHT NOW, THEY'LL TAKE CONTROL OF YOU THE SAME WAY THEY DID BATMAN.
WE NEED TO DO THIS TOGETHER. AS A TEAM. AS MORE THAN THAT.

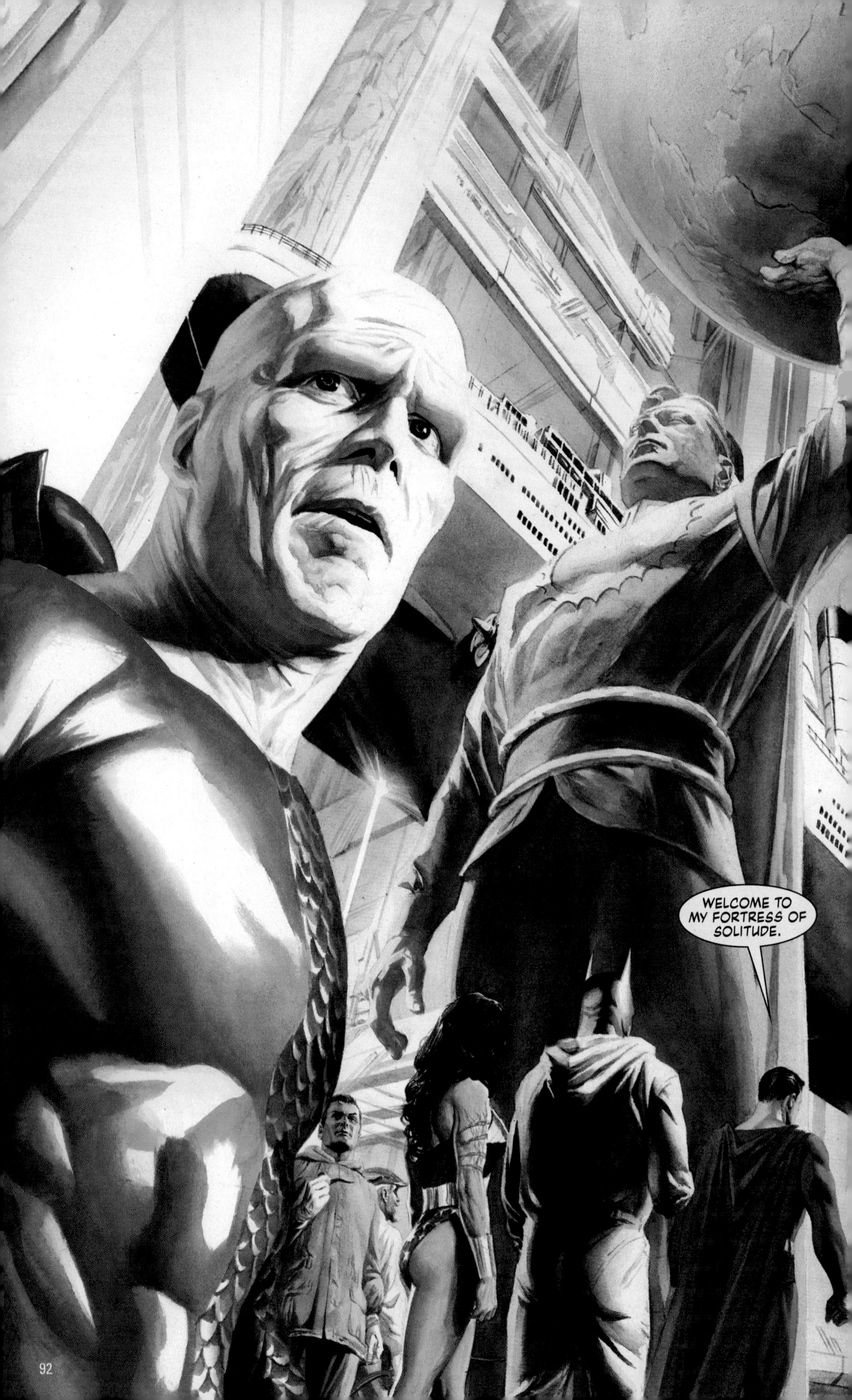
WELCOME TO MY FORTRESS OF SOLITUDE.

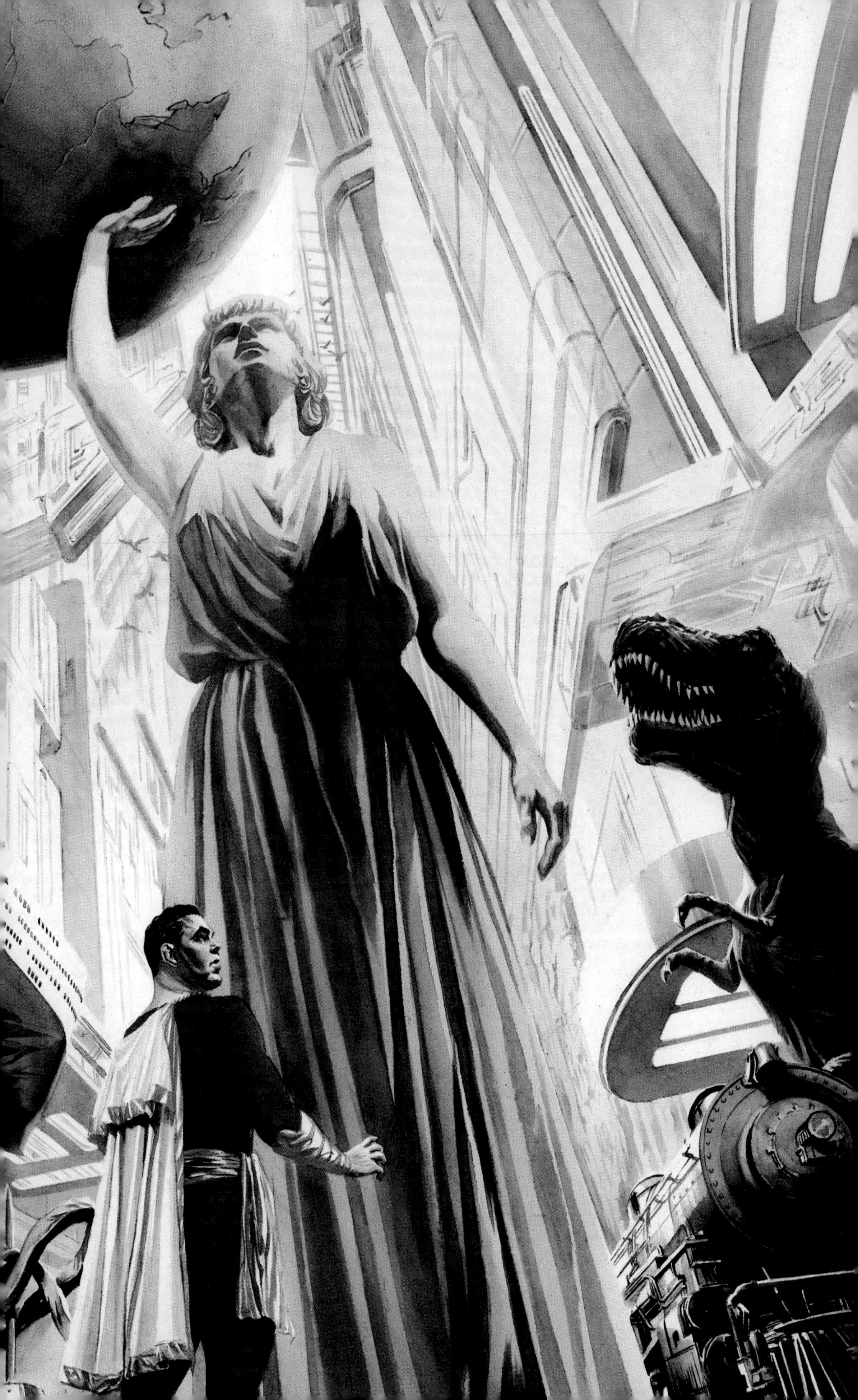

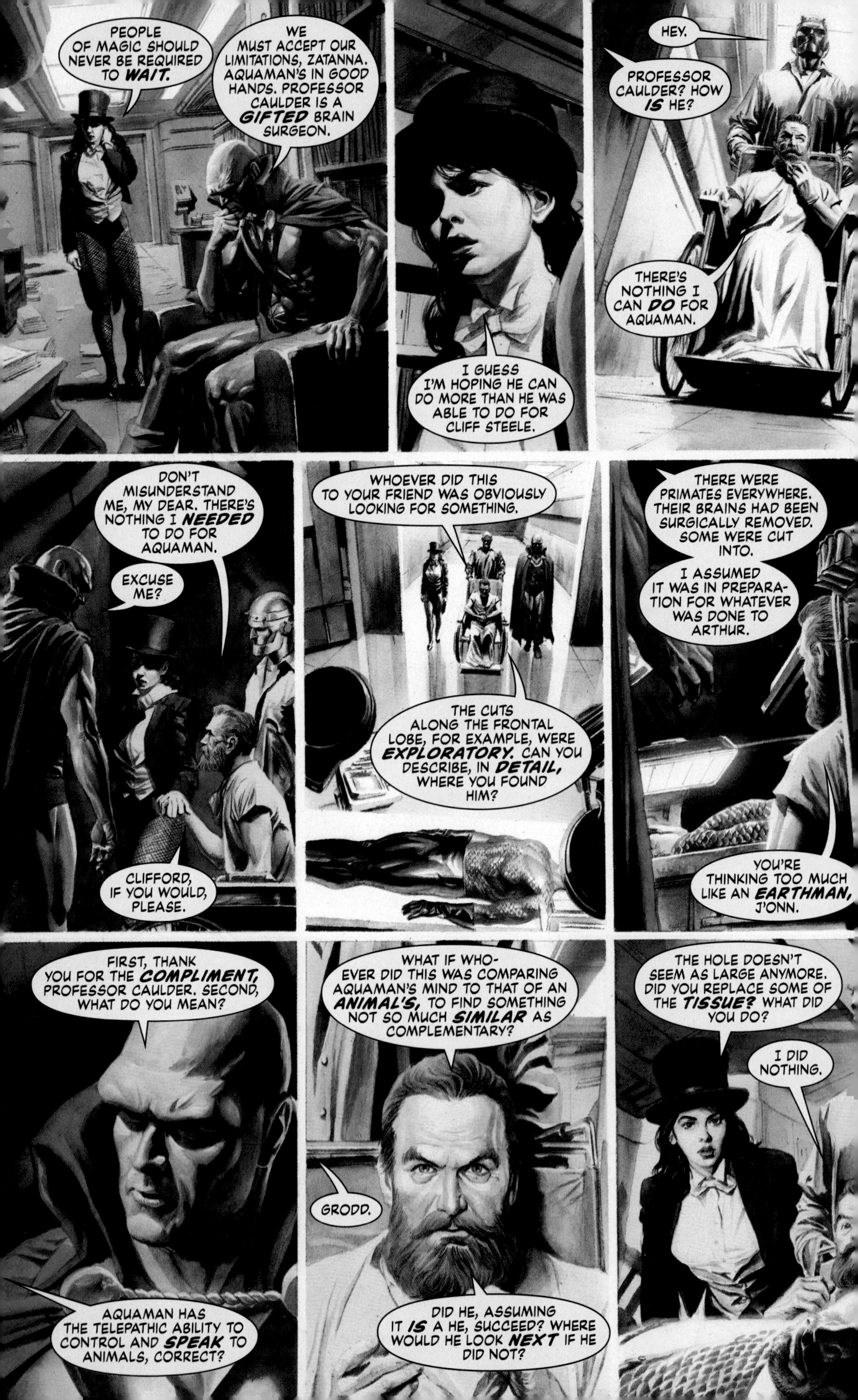
PEOPLE OF MAGIC SHOULD NEVER BE REQUIRED TO WAIT.
WE MUST ACCEPT OUR LIMITATIONS, ZATANNA. AQUAMAN'S IN GOOD HANDS. PROFESSOR CAULDER IS A GIFTED BRAIN SURGEON.
I GUESS I'M HOPING HE CAN DO MORE THAN HE WAS ABLE TO DO FOR CLIFF STEELE.
HEY.
PROFESSOR CAULDER? HOW IS HE?
THERE'S NOTHING I CAN DO FOR AQUAMAN.
DON'T MISUNDERSTAND ME, MY DEAR. THERE'S NOTHING I NEEDED TO DO FOR AQUAMAN.
EXCUSE ME?
CLIFFORD, IF YOU WOULD, PLEASE.
WHOEVER DID THIS TO YOUR FRIEND WAS OBVIOUSLY LOOKING FOR SOMETHING.
THE CUTS ALONG THE FRONTAL LOBE, FOR EXAMPLE, WERE EXPLORATORY. CAN YOU DESCRIBE, IN DETAIL, WHERE YOU FOUND HIM?
THERE WERE PRIMATES EVERYWHERE. THEIR BRAINS HAD BEEN SURGICALLY REMOVED. SOME WERE CUT INTO.
I ASSUMED IT WAS IN PREPARATION FOR WHATEVER WAS DONE TO ARTHUR.
YOU'RE THINKING TOO MUCH LIKE AN EARTHMAN, J'ONN.
FIRST, THANK YOU FOR THE COMPLIMENT, PROFESSOR CAULDER. SECOND, WHAT DO YOU MEAN?
AQUAMAN HAS THE TELEPATHIC ABILITY TO CONTROL AND SPEAK TO ANIMALS, CORRECT?
WHAT IF WHOEVER DID THIS WAS COMPARING AQUAMAN'S MIND TO THAT OF AN ANIMAL'S, TO FIND SOMETHING NOT SO MUCH SIMILAR AS COMPLEMENTARY?
GRODD.
DID HE, ASSUMING IT IS A HE, SUCCEED? WHERE WOULD HE LOOK NEXT IF HE DID NOT?
THE HOLE DOESN'T SEEM AS LARGE ANYMORE. DID YOU REPLACE SOME OF THE TISSUE? WHAT DID YOU DO?
I DID NOTHING.

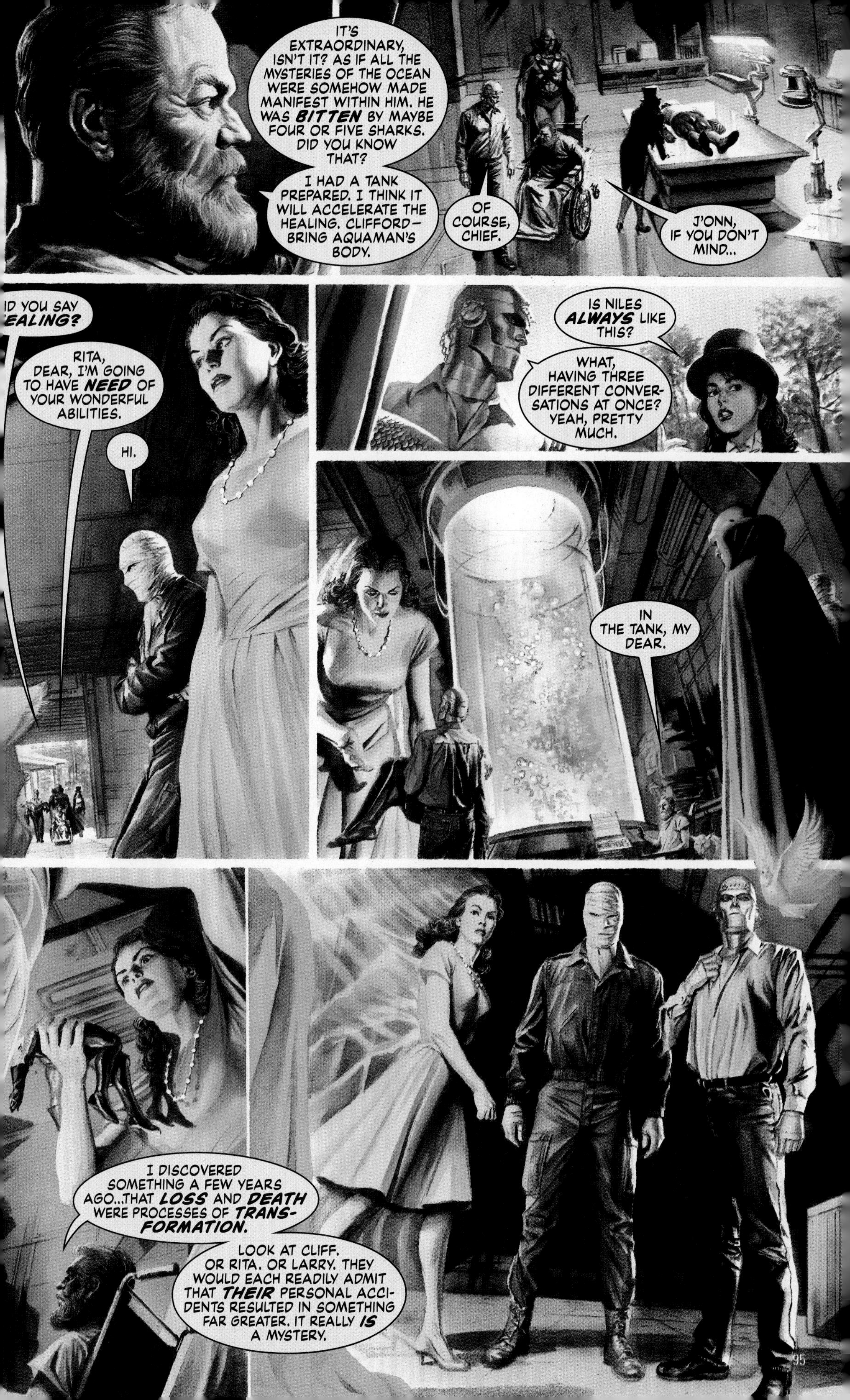
IT'S EXTRAORDINARY, ISN'T IT? AS IF ALL THE MYSTERIES OF THE OCEAN WERE SOMEHOW MADE MANIFEST WITHIN HIM. HE WAS BITTEN BY MAYBE FOUR OR FIVE SHARKS. DID YOU KNOW THAT?
I HAD A TANK PREPARED. I THINK IT WILL ACCELERATE THE HEALING. CLIFFORD—BRING AQUAMAN'S BODY.
OF COURSE, CHIEF.
J'ONN, IF YOU DON'T MIND...
ID YOU SAY EALING?
RITA, DEAR, I'M GOING TO HAVE NEED OF YOUR WONDERFUL ABILITIES.
HI.
IS NILES ALWAYS LIKE THIS?
WHAT, HAVING THREE DIFFERENT CONVERSATIONS AT ONCE? YEAH, PRETTY MUCH.
IN THE TANK, MY DEAR.
I DISCOVERED SOMETHING A FEW YEARS AGO...THAT LOSS AND DEATH WERE PROCESSES OF TRANSFORMATION.
LOOK AT CLIFF. OR RITA. OR LARRY. THEY WOULD EACH READILY ADMIT THAT THEIR PERSONAL ACCIDENTS RESULTED IN SOMETHING FAR GREATER. IT REALLY IS A MYSTERY.

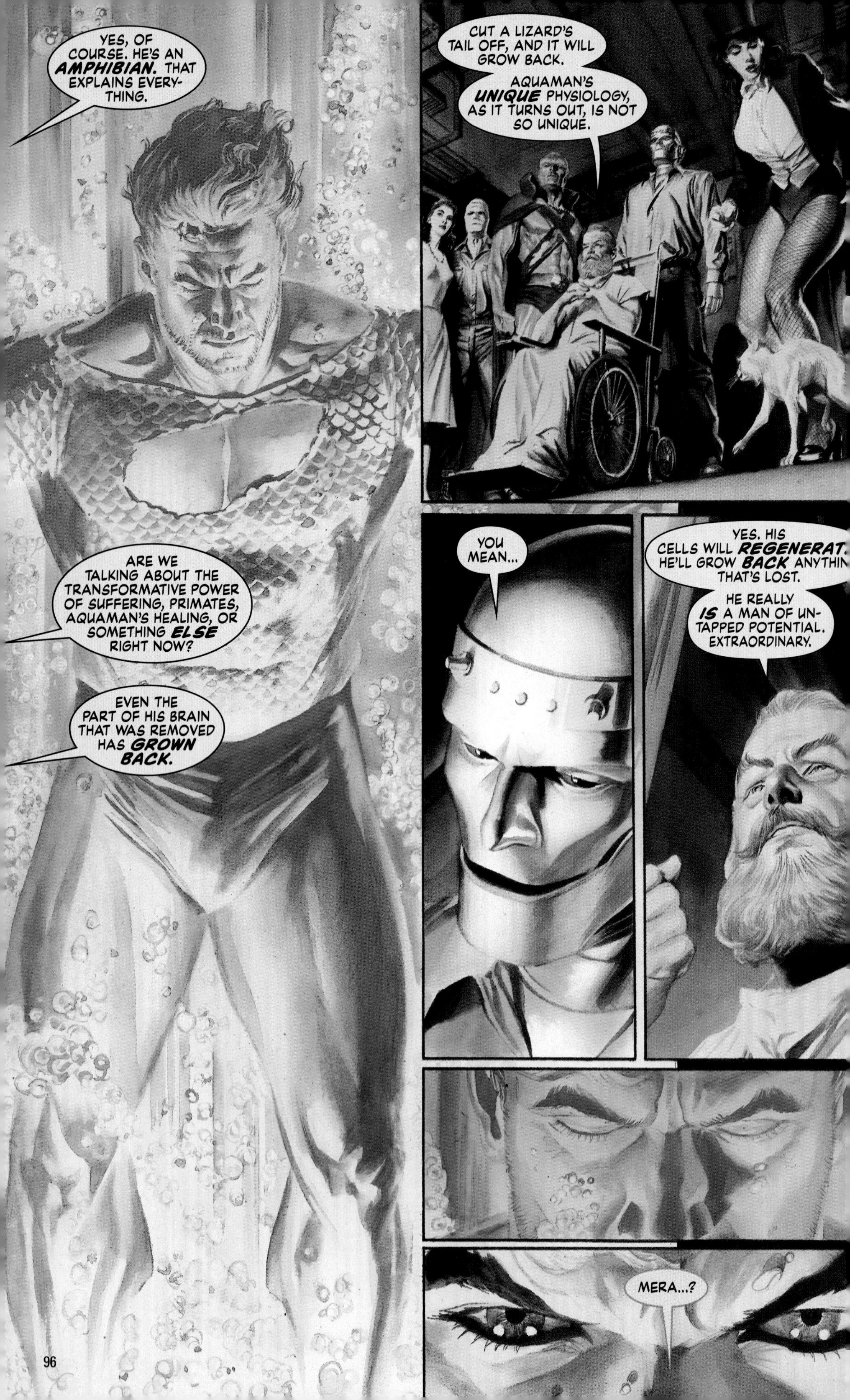
YES, OF COURSE. HE'S AN AMPHIBIAN. THAT EXPLAINS EVERY-THING.
ARE WE TALKING ABOUT THE TRANSFORMATIVE POWER OF SUFFERING, PRIMATES, AQUAMAN'S HEALING, OR SOMETHING ELSE RIGHT NOW?
EVEN THE PART OF HIS BRAIN THAT WAS REMOVED HAS GROWN BACK.
CUT A LIZARD'S TAIL OFF, AND IT WILL GROW BACK.
AQUAMAN'S UNIQUE PHYSIOLOGY, AS IT TURNS OUT, IS NOT SO UNIQUE.
YOU MEAN...
YES. HIS CELLS WILL REGENERAT HE'LL GROW BACK ANYTHIN THAT'S LOST.
HE REALLY IS A MAN OF UN-TAPPED POTENTIAL. EXTRAORDINARY.
MERA...?

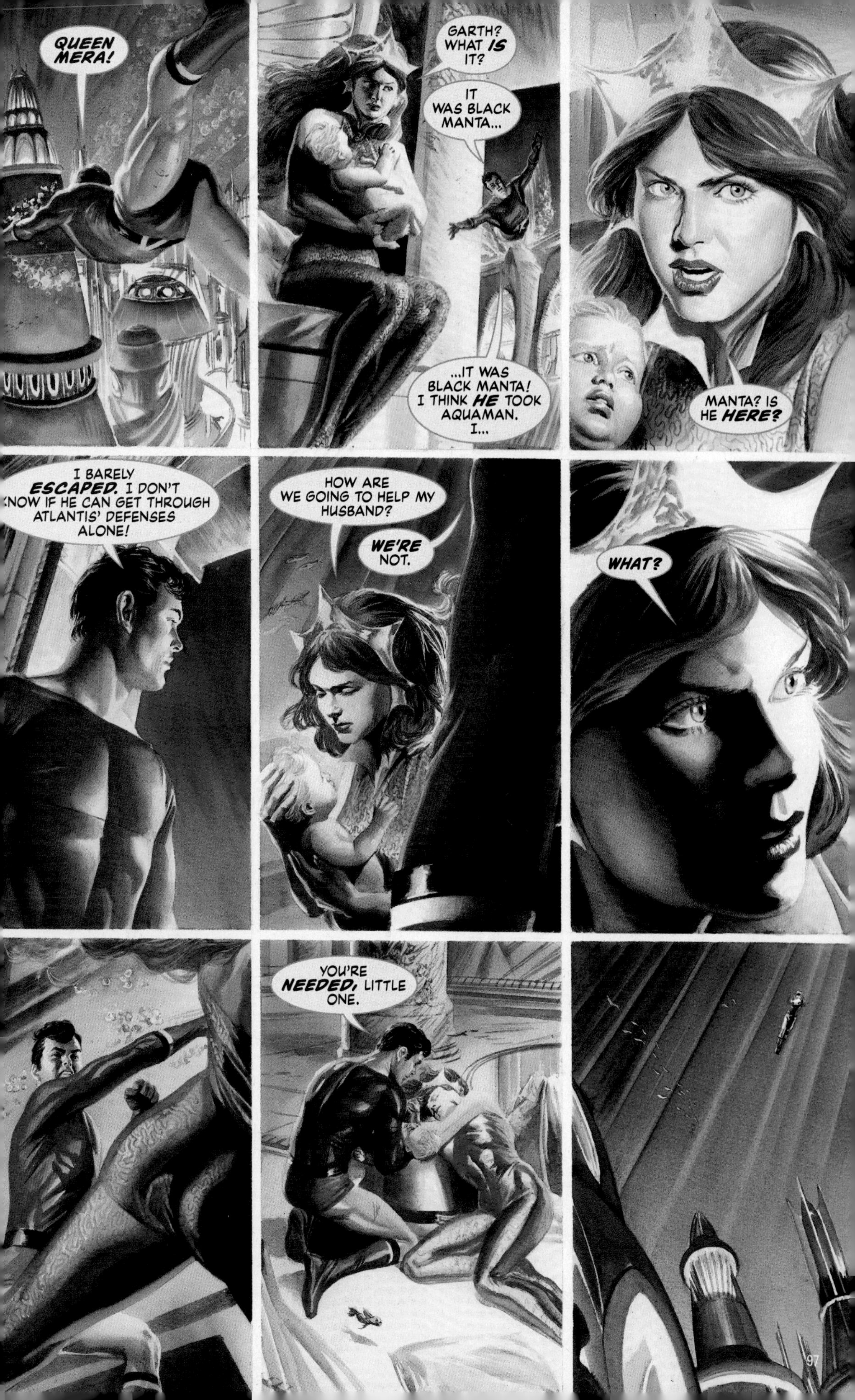
QUEEN MERA!
GARTH? WHAT IS IT?
IT WAS BLACK MANTA...
...IT WAS BLACK MANTA! I THINK HE TOOK AQUAMAN. I...
MANTA? IS HE HERE?
I BARELY ESCAPED. I DON'T KNOW IF HE CAN GET THROUGH ATLANTIS' DEFENSES ALONE!
HOW ARE WE GOING TO HELP MY HUSBAND?
WE'RE NOT.
WHAT?
YOU'RE NEEDED, LITTLE ONE.

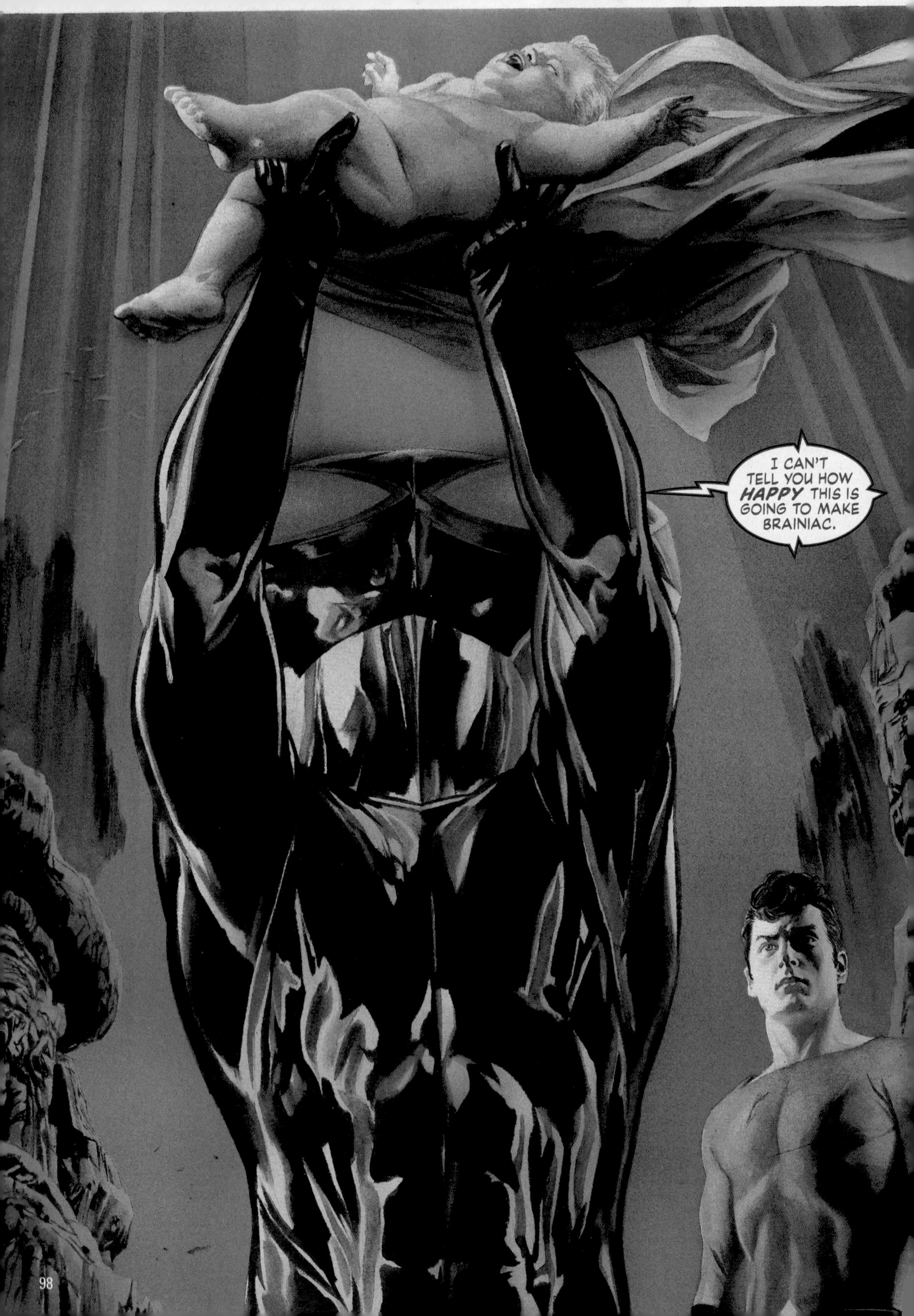
I CAN'T TELL YOU HOW *HAPPY* THIS IS GOING TO MAKE BRAINIAC.

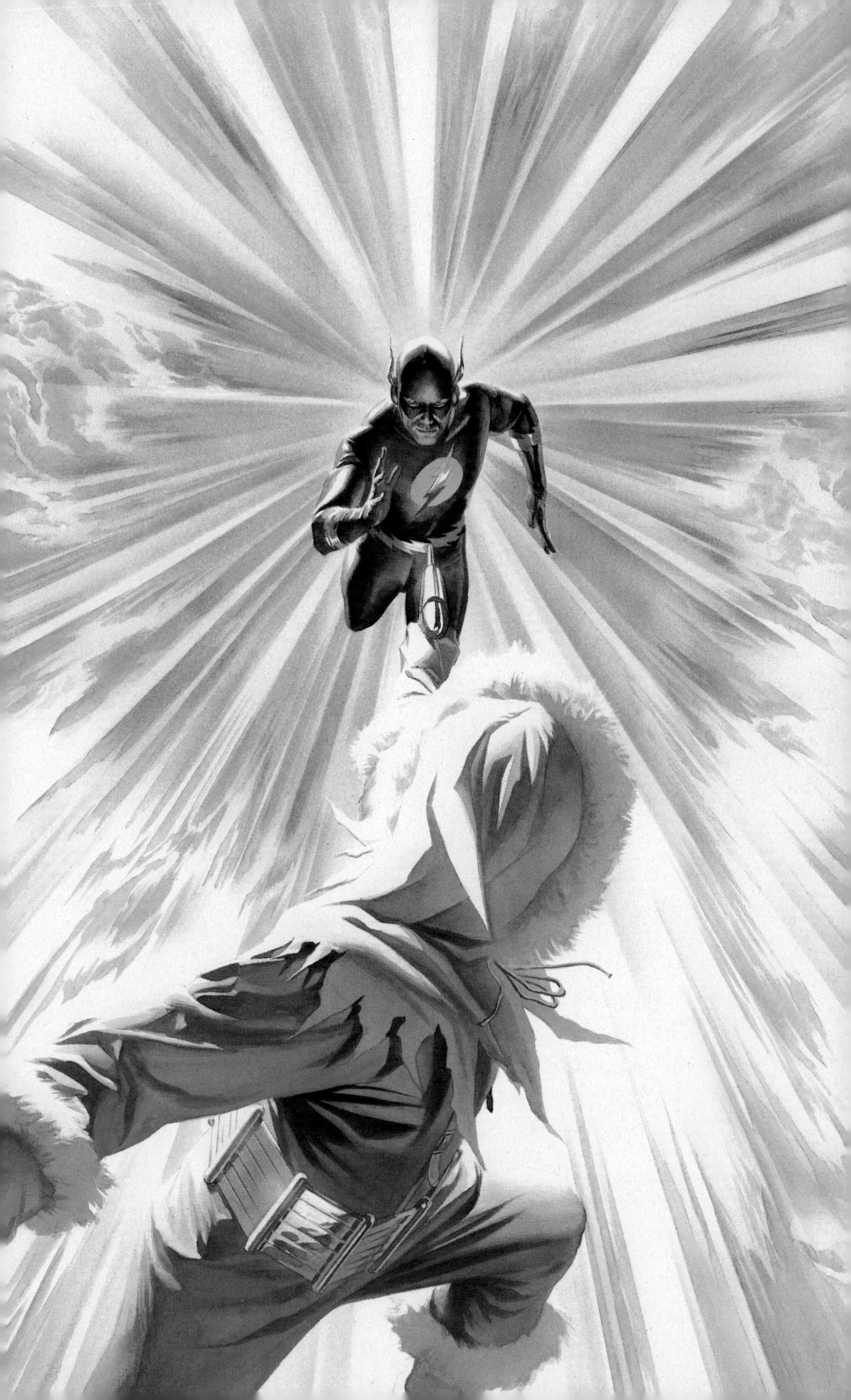

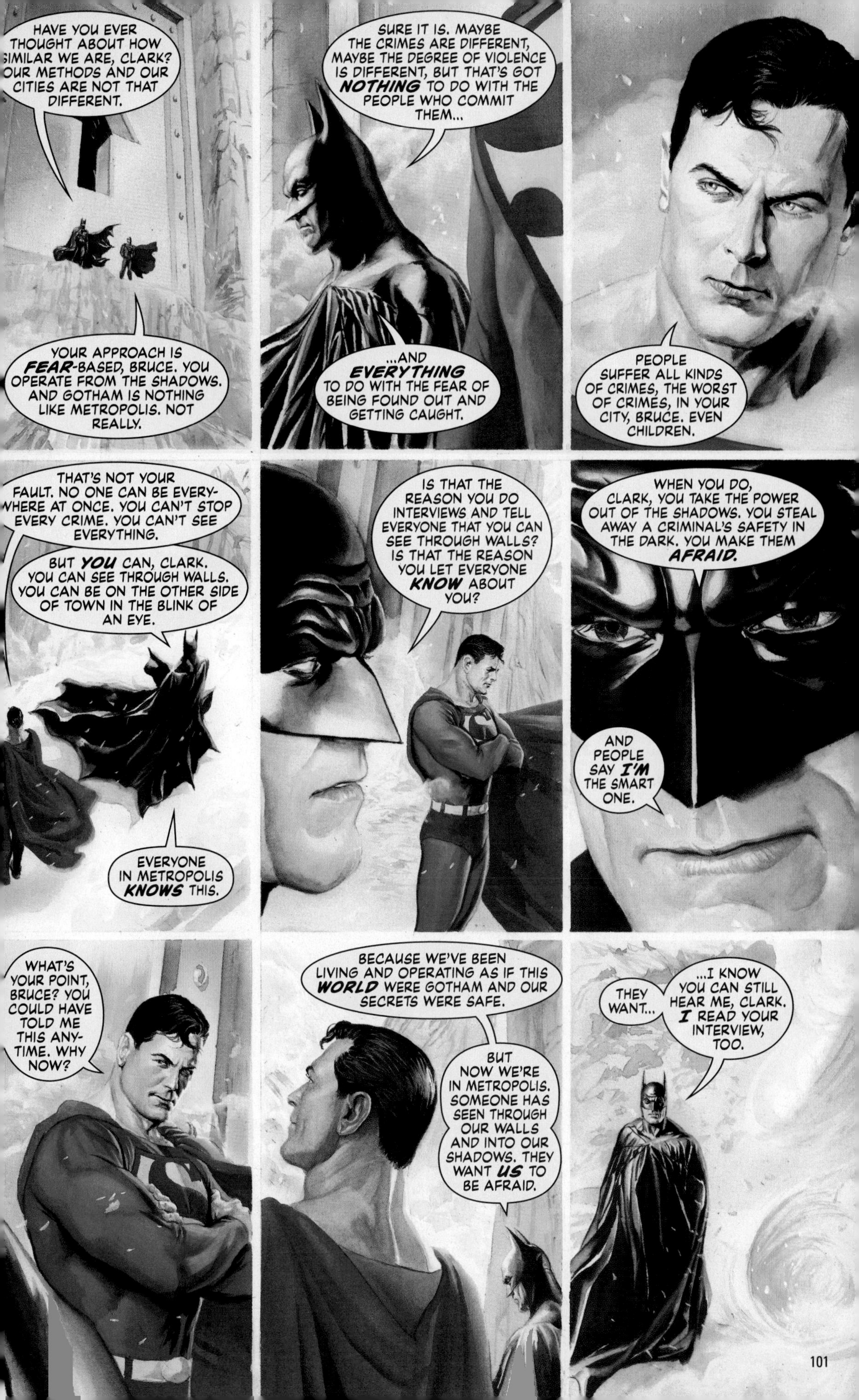
HAVE YOU EVER THOUGHT ABOUT HOW SIMILAR WE ARE, CLARK? OUR METHODS AND OUR CITIES ARE NOT THAT DIFFERENT.
YOUR APPROACH IS FEAR-BASED, BRUCE. YOU OPERATE FROM THE SHADOWS. AND GOTHAM IS NOTHING LIKE METROPOLIS. NOT REALLY.
SURE IT IS. MAYBE THE CRIMES ARE DIFFERENT, MAYBE THE DEGREE OF VIOLENCE IS DIFFERENT, BUT THAT'S GOT NOTHING TO DO WITH THE PEOPLE WHO COMMIT THEM...
...AND EVERYTHING TO DO WITH THE FEAR OF BEING FOUND OUT AND GETTING CAUGHT.
PEOPLE SUFFER ALL KINDS OF CRIMES, THE WORST OF CRIMES, IN YOUR CITY, BRUCE. EVEN CHILDREN.
THAT'S NOT YOUR FAULT. NO ONE CAN BE EVERY-WHERE AT ONCE. YOU CAN'T STOP EVERY CRIME. YOU CAN'T SEE EVERYTHING.
BUT YOU CAN, CLARK. YOU CAN SEE THROUGH WALLS. YOU CAN BE ON THE OTHER SIDE OF TOWN IN THE BLINK OF AN EYE.
EVERYONE IN METROPOLIS KNOWS THIS.
IS THAT THE REASON YOU DO INTERVIEWS AND TELL EVERYONE THAT YOU CAN SEE THROUGH WALLS? IS THAT THE REASON YOU LET EVERYONE KNOW ABOUT YOU?
WHEN YOU DO, CLARK, YOU TAKE THE POWER OUT OF THE SHADOWS. YOU STEAL AWAY A CRIMINAL'S SAFETY IN THE DARK. YOU MAKE THEM AFRAID.
AND PEOPLE SAY I'M THE SMART ONE.
WHAT'S YOUR POINT, BRUCE? YOU COULD HAVE TOLD ME THIS ANY-TIME. WHY NOW?
BECAUSE WE'VE BEEN LIVING AND OPERATING AS IF THIS WORLD WERE GOTHAM AND OUR SECRETS WERE SAFE.
BUT NOW WE'RE IN METROPOLIS. SOMEONE HAS SEEN THROUGH OUR WALLS AND INTO OUR SHADOWS. THEY WANT US TO BE AFRAID.
THEY WANT...
...I KNOW YOU CAN STILL HEAR ME, CLARK. I READ YOUR INTERVIEW, TOO.

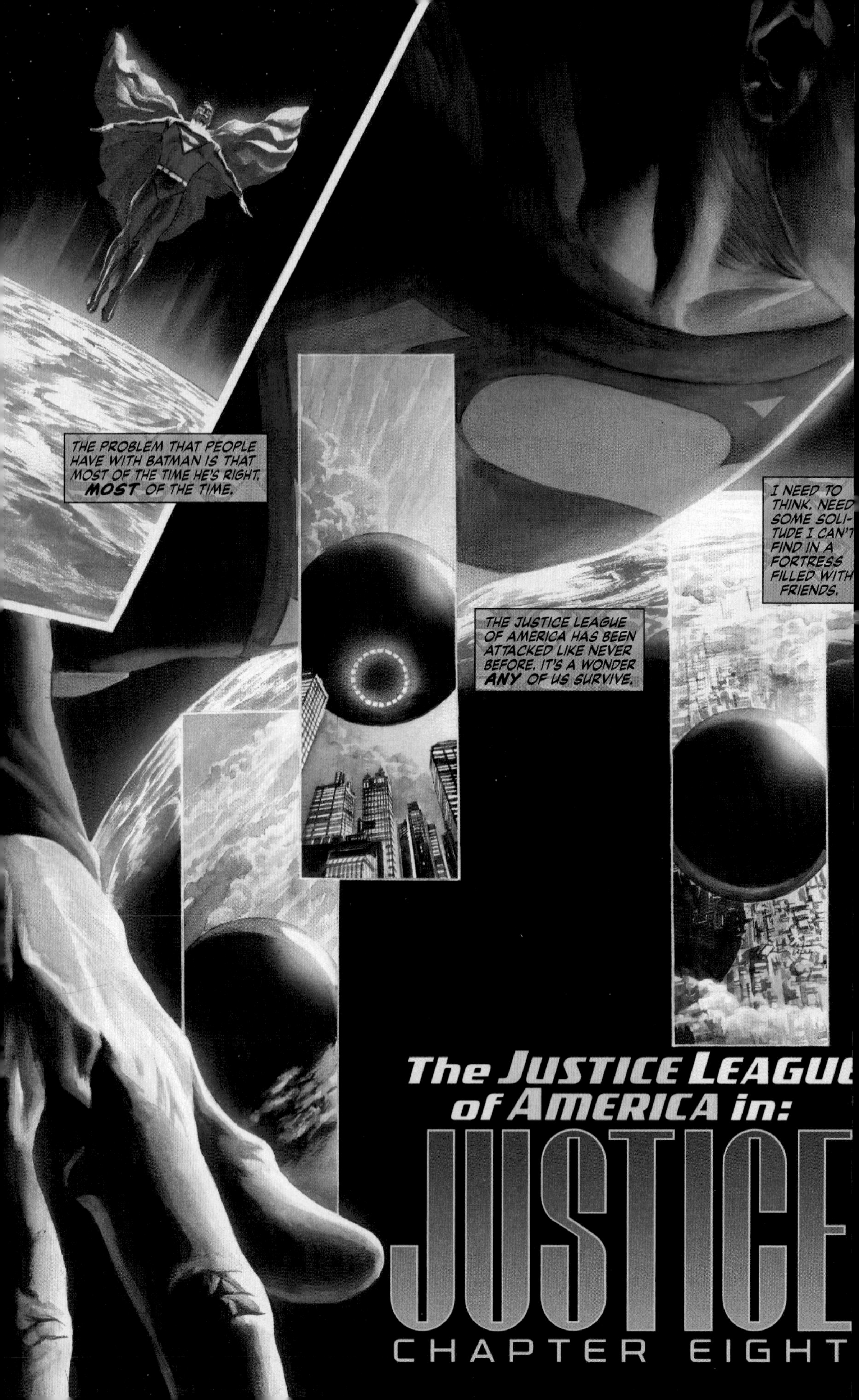
THE PROBLEM THAT PEOPLE HAVE WITH BATMAN IS THAT MOST OF THE TIME HE'S RIGHT. MOST OF THE TIME.
THE JUSTICE LEAGUE OF AMERICA HAS BEEN ATTACKED LIKE NEVER BEFORE. IT'S A WONDER ANY OF US SURVIVE.
I NEED TO THINK. NEED SOME SOLITUDE I CAN'T FIND IN A FORTRESS FILLED WITH FRIENDS.
The JUSTICE LEAGUE of AMERICA in:
JUSTICE
CHAPTER EIGHT

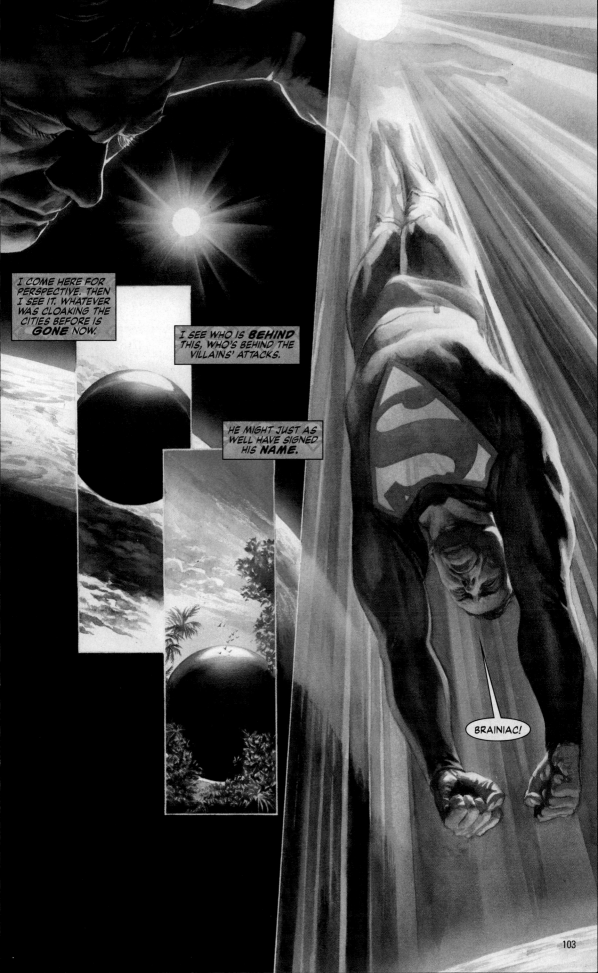

I COME HERE FOR PERSPECTIVE. THEN I SEE IT. WHATEVER WAS CLOAKING THE CITIES BEFORE IS *GONE* NOW.

I SEE WHO IS *BEHIND* THIS, WHO'S BEHIND THE VILLAINS' ATTACKS.

HE MIGHT JUST AS WELL HAVE SIGNED HIS *NAME.*

BRAINIAC!

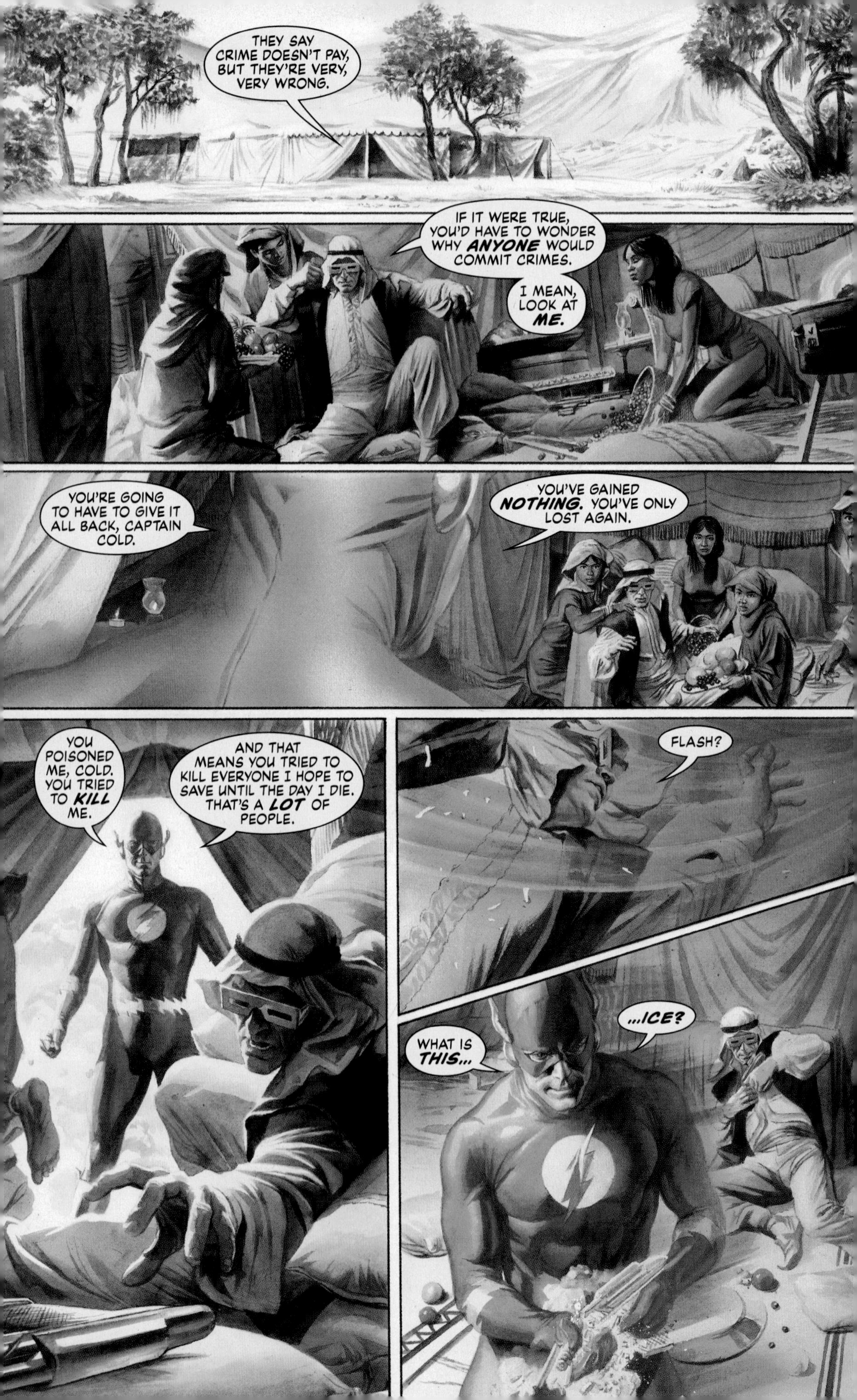
THEY SAY CRIME DOESN'T PAY, BUT THEY'RE VERY, VERY WRONG.
IF IT WERE TRUE, YOU'D HAVE TO WONDER WHY ANYONE WOULD COMMIT CRIMES.
I MEAN, LOOK AT ME.
YOU'RE GOING TO HAVE TO GIVE IT ALL BACK, CAPTAIN COLD.
YOU'VE GAINED NOTHING. YOU'VE ONLY LOST AGAIN.
YOU POISONED ME, COLD. YOU TRIED TO KILL ME.
AND THAT MEANS YOU TRIED TO KILL EVERYONE I HOPE TO SAVE UNTIL THE DAY I DIE. THAT'S A LOT OF PEOPLE.
FLASH?
WHAT IS THIS...
...ICE?

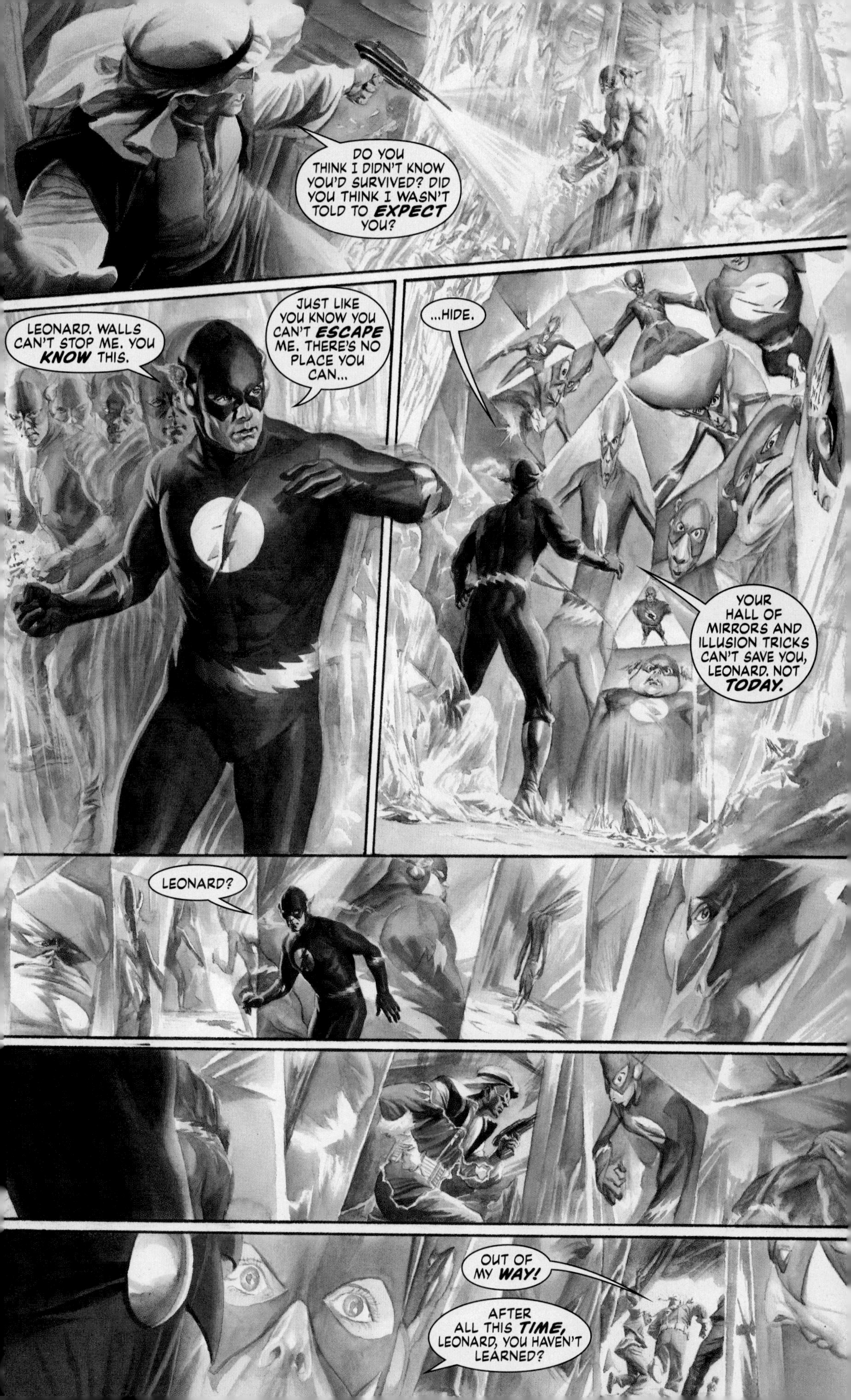
DO YOU THINK I DIDN'T KNOW YOU'D SURVIVED? DID YOU THINK I WASN'T TOLD TO EXPECT YOU?
LEONARD. WALLS CAN'T STOP ME. YOU KNOW THIS.
JUST LIKE YOU KNOW YOU CAN'T ESCAPE ME. THERE'S NO PLACE YOU CAN...
...HIDE.
YOUR HALL OF MIRRORS AND ILLUSION TRICKS CAN'T SAVE YOU, LEONARD. NOT TODAY.
LEONARD?
OUT OF MY WAY!
AFTER ALL THIS TIME, LEONARD, YOU HAVEN'T LEARNED?

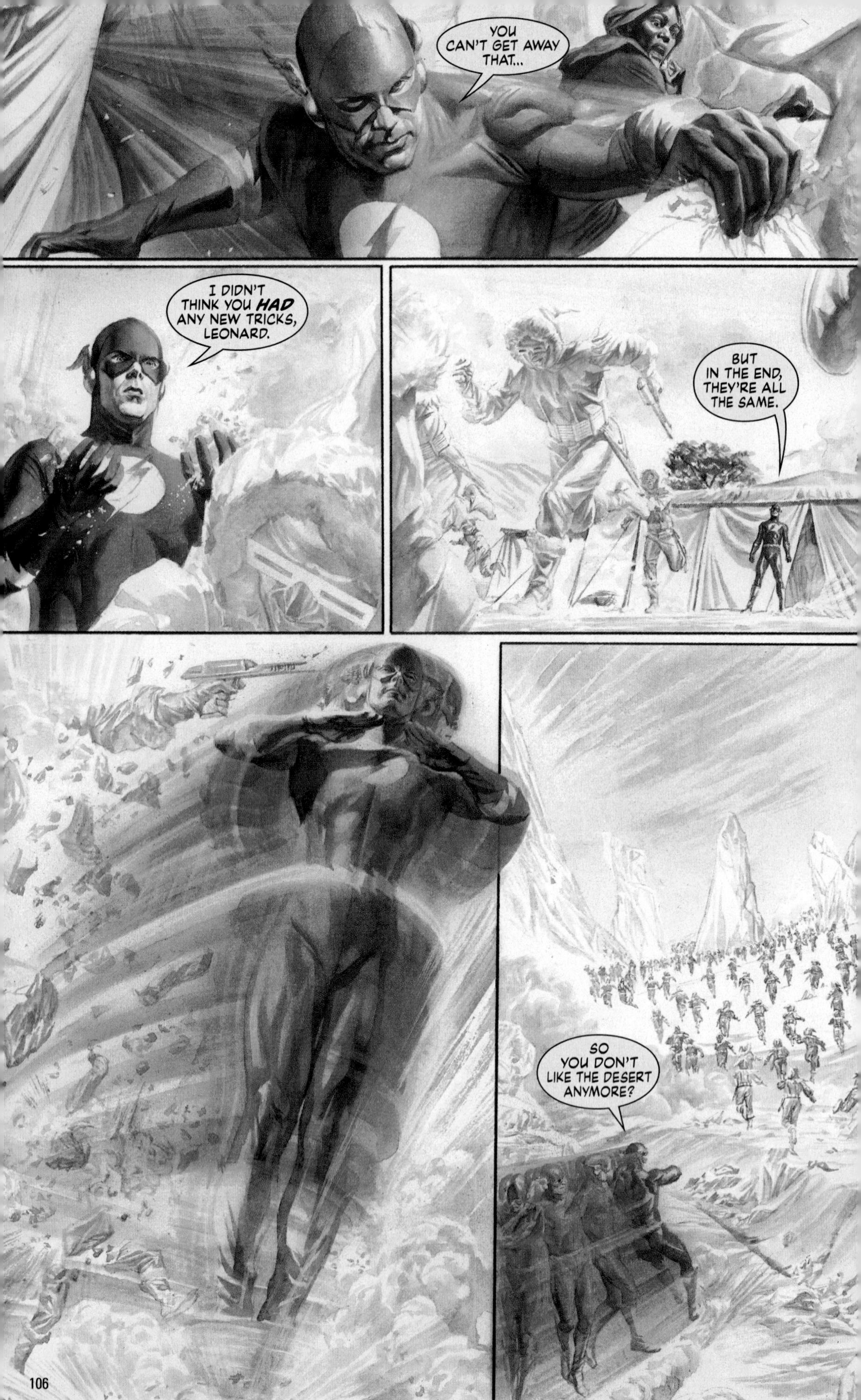
YOU CAN'T GET AWAY THAT...
I DIDN'T THINK YOU HAD ANY NEW TRICKS, LEONARD.
BUT IN THE END, THEY'RE ALL THE SAME.
SO YOU DON'T LIKE THE DESERT ANYMORE?

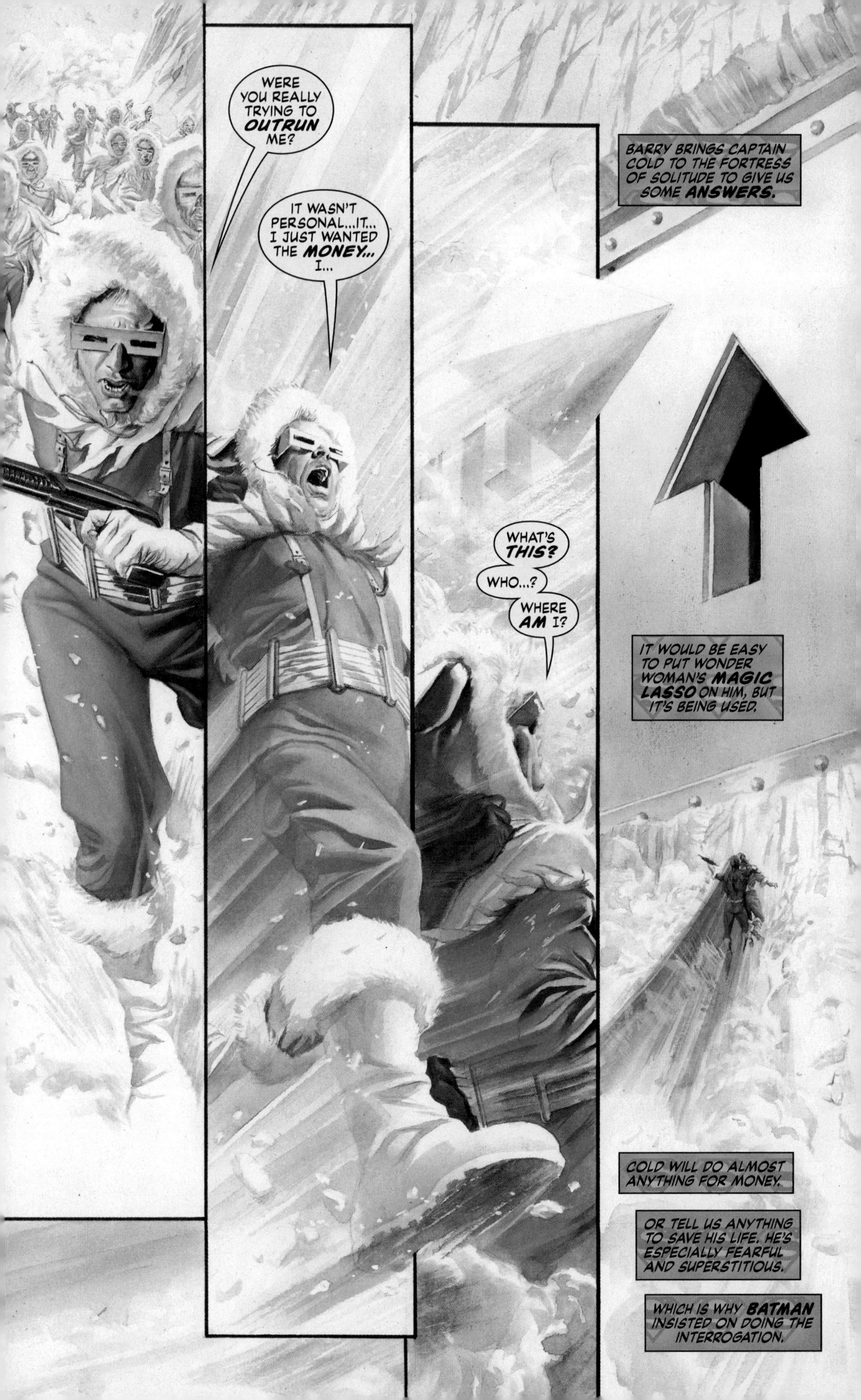
WERE YOU REALLY TRYING TO OUTRUN ME?
IT WASN'T PERSONAL...IT... I JUST WANTED THE MONEY... I...
BARRY BRINGS CAPTAIN COLD TO THE FORTRESS OF SOLITUDE TO GIVE US SOME ANSWERS.
WHAT'S THIS?
WHO...?
WHERE AM I?
IT WOULD BE EASY TO PUT WONDER WOMAN'S MAGIC LASSO ON HIM, BUT IT'S BEING USED.
COLD WILL DO ALMOST ANYTHING FOR MONEY.
OR TELL US ANYTHING TO SAVE HIS LIFE. HE'S ESPECIALLY FEARFUL AND SUPERSTITIOUS.
WHICH IS WHY BATMAN INSISTED ON DOING THE INTERROGATION.

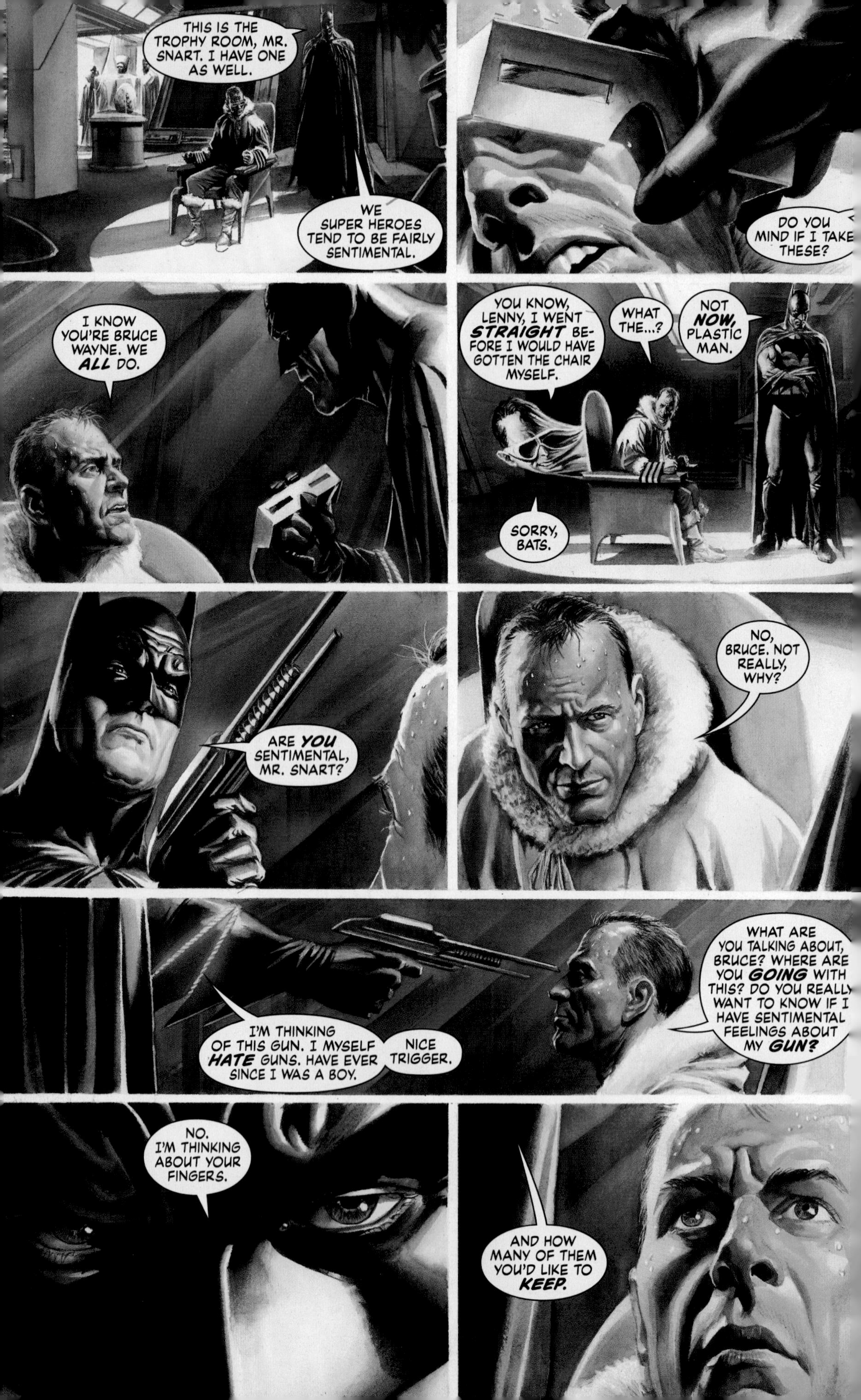

THIS IS THE TROPHY ROOM, MR. SNART. I HAVE ONE AS WELL.
WE SUPER HEROES TEND TO BE FAIRLY SENTIMENTAL.
DO YOU MIND IF I TAKE THESE?
I KNOW YOU'RE BRUCE WAYNE. WE ALL DO.
YOU KNOW, LENNY, I WENT STRAIGHT BEFORE I WOULD HAVE GOTTEN THE CHAIR MYSELF.
WHAT THE...?
NOT NOW, PLASTIC MAN.
SORRY, BATS.
ARE YOU SENTIMENTAL, MR. SNART?
NO, BRUCE. NOT REALLY, WHY?
I'M THINKING OF THIS GUN. I MYSELF HATE GUNS. HAVE EVER SINCE I WAS A BOY.
NICE TRIGGER.
WHAT ARE YOU TALKING ABOUT, BRUCE? WHERE ARE YOU GOING WITH THIS? DO YOU REALLY WANT TO KNOW IF I HAVE SENTIMENTAL FEELINGS ABOUT MY GUN?
NO. I'M THINKING ABOUT YOUR FINGERS.
AND HOW MANY OF THEM YOU'D LIKE TO KEEP.

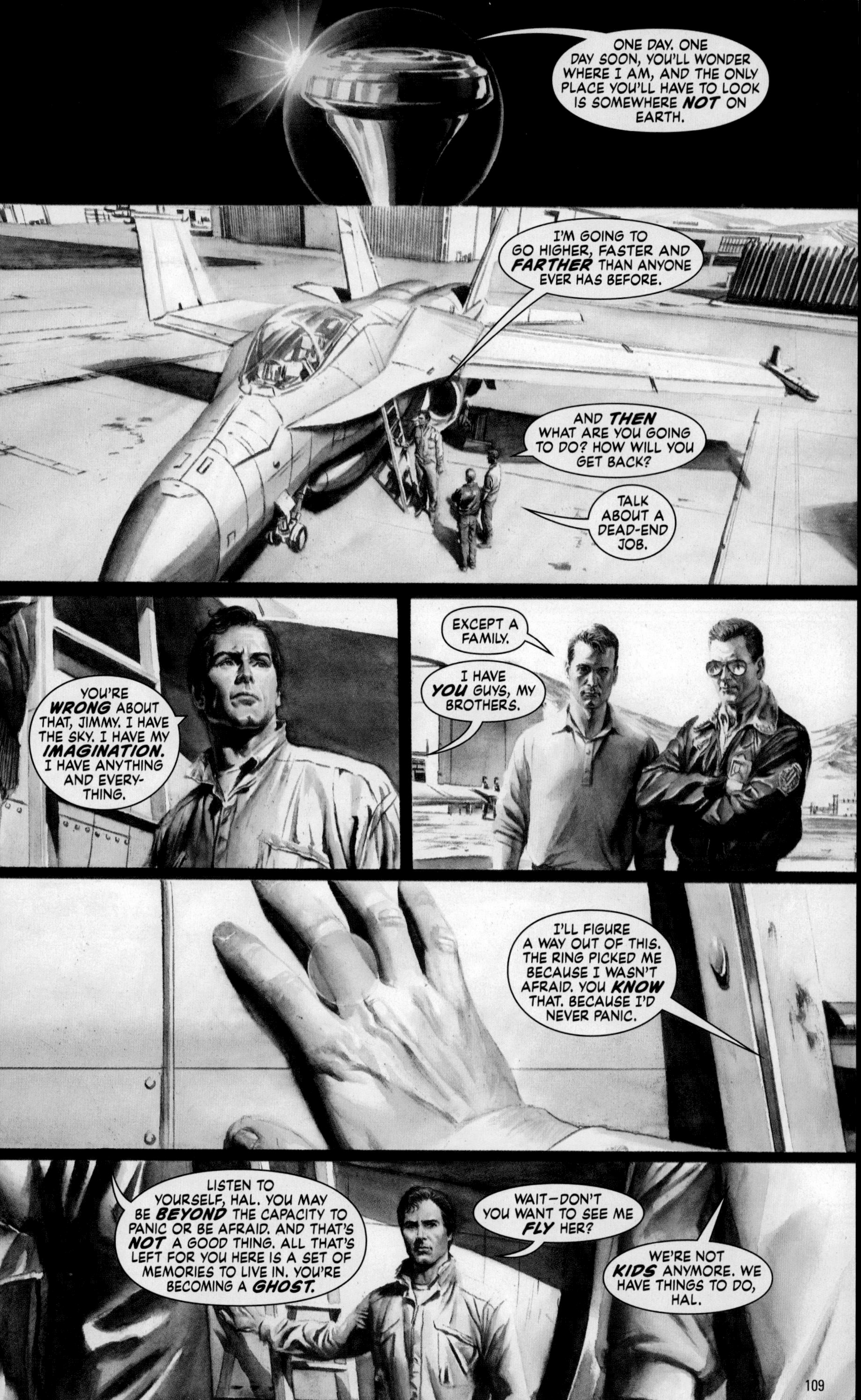
ONE DAY. ONE DAY SOON, YOU'LL WONDER WHERE I AM, AND THE ONLY PLACE YOU'LL HAVE TO LOOK IS SOMEWHERE NOT ON EARTH.
I'M GOING TO GO HIGHER, FASTER AND FARTHER THAN ANYONE EVER HAS BEFORE.
AND THEN WHAT ARE YOU GOING TO DO? HOW WILL YOU GET BACK?
TALK ABOUT A DEAD-END JOB.
YOU'RE WRONG ABOUT THAT, JIMMY. I HAVE THE SKY. I HAVE MY IMAGINATION. I HAVE ANYTHING AND EVERYTHING.
EXCEPT A FAMILY.
I HAVE YOU GUYS, MY BROTHERS.
I'LL FIGURE A WAY OUT OF THIS. THE RING PICKED ME BECAUSE I WASN'T AFRAID. YOU KNOW THAT. BECAUSE I'D NEVER PANIC.
LISTEN TO YOURSELF, HAL. YOU MAY BE BEYOND THE CAPACITY TO PANIC OR BE AFRAID. AND THAT'S NOT A GOOD THING. ALL THAT'S LEFT FOR YOU HERE IS A SET OF MEMORIES TO LIVE IN. YOU'RE BECOMING A GHOST.
WAIT—DON'T YOU WANT TO SEE ME FLY HER?
WE'RE NOT KIDS ANYMORE. WE HAVE THINGS TO DO, HAL.

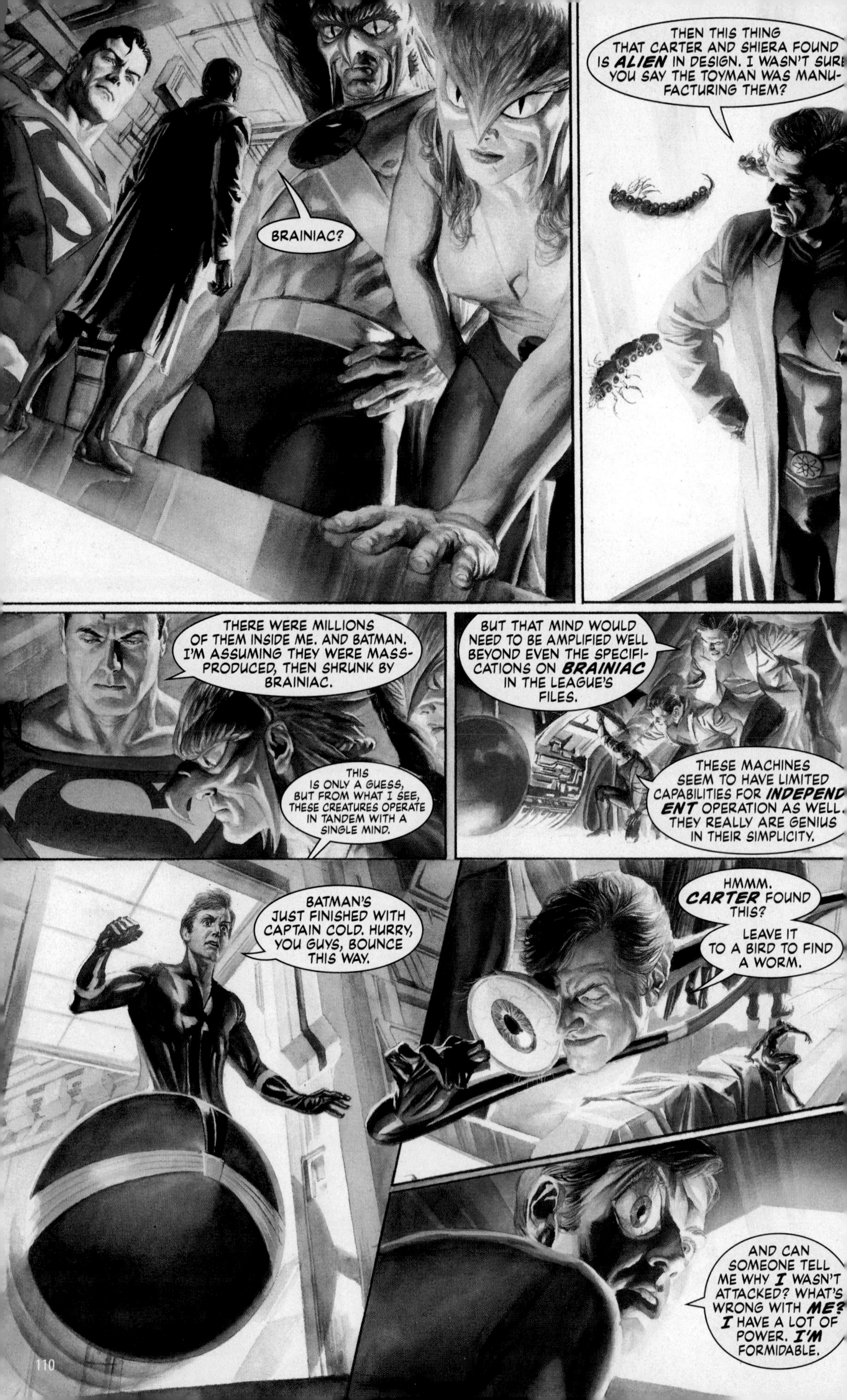
BRAINIAC?
THEN THIS THING THAT CARTER AND SHIERA FOUND IS ALIEN IN DESIGN. I WASN'T SURE YOU SAY THE TOYMAN WAS MANUFACTURING THEM?
THERE WERE MILLIONS OF THEM INSIDE ME. AND BATMAN. I'M ASSUMING THEY WERE MASS-PRODUCED, THEN SHRUNK BY BRAINIAC.
THIS IS ONLY A GUESS, BUT FROM WHAT I SEE, THESE CREATURES OPERATE IN TANDEM WITH A SINGLE MIND.
BUT THAT MIND WOULD NEED TO BE AMPLIFIED WELL BEYOND EVEN THE SPECIFICATIONS ON BRAINIAC IN THE LEAGUE'S FILES.
THESE MACHINES SEEM TO HAVE LIMITED CAPABILITIES FOR INDEPENDENT OPERATION AS WELL. THEY REALLY ARE GENIUS IN THEIR SIMPLICITY.
BATMAN'S JUST FINISHED WITH CAPTAIN COLD. HURRY, YOU GUYS, BOUNCE THIS WAY.
HMMM. CARTER FOUND THIS?
LEAVE IT TO A BIRD TO FIND A WORM.
AND CAN SOMEONE TELL ME WHY I WASN'T ATTACKED? WHAT'S WRONG WITH ME? I HAVE A LOT OF POWER. I'M FORMIDABLE.

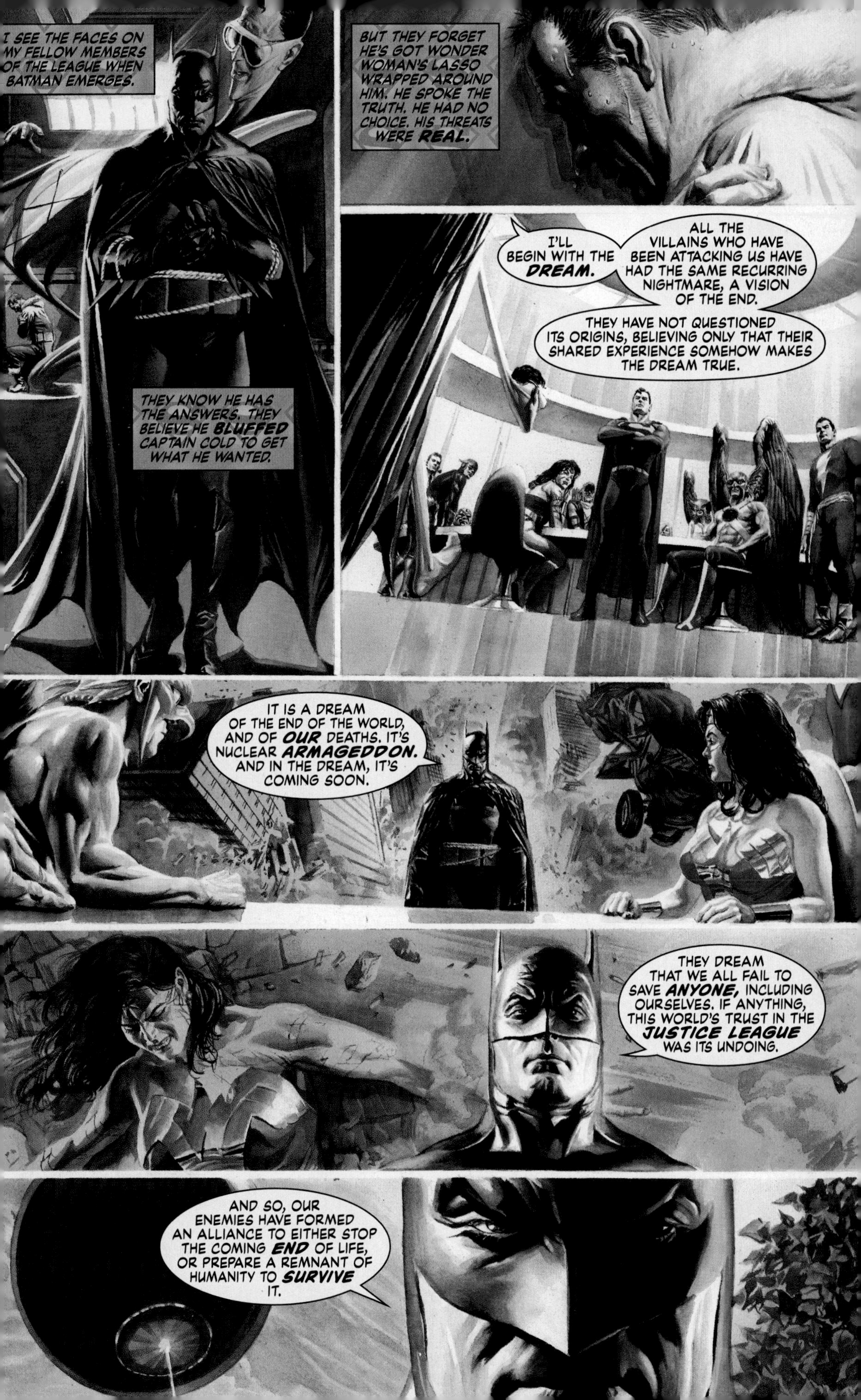
I SEE THE FACES ON MY FELLOW MEMBERS OF THE LEAGUE WHEN BATMAN EMERGES.
THEY KNOW HE HAS THE ANSWERS. THEY BELIEVE HE BLUFFED CAPTAIN COLD TO GET WHAT HE WANTED.
BUT THEY FORGET HE'S GOT WONDER WOMAN'S LASSO WRAPPED AROUND HIM. HE SPOKE THE TRUTH. HE HAD NO CHOICE. HIS THREATS WERE REAL.
I'LL BEGIN WITH THE DREAM.
ALL THE VILLAINS WHO HAVE BEEN ATTACKING US HAVE HAD THE SAME RECURRING NIGHTMARE, A VISION OF THE END.
THEY HAVE NOT QUESTIONED ITS ORIGINS, BELIEVING ONLY THAT THEIR SHARED EXPERIENCE SOMEHOW MAKES THE DREAM TRUE.
IT IS A DREAM OF THE END OF THE WORLD, AND OF OUR DEATHS. IT'S NUCLEAR ARMAGEDDON. AND IN THE DREAM, IT'S COMING SOON.
THEY DREAM THAT WE ALL FAIL TO SAVE ANYONE, INCLUDING OURSELVES. IF ANYTHING, THIS WORLD'S TRUST IN THE JUSTICE LEAGUE WAS ITS UNDOING.
AND SO, OUR ENEMIES HAVE FORMED AN ALLIANCE TO EITHER STOP THE COMING END OF LIFE, OR PREPARE A REMNANT OF HUMANITY TO SURVIVE IT.

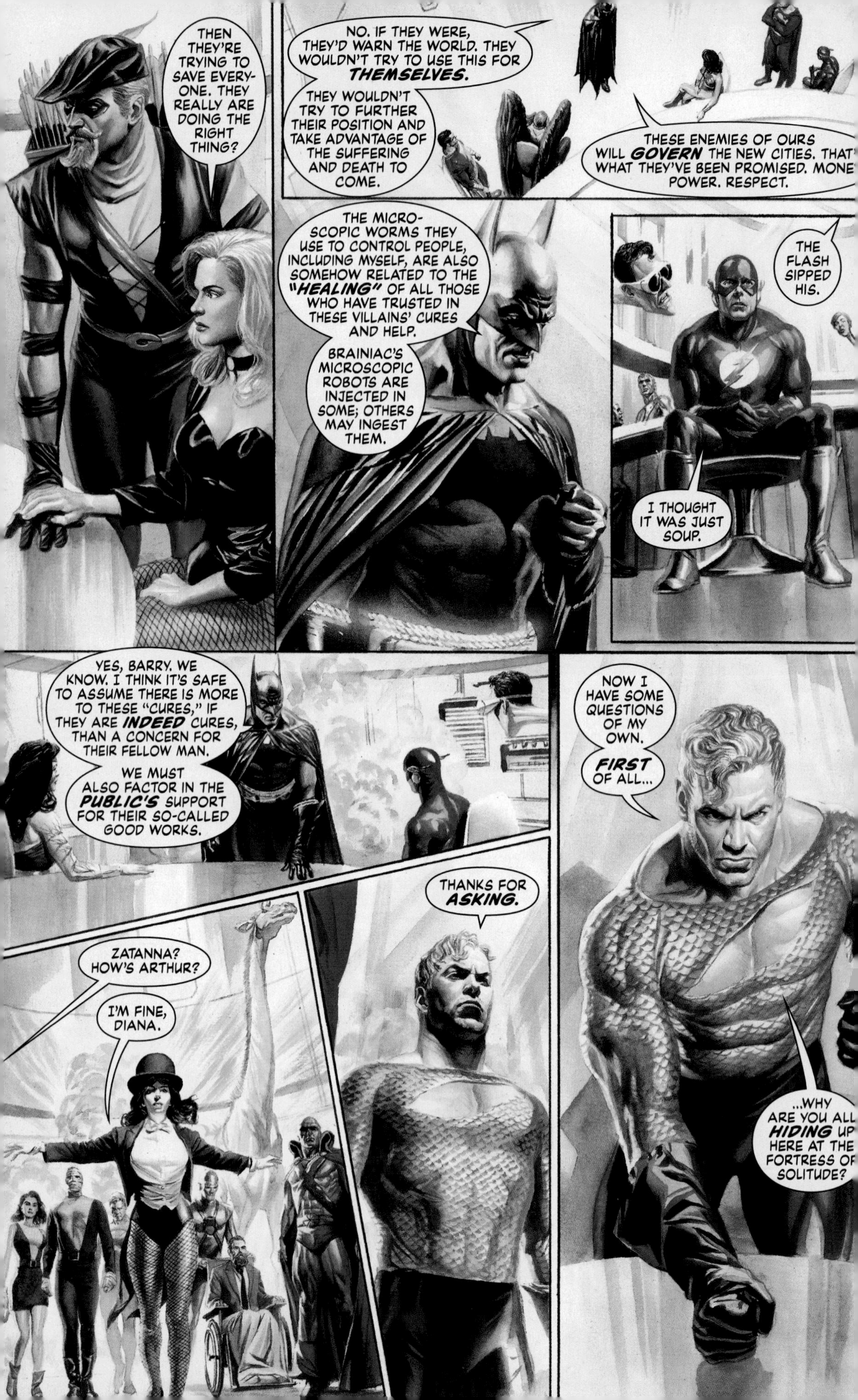

THEN THEY'RE TRYING TO SAVE EVERYONE. THEY REALLY ARE DOING THE RIGHT THING?
NO. IF THEY WERE, THEY'D WARN THE WORLD. THEY WOULDN'T TRY TO USE THIS FOR THEMSELVES.
THEY WOULDN'T TRY TO FURTHER THEIR POSITION AND TAKE ADVANTAGE OF THE SUFFERING AND DEATH TO COME.
THESE ENEMIES OF OURS WILL GOVERN THE NEW CITIES. THAT' WHAT THEY'VE BEEN PROMISED. MONE POWER. RESPECT.
THE MICROSCOPIC WORMS THEY USE TO CONTROL PEOPLE, INCLUDING MYSELF, ARE ALSO SOMEHOW RELATED TO THE "HEALING" OF ALL THOSE WHO HAVE TRUSTED IN THESE VILLAINS' CURES AND HELP.
BRAINIAC'S MICROSCOPIC ROBOTS ARE INJECTED IN SOME; OTHERS MAY INGEST THEM.
THE FLASH SIPPED HIS.
I THOUGHT IT WAS JUST SOUP.
YES, BARRY. WE KNOW. I THINK IT'S SAFE TO ASSUME THERE IS MORE TO THESE "CURES," IF THEY ARE INDEED CURES, THAN A CONCERN FOR THEIR FELLOW MAN.
WE MUST ALSO FACTOR IN THE PUBLIC'S SUPPORT FOR THEIR SO-CALLED GOOD WORKS.
ZATANNA? HOW'S ARTHUR?
I'M FINE, DIANA.
THANKS FOR ASKING.
NOW I HAVE SOME QUESTIONS OF MY OWN.
FIRST OF ALL...
...WHY ARE YOU ALL HIDING UP HERE AT THE FORTRESS OF SOLITUDE?

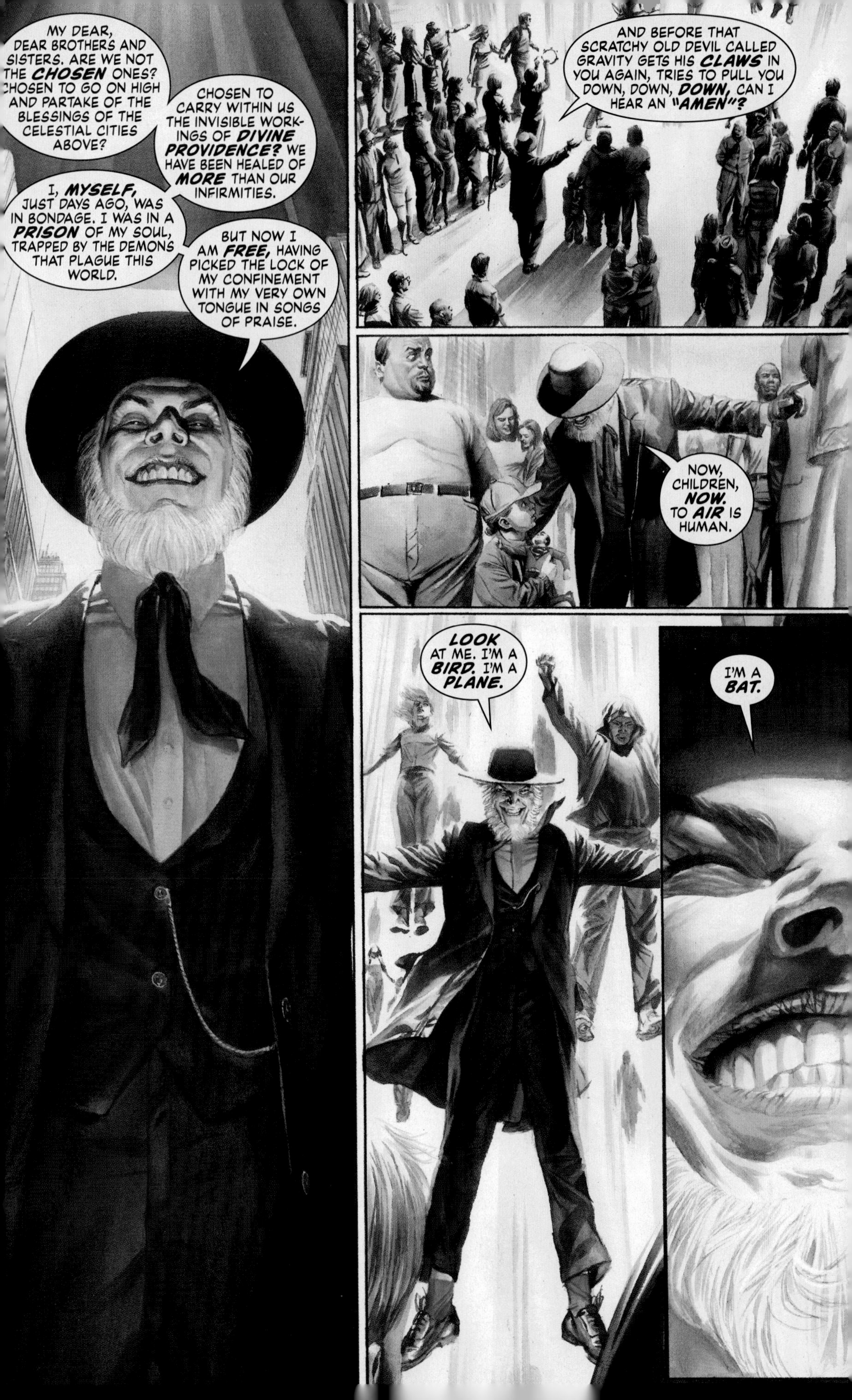

MY DEAR, DEAR BROTHERS AND SISTERS. ARE WE NOT THE CHOSEN ONES? CHOSEN TO GO ON HIGH AND PARTAKE OF THE BLESSINGS OF THE CELESTIAL CITIES ABOVE?
CHOSEN TO CARRY WITHIN US THE INVISIBLE WORKINGS OF DIVINE PROVIDENCE? WE HAVE BEEN HEALED OF MORE THAN OUR INFIRMITIES.
I, MYSELF, JUST DAYS AGO, WAS IN BONDAGE. I WAS IN A PRISON OF MY SOUL, TRAPPED BY THE DEMONS THAT PLAGUE THIS WORLD.
BUT NOW I AM FREE, HAVING PICKED THE LOCK OF MY CONFINEMENT WITH MY VERY OWN TONGUE IN SONGS OF PRAISE.
AND BEFORE THAT SCRATCHY OLD DEVIL CALLED GRAVITY GETS HIS CLAWS IN YOU AGAIN, TRIES TO PULL YOU DOWN, DOWN, DOWN, CAN I HEAR AN "AMEN"?
NOW, CHILDREN, NOW. TO AIR IS HUMAN.
LOOK AT ME. I'M A BIRD. I'M A PLANE.
I'M A BAT.

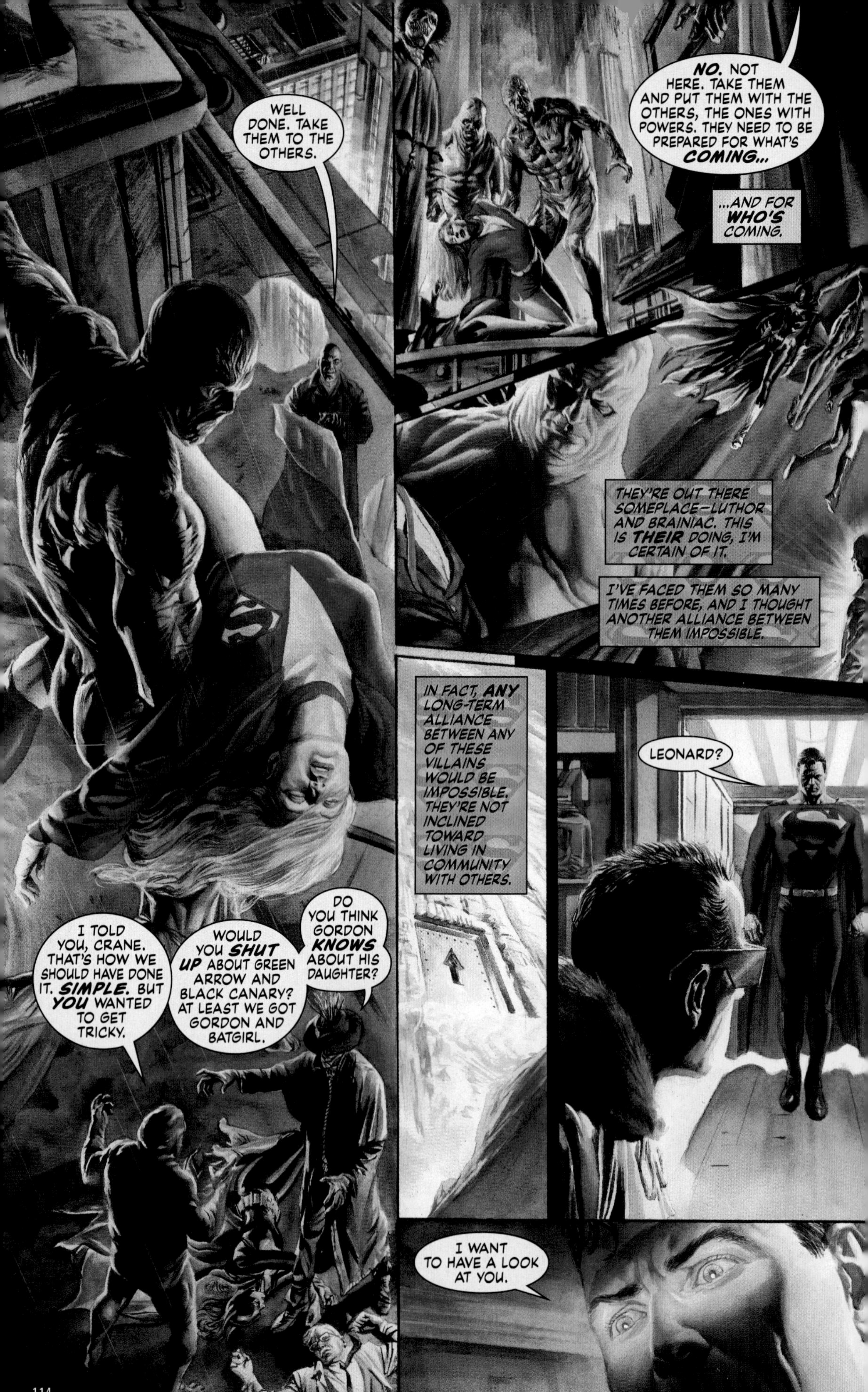
WELL DONE. TAKE THEM TO THE OTHERS.
NO. NOT HERE. TAKE THEM AND PUT THEM WITH THE OTHERS, THE ONES WITH POWERS. THEY NEED TO BE PREPARED FOR WHAT'S COMING...
...AND FOR WHO'S COMING.
THEY'RE OUT THERE SOMEPLACE—LUTHOR AND BRAINIAC. THIS IS THEIR DOING, I'M CERTAIN OF IT.
I'VE FACED THEM SO MANY TIMES BEFORE, AND I THOUGHT ANOTHER ALLIANCE BETWEEN THEM IMPOSSIBLE.
I TOLD YOU, CRANE. THAT'S HOW WE SHOULD HAVE DONE IT. SIMPLE. BUT YOU WANTED TO GET TRICKY.
WOULD YOU SHUT UP ABOUT GREEN ARROW AND BLACK CANARY? AT LEAST WE GOT GORDON AND BATGIRL.
DO YOU THINK GORDON KNOWS ABOUT HIS DAUGHTER?
IN FACT, ANY LONG-TERM ALLIANCE BETWEEN ANY OF THESE VILLAINS WOULD BE IMPOSSIBLE. THEY'RE NOT INCLINED TOWARD LIVING IN COMMUNITY WITH OTHERS.
LEONARD?
I WANT TO HAVE A LOOK AT YOU.

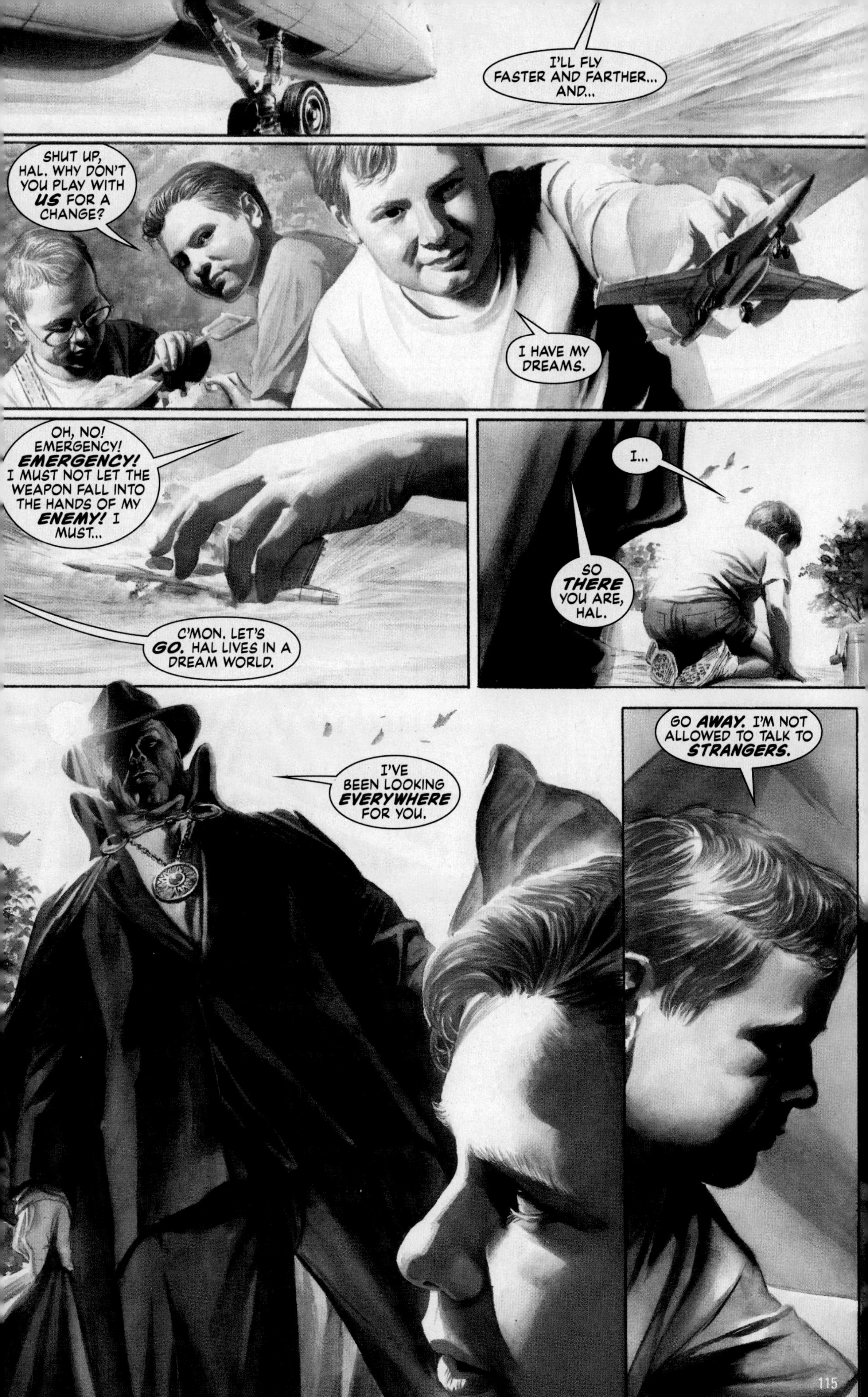
I'LL FLY FASTER AND FARTHER... AND...
SHUT UP, HAL. WHY DON'T YOU PLAY WITH US FOR A CHANGE?
I HAVE MY DREAMS.
OH, NO! EMERGENCY! EMERGENCY! I MUST NOT LET THE WEAPON FALL INTO THE HANDS OF MY ENEMY! I MUST...
C'MON. LET'S GO. HAL LIVES IN A DREAM WORLD.
I...
SO THERE YOU ARE, HAL.
I'VE BEEN LOOKING EVERYWHERE FOR YOU.
GO AWAY. I'M NOT ALLOWED TO TALK TO STRANGERS.

WONDER WOMAN?

YES, BILL?

WHAT HAPPENED? WHAT DID CHEETAH *DO* TO YOU?

WE ARE BOTH BEINGS OF MAGIC, BILL. THAT IS ALSO WHERE WE ARE MOST *VULNERABLE.* AND I'VE BEEN *CURSED.*

I'M GOING TO DIE FROM THE SAME POISON THAT KILLED HERCULES.

THE *CENTAUR'S* BLOOD?

BUT WHERE HERCULES' DEATH RETURNED HIM TO THE *GLORY* WHICH WAS HIS BY RIGHT AND BIRTH...

...I AM RETURNING TO MY *ORIGINS.* THESE SCARS ARE *BAKING* ME FROM WITHIN.

I WAS CLAY ONCE, FORMED BY MY MOTHER'S HANDS. THE GODDESS MADE ME *REAL* IN ANSWER TO MY MOTHER'S PRAYER. I AM BECOMING *UNREAL* AGAIN.

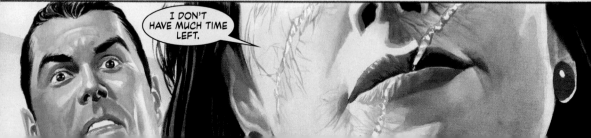

I DON'T HAVE MUCH TIME LEFT.

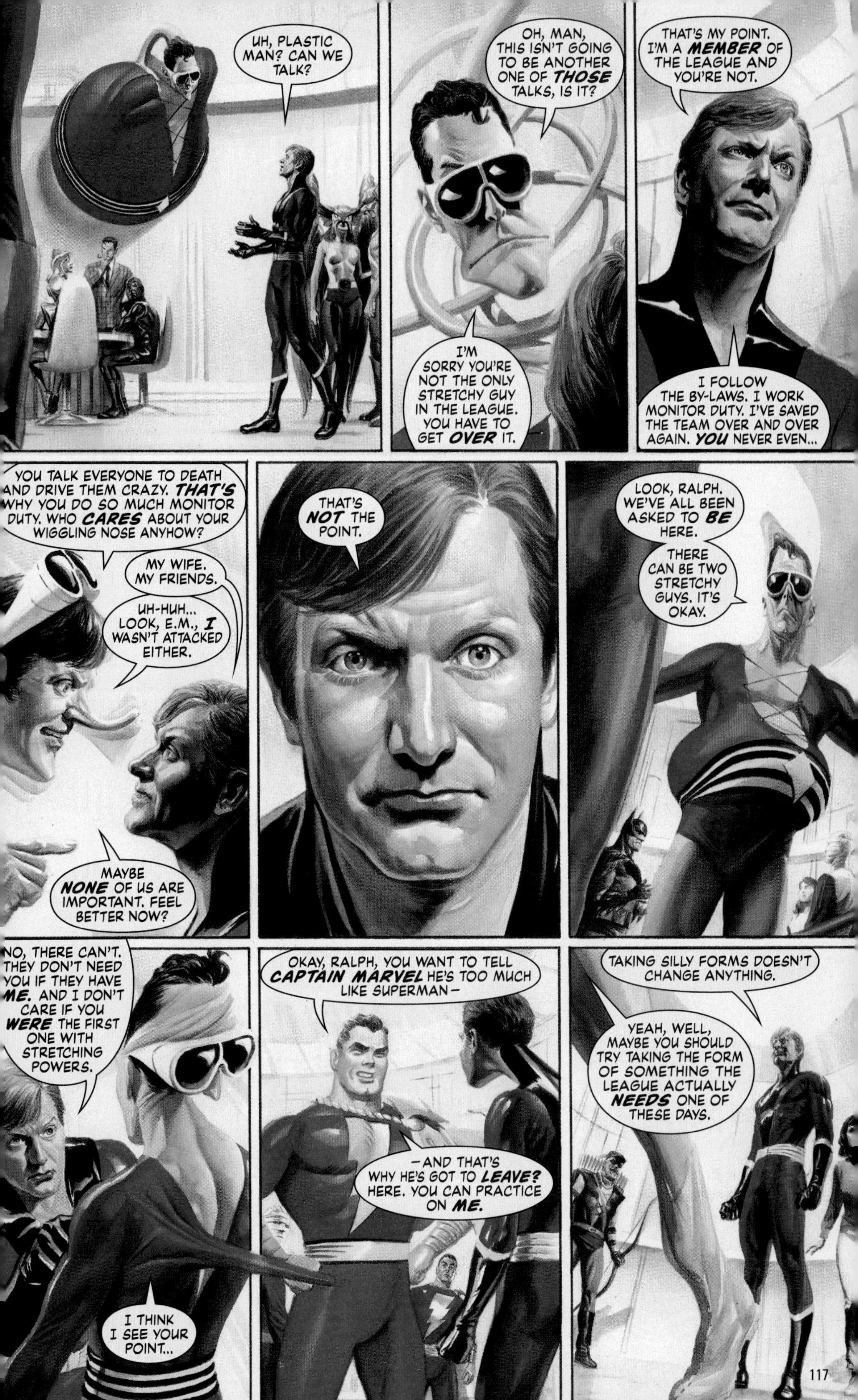
UH, PLASTIC MAN? CAN WE TALK?
OH, MAN, THIS ISN'T GOING TO BE ANOTHER ONE OF THOSE TALKS, IS IT?
I'M SORRY YOU'RE NOT THE ONLY STRETCHY GUY IN THE LEAGUE. YOU HAVE TO GET OVER IT.
THAT'S MY POINT. I'M A MEMBER OF THE LEAGUE AND YOU'RE NOT.
I FOLLOW THE BY-LAWS. I WORK MONITOR DUTY. I'VE SAVED THE TEAM OVER AND OVER AGAIN. YOU NEVER EVEN...
YOU TALK EVERYONE TO DEATH AND DRIVE THEM CRAZY. THAT'S WHY YOU DO SO MUCH MONITOR DUTY. WHO CARES ABOUT YOUR WIGGLING NOSE ANYHOW?
MY WIFE. MY FRIENDS.
UH-HUH... LOOK, E.M., I WASN'T ATTACKED EITHER.
MAYBE NONE OF US ARE IMPORTANT. FEEL BETTER NOW?
THAT'S NOT THE POINT.
LOOK, RALPH. WE'VE ALL BEEN ASKED TO BE HERE.
THERE CAN BE TWO STRETCHY GUYS. IT'S OKAY.
NO, THERE CAN'T. THEY DON'T NEED YOU IF THEY HAVE ME. AND I DON'T CARE IF YOU WERE THE FIRST ONE WITH STRETCHING POWERS.
I THINK I SEE YOUR POINT...
OKAY, RALPH, YOU WANT TO TELL CAPTAIN MARVEL HE'S TOO MUCH LIKE SUPERMAN—
—AND THAT'S WHY HE'S GOT TO LEAVE? HERE. YOU CAN PRACTICE ON ME.
TAKING SILLY FORMS DOESN'T CHANGE ANYTHING.
YEAH, WELL, MAYBE YOU SHOULD TRY TAKING THE FORM OF SOMETHING THE LEAGUE ACTUALLY NEEDS ONE OF THESE DAYS.

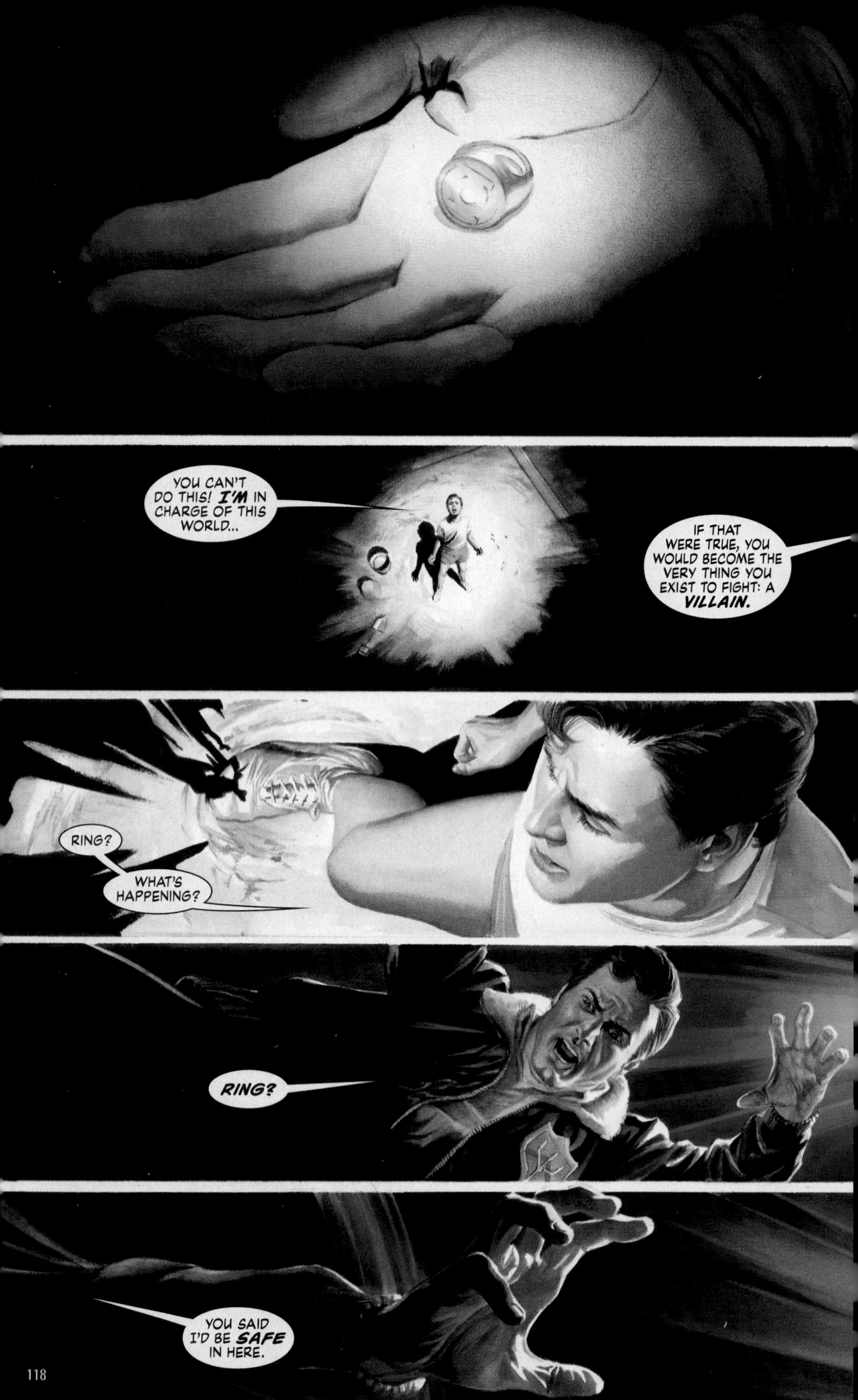
YOU CAN'T DO THIS! I'M IN CHARGE OF THIS WORLD...
IF THAT WERE TRUE, YOU WOULD BECOME THE VERY THING YOU EXIST TO FIGHT: A VILLAIN.
RING?
WHAT'S HAPPENING?
RING?
YOU SAID I'D BE SAFE IN HERE.

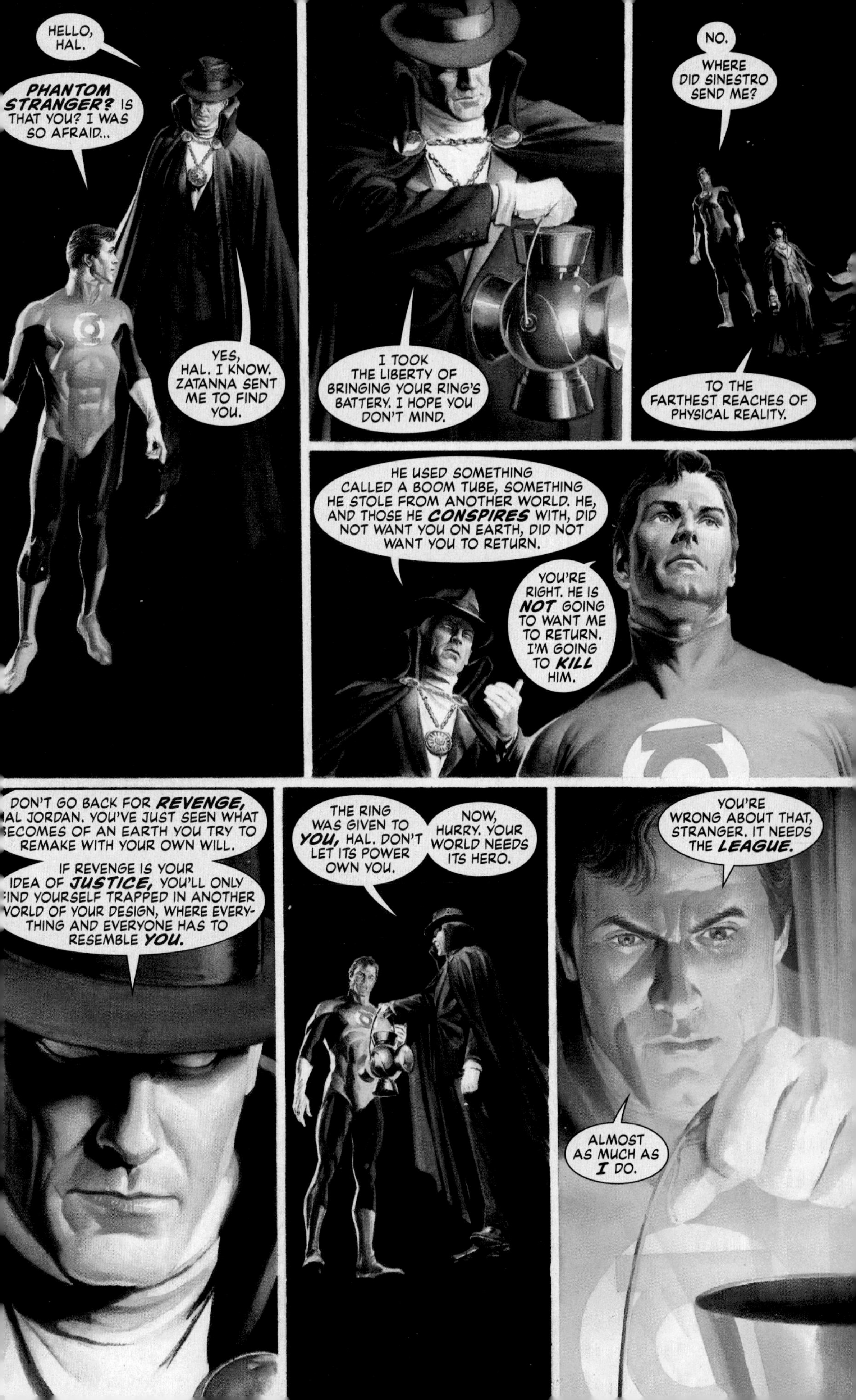
HELLO, HAL.
PHANTOM STRANGER? IS THAT YOU? I WAS SO AFRAID...
YES, HAL. I KNOW. ZATANNA SENT ME TO FIND YOU.
I TOOK THE LIBERTY OF BRINGING YOUR RING'S BATTERY. I HOPE YOU DON'T MIND.
NO.
WHERE DID SINESTRO SEND ME?
TO THE FARTHEST REACHES OF PHYSICAL REALITY.
HE USED SOMETHING CALLED A BOOM TUBE, SOMETHING HE STOLE FROM ANOTHER WORLD. HE, AND THOSE HE CONSPIRES WITH, DID NOT WANT YOU ON EARTH, DID NOT WANT YOU TO RETURN.
YOU'RE RIGHT. HE IS NOT GOING TO WANT ME TO RETURN. I'M GOING TO KILL HIM.
DON'T GO BACK FOR REVENGE, AL JORDAN. YOU'VE JUST SEEN WHAT ECOMES OF AN EARTH YOU TRY TO REMAKE WITH YOUR OWN WILL.
IF REVENGE IS YOUR IDEA OF JUSTICE, YOU'LL ONLY IND YOURSELF TRAPPED IN ANOTHER ORLD OF YOUR DESIGN, WHERE EVERYTHING AND EVERYONE HAS TO RESEMBLE YOU.
THE RING WAS GIVEN TO YOU, HAL. DON'T LET ITS POWER OWN YOU.
NOW, HURRY. YOUR WORLD NEEDS ITS HERO.
YOU'RE WRONG ABOUT THAT, STRANGER. IT NEEDS THE LEAGUE.
ALMOST AS MUCH AS I DO.

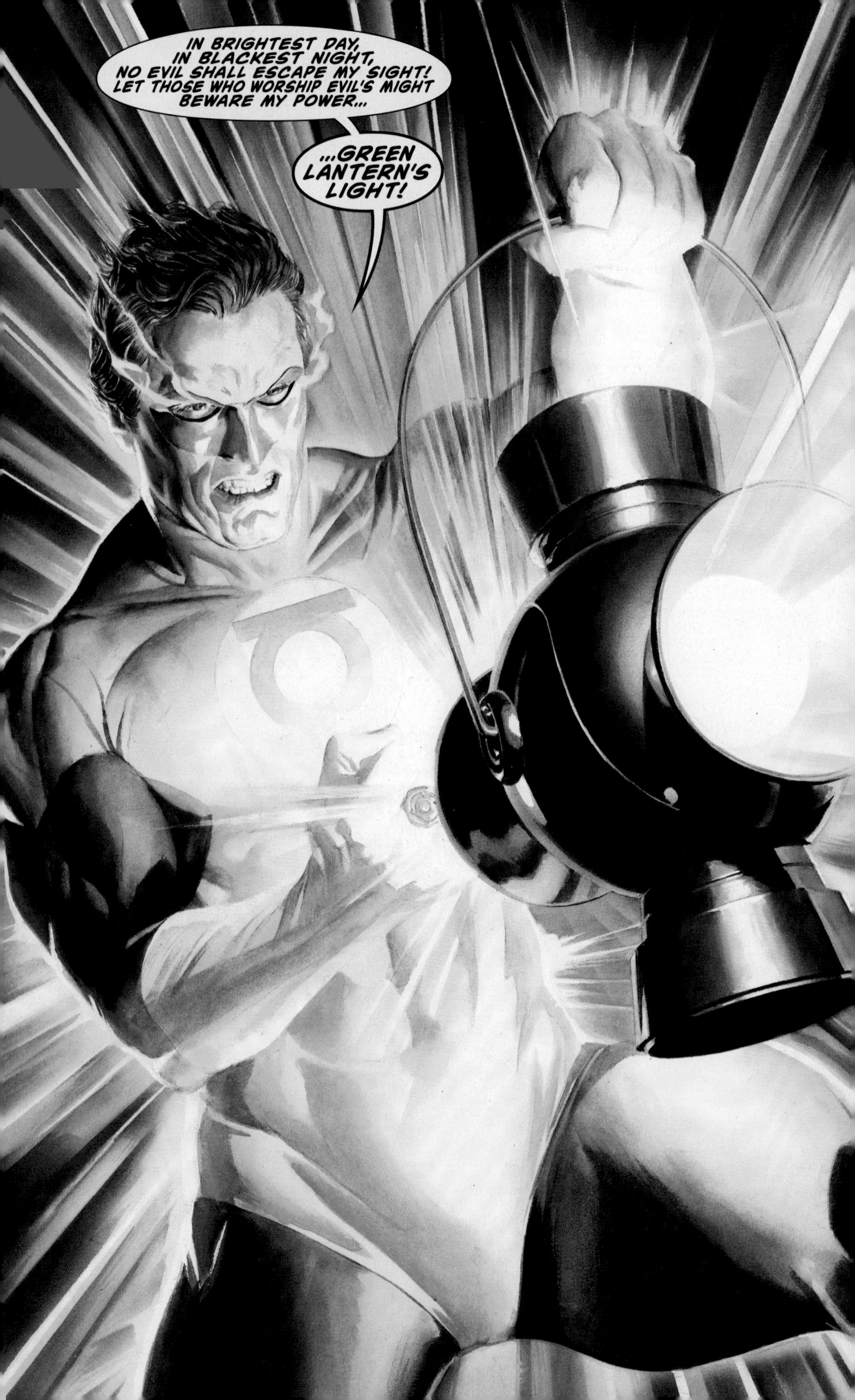
IN BRIGHTEST DAY, IN BLACKEST NIGHT, NO EVIL SHALL ESCAPE MY SIGHT! LET THOSE WHO WORSHIP EVIL'S MIGHT BEWARE MY POWER...
...GREEN LANTERN'S LIGHT!

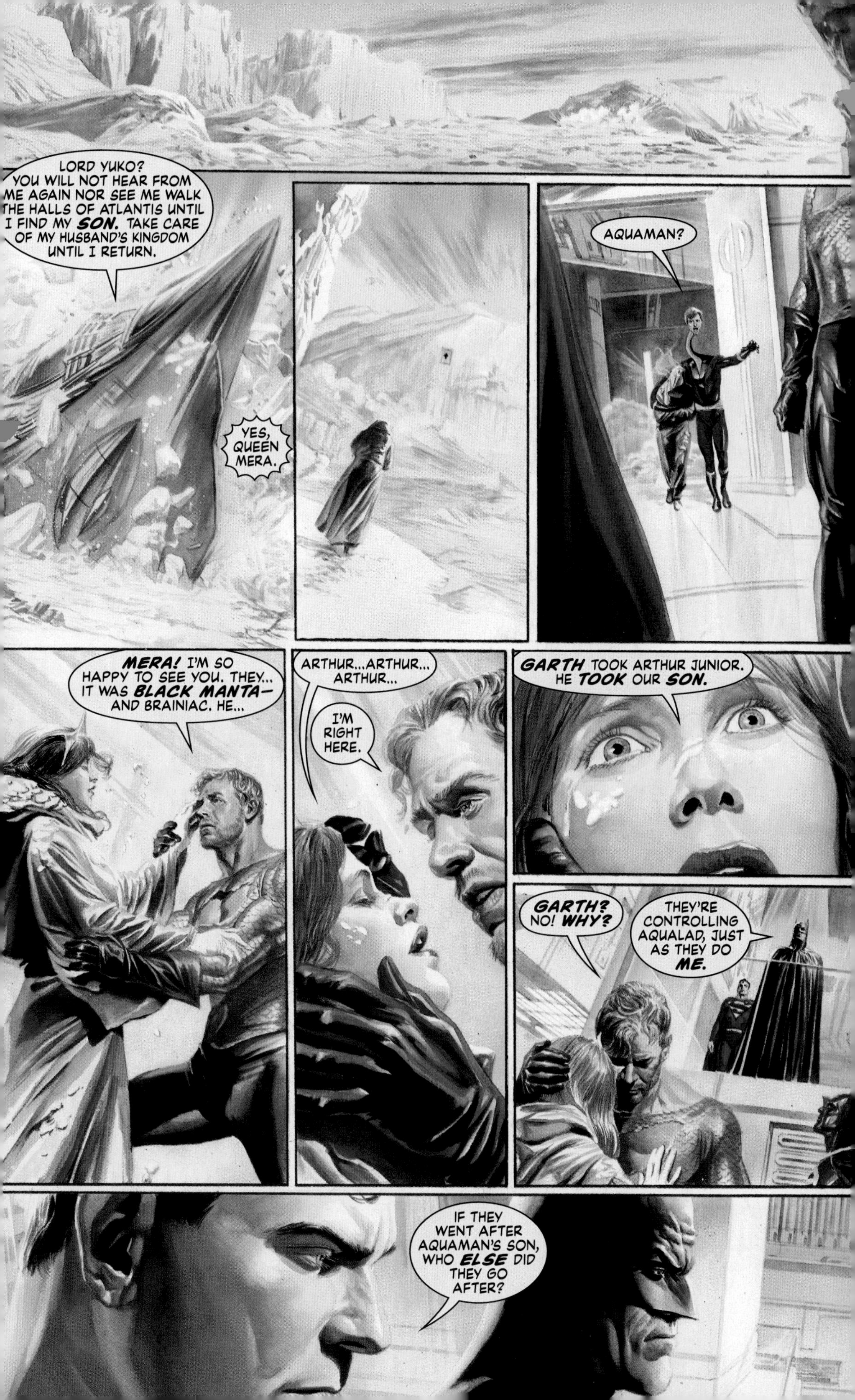
LORD YUKO? YOU WILL NOT HEAR FROM ME AGAIN NOR SEE ME WALK THE HALLS OF ATLANTIS UNTIL I FIND MY SON. TAKE CARE OF MY HUSBAND'S KINGDOM UNTIL I RETURN.
YES, QUEEN MERA.
AQUAMAN?
MERA! I'M SO HAPPY TO SEE YOU. THEY... IT WAS BLACK MANTA— AND BRAINIAC. HE...
ARTHUR...ARTHUR... ARTHUR...
I'M RIGHT HERE.
GARTH TOOK ARTHUR JUNIOR. HE TOOK OUR SON.
GARTH? NO! WHY?
THEY'RE CONTROLLING AQUALAD, JUST AS THEY DO ME.
IF THEY WENT AFTER AQUAMAN'S SON, WHO ELSE DID THEY GO AFTER?

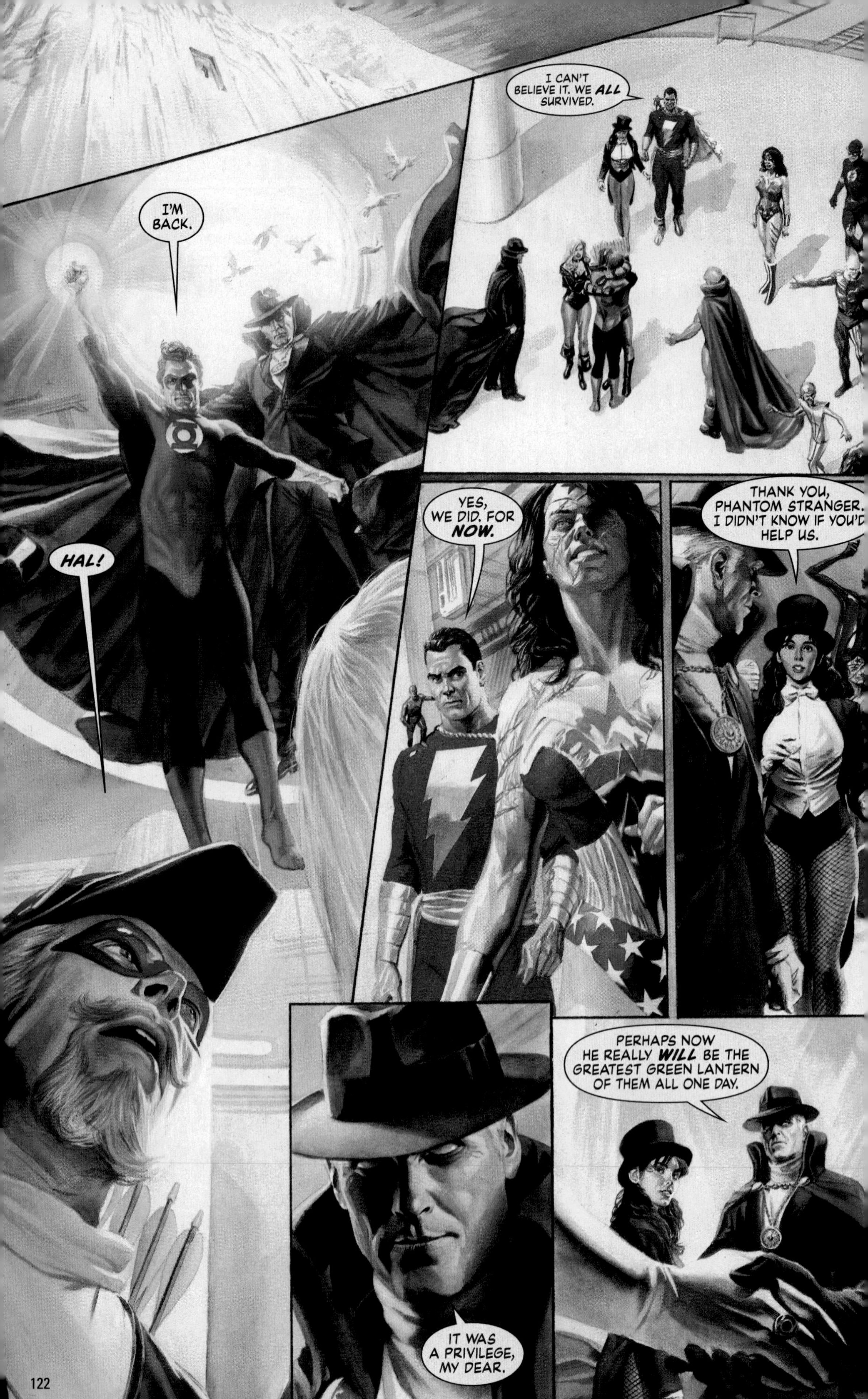
I'M BACK.
I CAN'T BELIEVE IT. WE ALL SURVIVED.
HAL!
YES, WE DID. FOR NOW.
THANK YOU, PHANTOM STRANGER. I DIDN'T KNOW IF YOU'D HELP US.
IT WAS A PRIVILEGE, MY DEAR.
PERHAPS NOW HE REALLY WILL BE THE GREATEST GREEN LANTERN OF THEM ALL ONE DAY.

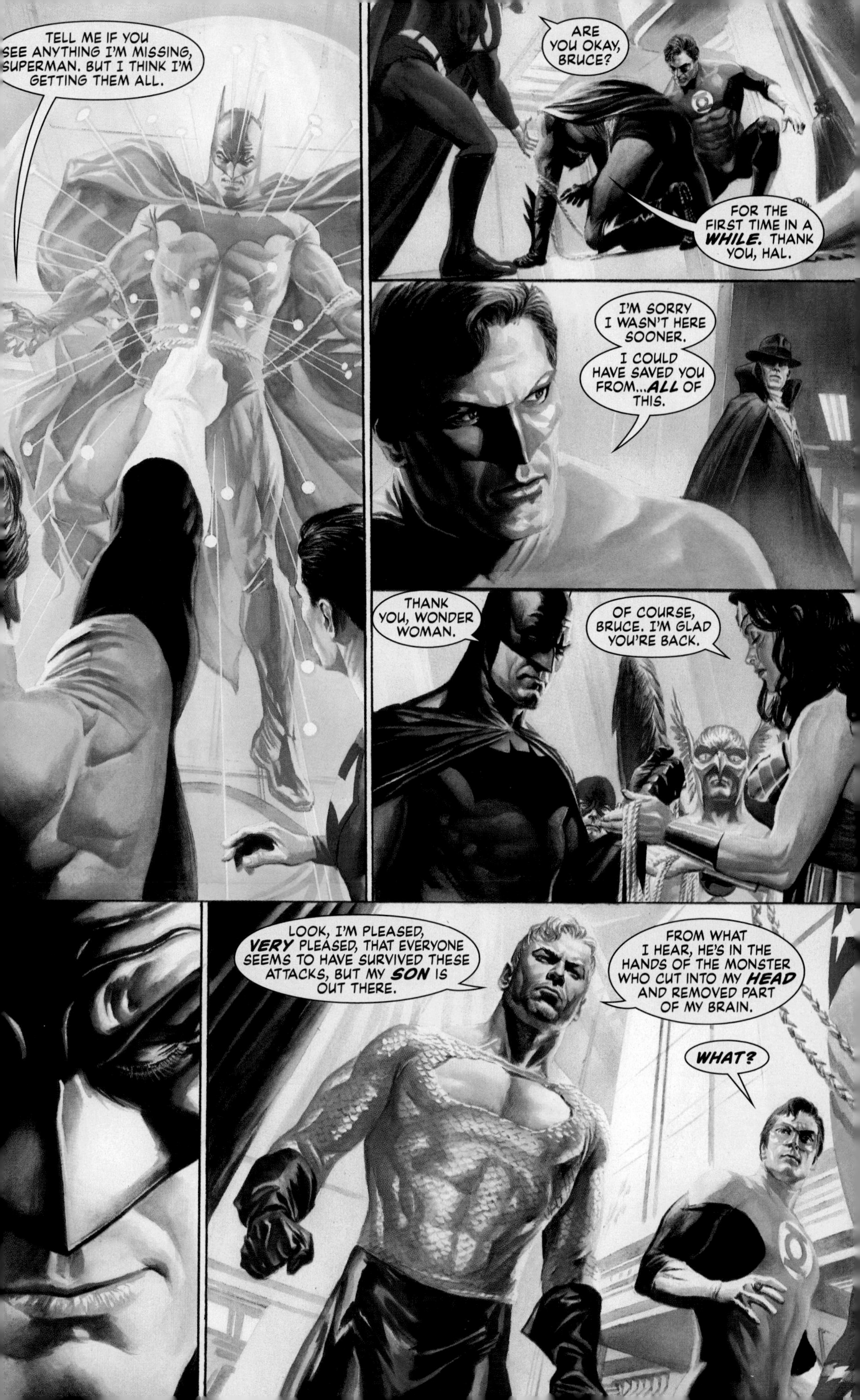
TELL ME IF YOU SEE ANYTHING I'M MISSING, SUPERMAN. BUT I THINK I'M GETTING THEM ALL.
ARE YOU OKAY, BRUCE?
FOR THE FIRST TIME IN A WHILE. THANK YOU, HAL.
I'M SORRY I WASN'T HERE SOONER.
I COULD HAVE SAVED YOU FROM...ALL OF THIS.
THANK YOU, WONDER WOMAN.
OF COURSE, BRUCE. I'M GLAD YOU'RE BACK.
LOOK, I'M PLEASED, VERY PLEASED, THAT EVERYONE SEEMS TO HAVE SURVIVED THESE ATTACKS, BUT MY SON IS OUT THERE.
FROM WHAT I HEAR, HE'S IN THE HANDS OF THE MONSTER WHO CUT INTO MY HEAD AND REMOVED PART OF MY BRAIN.
WHAT?

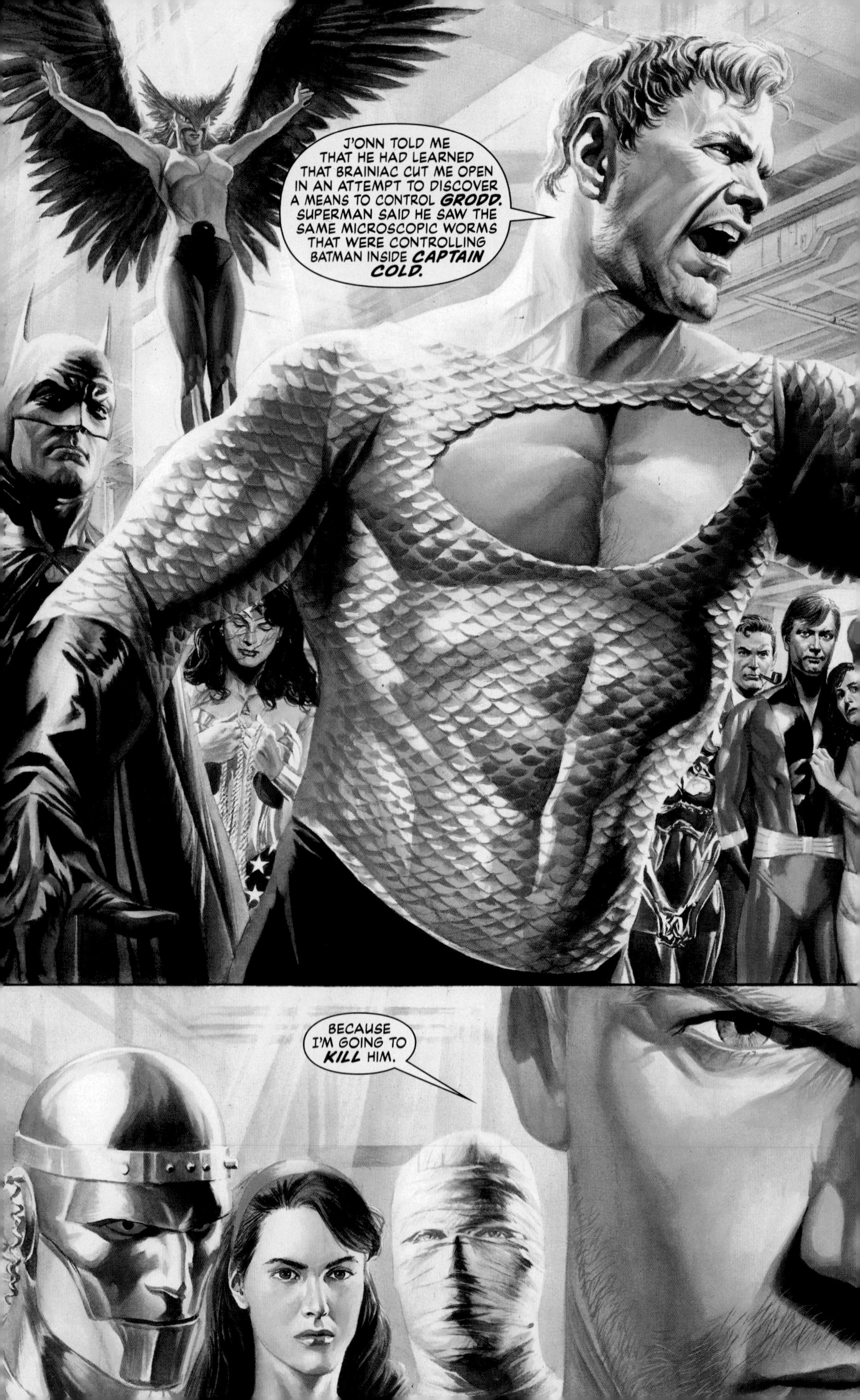
J'ONN TOLD ME THAT HE HAD LEARNED THAT BRAINIAC CUT ME OPEN IN AN ATTEMPT TO DISCOVER A MEANS TO CONTROL GRODD. SUPERMAN SAID HE SAW THE SAME MICROSCOPIC WORMS THAT WERE CONTROLLING BATMAN INSIDE CAPTAIN COLD.
BECAUSE I'M GOING TO KILL HIM.

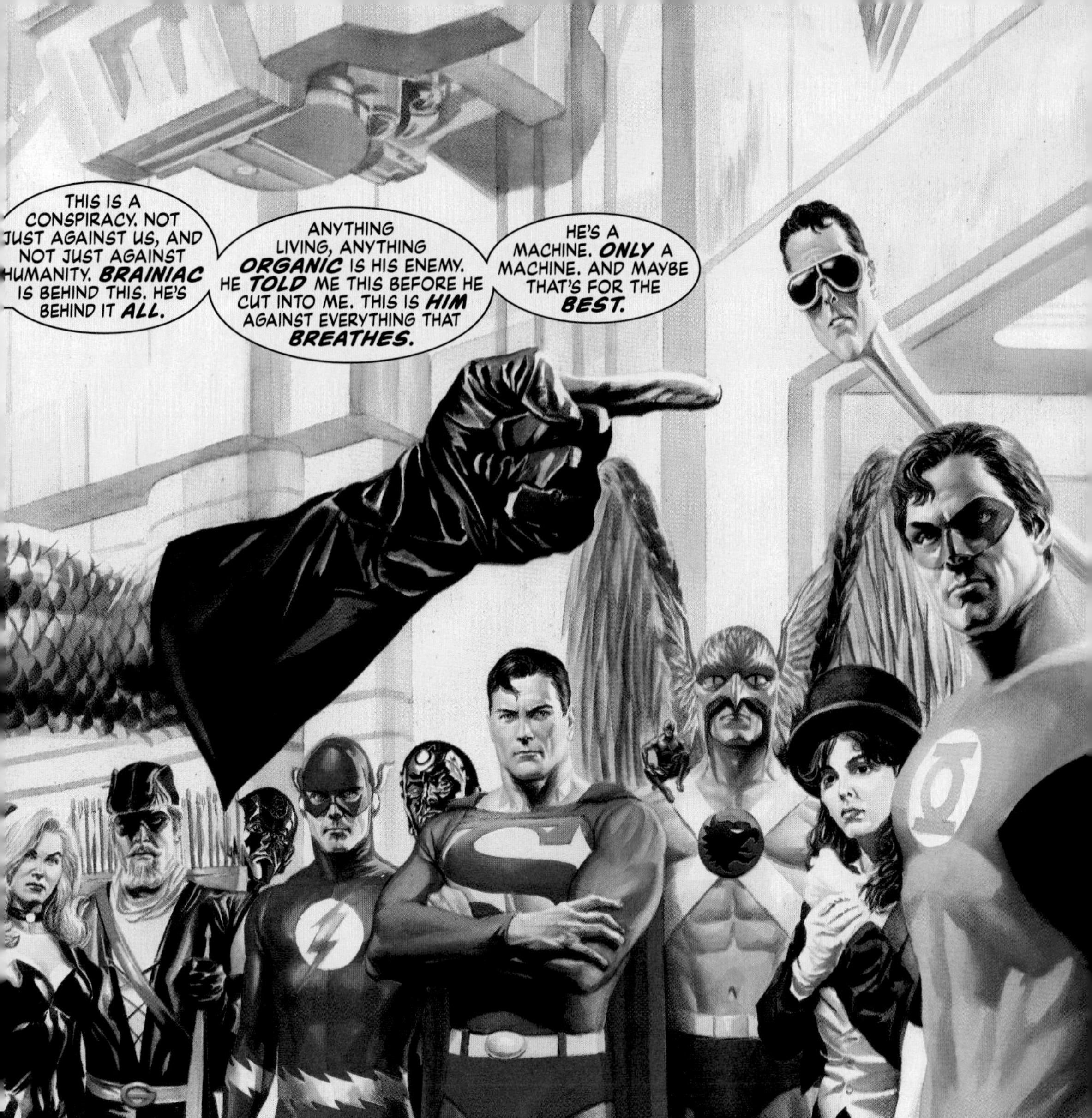
THIS IS A CONSPIRACY. NOT JUST AGAINST US, AND NOT JUST AGAINST HUMANITY. BRAINIAC IS BEHIND THIS. HE'S BEHIND IT ALL.
ANYTHING LIVING, ANYTHING ORGANIC IS HIS ENEMY. HE TOLD ME THIS BEFORE HE CUT INTO ME. THIS IS HIM AGAINST EVERYTHING THAT BREATHES.
HE'S A MACHINE. ONLY A MACHINE. AND MAYBE THAT'S FOR THE BEST.

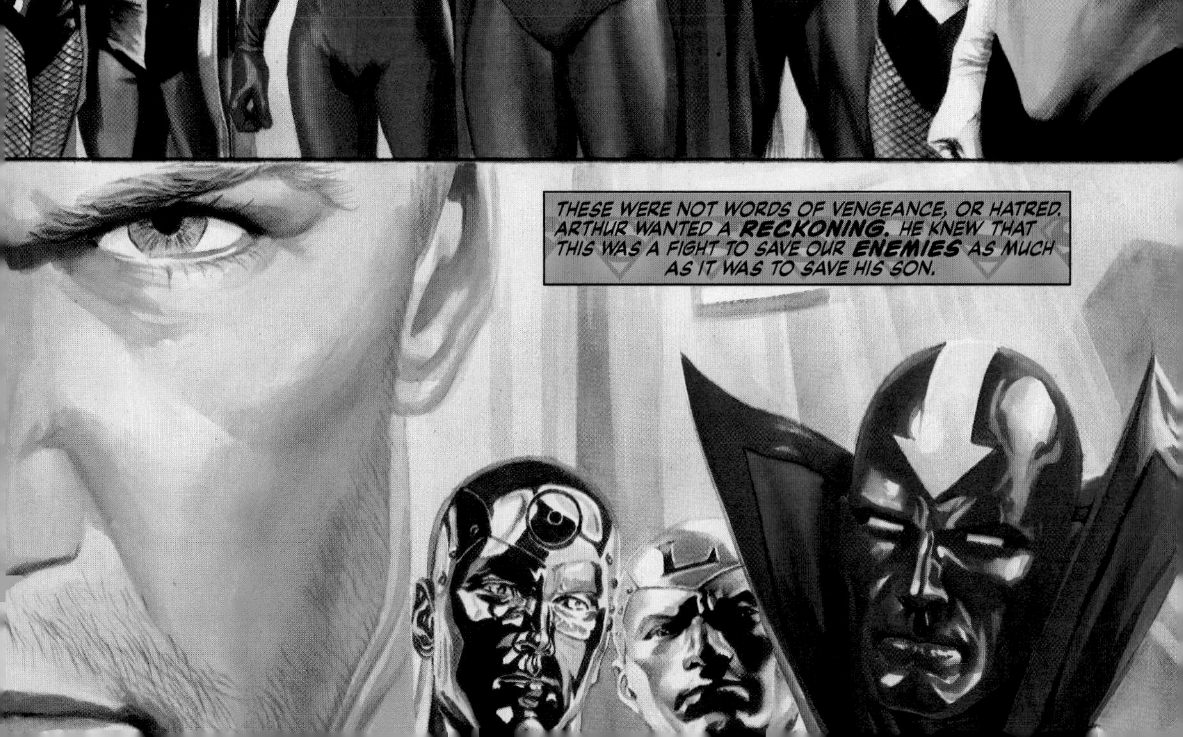
THESE WERE NOT WORDS OF VENGEANCE, OR HATRED. ARTHUR WANTED A RECKONING. HE KNEW THAT THIS WAS A FIGHT TO SAVE OUR ENEMIES AS MUCH AS IT WAS TO SAVE HIS SON.

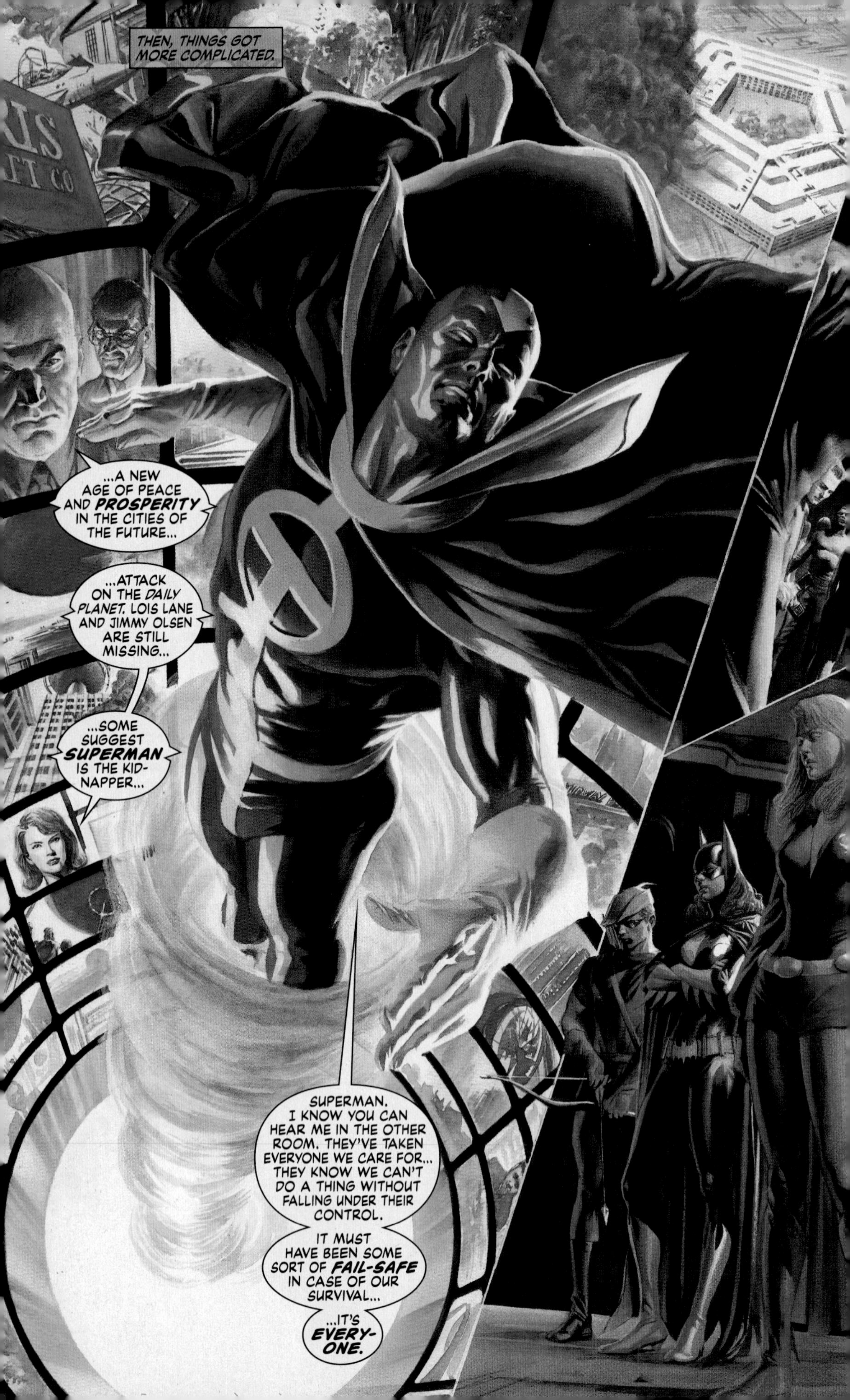
THEN, THINGS GOT MORE COMPLICATED.
...A NEW AGE OF PEACE AND PROSPERITY IN THE CITIES OF THE FUTURE...
...ATTACK ON THE DAILY PLANET. LOIS LANE AND JIMMY OLSEN ARE STILL MISSING...
...SOME SUGGEST SUPERMAN IS THE KID-NAPPER...
SUPERMAN. I KNOW YOU CAN HEAR ME IN THE OTHER ROOM. THEY'VE TAKEN EVERYONE WE CARE FOR... THEY KNOW WE CAN'T DO A THING WITHOUT FALLING UNDER THEIR CONTROL.
IT MUST HAVE BEEN SOME SORT OF FAIL-SAFE IN CASE OF OUR SURVIVAL...
...IT'S EVERY-ONE.

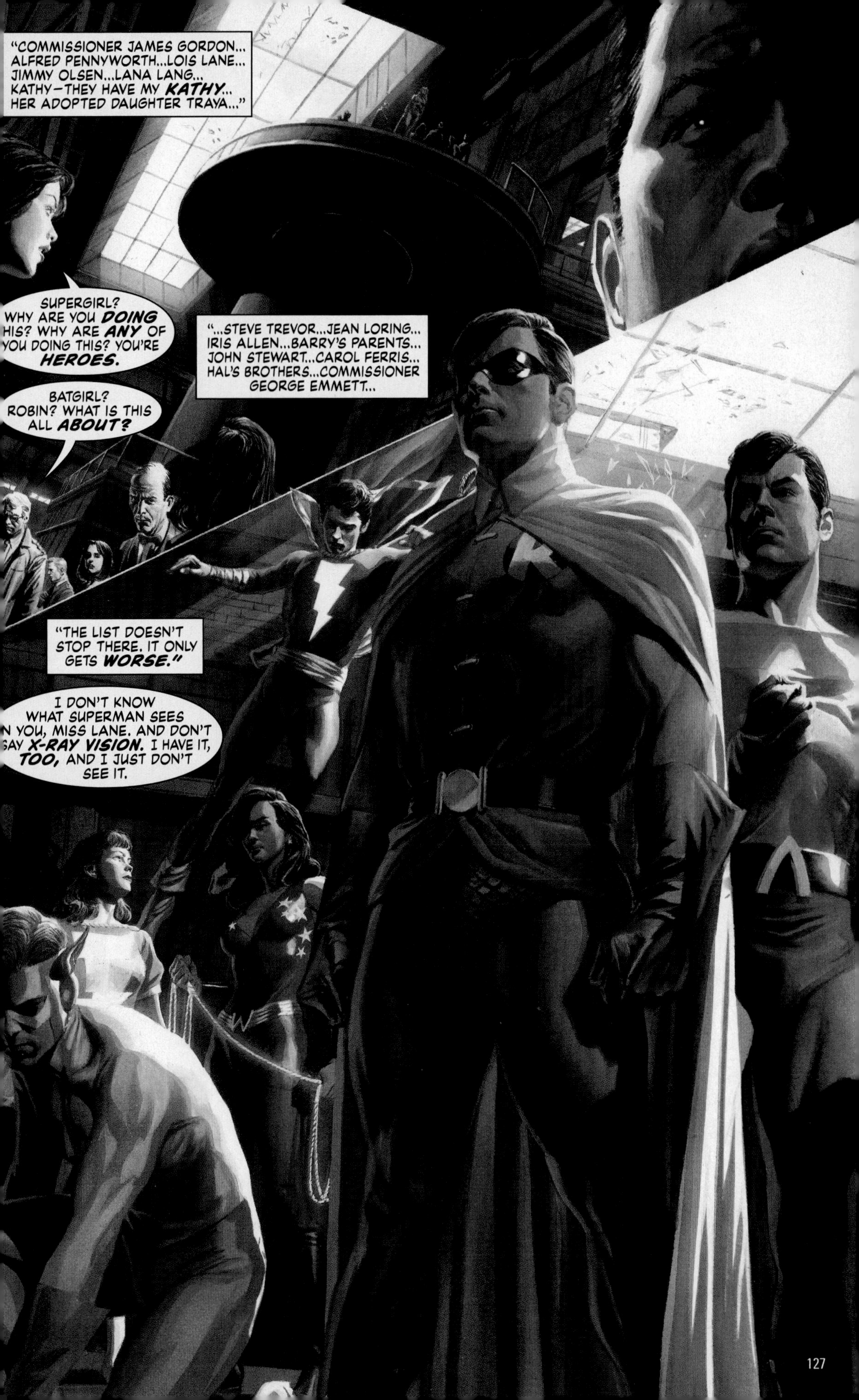
"COMMISSIONER JAMES GORDON... ALFRED PENNYWORTH...LOIS LANE... JIMMY OLSEN...LANA LANG... KATHY—THEY HAVE MY KATHY... HER ADOPTED DAUGHTER TRAYA..."
SUPERGIRL? WHY ARE YOU DOING HIS? WHY ARE ANY OF YOU DOING THIS? YOU'RE HEROES.
"...STEVE TREVOR...JEAN LORING... IRIS ALLEN...BARRY'S PARENTS... JOHN STEWART...CAROL FERRIS... HAL'S BROTHERS...COMMISSIONER GEORGE EMMETT...
BATGIRL? ROBIN? WHAT IS THIS ALL ABOUT?
"THE LIST DOESN'T STOP THERE. IT ONLY GETS WORSE."
I DON'T KNOW WHAT SUPERMAN SEES N YOU, MISS LANE. AND DON'T SAY X-RAY VISION. I HAVE IT, TOO, AND I JUST DON'T SEE IT.

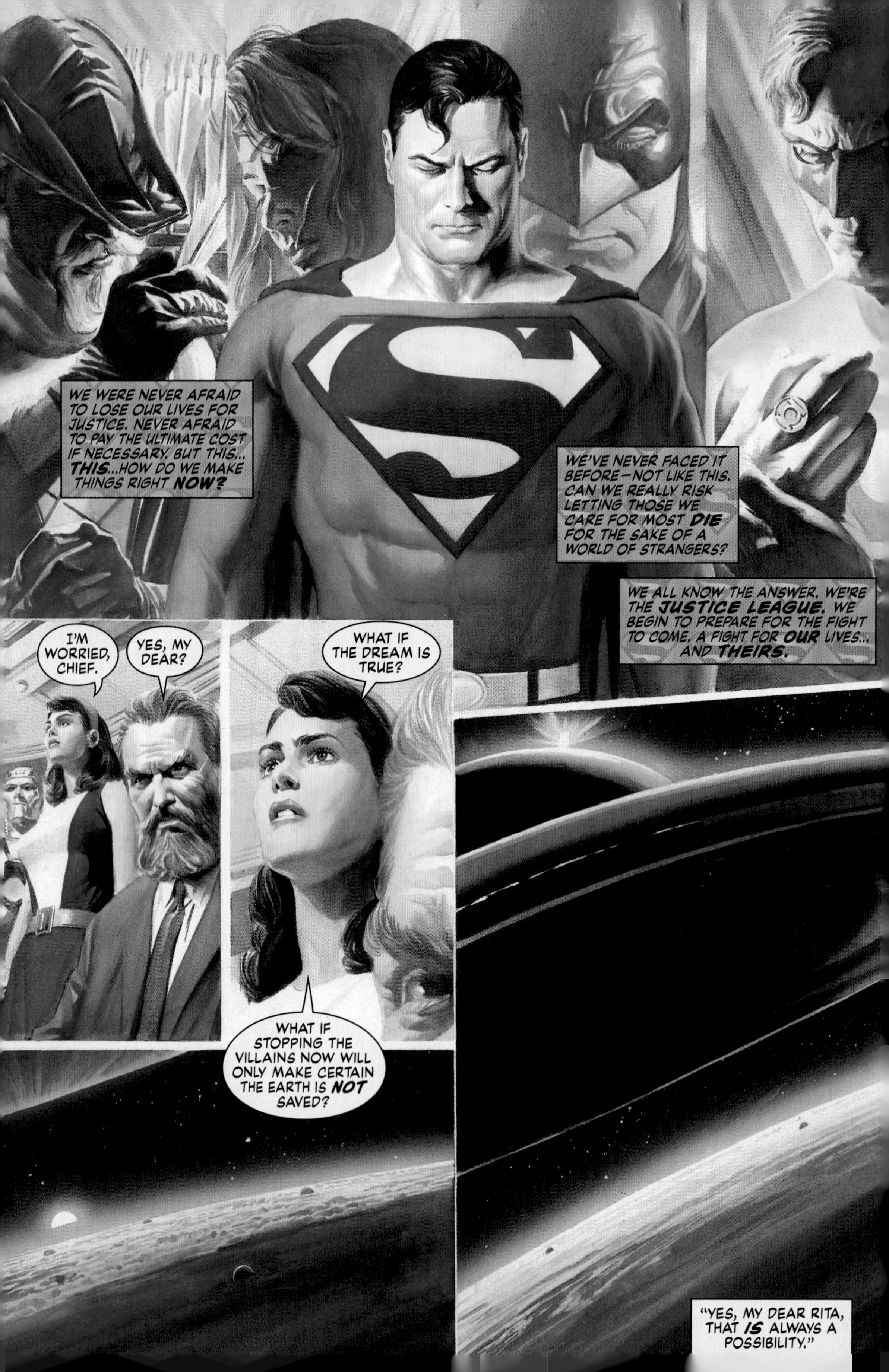
WE WERE NEVER AFRAID TO LOSE OUR LIVES FOR JUSTICE. NEVER AFRAID TO PAY THE ULTIMATE COST IF NECESSARY. BUT THIS... THIS...HOW DO WE MAKE THINGS RIGHT NOW?
WE'VE NEVER FACED IT BEFORE—NOT LIKE THIS. CAN WE REALLY RISK LETTING THOSE WE CARE FOR MOST DIE FOR THE SAKE OF A WORLD OF STRANGERS?
WE ALL KNOW THE ANSWER. WE'RE THE JUSTICE LEAGUE. WE BEGIN TO PREPARE FOR THE FIGHT TO COME. A FIGHT FOR OUR LIVES... AND THEIRS.
I'M WORRIED, CHIEF.
YES, MY DEAR?
WHAT IF THE DREAM IS TRUE?
WHAT IF STOPPING THE VILLAINS NOW WILL ONLY MAKE CERTAIN THE EARTH IS NOT SAVED?
"YES, MY DEAR RITA, THAT IS ALWAYS A POSSIBILITY."

FROM BRUCE WAYNE'S PRIVATE FILES IN THE BATCOMPUTER

SUPERMAN

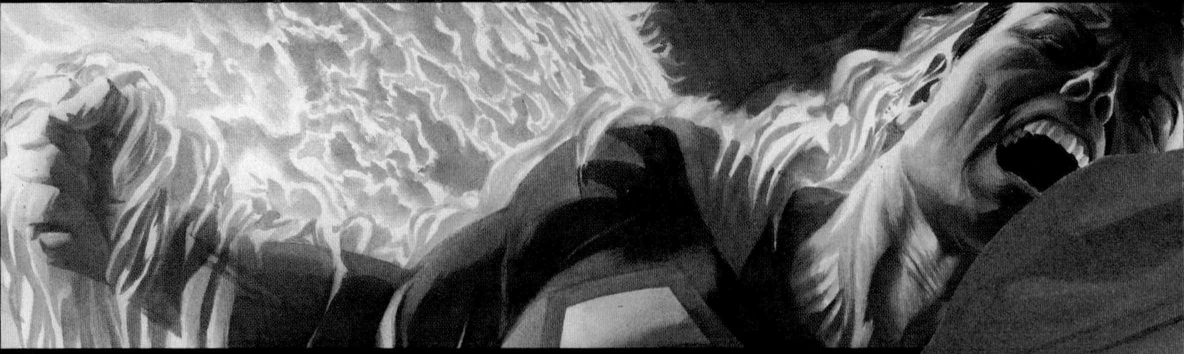

. . .Jor-El and his wife, Lara, sent their son in an experimental spacecraft to find new life and safety across the universe on a small planet known as Earth.

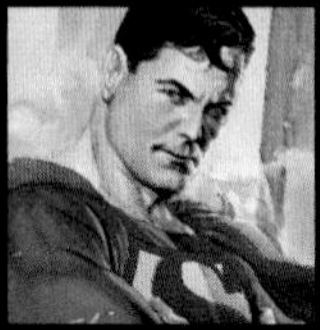

All our stories somehow involve the loss of parents at some point in our lives. But **SUPERMAN** lost far more than that. He is the last surviving member of an alien race from a planet called Krypton, a world he has learned collapsed at its core due to its people's abuses of its natural resources. Moments before its destruction, Superman's parents, Jor-El and his wife Lara, sent their son in an experimental spacecraft tofind new life and safety across the universe on a small planet known as Earth. A childless couple, the Kents, found thecrashed craft and child within. They never reported the rocket or the orphan to the authorities, but instead, believing their prayers for a child had been answered, raised the boy as their own, naming him Clark Kent.

While he seems almost invulnerable by human standards, his major physiological weakness, ironically, is the shattered remnants of his home planet, Krypton. This Kryptonite, depending on quantity and exposure, will kill Superman.

Superman was adopted. Perhaps that is what has determined his course in this world. This has formed his primary sense of hope, even after destruction. He believes that this world can be changed to a better one. But this hope may be a weakness to him just as Kryptonite is. He has taken a human disguise, operating among us as a reporter for the Daily Planet in Metropolis. That is how he remains aware of world events and is able to be anywhere, almost at any time.

His alien-inherited physiology enables him to fly. All his senses are heightened to the degree that they can be used offensively as well as defensively. And those bullets he chooses not to outrace bounce off him. Not like us. Not like the people of Earth. Still, he is similar to us in that Superman's compassion is both a strength and weakness. There is not a day that he does not risk his very life, heedless of the

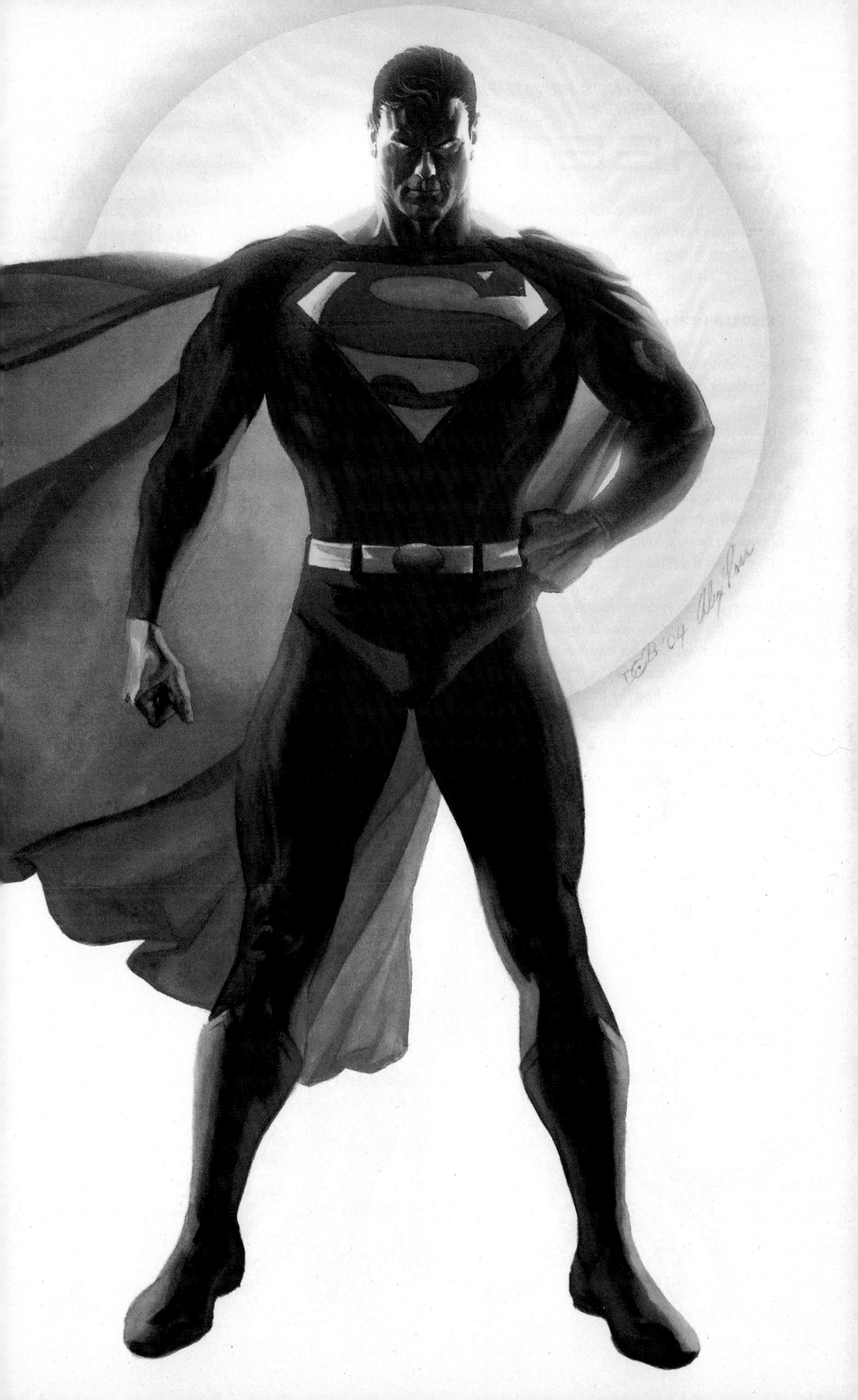

FROM BRUCE WAYNE'S PRIVATE FILES IN THE BATCOMPUTER

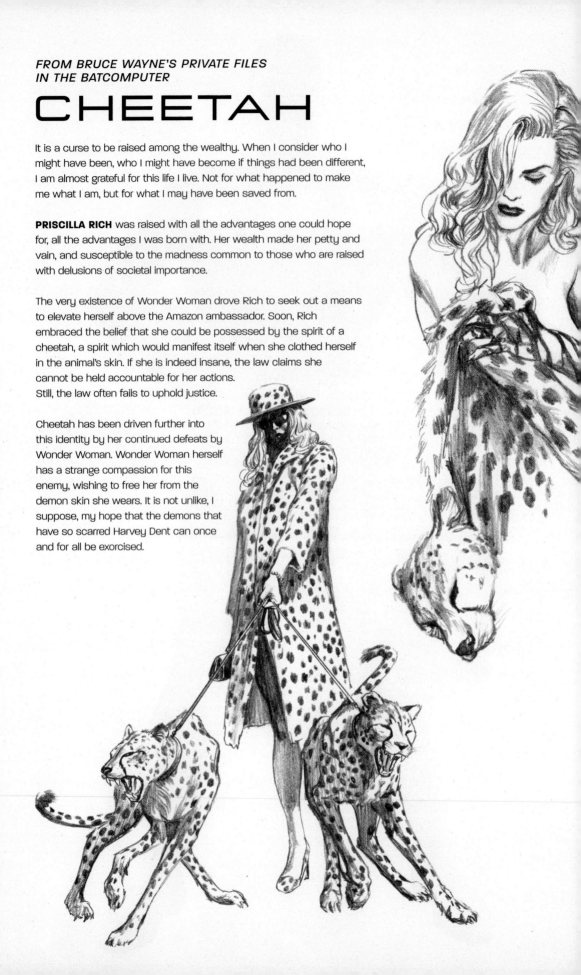

CHEETAH

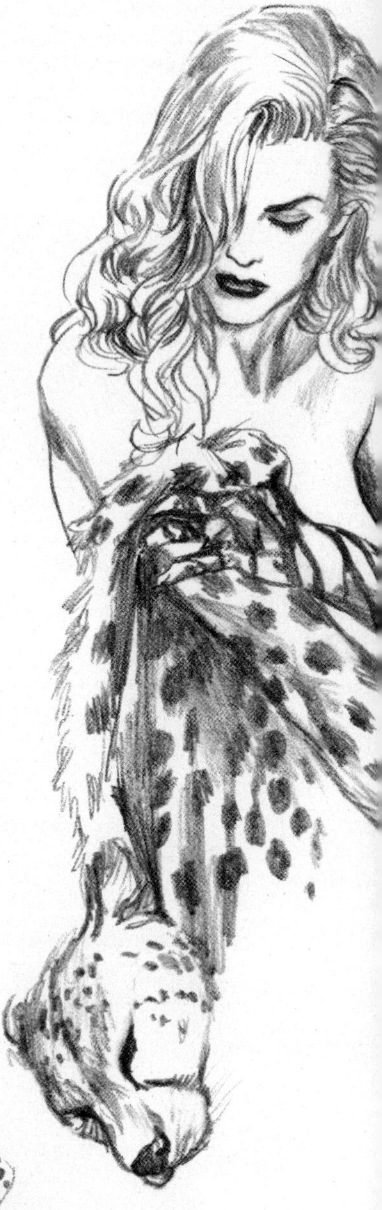

It is a curse to be raised among the wealthy. When I consider who I might have been, who I might have become if things had been different, I am almost grateful for this life I live. Not for what happened to make me what I am, but for what I may have been saved from.

PRISCILLA RICH was raised with all the advantages one could hope for, all the advantages I was born with. Her wealth made her petty and vain, and susceptible to the madness common to those who are raised with delusions of societal importance.

The very existence of Wonder Woman drove Rich to seek out a means to elevate herself above the Amazon ambassador. Soon, Rich embraced the belief that she could be possessed by the spirit of a cheetah, a spirit which would manifest itself when she clothed herself in the animal's skin. If she is indeed insane, the law claims she cannot be held accountable for her actions.
Still, the law often fails to uphold justice.

Cheetah has been driven further into this identity by her continued defeats by Wonder Woman. Wonder Woman herself has a strange compassion for this enemy, wishing to free her from the demon skin she wears. It is not unlike, I suppose, my hope that the demons that have so scarred Harvey Dent can once and for all be exorcised.

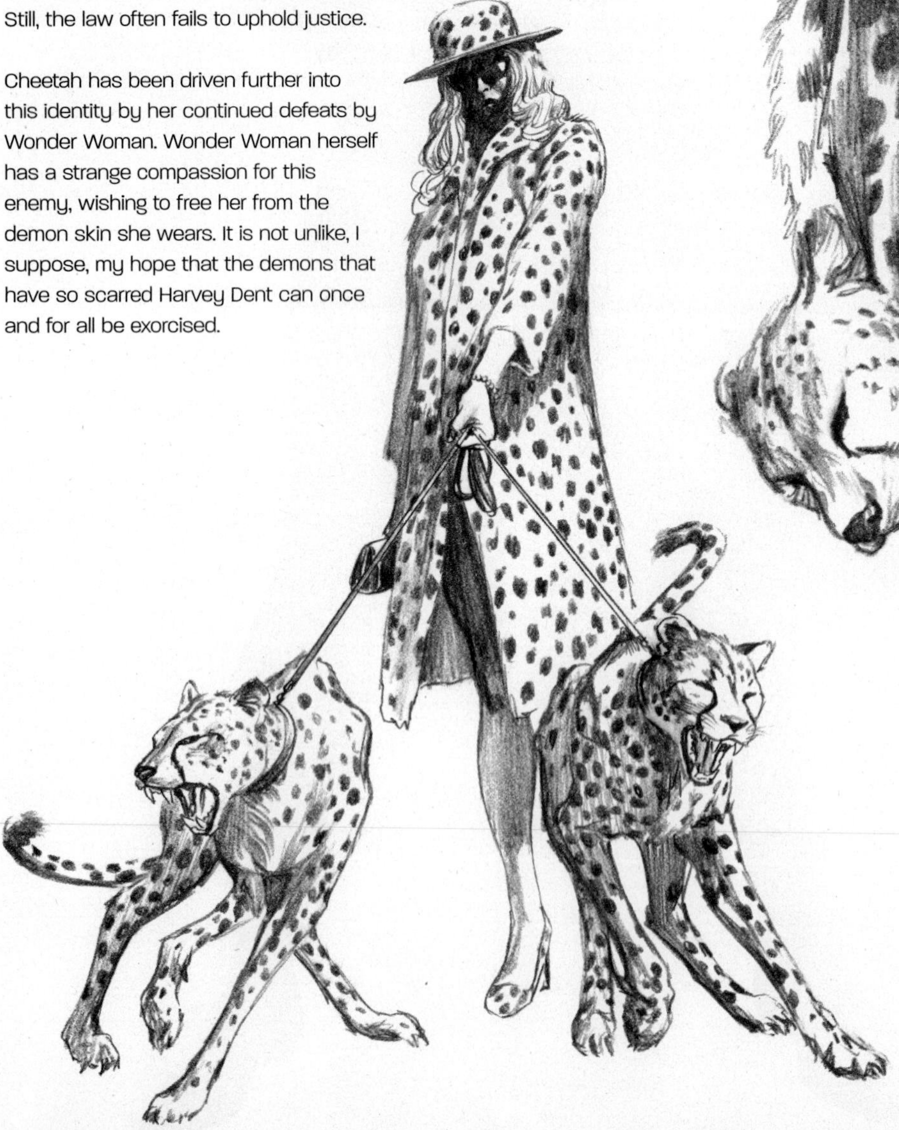

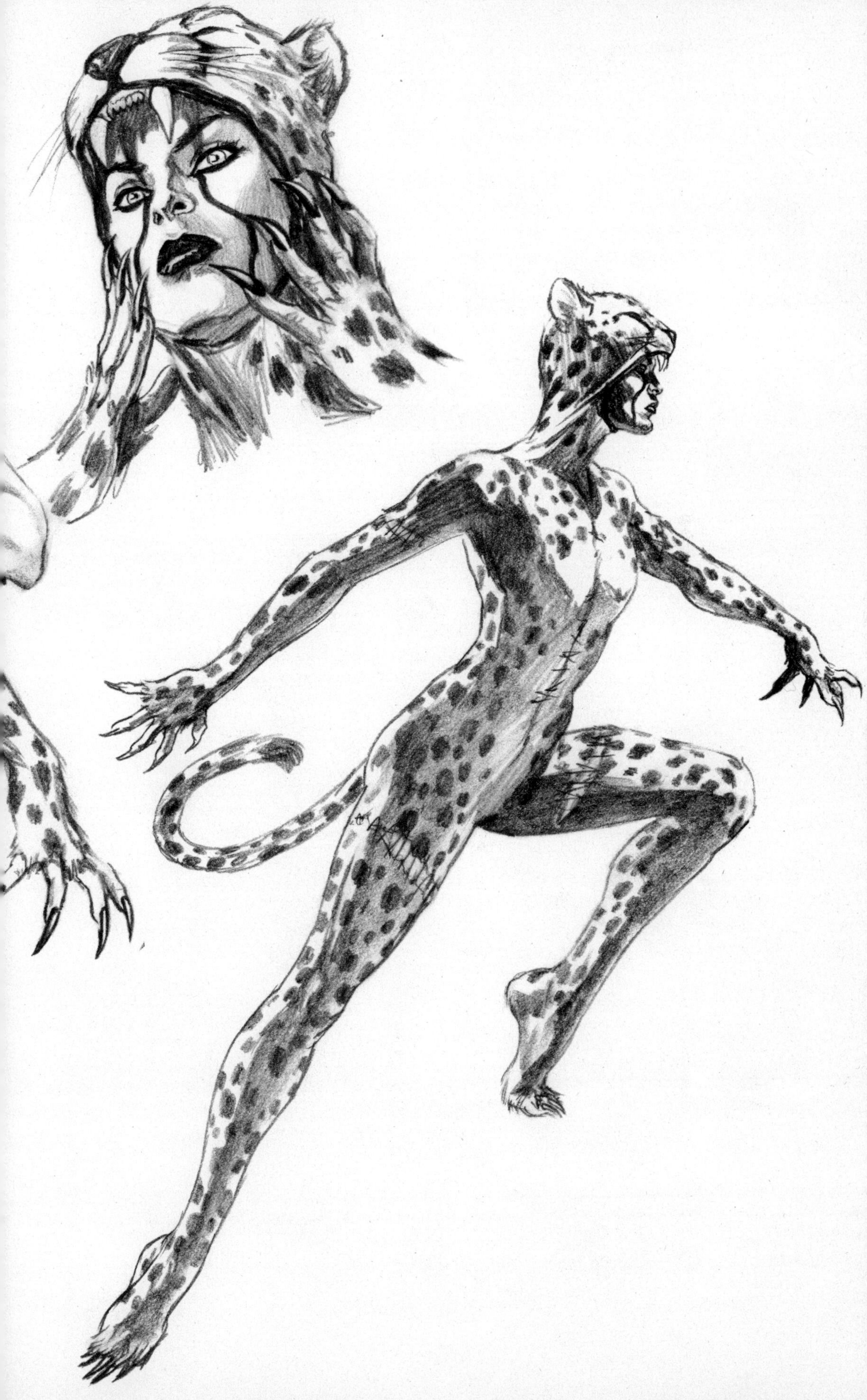

FROM BRUCE WAYNE'S PRIVATE FILES IN THE BATCOMPUTER

WONDER WOMAN

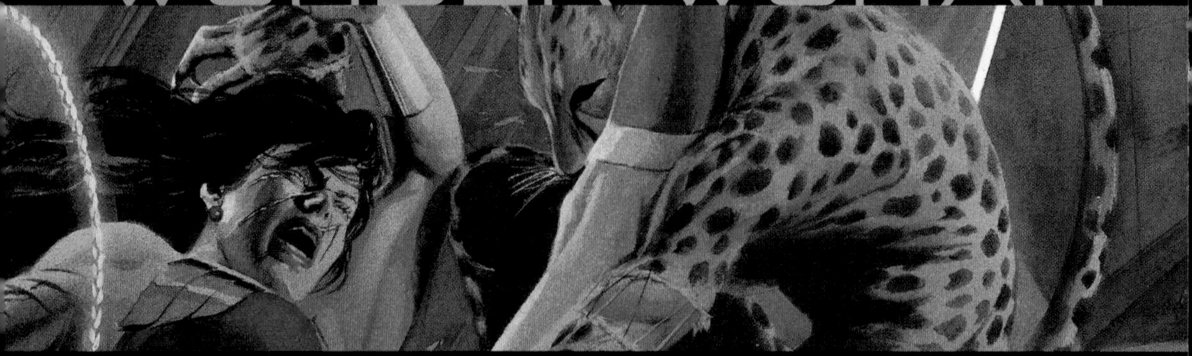

It is a mistake many make to categorize her as a warrior. She is far more than her training and skill suggest.

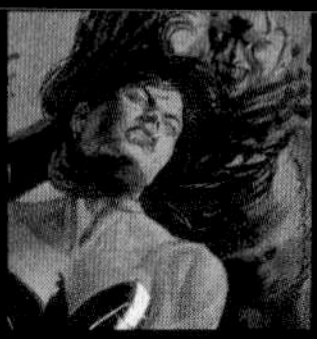

Her name is **PRINCESS DIANA**. Sometimes she hides her nature and identity, if such a thing were possible, under the name Diana Prince. By combat and contest she was chosen to represent an island nation of Amazon women who claim to be descendants of the Greek gods. She was one of the first members of the Justice League of America, and lives not to fight, but to work for peace. It is a mistake many make to categorize her as a warrior. She is far more than her training and skill suggest.

Evidence of her divine lineage includes a number of gifts, like those in myth, given by the gods. She carries a "Golden Lasso." It is unbreakable, and those confined by it are compelled to speak the truth. Its nature, by my inspection, is not scientific, but mysterious. I can find no reason for its properties. She wears bulletproof bracelets that she uses to defend herself, and has an invisible jet that allows her to travel the globe undetected, even by radar or heat-sensitive tracking devices.

Some have suggested that she is a perfect woman. And it is easy to see why popular speculation would see her as a possible mate for Superman. But I do not believe such a pairing ever to be possible. She understands too well the role we have chosen. She knows, unlike many in the League itself, that we cannot risk loved ones. They could become targets, our vulnerabilities.

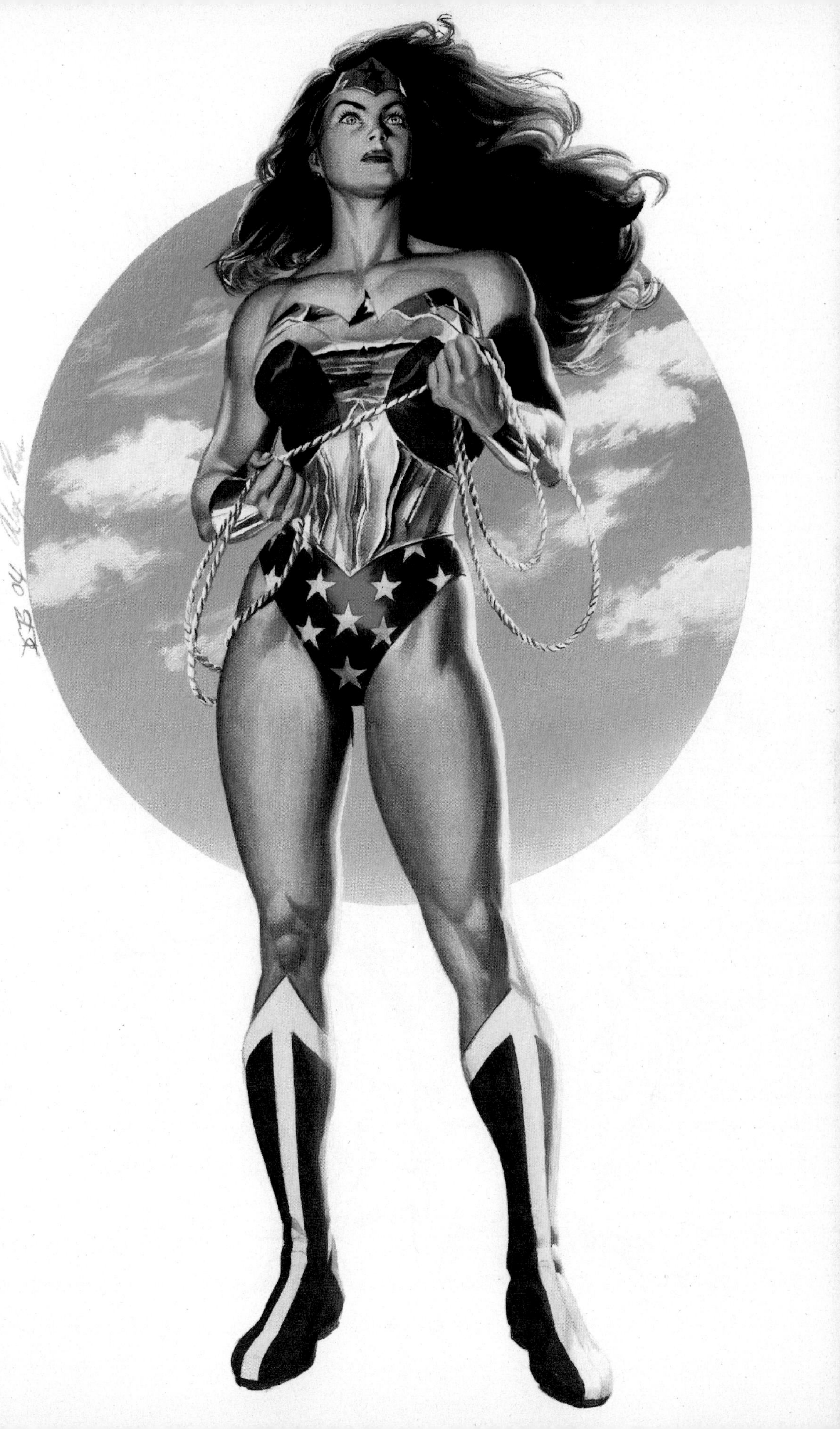

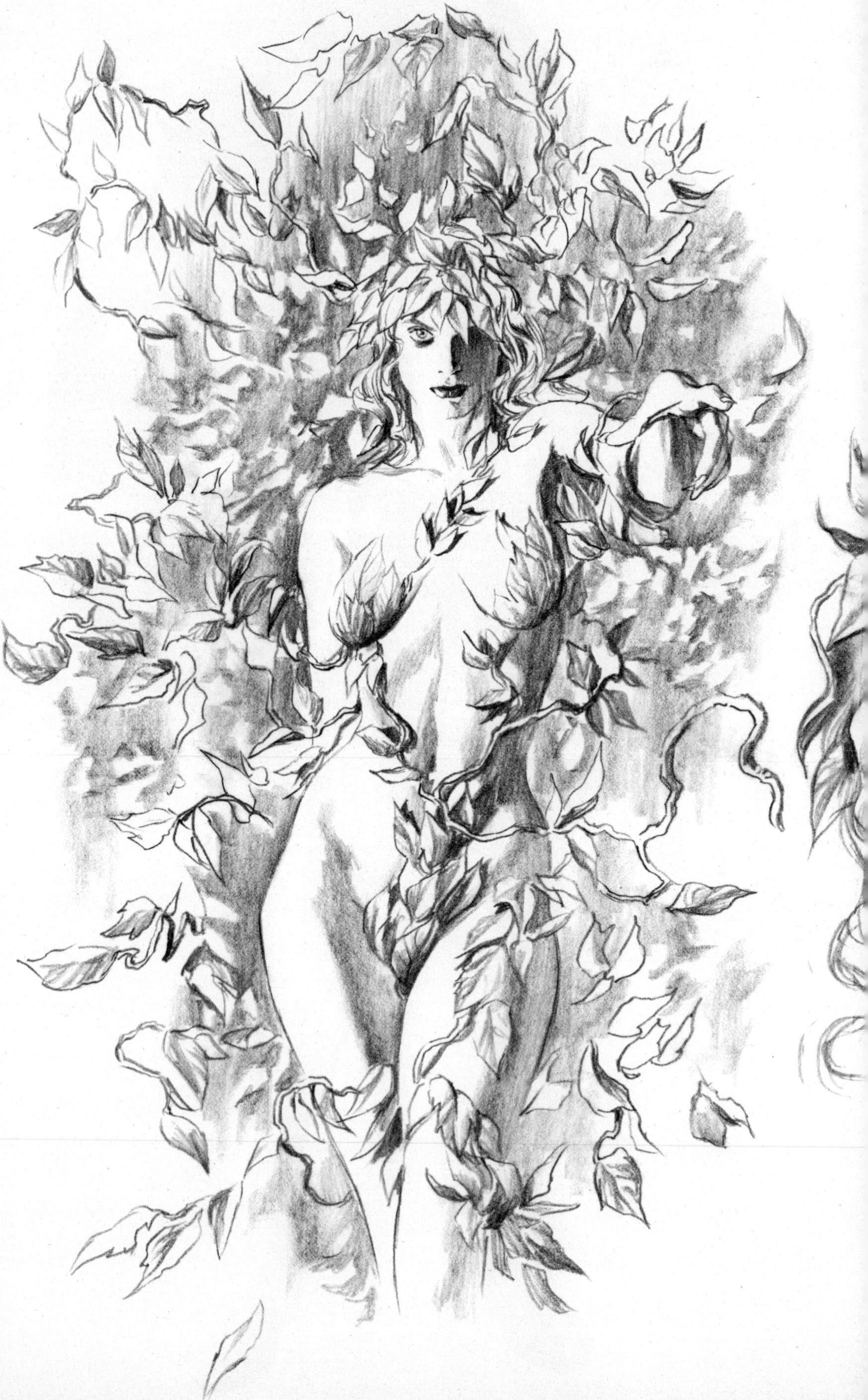

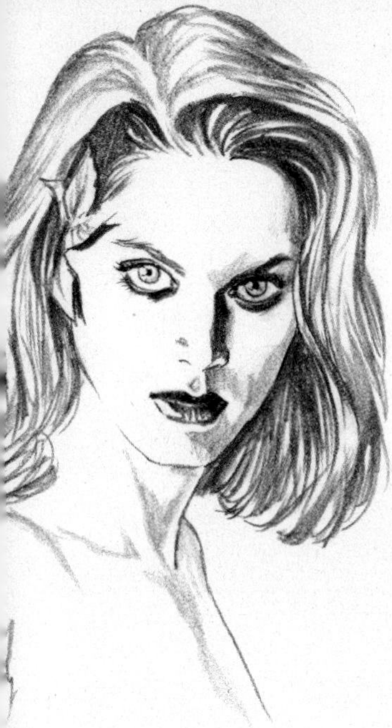

FROM BRUCE WAYNE'S PRIVATE FILES IN THE BATCOMPUTER

POISON IVY

PAMELA ISLEY is insane, dangerously so. Because of this, she cannot be dealt with by appealing solely to her mind. This is the mistake, I believe, of so many modern psychological treatments. We are far more complex than any one system of thought can claim to explain.

She became a criminal because of love, or what many mistake for it. Isley came from a rich family and had what would be considered a normal upbringing. In college, she majored in botany and fell in love with her professor. Her teacher fooled her with promises of love and marriage, and tricked her into stealing from a local museum's new Egyptian exhibit.

What she stole was an urn containing ancient poisonous herbs. But the herbs, intended to poison and kill Isley, instead mixed with her unique physiology, changing her, transforming her, making her immune to all poisons. Her sex appeal is now a weapon that she uses against all men, usually through the use of poisonous lipstick. My refusal to be manipulated by her allure has only caused her hatred of me to grow.

Her immunity to poison and her wild femininity are not her only weapons. In fact, these abilities are nothing compared to her intelligence and knowledge of plant life. She commands and is capable of manipulating the very life form necessary for every creature on Earth to breathe. That alone makes her one of the most dangerous beings alive.

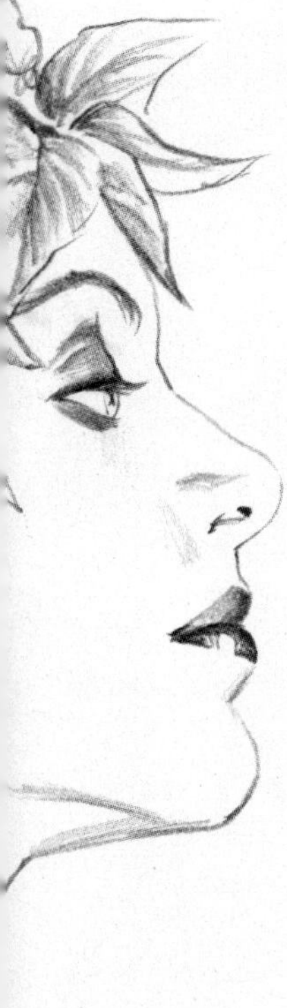

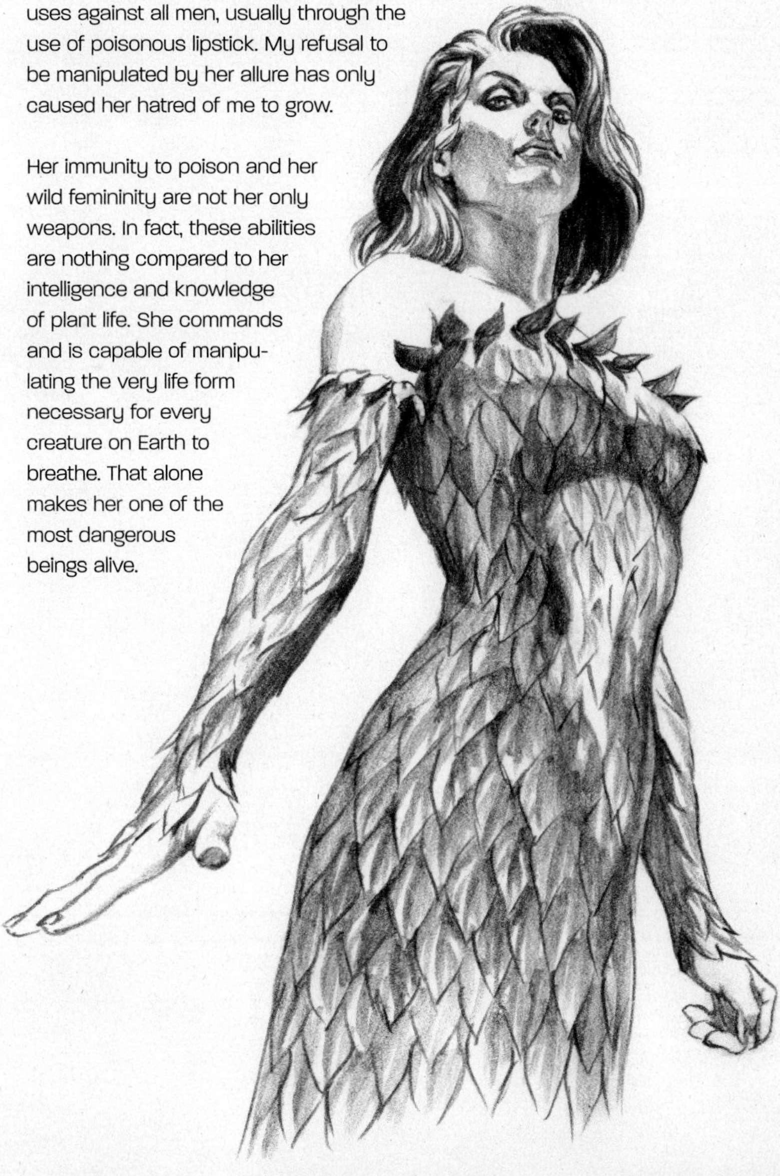

FROM BRUCE WAYNE'S PRIVATE FILES IN THE BATCOMPUTER

ATOM

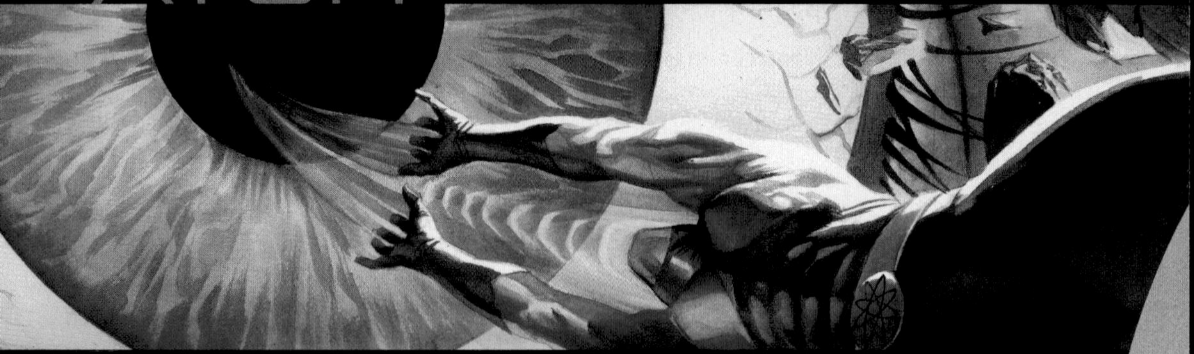

PROFESSOR RAY PALMER is a genius, a physicist who stumbled upon the remains of a white dwarf star. Palmer used fragments of the star to further his experiments in matter reduction. His experiments failed time and time again, but necessity and his belief that he could not fail forever forced Palmer to experiment upon himself, with success.

Palmer graduated from college and married Jean Loring. He became the Atom and used his life as a hero to fight crime and establish his wife's career as one of the predominant criminal lawyers in the state. Palmer became a hero for love. It is this notion that separates him from so many of the other members of the League. But I wonder, what would happen if Loring were not a part of the equation? I cannot believe the cavalier basis on which he fights crime. We cannot have relationships.

Palmer became a hero for love. It is this notion that separates him from so many of the other members of the League.

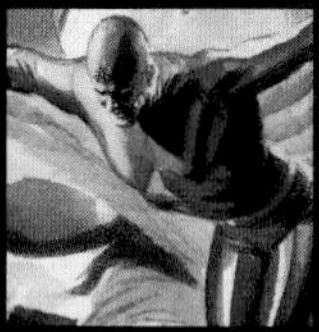

Palmer is capable of reducing himself to tiny, even subatomic, size. He can ride electronic impulses through phone lines. Despite all his discoveries, and all his experience battling crime, he has yet to find anything at a subatomic level that suggests a propensity for crime.

Crime is a choice, a matter of will. Modern sociology is the crime of suggesting that it is not.

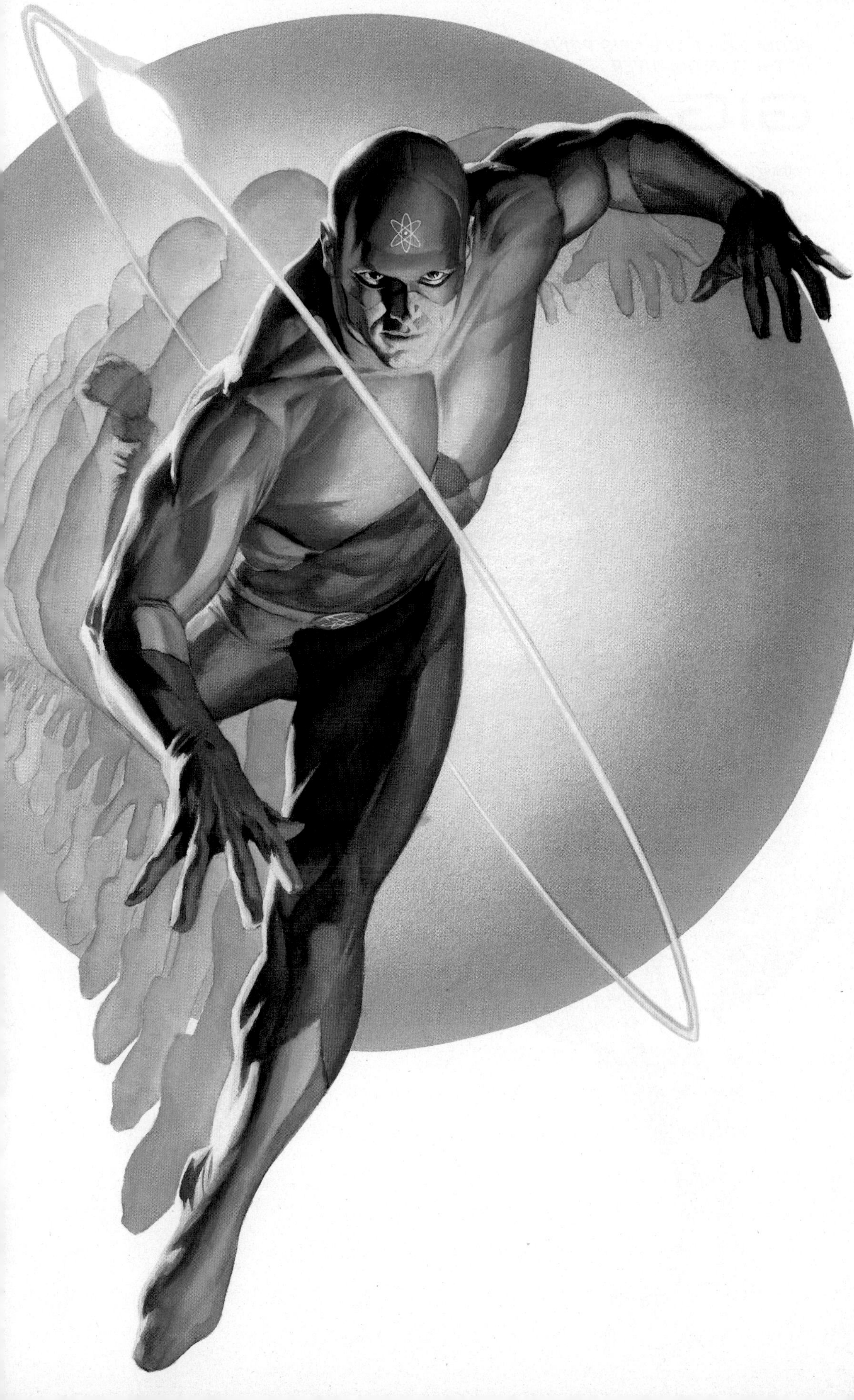

FROM BRUCE WAYNE'S PRIVATE FILES IN THE BATCOMPUTER

GIGANTA

Nothing is known about **GIGANTA**, except that she was somehow evolved from an ape by technology that originated in Gorilla City. I do not yet know if there is a Grodd connection. Giganta's aggression suggests that she is not a citizen of Gorilla City, as Solovar and all the denizens of Gorilla City are dedicated to peace.

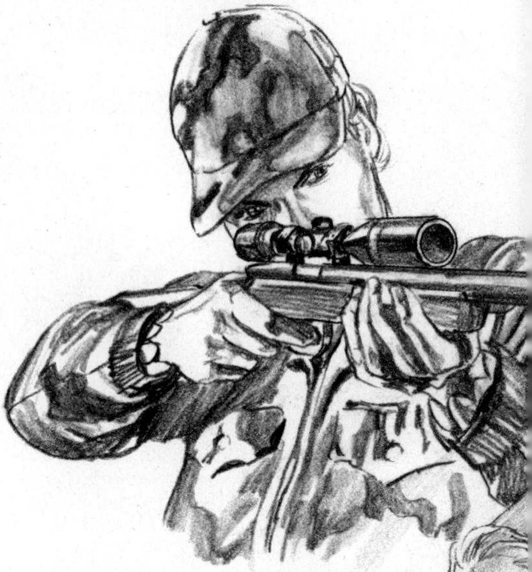

Her ability to manipulate her size suggests powers similar to those of the Atom. Perhaps he'll, one day, have to face her. I'm not sure Ray has it in him to strike her. I'll have to impress upon Ray the fact that she's a gorilla. And evil.

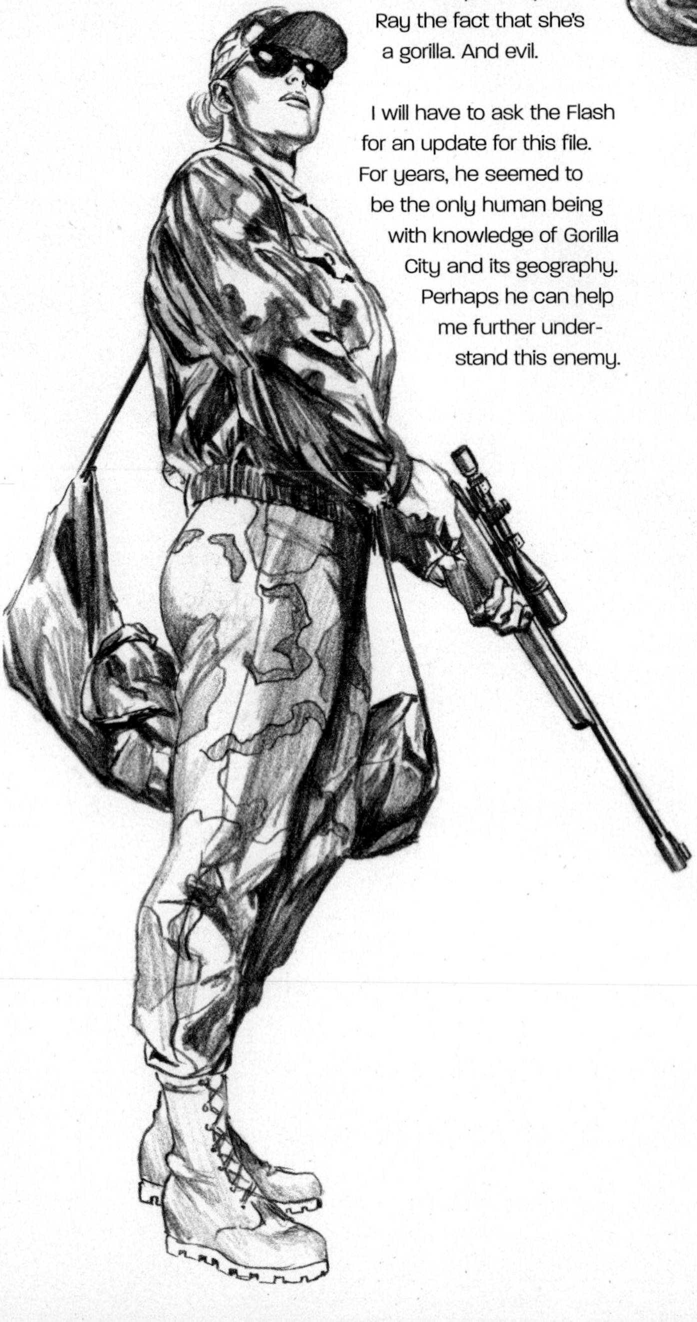

I will have to ask the Flash for an update for this file. For years, he seemed to be the only human being with knowledge of Gorilla City and its geography. Perhaps he can help me further understand this enemy.

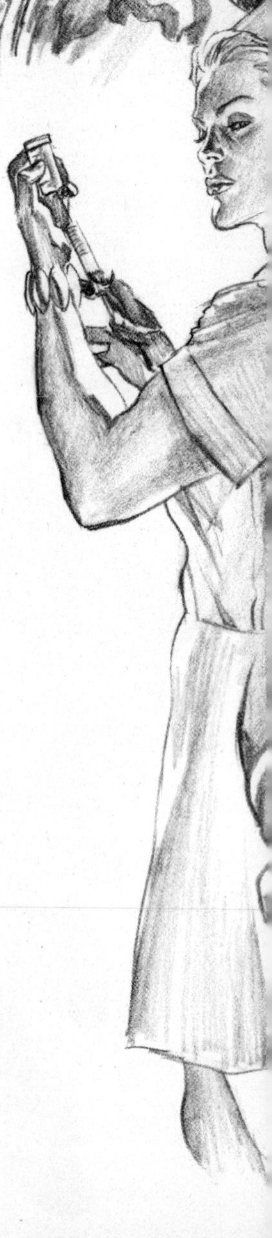

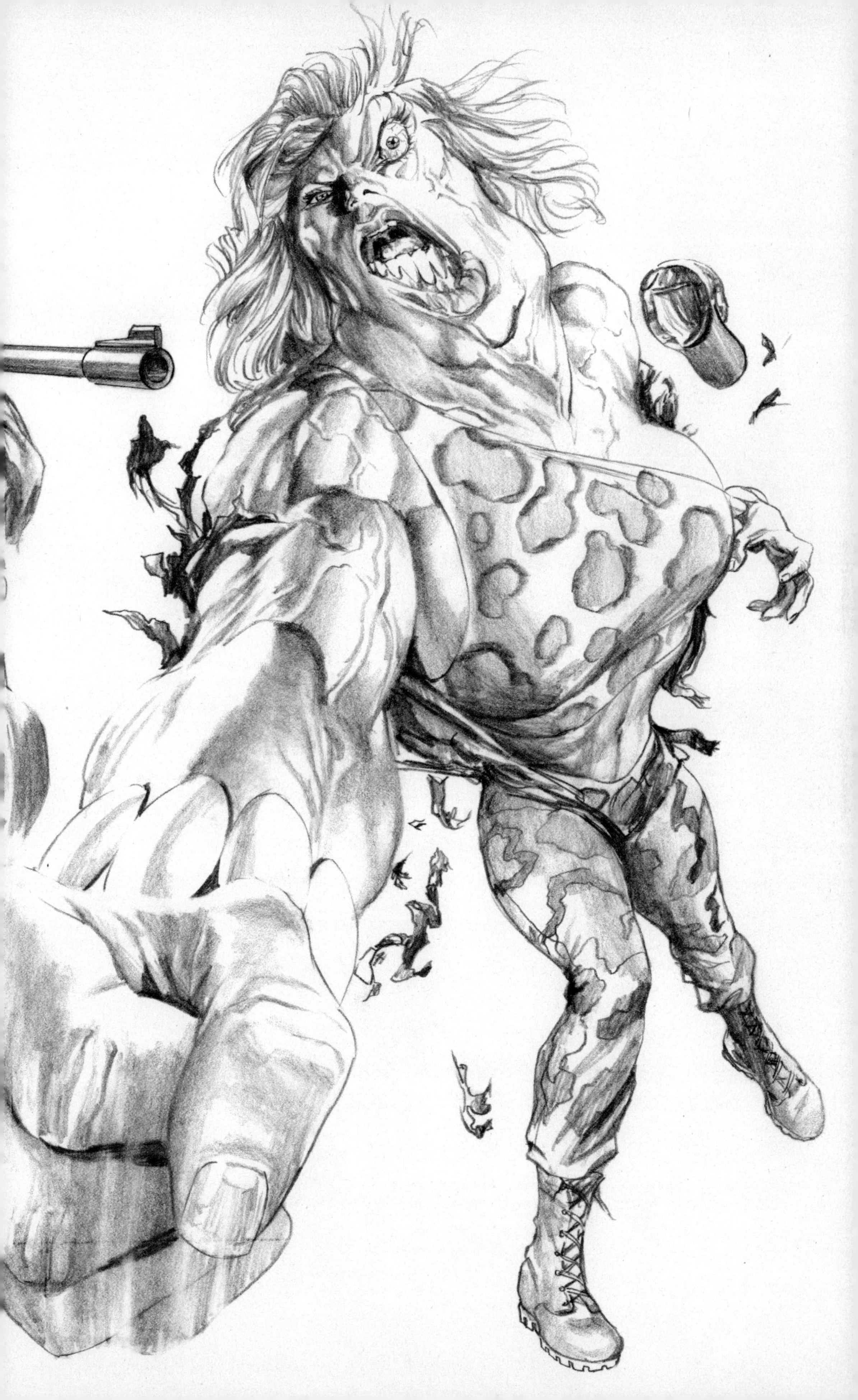

FROM BRUCE WAYNE'S PRIVATE FILES IN THE BATCOMPUTER

HAWKMAN

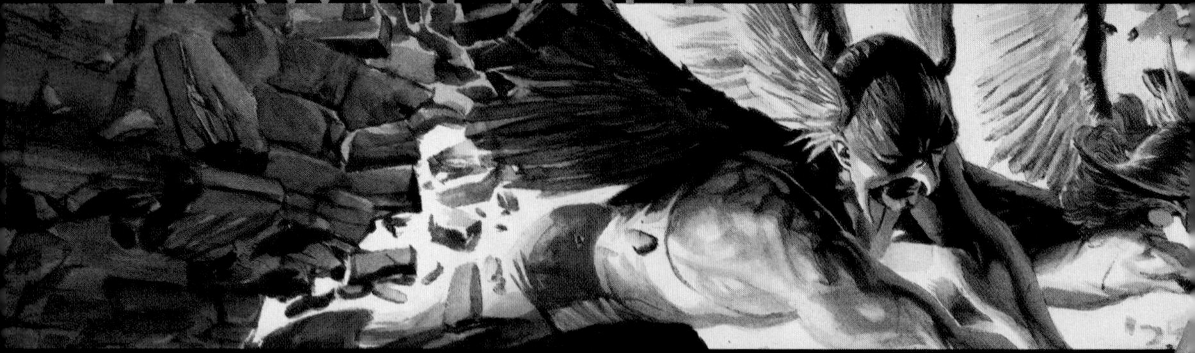

KATAR HOL was the equivalent of a policeman on his home planet of Thanagar. He and his wife, Shayera, came to Earth in pursuit of a criminal from their own planet. To them, crime is a disease, one that all but destroyed their once prison-free world. This disease was like a cancer: it spread. Attempting to contain it brought them to Earth.

It was here that they adopted the roles of Hawkman and Hawkgirl, recognizing humanity's willingness to accept an alien super hero more quickly than an alien manhunter. Katar and Shayera, married on Thanagar, altered the pronunciation of their names to fit human dialects, becoming Carter and Shiera Hall, and members of the Justice League of America.

Both can fly at great speeds due to artificial wings and antigravity belts. While they have a Thanagarian ship filled with weapons hidden just outside Earth's orbit, it is their study of Earth's history and weaponry that has become their primary passion. Carter and Shiera act as co-directors of the Midway City Museum, a cover set up by their human policeman ally, Commissioner George Emmett.

Perhaps the driving imperative for why Carter remains on Earth is this: he remembers a time before there was crime on his world. He can envision what this world might look like should crime be eliminated. For me, this notion seems to be impossible. Still, if it is not possible, why do we fight? Is it just to keep the world from becoming impossibly corrupt?

Perhaps the driving imperative for why Carter remains on Earth is this: he remembers a time before there was crime on his world.

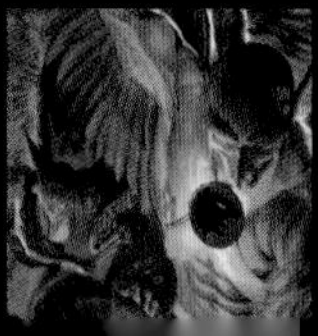

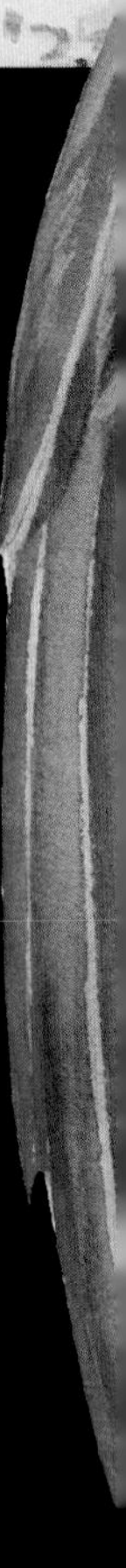

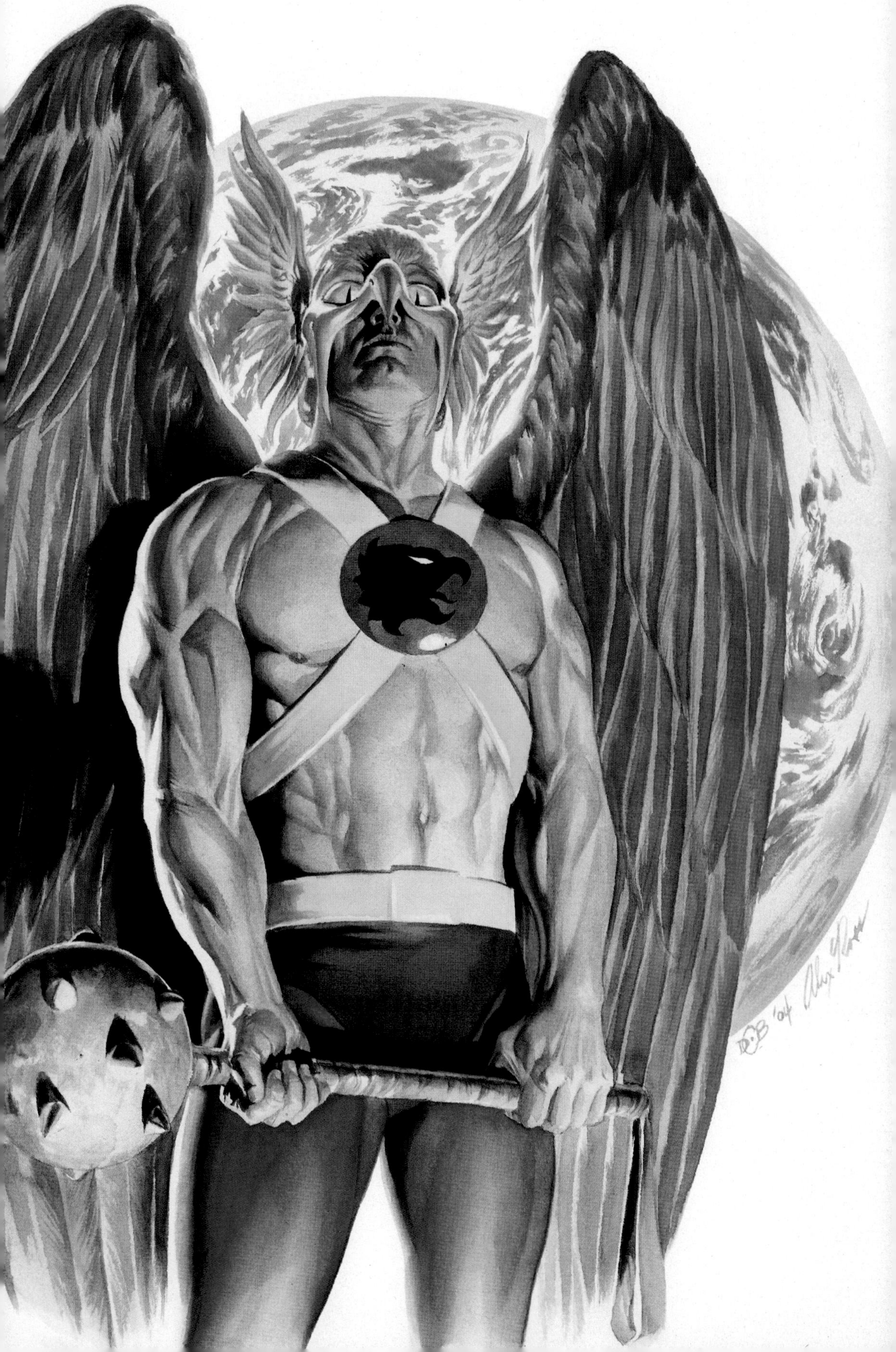

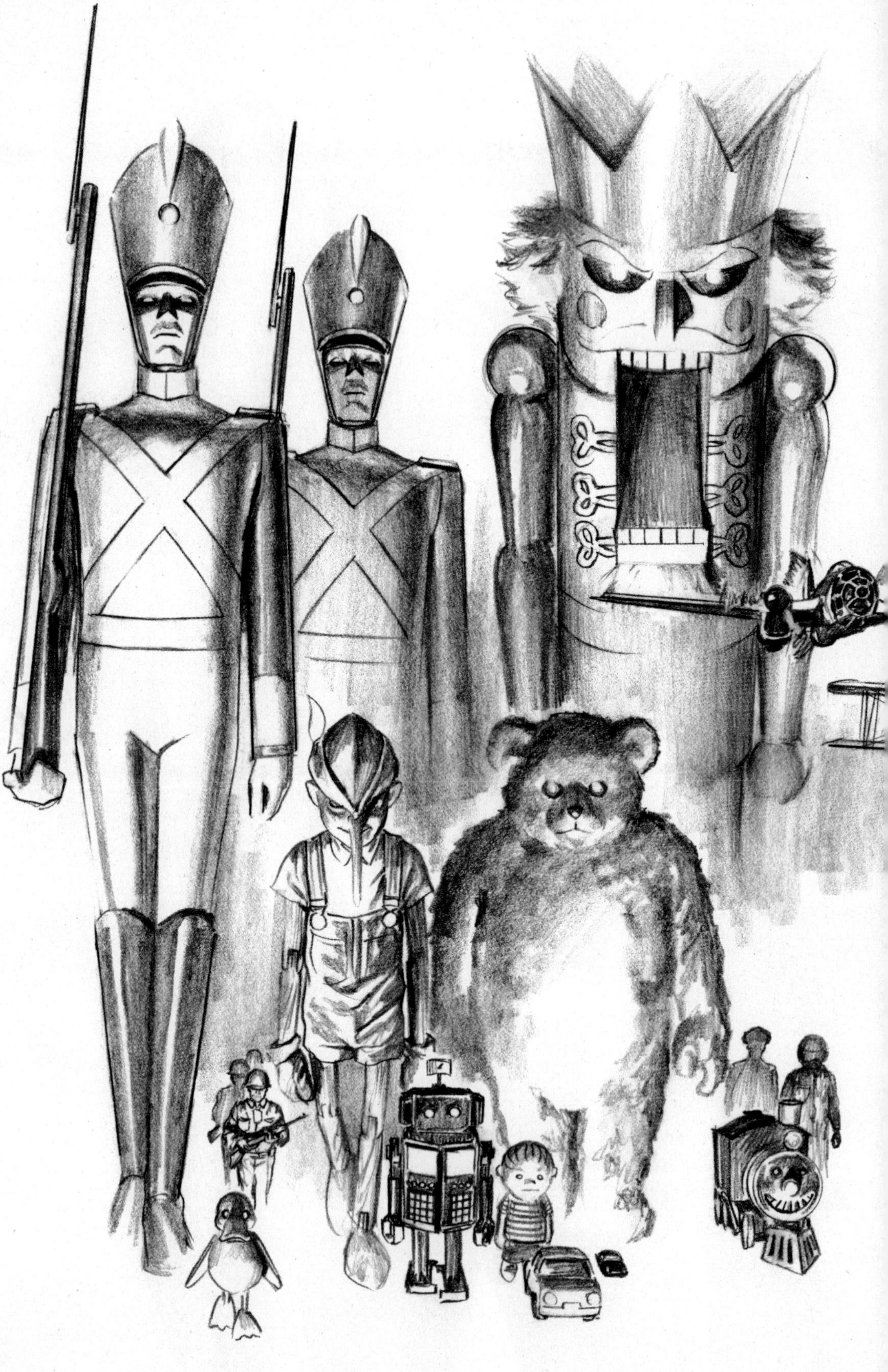

FROM BRUCE WAYNE'S PRIVATE FILES IN THE BATCOMPUTER

TOYMAN

Crimes with children as victims or witnesses must be the worst of all. In the case of **WINSLOW P. SCHOTT**, the crime was theft. When still a boy genius, Winslow built his first toy, a model plane, and had it stolen from him. The criminal in question, Winslow's next-door neighbor, was a boy about his own age.

Many would say this was merely a child wanting another child's toy. That it is completely natural. Are we all so naïve? For Winslow, it was far more than the theft, though. It is the compulsion of the criminal that leads him or her to crime. If Winslow's toys could be stolen by another child, why couldn't Winslow steal from others? Moreover, why couldn't he commit thefts using toys that he had built?

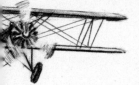

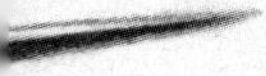

Schott's obsession is more than his proclivity toward crime. It's a desire for publicity, a childlike and almost l imitless need to be in the center of everything. His aspiration to be known for his genius is one of the primary reasons he has spent as much time behind bars as he has.

The Toyman has no special physical abilities save his ability to create toys of all forms and sizes — toys that can crack safes, deliver explosives, murder and far more. His killer toys have all but defeated Superman in the past.

Crime twists the entire world. It can turn the weapons of an adult against a child, and it can turn toys against those meant topro

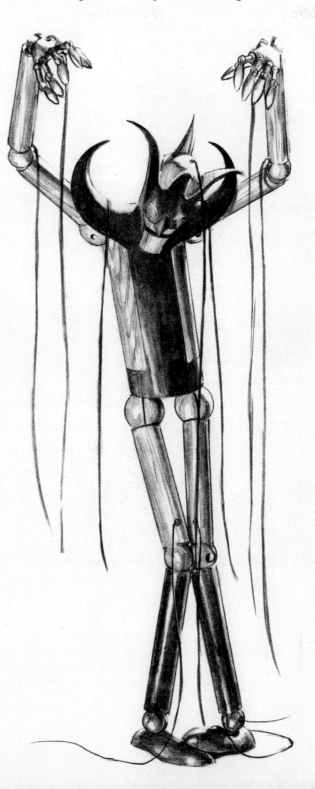

FROM BRUCE WAYNE'S PRIVATE FILES
IN THE BATCOMPUTER

THE FLASH

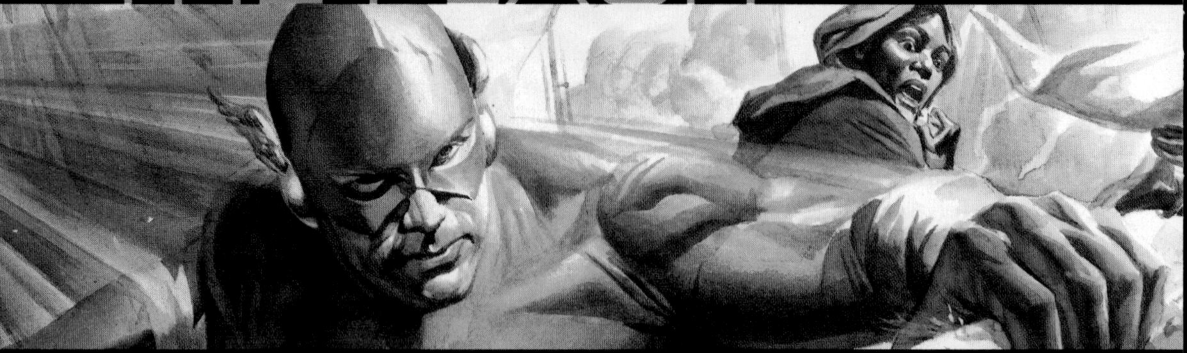

There is no place Allen cannot be in seconds, no foe he cannot outrun or outrace.

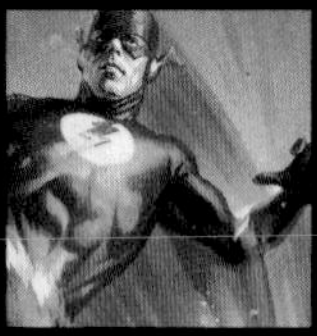

BARRY ALLEN is the kind of man I would have hoped to become had my parents not been murdered before my eyes. He is a forensic specialist for the Central City Police Department. There is no shadow on his record or his past. And when he is the Flash, he may move too fast to even cast a shadow.

Years ago, Barry Allen was working late in his laboratory when it was struck by lightning. The bolt struck him as well as certain chemicals in a nearby cabinet. The chemicals — their composition changed by the lightning — exploded in Allen's face and transformed him into a being who could move at super-human speed. There is no place Allen cannot be in seconds, no foe he cannot outrun or outrace. He has trained himself to vibrate his molecules at such high velocity that he can pass through walls and even step into different dimensions and eras.

Allen is married. His wife's name is Iris. As our identities must be guarded at all costs, the same applies to our families. The exposure of one is the exposure of both.

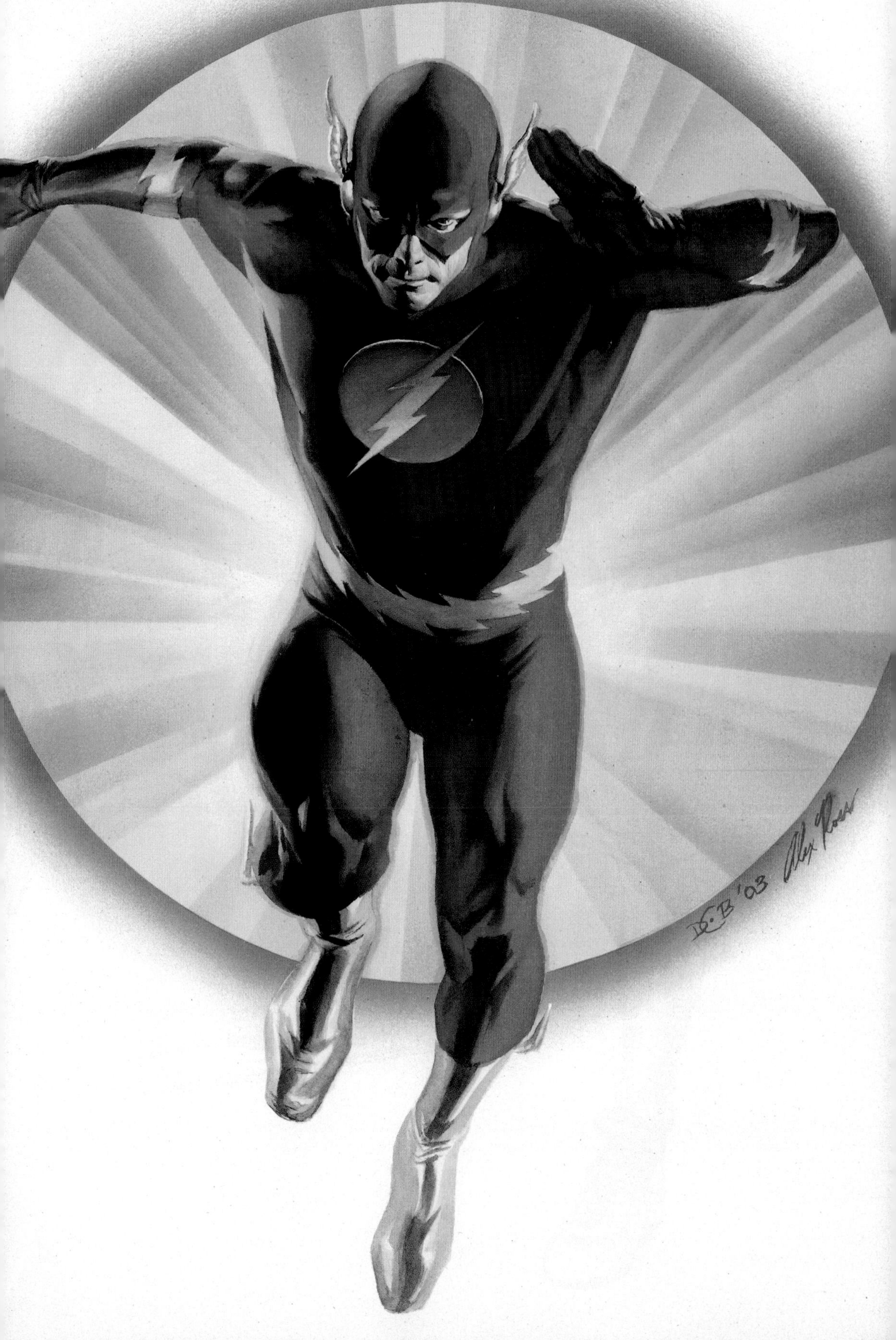

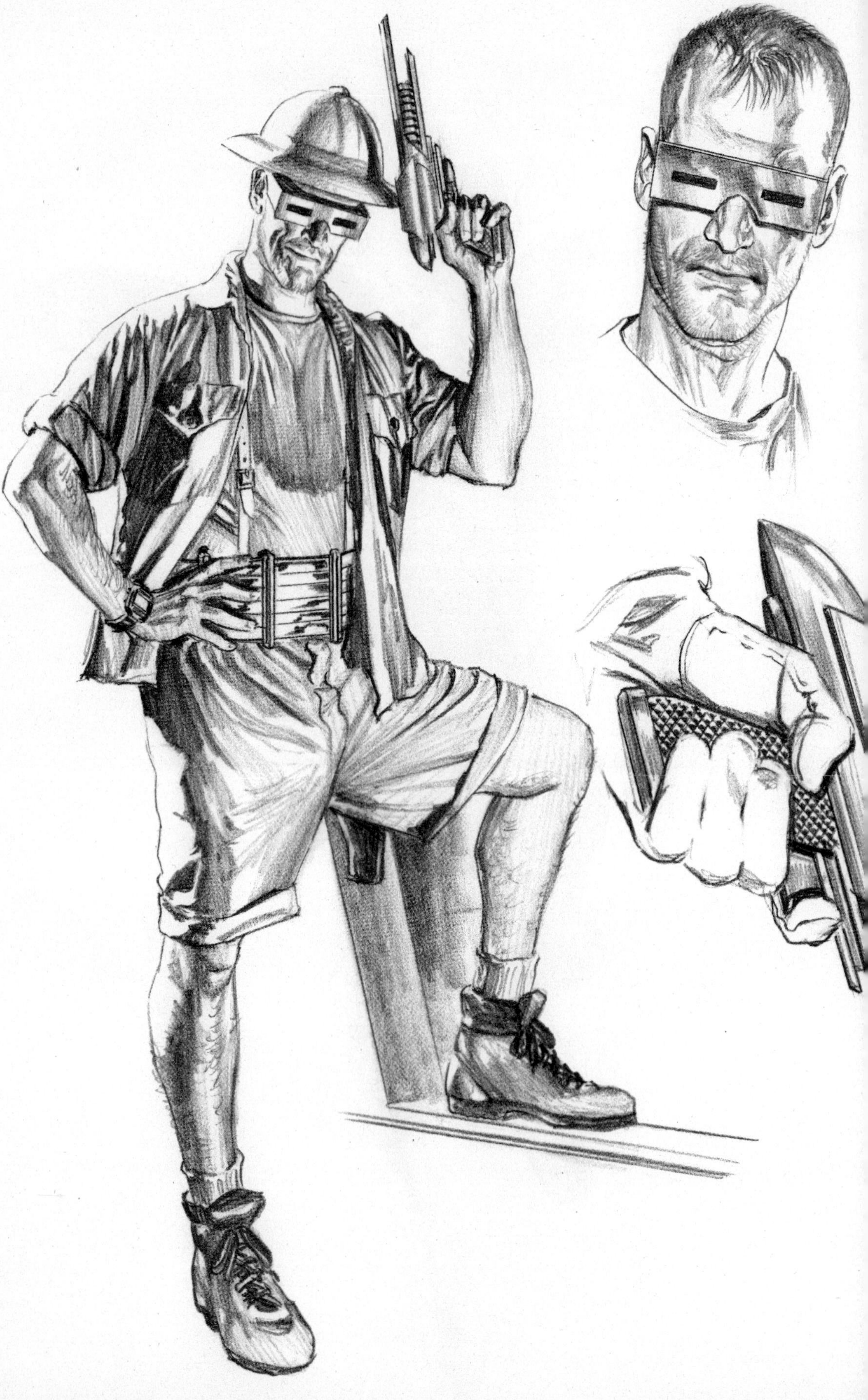

FROM BRUCE WAYNE'S PRIVATE FILES IN THE BATCOMPUTER

CAPTAIN COLD

LEONARD SNART is a professional criminal and, oddly enough, a man with little vision. He desired a criminal career in Central City and therefore dedicated himself to killing the Flash as a start. Despite his rational mind, he is a fool. Believing a cyclotron could stop the Flash, he attempted to steal one, but in the process he triggered the cyclotron. It irradiated Snart's experimental handgun and transformed it into a freezing device that he has used on the Flash and Central City numerous times.

It is surprising to think how many of the Justice League members or superpowered criminals seem to be created as a result of accidents. Snart now calls himself Captain Cold. He seems satisfied with the basest of crimes, selling his services for wealth more than for power. For comfort more than for control.

His wants are petty. And that is the way to defeat him.

Justice #5 third printing.

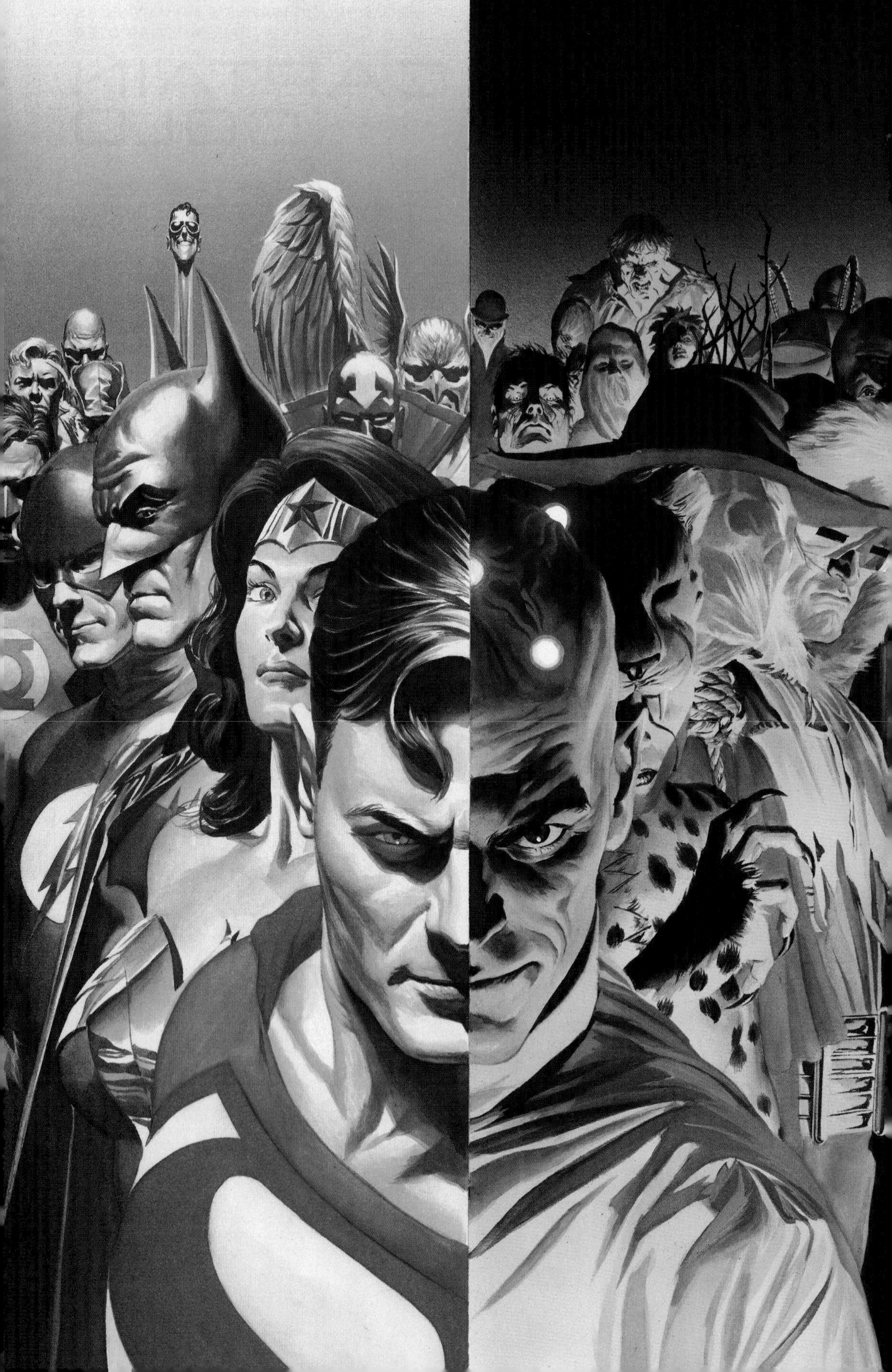

ORIGINAL PENCILS

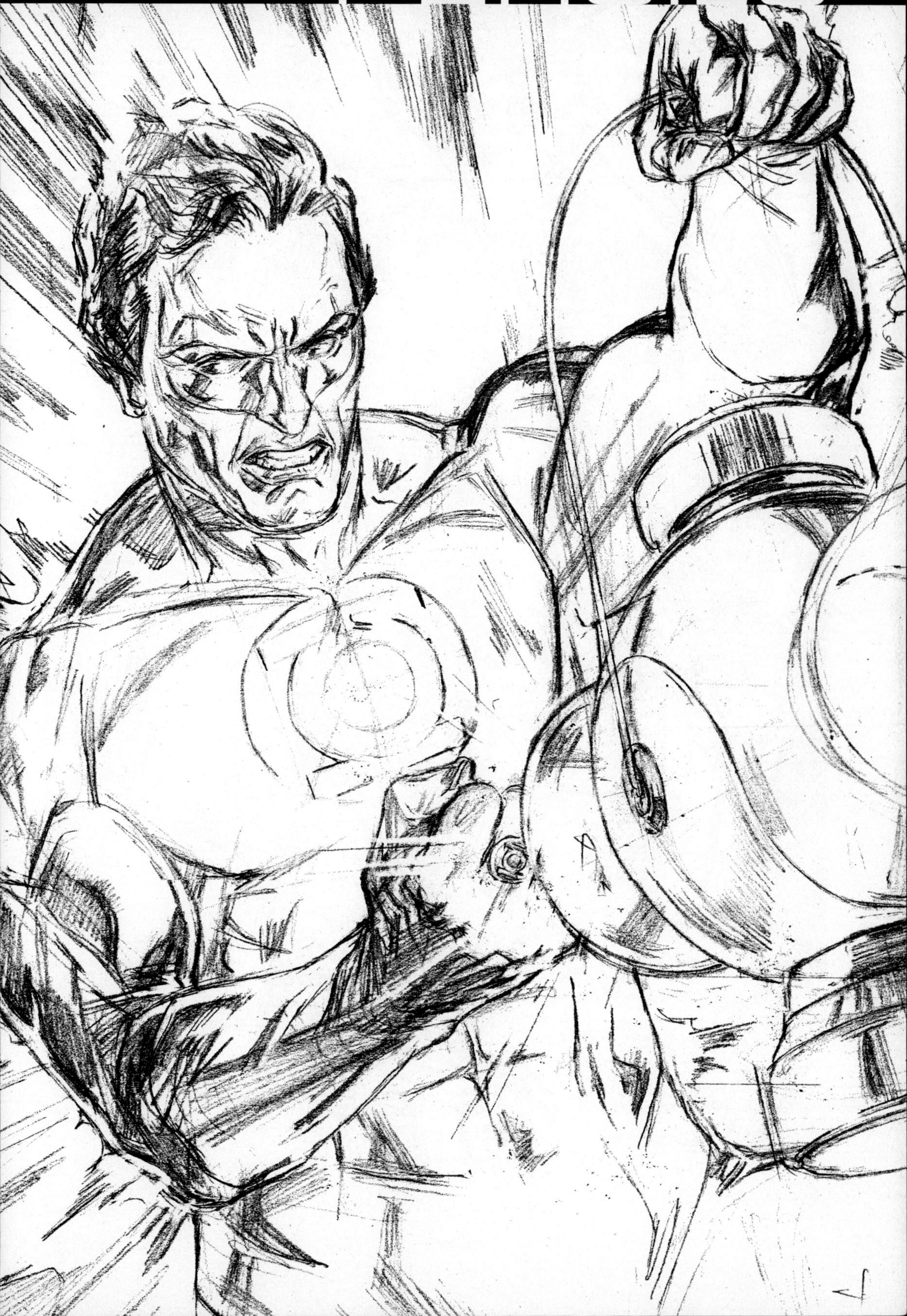

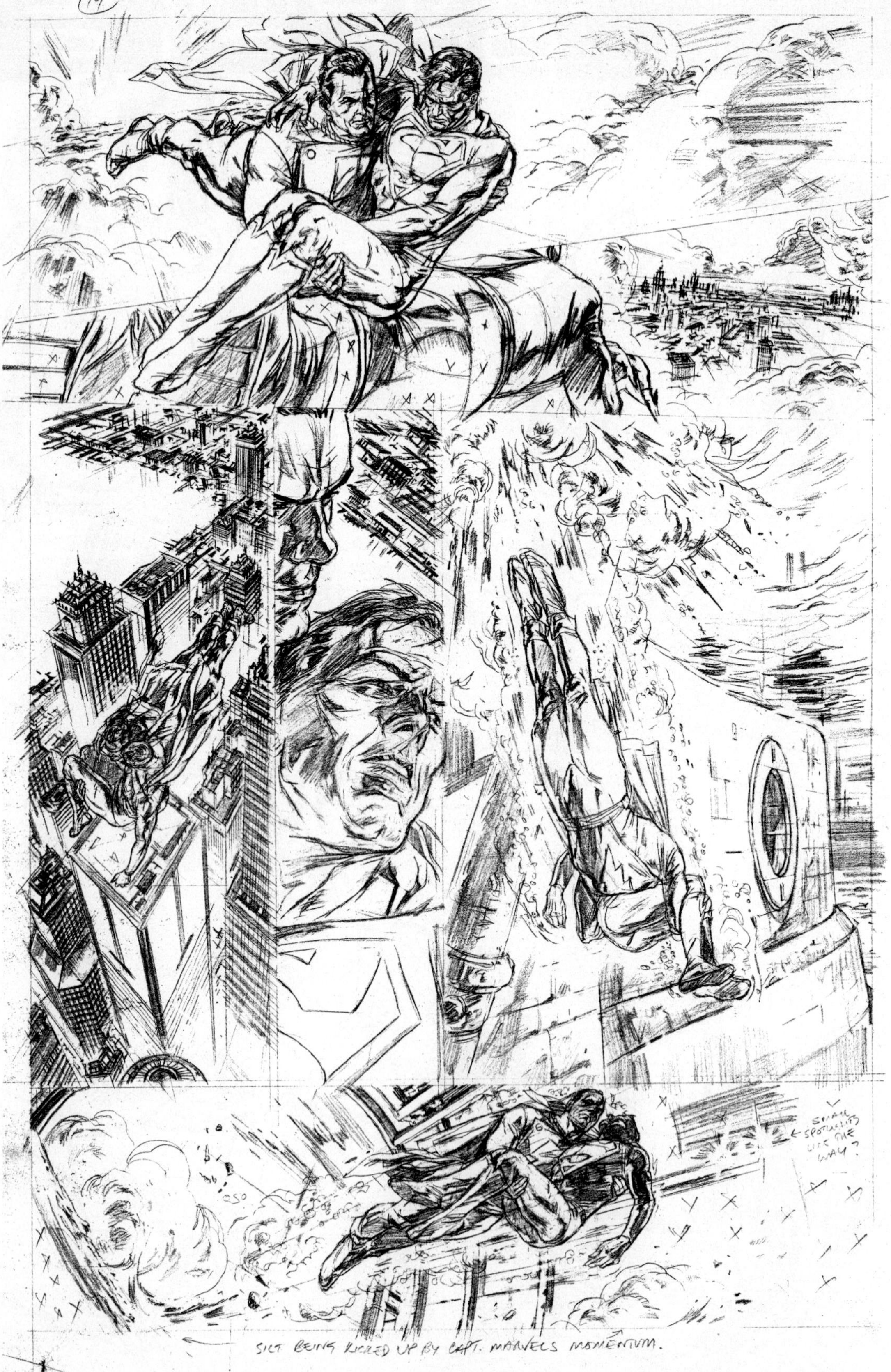

SMALL SPOTLIGHTS LIKE THE WAY?
SILT BEING KICKED UP BY CAPT. MARVELS MOMENTUM.

(8)

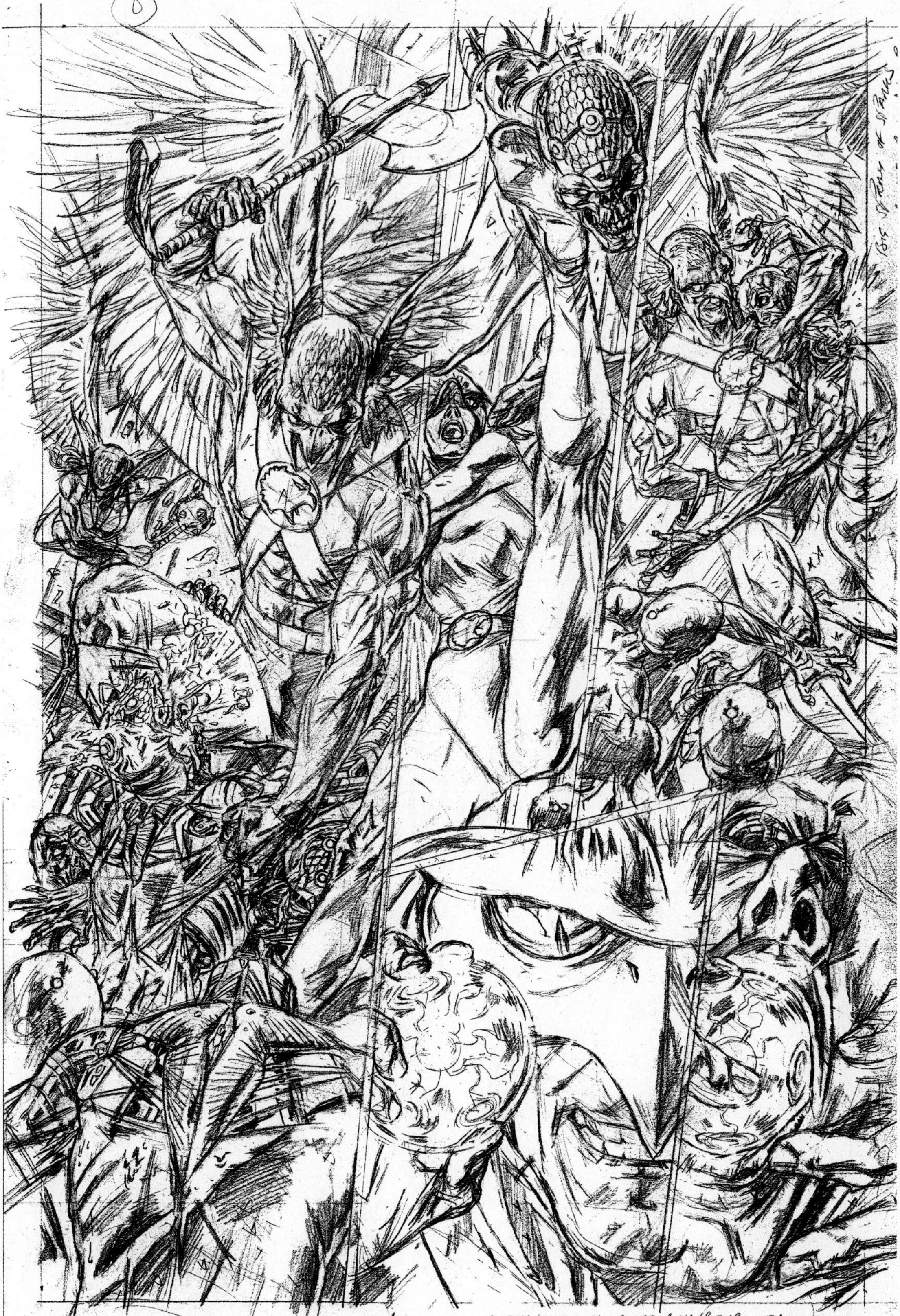

BIG SPRAY OF SPARKS

17.

GOLDEN COLORED GLASS BALL/BOMB. WITHIN IT WE SEE A MINI ENERGY SOURCE WITH TENDRILS COMING OFF OF IT BOUNCING OFF THE INSIDE.

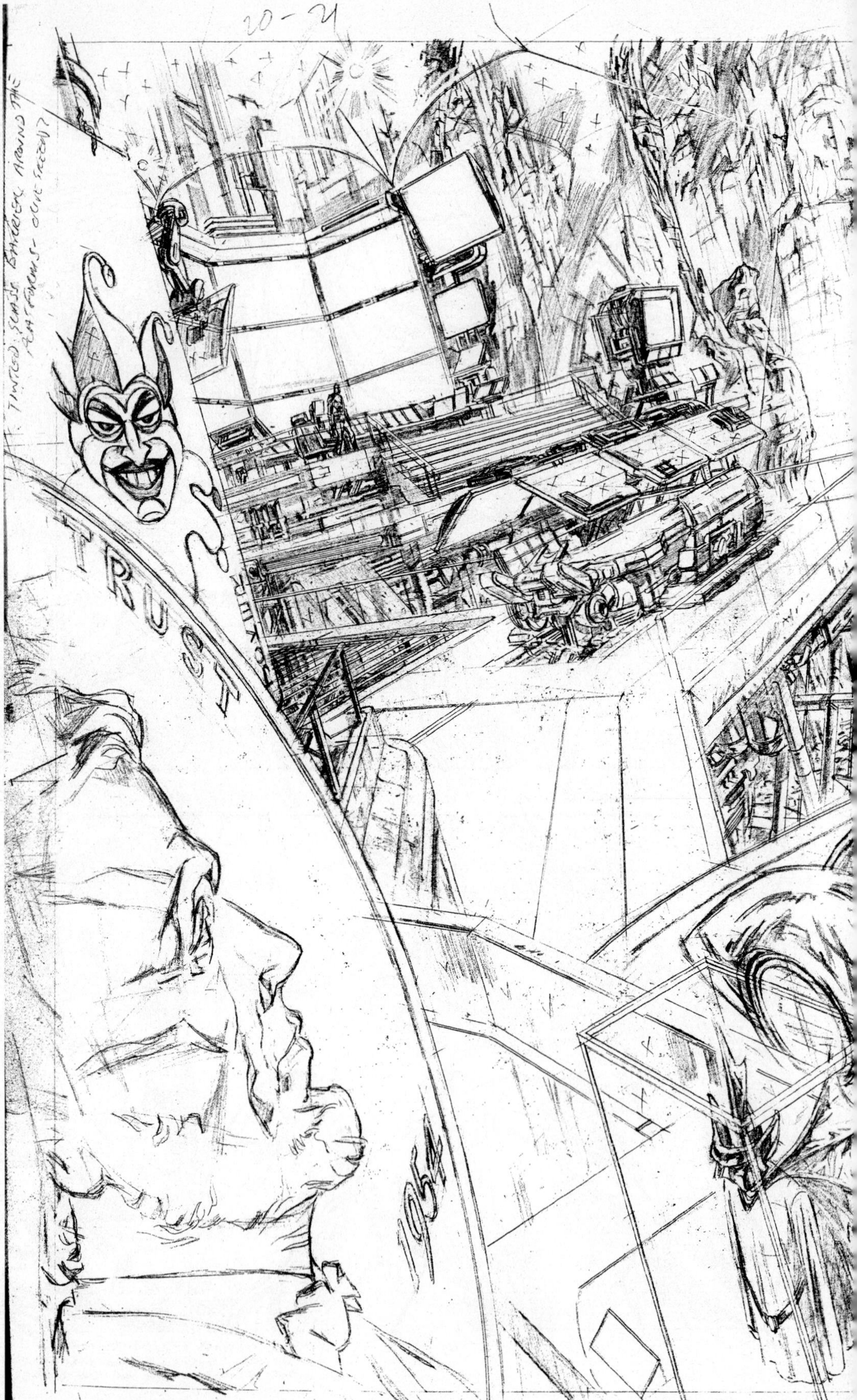

20-21
TINTED GLASS BARRIER AROUND THE PLATFORMS - OVERSEEN?
TRUST
1054

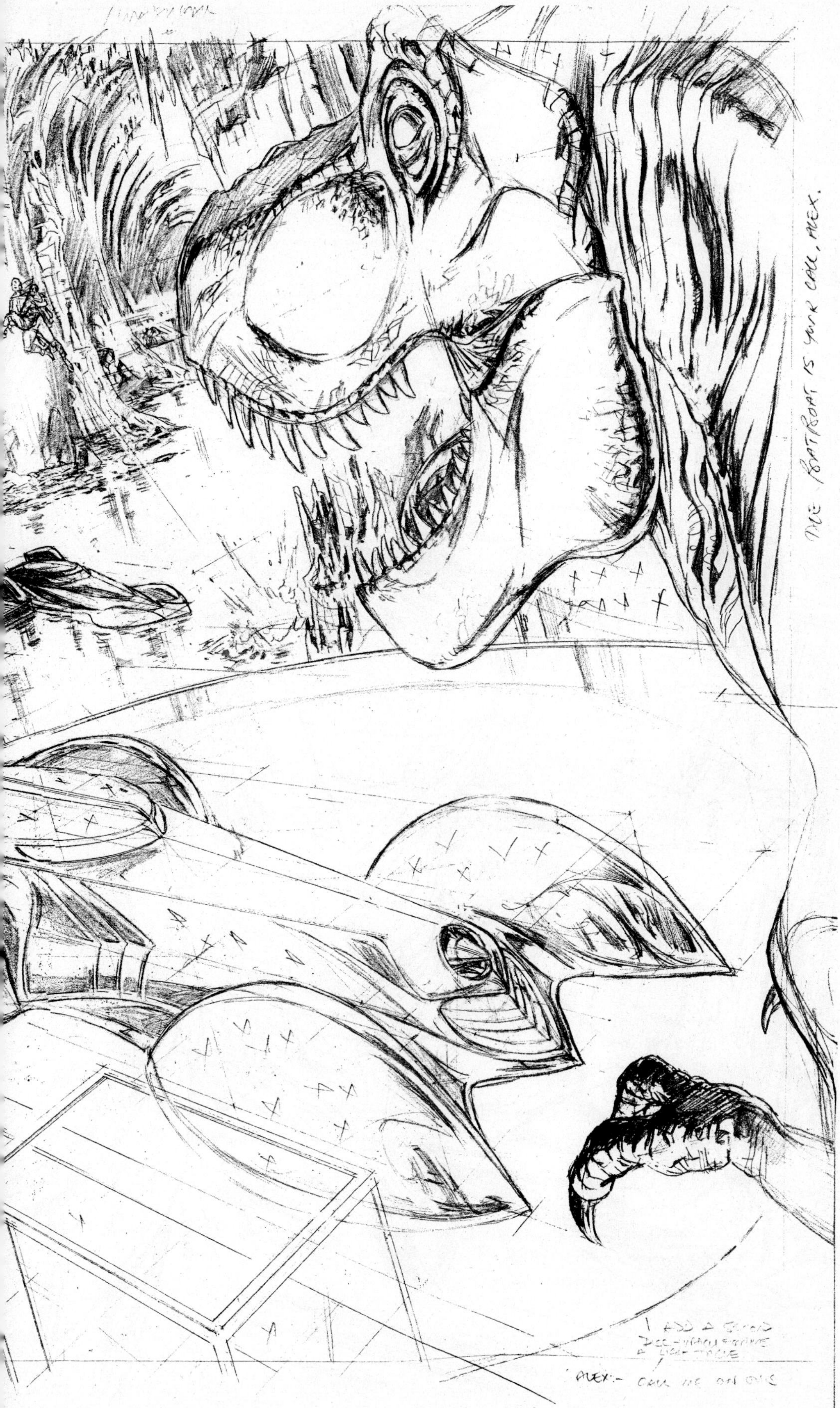

THE BATBOAT IS YOUR CALL, ALEX.
I ADD A SECOND
ALEX:- CALL ME ON ONE

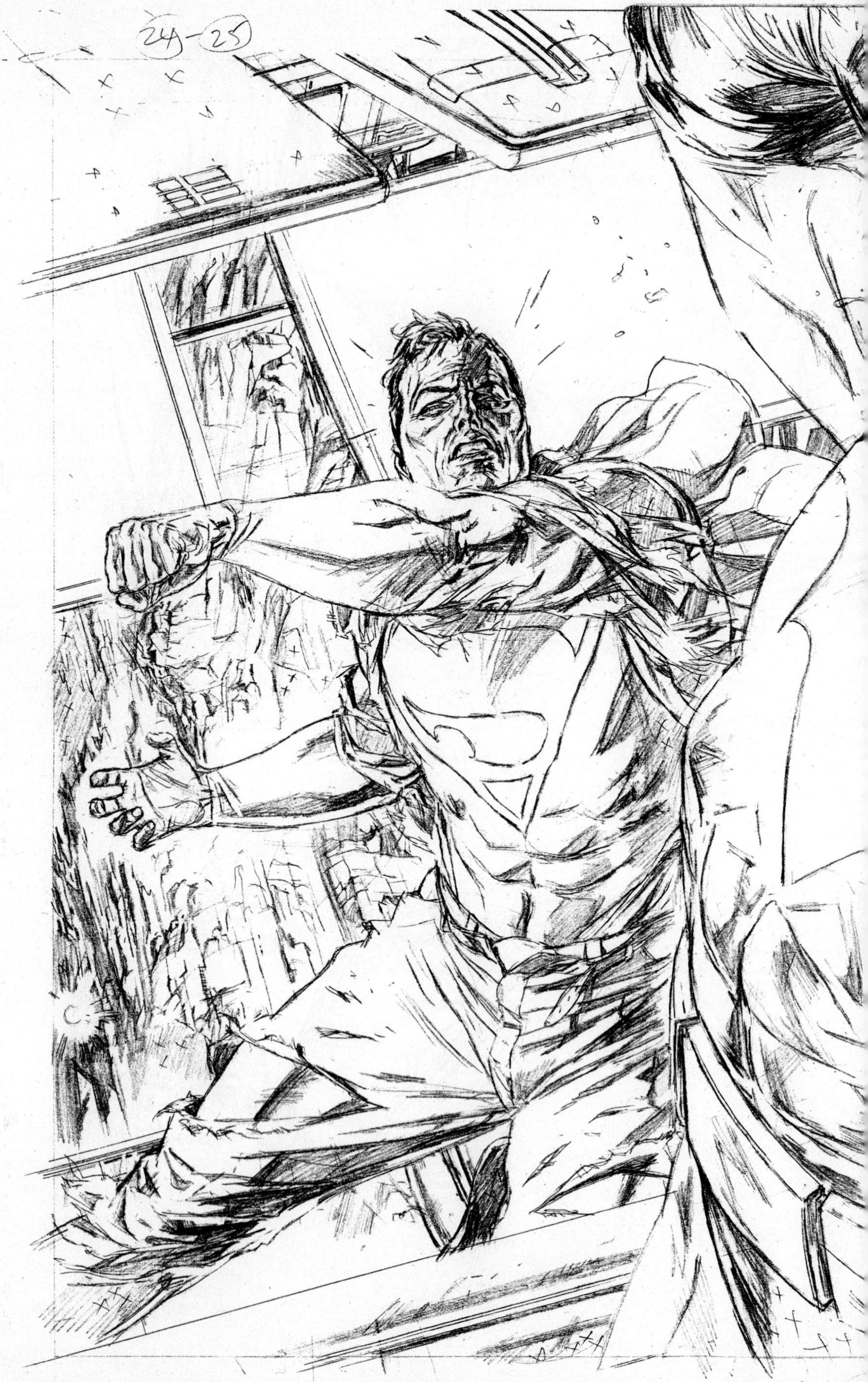
24-25

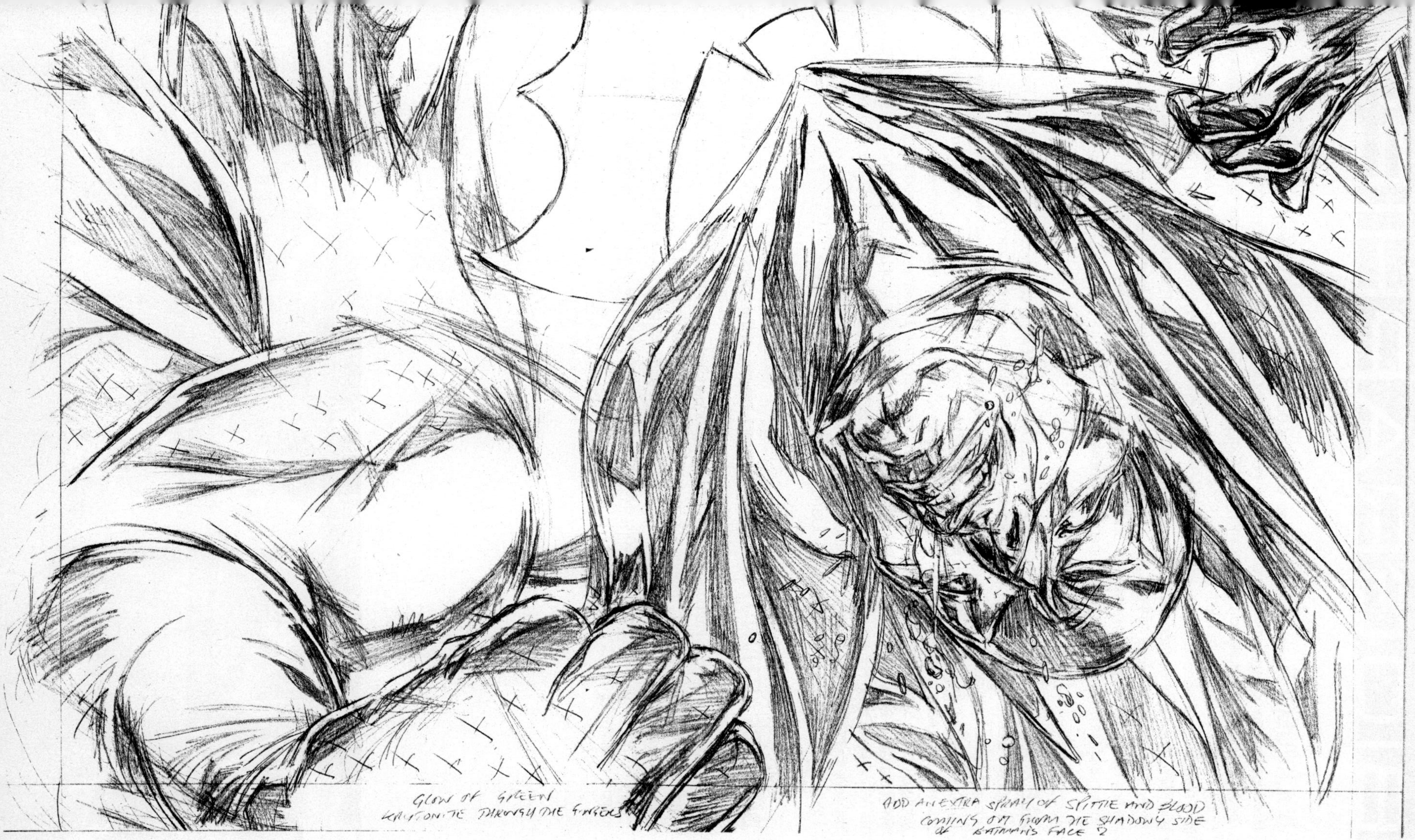
GLOW OF GREEN
KRYPTONITE THROUGH THE FINGERS
ADD AN EXTRA SPRAY OF SPITTLE AND BLOOD
COMING OUT FROM THE SHADOWY SIDE
OF BATMAN'S FACE ?

BIOGRAPHIES

JIM KRUEGER was a creative director at Marvel Comics before eventually leaving to become a freelance writer/property creator. His comics work includes *The Clock Maker* and *Micronauts* for Image Comics, *The Matrix Comics* for Burlyman Entertainment, and *Foot Soldiers*, *Galactic* and *Star Wars* for Dark Horse Comics. Krueger has also collaborated with artist Alex Ross on numerous projects for Marvel, including *Earth X*, *Universe X* and *Paradise X*. Besides writing for comics, Krueger is also a filmmaker who wrote, directed and produced the short film *They Might Be Dragons* (which was awarded "Best Short Film" at The New York Independent Film Festival), directed *Eleven* for RIPFEST 2006, and is preparing to direct his first feature. He has also just finished his first novel, *The Frankincense Monster and Other Haunted Christmas Stories*. Krueger is president and publisher of his own entertainment company, 26 Soldiers.

ALEX ROSS studied illustration at the American Academy of Art in Chicago, then honed his craft as a storyboard artist before entering the comics field. His miniseries *Marvels* (Marvel Comics, 1993) created a wider acceptance for painted comics. He moved on to produce the equally successful KINGDOM COME (DC Comics, 1996). Receiving critical acclaim and multiple awards for these best-selling works, Ross made a name as both an artist and storyteller, dedicating himself to bold experiments within the comics medium. With a miniseries for Vertigo (UNCLE SAM, 1997), several projects for Marvel Comics *(Earth X, Universe X* and *Paradise X)*, and six oversized graphic novels focusing on DC's iconic characters (collected in THE WORLD'S GREATEST SUPER-HEROES), he continues to bring comics to a broader audience. In 2003, Ross was the subject of a ten-year retrospective of his work for DC Comics, *Mythology* (Pantheon Books), written and designed by Chip Kidd. He is currently continuing work on the 12-part maxiseries JUSTICE for DC. Alex Ross lives in Illinois.

DOUG BRAITHWAITE broke into the comics industry at the age of 17 when he did work for Marvel UK. Soon he was working for comics companies in America, where his first assignment was pencilling an issue of DC Comics' DOOM PATROL. From there, Braithwaite's elegant pencilling style has graced many of DC's top-tier characters, including Superman, Batman, Wonder Woman, Green Arrow, and the JLA. He was also a penciller on Marvel's *Punisher* series. His first collaboration with Jim Krueger and Alex Ross was for Marvel's *Universe X* and *Paradise X,* where ultimately pencilled nearly every Marvel character. A native of London, England, he continues to work on JUSTICE for DC.

KINGDOM COME

THE GREATEST SUPER HERO EPIC OF TOMORROW!

KINGDOM COME

Mark WAID   Alex ROSS

Mark Waid and **Alex Ross** deliver a grim tale of youth versus experience, tradition versus change and what defines a hero. KINGDOM COME is a riveting story pitting the old guard — Superman, Batman, Wonder Woman and their peers — against a new uncompromising generation.

WINNER OF FIVE EISNER AND HARVEY AWARDS, INCLUDING BEST LIMITED SERIES AND BEST ARTIST

IDENTITY CRISIS

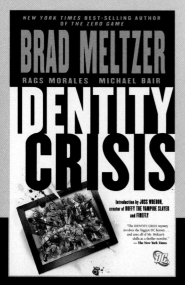

BRAD MELTZER
RAGS MORALES
MICHAEL BAIR

CRISIS ON INFINITE EARTHS

MARV WOLFMAN
GEORGE PÉREZ

DC: THE NEW FRONTIER VOLUME 1

DARWYN COOKE
DAVE STEWART

DON'T MISS THESE OTHER GREAT TITLES FROM AROUND THE **DCU!**

SUPERMAN: BIRTHRIGHT

**MARK WAID
LEINIL FRANCIS YU
GERRY ALANGUILAN**

BATMAN: DARK VICTORY

**JEPH LOEB
TIM SALE**

WONDER WOMAN: GODS AND MORTALS

**GEORGE PÉREZ
LEN WEIN/GREG POTTER
BRUCE PATTERSON**

GREEN LANTERN: NO FEAR

**GEOFF JOHNS
CARLOS PACHECO
ETHAN VAN SCIVER**

GREEN ARROW: QUIVER

**KEVIN SMITH
PHIL HESTER
ANDE PARKS**

TEEN TITANS: A KID'S GAME

**GEOFF JOHNS
MIKE McKONE**

SEARCH THE GRAPHIC NOVELS SECTION OF
WWW.DCCOMICS.COM
FOR ART AND INFORMATION ON ALL OF OUR BOOKS!